CRUISING GUIDE
TO
THE HAWAIIAN ISLANDS

BY
CAROLYN AND BOB MEHAFFY

CRUISING GUIDE
TO
THE HAWAIIAN ISLANDS

BY
CAROLYN AND BOB MEHAFFY

Paradise Cay Publications, Inc.
P. O. Box 29
Arcata, CA 95518-0029

Legal Disclaimer: In devising the sailing directions and sketches of anchorages and harbors, we have relied on NOAA charts and personal observations and have made every effort to insure that the directions and sketches are accurate. However, they should not supplant your use of official charts and your own careful observations of conditions that may have changed since the publication of this book. Neither the publisher nor the authors assume any responsibility for property loss or risk to persons that might occur from the use or interpretation of any information in this book.

ISBN 0-939837-73-0, 978-0-939837-73-0

Published by Paradise Cay Publications, Inc.

COVER by Rob Johnson, www.johnsondesign.org

MAPS by Allan Cartography

Front Cover Photo: Offshore of Molokai by Carolyn and Bob Mehaffy

Title Page: Rainbow over ʻAlenuihāhā Channel and Maui

Authors' photo by Sandra Cavey

Historical Sketches, Photographs, and Clip Art: Guava Graphics, Honolulu, Hawaiʻi
(pp. vi, vii, viii, 3, 4, 5, 6, 7, 8, 10, 25, 51, 65, 66, 89, 95, 117, 123, 131, 135, 150, 178, 210, 212, 222, 231, 242, 247, 258, 271, 275, 286, 295)

CONTENTS

ABOUT THE HAWAIIAN ISLANDS

DESTINATIONS

APPENDIX

PREFACE

Hawai'i is, in many ways, a cruiser's paradise. No other state has such remarkable weather, beautiful and varied scenery, or secluded anchorages. But sailing the Hawaiian waters presents boaters with unique challenges. The trade winds that cool Hawai'i require a high degree of readiness on the part of both the boaters and their boats. And because of the variable conditions of the channels between the islands, those who cruise Hawai'i must be skilled boaters and navigators.

The *Cruising Guide to the Hawaiian Islands* is a boaters' companion designed to aid resident and visiting boaters alike in their enjoyment of the Islands. The first ten chapters offer a brief look at the geological, historical, and political history of the Islands, as well as information on weather, boat equipment, provisions, medical supplies, and passage-making.

Chapters 10-19 describe 68 destinations in the Islands, grouped by island. The entry for each destination includes background about the area, a few suggestions about what you can see and do there, directions on getting to the destination, and suggestions for anchoring or mooring there. To help you visualize the destinations, each entry also has a sketch based on our most recent observations of the harbor or anchorage. **As with all sketches, ours are subjective; that is, they represent what we saw at the time we were there.** In the continually changing world we sail in, buildings and church steeples that we used for reference marks when we were at a particular destination may be gone by the time you arrive. The placement and color of navigation lights sometimes change without warning. To be safe, you must remain alert for these and other possible changes when you visit any of these beautiful anchorages or harbors.

We based the sketches on NOAA charts whenever they were available for a specific location. **However, as with any cruising guide, nothing in this book is intended to replace any other charts.** It is a supplement to help you arrive at your destination, anchor in a suitable area, and enjoy yourself while you're there.

In preparing this *Cruising Guide*, we visited every anchorage we describe, except for the island of Ni'ihau. As we cruised the Islands, we interviewed other cruisers, charter boat skippers, tug boat captains, harbormasters, Fish and Wildlife Service personnel, Islands residents, university professors who specialize in Hawaiian culture, history, and language, and anyone else who could help us make this book more accurate and more complete.

We have not included all the bays and roadsteads that, in certain weather conditions, might be good destinations. Though our sources suggested we try other anchorages that they liked, we sometimes decided that these destinations were either unsafe and/or too uncomfortable to include them. Undoubtedly, you will discover on your own some of these destinations and, in the right weather, find them entirely satisfactory.

Whenever we give you a course to follow, such as that for a channel into a harbor, we give you the magnetic bearing from our compass. This reading will most likely be slightly different from what you see on your compass as you enter the same channel because of the differences resulting from the individual adjustments to every compass.

At the beginning of every destination, we have provided the GPS coordinates of either the entrance to a harbor or of the place we were anchored. Use these coordinates with care because of the very nature of GPS. Before you enter these coordinates into your GPS, check them carefully on your chart.

In this book we refer to all personnel in small boat harbors as *harbormasters*, as is the custom in other states. The State of Hawai'i does not follow this custom, however. Instead, many harbors are supervised by harbor *agents*. To avoid confusion, we have simply called them all *harbormasters*, even though that is not always the State-approved designation.

At the beginning of each chapter, you'll find an appropriate quotation in Hawaiian from a chant, poem, proverb, or myth. We hope these quotations give you a greater appreciation for the beauty and complexity of the Hawaiian language and of the people who have spoken it for many centuries. You will also notice that we have used two marks, the *kahakō* (or macron) and the '*okina* (') in our writing of Hawaiian words. These marks indicate pronunciation and, in turn, help to clarify meanings.

ACKNOWLEDGMENTS

The following people freely offered us help, sometimes spending hours with us to make certain we understood. To all of them we extend our heartfelt thanks. To anyone we've inadvertently left off our list, we apologize most sincerely.

We extend our thanks to the following boaters who offered encouragement and help:

Ralph Blancato on *Maile;* Tom Campanelli on *Suta;* Jeff Curran on *Mandarin;* John Koon on *Wind's Way;* Bob Leary on *Kanaloa;* Matt Klocek on *Ariel;* Ben McCormack on *Moana;* Skip Price on *Silent Lady;* Rick Taylor on *Trilogy IV;* Capt. Reuben Wahineho'okai on the tug *Joe Sevier.*

We also thank these people from various organizations who went far out of their way to help us:

William Aila, Harbormaster, Wai'anae; Ray Balagan, Harbormaster, Port Allen; Clay Bertelmann, Cultural Resources Coordinator, Hawai'i; Ian Birnie, District Manager, Hawai'i Harbors Division; Hal Campbell, District Manager, Maui Harbors Division; Delores Clark, Public Affairs Officer, National Weather Service; Bob Farrell, NOAA Weather Office; Mike Gautreaux, General Island Manager, Midway Atoll; Nick Giaconi, Harbormaster, Mā'alaea; Kimo Alama Keaulana, Professor of Hawaiian Studies, Honolulu Community College; Dr. Peter Kessinger, Provost, Honolulu Community College; Steve Lewis, Manager, Ala Wai Marine; Sherry Menze, Harbormaster, Mānele Bay; Nancy Murphy, Harbormaster, Ke'ehi Lagoon; Earl Okomoto, Harbormaster, He'eia Kea; Stella Pihana, Program Coordinator, Cultural Center at Ka'ala; Brad Rimell, Port Captain, Sause Brothers Tug and Barge; Robert Rushforth, Harbormaster, Ala Wai; Rob Schallenberger, Manager, Fish & Wildlife Service, Midway Atoll; Robert Smith, Manager, Fish & Wildlife Service, Pacific Region; Hal Silva, Harbormaster, Lahaina; Bernie Strehler, Harbormaster, Kaunakakai; Richard Waltjen, Harbormaster, Nāwiliwili; Bob Wilson, Harbormaster, Midway Atoll.

This edition of the *Cruising Guide to the Hawaiian Islands* would not have been accurate without the details and suggestions of many. We sincerely appreciate the unflagging assistance of the following people:

Manny Andrade, Harbormaster, Port Allen; Ian Birnie, District Manager, Hawai'i Harbors Division; Bill Bolton, Port Captain, Hawai'i Yacht Club; Ken Chee, Harbor Agent, Ke'ehi Lagoon Harbor; Scott Cunningham, Harbormaster, Kahului Harbor; Russell Doane, Harbormaster, Ko Olina Marina; Nicholas Giaconi, Harbormaster, Ma'alaea Harbor; John Gomersall, Manager, The Phoenician; Jerry Leineke, Director, U. S. Fish and Wildlife Service, Pacific Region; Sherry Menze, Harbormaster, Mānele Bay; Daniel Mersbaugh, Harbormaster, Honokōhau Harbor; Nancy Murphy, Hawaii District Manager, DLNR; Earl Omoto, Harbormaster, He'eia Kea Harbor; Paul Sensano, Harbormaster, Hale'iwa Harbor; Hal Silva, Harbormaster, Lahaina Harbor; Meghan Staats, Harbormaster, Ala Wai Harbor; Bernie Strehler, Harbormaster, Kaunakakai Harbor; Steve Thompson, O'ahu District Manager, DLNR; Vaughn Tyndzik, Kaua'i District Manager, DLNR; Ed Underwood, O'ahu Assistant Manager, DLNR.

Nu'uanu Falls, O'ahu

ABOUT THE AUTHORS

For many years, Carolyn and Bob Mehaffy have called San Francisco Bay home port. After retiring from American River College in Sacramento, California, they set sail for Hawaii and a new career as full-time cruising sailors and free-lance writers. Their previous books for sailors are *Destination Mexico: Planning a Cruise to Mexico* and *Cruising Guide to San Francisco Bay.* Both are available from Paradise Cay Publications, Inc. (www.paracay.com) The Mehaffys' articles appear regularly in *Cruising World, Ocean Navigator,* and *Sail Magazine.*

HAWAI'I: "THE LOVELIEST FLEET OF ISLANDS"

He home aloha 'ia na ke 'ala me ke onaona
("The beloved home of fragrance and sweetness")

In an ancient time a small cadre of sailors and their families piled provisions into every available space on their double-hull sailing canoe and struck out across the Pacific Ocean, confident their navigational skills would take them to distant islands. They sailed north, in swells that lifted the two bows of their canoe gently above the line of the horizon and in wind waves that slashed across the decks. When they reached their uncharted destination, they rejoiced to have found a new homeland as lovely as the one they'd left behind. Perhaps it was even lovelier, with its high land and its valleys covered in green and its shores lapped by sapphire and aquamarine water. They gave to the islands they inhabited the names *Hawai'i, Maui, Moloka'i, Lāna'i, O'ahu, Kaua'i, Ni'ihau, Nihoa,* and *Mokumanamana.*

Beautiful black sand beach on the Big Island

In 1866 the steamer *Ajax* docked in Honolulu Harbor, and a newspaper reporter for the Sacramento *Union,* using the pen name "Mark Twain," landed in these islands that he called *"the loveliest fleet of islands that lies anchored in any ocean."* They were to become the permanent home for his heart. After four months in the Hawaiian Islands, he returned to the Mainland, never to see Hawai'i again, but it remained clear and unchanged in his imagination:

No alien land in all the world has any deep strong charm for me but that one, no other land could so longingly and so beseechingly haunt me, sleeping and waking, through half a lifetime, as that one has done. Other things leave me, but it abides; other things change, but it remains the same. For me its balmy airs are always blowing, its summer seas flashing in the sun; the pulsing of its surfbeat is in my ear, I can see its garlanded crags, its leaping cascades, its plumy palms drowsing by the shore, its remote summits floating like islands above the cloud wrack; I can feel the spirit of its woodland solitudes, I can hear the splash of its brooks; in my nostrils still lives the breath of flowers that perished twenty years ago.

One hundred years after the *Ajax* and probably 1500 years after the double-hull canoes of the Polynesians, cruising boats, primarily from the west coast of North America, became the latest voyagers to these islands that writer and sailor Jack London called *"a lotus land . . . where every day is a paradise of days. It is not too hot. It is not too cold."*

Piling provisions into every available space on their boats, these 20th Century sailors rediscover, for one more time in its long history, the lotus land of Hawai'i. The lucky cruisers are those who make the three-week crossing of the Pacific and then have time to spend several weeks or even months in further exploration of this paradise. (Those who can't manage to spend much time in the Islands are not the unlucky ones, though. The passage across the Pacific, along a route bending ever more southwesterly into balmier and balmier days, can be its own reward.)

The climate of the Islands—distinctly tropical, unlike any other place in the United States— is perhaps the first attraction for many cruising sailors. Neither Florida nor Southern California can match Hawai'i, where the weather along the coasts is balmy year round, rarely getting warmer than 85 degrees nor cooler than 65 degrees. The water is always just right for swimming, snorkeling, surfing, and scuba diving. But wait. You say you might grow weary of all this balminess, that you may tire of a place where all you have to do is, *"To sit together/Drinking the blue ocean, eating the sun/Like a fruit . . ."* (from "The Luau," by Genevieve Taggard). The uplands of each island are cooler, with two of the islands not uncommonly having snow on their highest peaks. A short drive can take you away from the coastal paradises to a place where you can snow ski or hike on mountain trails.

While you can't anchor or moor your boat in the snow and ice, you can choose from an enormous variety of other possibili-  ties in these islands, from being in the heart of a city of 400,000 (the Ala Wai in Honolulu) to mooring off an uninhabited island (Molokini). You can choose the leeward side of any island, where you'll have warm, sunny days rarely marred by rain but still within view of the voluminous clouds that sit atop the islands' upper ridges most of the time. Or you can visit one of the tropical jungle settings on the wind-ward sides of the islands, where tropical vines and trees and flowers grow in profusion and where you may experience rainfall for some part of many of the days you're there.

Pā'ū rider, Aloha Week, Moloka'i

To most cruising sailors who come from the North American continent, the Hawaiian Islands will seem both familiar and foreign—two opposite qualities that also make Hawai'i an ideal cruising destination. The fiftieth state of the United States is recognizably American, despite its location more than 2,000 miles from any other portion of the U. S. and on the latitude of Cabo San Lucas, Mexico. Its business face is decidedly American. In the markets and shops are all the products one could find in Lubbock, Texas, or Pittsburgh, Pennsylvania, or Los Angeles. Many of the markets and shops are, in fact, parts of the same chains found on the continent. Its road signs, its restaurants, its governing bodies are the same as those in Lubbock, Pittsburgh, and Los Angeles. And the official language is American English. Thus visitors from the Mainland feel right at home here, comfortable and secure.

Yet you will nevertheless constantly have the sense of being in a foreign country, much like, for example, being in Mexico. The face of the culture is decidedly different from that in the other states of the U. S. Most of the residents you'll meet are dark skinned and have dark hair and eyes. Many of them speak American English with an accent but speak at least one other language fluently. And they react quite differently to strangers, being much more open, friendly, generous, and eager to help than one is accustomed to finding in Texas or Pennsylvania or California. Travel agents and promoters may have invented the phrase "the Aloha Spirit," but the spirit of *aloha* is nonetheless real.

Woven into every language, regardless of its origin, are words from the melodious and expressive language of Hawai'i. Some Hawaiian words are far more commonly used than their English equivalents, for example, *mauka* ("inland, the mountains") and *makai* ("the sea") to give directions. Rare is the town or bay or street that doesn't have a Hawaiian name, these often multi-syllabic names that roll sweetly off the tongues of native speakers.

Just as everywhere else around the globe, here fast food stands offering hamburgers, pizza, and tacos are in towns of any size at all. The local fare, however, is more likely to be *poi, sushi, manapua,* or Spam *musubi.* Alongside doughnuts and apple pie are loaves of Portuguese sweet bread and cookie-like pastries, *manju,* filled with coconut or sweet bean paste. Roadside stands feature apple bananas, soursops, coconuts, papayas, and mangos instead of apples, cherries, peaches, and strawberries.

What these many facets of the Hawaiian Islands add up to is a cruising destination that is just about perfect, especially for a first-time cruise. You can feel secure and comfortable while in an exotic land.

The poet William Meredith captured the essence of Hawai'i:

A place to live when you are reconciled
To beauty, and unafraid of time.

He might have said the same thing about a cruising boat, no matter what length the cruise. Imagine the joy when these two places, Hawai'i and the cruising boat, come together.

Valley on O'ahu

THE PEOPLE OF HAWAI'I

Eia nā waʻa; kau mai ai,
E hoʻi, e noho ia Hawaiʻi-kua-uli,
He ʻāina loaʻa i ka moana,
I hōʻea mai loko o ka ʻale,
I ka halehale poʻi pū a Kanaloa.

("Here are the canoes; get on board,
Come, and dwell in Hawaiʻi-with-the-green-back,
A land that was found in the ocean,
That was thrown up from the sea,
From the very depths of Kanaloa.")

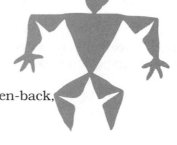

Over the many, many centuries after the Hawaiian Islands "were thrown up from the sea," if not from the underworld ruled by Kanaloa then from the volcano beneath the ocean's floor, life slowly came to these remote islands. Carried here by the wind or the sea, at least 2,200 species of plants and 67 species of birds, along with a number of insects and 2 higher order animals, the hoary bat and the monk seal, made the journey and were still prospering when the first Polynesians arrived.

Anthropologists and historians debate the arrival date of the first group of people, but all agree the Islands were discovered by migrating Polynesians at least by AD 700. Some people propose a date as early as AD 100.

Generally, they agree that the first groups to arrive sailed the 2,000 miles from the Marquesas in large, double-hull canoes. Evidence supports the theory that the Polynesians had been making ocean voyages of as much as 1,000 miles for at least 1,000 years before Western sailors attempted such lengthy voyages. With no navigation equipment, these skillful Polynesian explorers relied on the paths of birds in flight and the routes of dolphins, on wave patterns and ocean currents, and, most impressively, on the stars to navigate across the uncharted ocean. The brightest stars in the sky, Sirius and Arcturus *(Hōkūleʻa)*, a reddish star off the handle of the Big Dipper, are believed to have been the key navigational stars for these voyagers.

The supposition is that a group of people set out to look for this land to the north after observing the yearly return of migrating birds (perhaps Pacific golden plovers, which migrate each fall from Siberia and Alaska to the Hawaiian Islands and as far beyond as the Marquesas, Tahiti, and New Zealand).

No one assumes the first settlers on Hawaiʻi found the Islands accidentally, for they apparently brought with them plants and animals to establish as food sources—taro, coconuts, bananas, yams, breadfruit, sugar cane, pigs, dogs, and chickens. To make *kapa* (barkcloth), they brought paper mulberry, and, for woven matting, the *tī* (related to the lily).

They also brought from their homeland their beliefs, practices, and history, preserved in rituals and *mele* (chants). From the chants that have survived and the archeological evidence, we must piece together the history of the ancient Hawaiians, for they had no written language until after the American missionaries set

Missionary preaching at Kailua

up schools in the Islands in the early 1800s. (The first written history of the Hawaiian people did not appear until 1838, when students of the Reverend Sheldon Dibble at Lahainaluna School produced it in the Hawaiian language.)

These Polynesians who settled Hawai'i worshipped a set of nature gods that figured in every facet of their daily lives. They assigned the word *akua,* their word for "god," to a wide range of subjects. An object of nature, a person, living or dead, a created image—any of these, if worshipped, would merit the name *akua.* The early Hawaiians also had gods that were like chiefs who dwelt in far lands or in the heavens and who visited the Islands periodically. Ku, Kāne, Kanaloa, and Lono were apparently the most powerful of these. At the numerous *heiau* (temples) throughout the Islands, the Hawaiians worshipped these gods for their special qualities, much as the citizens of classical Greece worshipped their various gods.

Hawai'i boxers

Ku, the male aspect of nature, had dominion over the land and farming and fishing, but Ku "the island snatcher" was also the god of war and demanded human sacrifice from those who worshipped him. He and his mate, the great goddess Hina, the female aspect of nature, were believed to be the earliest gods. The god Kāne, the ancestor of all Hawaiian people, came out of *pō* ("darkness" or "the realm of the gods") and created mankind, ushering in the period of light (*ao*). Kanaloa was the ruler of the dead and the underworld and therefore the antithesis of Kāne; however, the Hawaiians also worshipped him as a fishing deity and as the god of the narcotic beverage *awa.*

The Hawaiian people venerated Lono, the benevolent god of clouds, harvests, and the rain and a renowned boxer, at the *makahiki,* a harvest festival held each year from October to February. During the *makahiki,* boxing (the sport of Lono), along with surfing, sledding, and

Fierce *ki'i* at a *heiau*

maika (similar to bowling), was a popular event. In the evenings the people gathered for the *lū'au* and the *hula,* a religious ceremonial dance performed only by celibate men and women. The chiefs observed a *kapu* on war for the duration of the *makahiki.*

Though not as powerful as these four great gods, Pele, Māui, Laka, and Hi'iaka are the subject of many popular myths. These deities are of later origin than the other four gods, but their all-too-human qualities have endeared them to the people. Pele, the fiery goddess of the volcano, still "lives" in the active volcano Kīlauea, and the trickster demi-god Māui is the only Hawaiian deity to have an island named after him. Laka and Hi'iaka are the goddesses of *hula.*

The Hawaiians had many other shared deities, but they also had their family or personal gods, known as *'aumākua.* These *'aumākua* might assume the shape of sharks, eels, owls, birds, rocks, clouds, and other figures of the natural world. Mortals did not harm their *'aumākua,* and, in return, the *'aumākua* served the mortals who worshipped them by warning the mortals of dangers or reprimanding them for their actions.

The Marquesans who first came here are believed to have been a fierce, cannibalistic people who grew mellower over the centuries of their isolation

Faces of Hawai'i

on the Islands, coming to worship most fervently the gentle god Lono. Around the 12th Century, warring Tahitians invaded Hawai'i, supplanting the chiefs as rulers on each island and also replacing the gentle fertility god Lono as the most venerated god with the fierce war god, Ku the Island Snatcher.

Apparently this 12th Century invasion was the last contact between the Islanders of the South Pacific and the Hawaiians. For the next five centuries the Hawaiian culture and people evolved, apparently without any outside influences. (A Spanish galleon sailing between Mexico and the Philippines may have been blown off course and wrecked somewhere in the Hawaiian Islands in the 16th or 17th century. Some historians base this hypothesis on a few pieces of metal and a piece of woven fabric resembling sailcloth present on the Islands before Cook came and on a chart a British captain took off a captured Spanish galleon in 1742. This chart showed two islands at the correct latitude for Hawai'i, though the longitude was slightly off.)

A strict *kapu* system of laws with a religious foundation regulated the religious, political and social life of every Hawaiian from birth to death. One result was a society of rigid classes, a caste system in which the highest value was placed on the purity of one's lineage. The highest of the *ali'i*, or nobles, traced their ancestry directly to the gods. Mothers as well as fathers passed their ranking on to their children. In Hawaiian *mele* concerned with genealogy, the names of both the fathers and the mothers appear. The last verse of the great creation myth *Kumulipo*,

Tatooed *hula* dancer in *kapa* skirt

for example, includes this genealogy of I, a high chief of Hilo whose grandfather, Kumalaenui, was an ancestor of the last two reigning royalty, Kalākaua and Lili'uokalani :

    Kumalaenui of 'Umi was the husband of Kunu'unuipu'awa-lau.
    Their son, Makua, was the only high chief (wohi kukahi) of the island.
    Kapohelemai, his wife, whose rank as sacred wohi Ali'i and Honor.
    So their heir I, the I of the Kingdom
           (from the translation of Queen Lili'uokalani, 1897).

Despite their prominence, the lives of the *ali'i* were circumscribed by the *kapu* just as were those of the *maka'āinana* (literally, "the people who tended the land") and the *kauā* ("slave caste"). The punishment for *kapu* breakers was typically a brutal death by stoning, clubbing, incinerating, or burying alive, but the *kapu* breaker had one court of appeal. If he or she could get to one of the *pu'uhonua*, a "place of refuge," such as that at Hōnaunau, before being captured by the chief's warriors, the *kapu* breaker would be absolved of the wrongdoing.

The many *kapu* on women of every class were particularly restrictive. A *kapu* forbidding women to eat pork, coconuts, bananas, and shark meat must have meant some lean days for the women. They also were forbidden from performing certain tasks, such as *poi* pounding, and, though they could dance the *hula*, they could not dance it in the *heiau*.

As with systems of governing laws everywhere, unethical and capricious chiefs and priests sometimes abused their power to institute the *kapu*, using religion as the basis for punishing their enemies or acquiring control of more territory.

Helmeted warrior

Woman wearing feather *lei* set

However we may judge the *kapu* system now, the pre-contact Hawaiians were an industrious, religious people with a strong allegiance to their families and *ohana* ("clan") and great respect for their elders. Their verbal dexterity and sense of humor show clearly in the artistry and ironic subtleties of the *mele* they composed on a variety of topics. Other artistic urges took form in the *hula* and the music accompanying both the *mele* and the *hula*. For this accompaniment, they used drums made of coconut trees and gourds, bamboo rattles, and castanets of pipes, sticks, and pebbles.

They carved stone and wooden statues, created wicker and feather sculptures, and incised petroglyphs on *pāhoehoe* lava or boulders. Their woven baskets and mats are more skillfully wrought than any others in all of Polynesia. Elaborately painted *kapa* adorned their oracle towers and their bodies. In praising the *kapa*, Captain Cook wrote, "*. . . in coloring or staining it [kapa], the people of Atooi [Kaua'i] display a superiority of taste, by the endless variations of figures which they execute.*" Their featherwork in cloaks, capes, and helmets was described by Cook as comparable to the "thickest and richest velvet."

Perhaps in no other medium was their artistic impulse more creatively expressed than in the adornment of their bodies. In addition to the wreaths, headbands, necklaces, and anklets they fashioned, both men and women ornamented their faces, limbs, and torsos by tattooing, burning, or blistering elaborate designs on them.

What we would call "artistry" today for the Hawaiians extended to everything they created. They lived within a world they saw as beautiful and meaningful, one from which they drew both physical and spiritual sustenance. Nothing in their lives, then, was lacking in significance or esthetics. They polished their fishhooks and rubbed and oiled their calabashes. Nothing was what we know today as a "throwaway." This sensitivity to their world suffuses their art, which many anthropologists believe surpasses any other among the Polynesians and is among the finest of its kind in the world.

WESTERN CONTACT

In July, 1776, two ships under the command of Captain James Cook, one of the greatest navigators ever known, sailed from England on a quest to find the mythical Northwest Passage across the top of the North American Continent. In December, 1777, Cook sailed north from Tahiti, expecting not to see land again for thousands of miles. The charts of the English Admiralty showed only a great expanse of empty ocean between Tahiti and the northwest coast of America. Far too soon, while still thousands of miles from their destination, the ships' crews began to spot turtles and birds in the ocean and then high land in the wrong direction, the northeast. Cook and his men had stumbled upon the Hawaiian Islands, the first Westerners in recorded history to do so.

When the people of these isolated islands first saw the HMS *Resolution* and *Discovery*, those "floating islands," as they later called them, off the coast of Kaua'i, a *kahuna* told them the ships could be "nothing else than the *heiau* of Lono, the tower of Keolewa, and the place of sacrifice at the altar." And, indeed, the Hawaiians came to believe, at least temporarily, that Captain Cook was the god Lono. After a fruitless attempt to find the Northwest Passage, Cook returned to the "Sandwich Islands," the name he gave to Hawai'i in honor of the Earl of Sandwich, for food

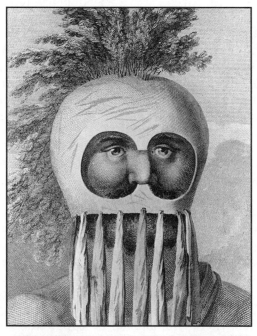

Hawaiian man in gourd mask

and water. When he anchored in Kealakekua Bay, on the Big Island, the Hawaiians greeted Cook with all pomp and ceremony. Coincidentally, but to the Islanders significantly, he had arrived at Kealakekua during the *makahiki*, the festival celebrating the god Lono.

In less than a month after the Hawaiians honored Cook as if he were a god, they had killed him. Tensions had begun to arise among both the Hawaiians and the English for a variety of reasons. For one, the Hawaiians began to question what they perceived as weaknesses in this "Lono," who was powerless to avoid damage to his ships in storms. For their part, the English did not look kindly on the casual thefts perpetrated by the Hawaiians. Any kind of metal, for instance, was not secure; the Hawaiians were particularly covetous of iron nails, from which they made fish hooks. When the cutter from the *Discovery* was stolen, Cook went ashore with nine other sailors to abduct the chief, Kalaniopu'u, planning to hold him hostage until the Hawaiians returned the cutter. In protecting their chief, the Hawaiians killed Cook and four of the sailors. To avenge these deaths, the sailors destroyed villages and *heiau* and killed scores of Hawaiians, decapitating two of them and displaying their heads on the bow of a row boat.

The legacy of Cook and the sailors aboard these two ships is far reaching and complex, and in many ways inexpressibly sad. They brought Western diseases to these people who had no defenses against them, diseases that decimated the population. The most immediately ravaging of those diseases were syphilis and gonorrhea. Sailors aboard Cook's ships infected the Hawaiian women during the first brief contacts on Kaua'i and Ni'ihau and at every place they landed after that. In keeping with the Hawaiians' easy acceptance of everything natural, including their sexuality, the women were eager partners for the equally eager sailors, who had been at sea for many months. The women infected soon spread the disease among the Hawaiian men. Other diseases previously unknown in the Islands, and deadly to the Hawaiians—small pox, measles, whooping cough, and typhus—came with other visitors in the years to follow. From an estimated 300,000 Hawaiians in 1778, the population dropped to under 50,000 in only 100 years. Today the estimated number of pure Hawaiians is fewer than 5,000; however, on surveys over 80,000 people identify themselves as native Hawaiians.

Though no other Western ships came through the Islands for the next five years, soon after that, ships from many nations—Russia, Spain, England, and America, particularly—stopped in Hawai'i for food and water as they carried goods to and from Asia.

THE KINGDOM OF HAWAI'I

Two other legacies of Western contact were to become instrumental in the unification of the Hawaiian Islands. Previous to 1790, each island had had one or more ruling chiefs, with bloody civil wars regularly breaking out among them. Occasionally chiefs and warriors from one island would invade another, but no single chief had been able to control more than one of the four large islands.

Kamehameha I, a high-born chief of the Big Island, was both ambitious and shrewd. He quickly recognized the enormous advantages of the Western cannons, guns and sailing ships in warfare. With the help of these weapons and ships and the military expertise of Western sailors, Kamehameha conquered Maui (1790), the remainder of the Big Island (1791), and O'ahu (1795). In 1796 and again in 1809, he planned to invade Kaua'i, but, because of bad weather in the Kaua'i Channel in the first instance and disease among his warriors in the second, he never touched the shores of Kaua'i. In 1810, Kaumuali'i, the king of Kaua'i and Ni'ihau, yielded to diplomatic pressure and agreed to serve as a tributary king under Kamehameha, thus accomplishing the unification of the Hawaiian Islands.

Under Kamehameha's rule came an end to the centuries of bloody and brutal civil wars in the Islands and the increased influence of the West on the economy of Hawai'i. A quick study, Kamehameha soon realized the valuable treasure his islands held in the mountains: the aromatic sandalwood so prized among the Asians. He traded this wood for the gold and silver that gave him an economic power among the world's markets. Consequently, today only one or two small stands of the slow-growing sandalwood remain in all Hawai'i.

During his reign, Kamehameha I strictly maintained the feudal *kapu* system, but six months after his death in 1819, his son, Liholiho, ruling as Kamehameha II, yielded to pressure from Queen Ka'ahumanu and abolished the system. Ka'ahumanu, the outspoken, independent, yet favorite wife of Kamehameha I, promulgated the abolition of altars for offerings and sacrifice, of temples, and of the hundreds of rules that had dictated the lives of the Hawaiians for centuries. One of those was that women and men could not eat together. To symbolize the death of *kapu*, the new king dined with Ka'ahumanu and his mother, the regal Queen Keōpūolani, whose royal lineage placed her so high that even the late king, her husband, had to crawl on his stomach to approach her.

After the decimation of the sandalwood on the Islands, whaling became the primary source of foreign revenue for the Islands. Between 1820 and 1860, as many as 500 whaling ships put into Hawaiian ports, notably Lahaina and Honolulu but also Hilo and Koloa, during the spring and fall hunting seasons.

At about the same time the first whaling ships arrived in Hawai'i, so did the first missionaries from New England, landing at Kailua on the Kona Coast in 1820. The Hawaiian people were receptive to this new religion, for their king had just abolished the traditional one. The missionaries, though horrified by the "pagans" they found here, stayed on to bring further dramatic changes to the islands.

These first missionaries brought to the Islands Western medicine and education. Hawaiian herbal medicine, according to some accounts, was more advanced than the medicine of the West when the first explorers came here, but the Hawaiians had no herbs or practices to ameliorate the effects of the many Western diseases the Hawaiians suffered from in the 19th Century. Through the mission schools, the missionaries facilitated the Hawaiians in developing a written language and in recording their oral histories. On the Islands' first printing press, set up in 1834 at Lahainaluna Mission School, these histories were printed.

But the missionaries also brought with them attitudes that would quash much of what remained of the Hawaiians' way of life. They condemned as barbaric not only the traditional gods but the dance, the music, the clothing, the sexual mores, and the carefree spirit of the people.

The second generation of these New England missionary families changed Hawai'i in another sphere. They became the entrepreneurs of the Hawaiian Islands. In 1840 Kamehameha III instituted a constitutional monarchy, with two houses of government and a supreme court, followed in 1847 by a separation of the lands of Hawai'i into three groups: the royal land, the chiefs' land, and the people's land. Beginning in 1850 foreigners could buy Hawaiian land. The sons of the missionaries were among the foreigners who rapidly began to acquire land in these islands, from a people whose culture had included no concept of the private "ownership" of property. Marriage was another means through which land came into the hands of the Westerners. With all this rich agricultural land in their possession, sons of the missionaries became the sugar barons of the Islands.

Harvesting sugar cane

Sugar cane probably came to Hawai'i with the first Polynesians, but the sugar industry began in Hāna, Maui, in 1849, with a small plantation begun by an ex-whaler, George Wilfong. The rapid populating of California during the Gold Rush and, later, the American Civil War insured an American market for all the sugar Hawai'i could produce.

Labor soon became the only impediment to supplying these expanding markets. The plantation owners could not find an adequate work force on the Islands because the Hawaiian population was too small and those who had worked on the plantations had become disenchanted with the working conditions. The passage of the Masters and Servants Act in 1850 allowed the importation of what were essentially indentured servants. The consequent influx of workers gave these Islands one of the most ethnically diverse populations in the world. Workers from China, Japan, Portugal, and the Philippines were the major groups, but others came from all around the Pacific as well as from Germany, Russia, Norway, and Puerto Rico.

James Dole began growing pineapple commercially on a small homestead in Wahiawā, O'ahu, canning the fruit for importation to the United States. In 1922 he bought the island of Lāna'i and turned it into the world's largest pineapple plantation. The pineapple industry, too, demanded large numbers of additional workers, assuring that the doors of Hawai'i would remain open to immigrants.

The Kingdom of Hawai'i lasted until 1893, when a group of businessmen in the Islands called the Annexation Club took over Honolulu and established the Provisional Government of Hawai'i under the leadership of Sanford Dole. Queen Lili'uokalani, who had assumed the throne upon the death of her brother Kalākaua, ruler of Hawai'i from 1874 to 1891, abdicated. The U.S. President, Democrat Grover Cleveland, was unsuccessful in his opposition to the Provisional Government and its successor, the Republic of Hawai'i, and in his attempts to have Lili'uokalani reinstated.

Shortly after the opposition party candidate William McKinley won the election and took office as President in 1898, he signed a Joint Resolution of Annexation, and Hawai'i became the possession of the United States. Former President Cleveland was to write later: "As I look back upon the first steps in this miserable business and I contemplate the means used to complete the outrage I am ashamed of the whole affair."

After many more years of political wrangling, Hawai'i became the 50th state of the Union in 1959, when its voters ratified 17 to 1 the recommendation of statehood by the U. S. Congress.

The State of Hawai'i includes all the islands in the chain, from Kure to the Big Island, except for Midway Atoll. (Midway has belonged to the Federal Government since it was annexed in 1867 under the provisions of the Guano Act.) The four counties of the state are Hawai'i (the Big Island), Maui (including Moloka'i, Lāna'i, and Kaho'olawe), Honolulu (comprising the island of O'ahu as well as all the islands in the Northwestern Chain, again except Midway, all of which are uninhabited), and Kaua'i (including Ni'ihau and the uninhabited islands of Ka'ula and Lehua).

HAWAI'I TODAY

In 2000 the U. S. census found that 43% of the permanent residents of Hawai'i were multiracial, about half (22%) of those part Hawaiian. Caucasians accounted for the largest single group (24%), followed by Japanese (16%), Filipino (12%), and Chinese (3%). Blacks, Koreans, Hawaiians, and Samoans were the other groups identified. This diversity has created a rich fusion of cultures that makes Hawai'i unique.

Hula students performing during Aloha Week, Moloka'i

Happily, for the last 30 or so years, many more resident Hawaiians, both native and transplanted, have become dedicated to promoting some of the traditions and customs of the Old Hawaiians. Increasing numbers of students study the Hawaiian language, and writers both public and private are spelling Hawaiian words as they were first written down. Careful speakers attempt to pronounce Hawaiian words as they were pronounced before they were anglicized. Books of ancient chants and myths, in Hawaiian and translated into English, are more common than ever.

On all the major islands are *hālau hula* (literally *hālau* is a longhouse for canoes or *hula* instruction, but now it also describes a class for *hula*), each with a *kumu hula*, who teaches the precepts as well as the movements of *hula*. Here students learn the *mele* and the music that, along with the dance, tell of ancient Hawaiians.

The musical tradition in the Islands is one of the richest cultural strands. From the missionaries came melody and four-part harmony, both unused in the traditional chants. To the percussion instruments of the ancient Hawaiians was added the guitar, probably first brought over by traders on ships from Mexico or California. In time the Hawaiian musicians loosened the strings and tuned them to suit their style, and so evolved that peculiarly Hawaiian instrument, the slack-key guitar. Later came the steel guitar, perhaps inspired by an East Indian stringed instrument, the *gottuvadyam*. From Portugal came the *braquino*, or *cavaquinho*, today known the world over as the Hawaiian *'ukulele* ("jumping flea").

Another milestone in the evolution of Hawaiian music came in 1868, when King Kalākaua decided to form a royal band for Hawai'i, much like those of the monarchies in Europe. Heinrich Berger came over from Germany to be the bandmaster. He served as director of the band from 1872 to 1915. His enormous influence on Hawaiian music has led to his being called the "Father of Hawaiian Music." He arranged more than 1,000 Hawaiian songs and composed 75 originals, his synthesis of Hawaiian and Western music traditions resulting in songs that people recognize around the world as "Hawaiian." He and Kalākaua, also a talented musician, collaborated on the Kingdom's national anthem, the moving "Hawai'i Pono'i." In this same musical style, Queen Lili'uokalani wrote the even better known "Aloha 'Oe."

In addition to the standard U. S. holidays, several holidays celebrate Hawaiian traditions, both old and not so old. Merrie Monarch Week in Hilo celebrates the *hula*, May Day is Lei Day, Kamehameha Day honors the first king of all the Hawaiian Islands, and Aloha Week (actually spread over several weeks in the fall) has taken the place of the *makahiki*, or harvest festival. And at the end of every week comes Aloha Friday, when men dress in Aloha shirts and women in *mu'umu'u* or *holomu'u* (a long, seamed dress), both the shirts and the dresses of colorful tropical prints, a specialty of Hawai'i.

Along with these holidays with specifically Hawaiian themes are the many holidays the various ethnic groups sponsor. The Japanese Cherry Blossom Festival, the Chinese Narcissus Festival, and the Fiesta Filipino are among the most prominent of these.

In Hawai'i, the cowboys who work the ranches are called *paniolo*, the name introduced in the 19th Century by the Spanish *vaqueros* brought over to help train the local wranglers. Today, several rodeos each year commemorate the tradition of riding and roping, the biggest of them all the annual Makawao Rodeo on Maui.

The *lū'au* is one Hawaiian tradition that seems never to have gone out of favor. Though contemporary *lū'au* often include many variations, the traditional meal features *kalua* pork, fish, chicken, *poi*, sweet potatoes, breadfruit, and bananas, all wrapped in *tī* leaves and baked in an *imu*, an underground oven. For a small meal, Hawaiians like to pick *'opihi* ("limpits") off the rocks and eat them raw. *Limu* ("seaweed") is also a local favorite.

When asked to name the food that, after the *lū'au*, most represents Hawai'i today, some locals will answer, "Loco Moco." A favorite breakfast treat for the stout of heart, this hearty meal shows the influence of other cultures. Over a bowlful of white rice are a hamburger patty, grilled onions, and two fried eggs; then the entire dish is drenched in thick brown gravy. Another favorite, the "Hawaiian Plate," served in many neighborhood restaurants, features pork, chicken, or fish and two scoops of rice and two of macaroni salad. Along with this mixture of starchy offerings are, of course, ethnic foods from around the world.

Snack foods come in the same variety. From the Chinese has come crack seed, with entire stores devoted to the sale of these preserved and seasoned fruits and seeds. An island institution is shave ice, a savory version of the snow cone. The many other snacks enjoyed here, from *lomi lomi* salmon to *sushi*, are called *pūpū*, the equivalent of the English "appetizers."

Limu (seaweed) harvesting, Pūko'o Bay

Fortunately, much of the best of Old Hawai'i has never disappeared: the close immediate and extended families, the generosity and acceptance of strangers, and the appreciation for the natural world. Perhaps the beautiful *lei* symbolize best the spirit of Hawai'i. These elegant necklaces made from shells or flowers and greenery express the joy the Hawaiians experience in the natural world as well as their love of color, texture, and design. Offered as tokens of esteem and love, the *lei* encircles the wearer in an embrace of Hawai'i *aloha*.

GEOLOGY AND GEOGRAPHY

Nou nō a o uka me kai,
Nou nō Hawaiʻi nei ā puni
("Yours is the upland, yours the sea,
Yours the whole of Hawaiʻi.")
Chant to Pele, the deity of volcanoes

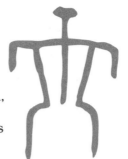

GEOLOGY

When Pele, the Hawaiian goddess of fire, brought her family to Hawaiʻi to find a suitable place for their new home, she began her search at the most northwesterly of the inhabited islands, Niʻihau, and then continued down the chain until she came to the last island. There, finally, she found the fire pit she was looking for, the Kīlauea Volcano.

In this early myth, by following the chain of islands from the oldest to the youngest, Pele found the birthplace of the islands of Hawaiʻi. Today, scientists believe that millions of years before the appearance of any of these islands, magma flowed up through a crevice in the floor of the Pacific Ocean, building up into a mound, called a shield volcano. After centuries of more or less continual oozing, the first island appeared, some 25-40 million years ago. That first island, geologists theorize, is now the northwestern most of the Emperor Seamounts, which extend northwest beyond the island of Kure.

The lovely results of erosion

Two different theories account for the oldest of the volcanic islands being the most northwestern and the youngest being the Big Island at the southeastern tip. One theory is that the plate on which these islands formed has moved and continues to move northwest at a consistent rate of almost 3 inches each year. The "hot spot," however, has remained in approximately the same position below the plate. As a new island develops, the plate takes it gradually away from the volcanic activity.

In recorded history, only Haleakalā (1790) on Maui and Hualālai (1801), Mauna Loa (1859-1975), and Kīlauea (1840-present) on the Big Island, have had volcanic eruptions, lending support to this theory. Perhaps even more persuasive is Lōʻihi Seamount, now building 15 miles southeast of the Big Island. Still 500 fathoms below the ocean's surface, Lōʻihi Seamount will perhaps not be an "island" for another thousand years or so, but it is growing steadily as the submarine volcano continues to push magma through the earth's crust.

The second theory is that the ocean floor beneath the Hawaiian archipelago has a series of cracks that run generally in a northwest-southeast line and that out of this series of cracks seeped the lava that formed this chain of islands.

Thus, over the course of millions of years, volcanic activity has created these islands, but erosion has altered their shapes. Streams cut valleys into the rounded slopes, and waves carved some of the world's highest sea cliffs. Gravel, sand, and clay washed down to cover the valley floors and the edges of the islands. At the same time colonial corals and algae were building fringing reefs around the islands. Most of the islands of this archipelago are so eroded now that they are no longer islands at all but seamounts, the peaks in many instances several hundred fathoms below the surface of the Pacific Ocean.

By reversing Pele's route and following the Hawaiian islands and atolls from the Big Island northwestward to Kure Atoll, one can follow the geologic history of the chain back in time. What the Big Island is today the other islands and atolls were in millennia past.

As one would expect, the youngest of the landforms of the chain (discounting Lōʻihi and other seamounts building to the southeast), the Big Island, is also the largest, with 4,038 square miles of land area, and still growing on apace. (Kīlauea is the world's most continuously active volcano.) Formed by five shield volcanoes—Kohala, Mauna Kea, Hualālai, Mauna Loa, and Kīlauea—it makes up almost two thirds of the land area of the entire state.

Snowy peaks of Mauna Loa

Because it is younger, it is less eroded than the other islands. One result, in addition to its size, is its elevation. Mauna Kea (13,796 feet) and Mauna Loa (13,769 feet) are the highest peaks in the Hawaiian Islands, and, when measured from its base in the Hawaiian Trough, Mauna Kea, at 33,476 feet, is the tallest in the world.

Together with size, this height gives the Big Island the greatest variation in climate zone. On the windward slopes of Mauna Loa rainfall may exceed 300 inches annually, and snow covers the peaks of Mauna Loa and Mauna Kea each winter. Yet much of the Kona Coast, one of the warmest and driest spots in the Islands, is properly classified as a desert.

Another indication of the geologic youth of this island is its beaches. They are fewer in number than those of the other major islands, and a large percentage of them are black sand, from the breakdown of lava rather than of the reefs.

The next island northwestward in the chain and the second largest, Maui consists of two shield volcanoes connected by an isthmus formed from lava flows. The older of the volcanoes is now the West Maui Mountains, with its exquisitely carved valleys, ridges, and peaks. The younger volcano, Haleakalā, last erupting in 1790, has created East Maui, much more rounded than West Maui because it has seen much less erosion. Because of their elevations, the two volcanoes of Maui assure that the windward slopes get more than abundant rainfall: over 350 inches per year on the slopes of Haleakalā (10,023 feet) and 400 inches on the West Maui summit, Puʻu Kukui (5,788 feet).

Geologists believe that Maui, Molokini, Kahoʻolawe, and Lānaʻi were once connected but that the connections were inundated after the last ice age. Tiny Molokini, 2.5 miles offshore of the west coast of East Maui, is but one side of the rim of a small volcanic cone. The cove on the north side of the rim is over the crater of the cone. This island in the rain shadow of Haleakalā is dry and shows no evidence of ever having been inhabited. Kahoʻolawe, too, is a small island (45 square miles) in the shadow of Haleakalā. Though archeological remains on the island suggest earlier human habitation, it is now too dry to sustain even range land for cattle.

The three volcanoes that formed the island of Molokaʻi have given it three diverse areas. The earliest of the volcanoes resulted in West Molokaʻi, where the shield volcano Mauna Loa is presently a relatively low, dry tableland, with one of the longest white sand beaches in the Hawaiian Islands on its west shore.

The second shield volcano formed East Molokaʻi, because of its elevation—4,950 feet at its peak, Kamakou—much wetter and therefore much more dramatically etched with gulches and valleys. Almost vertical sea cliffs on the northeast shore enhance the drama. On the side of one of these sea cliffs, a later and much smaller volcano erupted to form the Kalaupapa Peninsula, a flat tongue of land virtually inaccessible by land.

Lāna'i, though undoubtedly as old as Moloka'i and Maui, retains the classic rounded shape of the single shield volcano that was its creator. In the rain shadow of the West Maui Mountains, it receives little rain and thus has been subject to much less water erosion than the other major islands. Yet it does boast some of Hawai'i's highest sea cliffs on its southwest coast, which is exposed to the open ocean.

The two old shield volcanoes of O'ahu, the Wai'anae and the Ko'olau, are both greatly eroded. Lava flows from the two joined to create the Leilehua Plateau. The younger of the two, Ko'olau, is the wetter and has the more spectacular *pali*, though Wai'anae, too, has magnificent cliffs. Both have classic examples of amphitheater-headed valleys. Some of the landmarks on O'ahu are the result of much later volcanic activity. Diamond Head, Punchbowl, and Koko Head are all examples of tuff cones (a cone forms when volcanic ash built up around a vent is cemented together). White sand beaches dot the entire perimeter of O'ahu.

photo by Vickie Buck

Jon Petersen and friendly gooney on Midway

The oldest of the major Hawaiian Islands, Kaua'i is in the minds of its many admirers also the most beautiful. The elevations of the two peaks of the single shield volcano result in large amounts of rainfall. Wai'ale'ale, one of those peaks, with its recorded rainfall of more than 450 inches a year is one of the wettest spots on earth. This abundance of water running off the slopes has resulted in geologic and aesthetic wonders, notably Waimea Canyon and the Alaka'i Swamp. In conjunction with the action of the ocean waves, the runoff has created the magnificent sea cliffs, Nā Pali.

Little Ni'ihau, once probably connected to the island of Kaua'i, suffers from being in the lee of Kaua'i. The 73 square miles of this single shield volcano includes some of the driest spots in the Hawaiian Islands. Ironically, one of its claims to geologic uniqueness is the presence on the island of two large *playa* lakes, the Hālāli'i and the Halulu (in some years having more mud than water).

After Ni'ihau begins the chain of islands and atolls known as the Northwestern Hawaiian Islands. (Geographically, all these islands and atolls except Midway belong to the State of Hawai'i, though they are National Wildlife Refuges.)

In this group, according to geologists, are the oldest of the landforms in the chain still having enough land mass above the ocean's surface to be called islands: Nihoa, Necker, French Frigate Shoals, Gardner Pinnacles, and Laysan. All are relative low in elevation, from Nihoa, the most southeasterly and therefore the youngest and highest at 910 feet, to Laysan at 35 feet. As a result, these islands are all dry, with little to no vegetation. Several *heiau*, extensive agricultural terraces, and other remains indicate that Polynesians with a culture similar to that of Tahiti once inhabited Nihoa and Necker, but the birds are the primary residents on all the Northwestern Islands now. In all the Northwestern Islands, only French Frigate Shoals, Laysan, and Midway Atoll are occupied, each having a few resident biologists to study the wildlife and habitat. Additionally, Midway has a permanent maintenance crew and, periodically, a handful of volunteers who assist the biologists.

In the Northwestern Hawaiian Islands are the atolls Maro, Lisianski, Pearl and Hermes, Midway, and Kure. These atolls, barely rising above sea level, are thought to be the remains of shield volcanoes similar to those found among the major islands to the southeast. Over the course of millions of years wind and water have eroded them so that only parts of the fringing reefs and, in some cases, small sand islands remain above the surface of the ocean. Ideal wildlife habitats, these are also a part of the Hawaiian Islands National Wildlife Refuge.

Boaters interested in geology have but to follow this chain northward from the Big Island to Midway Atoll to see on exhibit the evolution of these diverse islands of Hawai'i. (Kure is the last island in the chain, but Midway is the only destination in the Northwestern Islands open to cruising sailors.) Though scientists believe the islands and atolls have all come from the same source, their land masses having bubbled up out of fissures in the ocean floor, each is geologically unique because of its location on the shifting plate on the earth's crust. This diversity is, of course, interesting in itself, but for boaters it's another reason for choosing Hawai'i as a cruising ground.

GEOGRAPHY

The State of Hawai'i, the 50th state, is the southernmost of the states and is one of the most remote places on the earth. It sits almost in the center of the Pacific Ocean, its 132 islands, reefs, and shoals stretching over 1,523 miles of ocean, from Kure Atoll southeast to the Big Island. The nearest continent, North America, lies 2,100 miles to the east, and the Marquesas, the likely origin of the earliest settlers on the islands, are 1,900 miles to the south.

This isolation undoubtedly meant that plant and animal life came slowly to the islands of Hawai'i. Whatever came here over the thousands of years before the first humans arrived had to have been brought by chance on the wind or on the ocean. Biologists estimate that perhaps no more often than once in every 100,000 years did a new species establish itself on the islands.

Because of this isolation, and the climate and volcanic soil of the Hawaiian Islands, some of those species that did prosper here evolved into unique flora and fauna. Hawai'i has species of birds, insects, snails, and plants found nowhere else in the world. For example, the state bird, the *nēnē*, is related to the Canada goose but is nevertheless a unique species. The state tree, the *kukui,* or candlenut, is also found nowhere else.

People, of course, have introduced thousands of other species, particularly since the arrival of the first Europeans. The early Polynesians are believed to have brought pigs, dogs, chickens, taro, banana, coconut, sugar cane, breadfruit, yams, and other plants. Rats apparently hitched a ride on one of those early journeys.

What all travelers, plant or animal, found when they arrived at these islands by chance was a climate as salubrious as any in the world. Along the archipelago, which stretches between approximately 19 and 29 degrees north latitude, the ocean acts as a thermostat for the islands' temperature. Varying from 73-74 degrees in February and March to near 80 in September and October, the ocean moderates the air, no matter from which direction, before it reaches the islands. With this proximity to the equator, the days and nights vary little in duration from summer to winter (those being the only two seasons). In the summer the days are about 13½ hours long; in the winter, about 11, another reason for little seasonal variation in temperatures.

Despite its isolation, Hawai'i draws to its sunny beaches and tropical forests people from around the world, and its location makes it an ideal destination for cruisers.

Conch shell blower

Diamond Head Light

Ahu (travelers' shrines) at Shipwreck Beach

17

WEATHER, TIDES, CURRENTS, WIND, AND STORMS

'A'ohe 'auwa'a pa'a i ka hālau i ka mālie.
("No canoes remain in the sheds in calm weather.")

WEATHER

The fabled weather in Hawai'i features mild temperatures throughout the year, with moderate humidity and cooling tradewinds on most days. Rain is falling somewhere on the Islands just about all the time, but rarely does it interfere with beach or other outdoor activities. Severe storms are rare.

Visitors from places that have markedly different seasons often claim that Hawai'i has no seasons. For the residents, though, the year divides into two distinct seasons: summer and winter. In the summer months, between May and October, the high temperature along the coasts is generally in the mid to upper 80s. The cooling tradewinds blow fairly

Rain clouds hovering over Lāna'i

persistently, as much as 90 percent of the days in some summers. When those tradewinds die out, as they often do intermittently in September and October, the temperatures may climb into the lower 90s.

In the winter, from November through April, the tradewinds are not as consistent, blowing as few as 50 percent of the days, but the temperature may nevertheless sometimes be a bit cooler because the ocean is a few degrees cooler. The record lows for the coastal areas are between 48-53, but these low readings are rare. (The mountain peaks have much colder winter weather because of their elevations; on some of the peaks the climate is classified as sub-arctic!)

The more significant difference is that weather fronts from the northern latitude and *kona* storms interrupt the tradewinds, bringing the heaviest and most frequent rains on the leeward sides of the islands. On the windward sides, of course, the tradewinds bring frequent and sometimes heavy rains throughout the summer as well.

For the residents of the Islands, the winter temperatures are cool enough for them to break out woolen jackets, long pants, and their electric blankets at night. For most visitors, though, even in February and March, typically the coldest months, it's still shorts, T-shirts, and sandals weather.

RAINFALL

In the ocean around the Hawaiian Islands, between 25 and 30 inches of rain falls each year. While some coastal areas in the Islands might also receive approximately that amount, the averages range dramatically. Some leeward coasts receive less than 10 inches a year, most of it falling in the winter months. By contrast, windward coasts may receive rainfall every month of a typical year, in some cases totaling well over 100 inches a year. Hilo, for instance, receives an average of 141 inches annually. Some of the mountain peaks, such as Mt. Wai'ale'ale on Kaua'i, receive well over 400 inches of rainfall in an average year.

The heaviest rainfall amounts are recorded between November and April on the leeward sides of the Islands. Typically, these areas receive no rainfall in the summer.

VISIBILITY

Every now and then one hears an old saying that appeals to us all: "If you're sailing around the Hawaiian Islands and you see fog, clean your glasses."

Fog is indeed non-existent in the Islands, but you still can't always see forever on a clear day. Some islands, the island of Hawai'i more than any others, have "vog," which looks like high fog to most who see it. Vog forms when the volcano at Kīlauea spews ash and other particles into the dense air; the vog becomes especially noticeable when a trade wind inversion keeps the volcanic debris below 5,000 feet. Occasionally, the vog is blown or drifts as far north as O'ahu. When vog is especially thick, visibility along the South Kona coast will be no more than 2 or 3 miles. Although it obscures the views of the island and makes photographs taken of landscapes look fuzzy, boaters don't have to worry about running into the island because of zero-visibility vog. And vog produces stunning sunsets!

The only other visibility-reducing situation boaters encounter when cruising the Islands is an occasional squall, but these cause few problems because they move quickly. So perhaps the old saying is almost correct. A few instances of vog and an occasional squall notwithstanding, visibility in Hawai'i comes as close to being perfect as a boater is likely to find.

TIDES

The tide range in Hawai'i is slight compared to that in most other places in the world. With a maximum tide range of only 2.5 feet, boaters don't have to worry excessively about going aground while they sleep.

Although a few dangers do exist, essentially boaters in Hawai'i concern themselves with tide only when they have to cross a reef to get into an anchorage or when they anchor in a shallow bay. Passages through reefs in Hawai'i rarely have less than 10 feet of water at the shallowest point, so tide causes few concerns. Some anchorages and small boat harbors, however, do have shallow water. For example, the anchorage area inside the breakwater at Mānele Bay, on Lana'i, has only 7 or 8 feet of water, at best. In some areas where shoaling has occurred, even less water covers the soft mud bottom; thus, most cruising boats will sometimes touch bottom when

Trade winds on an ocean passage

the tide is out. Because the mud on the bottom is soft, however, boats can generally power out.

To avoid tidal surprises, most boaters whose boats have a draft of 6 feet or more try not to anchor in less than 12 or 15 feet of water. If you don't anchor in the shallowest part of harbors and bays such as Hanalei, Kāne'ohe, Kaunakakai, Kahului, or Kamalō, you shouldn't have to worry about tides.

CURRENTS

Because of the small tide range, currents around the Islands are also insignificant. Rarely will you find an area where the current exceeds 1 knot. Some harbors on one of the major channels, such as Pūkoʻo, Kamalō, and Kaunakakai, have a current at the entrance that can be as strong as 1 knot.

In long passages around Hawaiʻi, you will occasionally find your boat set by a cross current. For instance, while we were enroute to Midway Atoll, the GPS sometimes showed that we were being pushed to one side or the other of our desired track by a current. To avoid being pushed too far off course, we plotted our GPS position on our chart every 2 or 3 hours.

TRADE WINDS

The persistent trade winds in the Hawaiian Islands are a result of the equally persistent Pacific High, a high pressure system, or anticyclone, that usually sits northeast of Hawaiʻi. The High has a seasonal shift, moving north in the summer and south in the winter. In the summer it is generally stronger and more consistent. But the terrain of the Islands exerts the greatest influence on both the speed and the direction of the winds. Because of the ruggedness and the variations of the terrain, trade winds in the exposed channels, near headlands, and in the lee of gorges, passes, and saddles may be stronger and gustier than in the open ocean.

The Pacific High is large, usually covering hundreds of miles of ocean. Because the High has a clockwise rotation, it causes significant wind patterns over the open ocean. On the north side of the High, above 40° N, the winds are most commonly westerly. But on the south side of the High, the winds are northeasterly. These northeasterly trade winds blow from a few hundred miles west of the Pacific coast of Mexico to Hawaiʻi, and even as far as Guam and the Philippines.

When writers talk about the "steady trade winds," they refer not to the strength but simply to the persistence. The trades that blow over the Hawaiian Islands range in strength from a whisper to 30 knots. The only quality of these winds that is "steady" is the winds themselves. Trade winds, which blow out of the northeast or east, do dominate the weather picture in Hawaiʻi. So dominant are these winds, in fact, that the term "windward" here always refers to the direction of the trades, no matter where the actual wind is coming from at the moment.

Boaters describe the strength of the wind in terms set down during the last century by Sir Francis Beaufort, a Royal Navy hydrographer. Fortunately, the meteorologists at the National Weather Service use the same scale, though slightly different descriptive terms, when they prepare weather forecasts.

The following chart shows the scale, with the right column showing the terms used by the Weather Service:

Force	Wind Speed (in knots)	Beaufort Description	Sea Height	Weather Service Description
0	0-1	Calm	0	Light & Var.
1	1-3	Light Airs	Less than 1'	Light & Var.
2	4-6	Light Breeze	Less than 1'	Light & Var.
3	7-10	Light Breeze	1-2'	Gentle
4	11-16	Moderate Breeze	2-4'	Moderate
5	17-21	Fresh Breeze	4-8'	Fresh
6	22-27	Strong Breeze	8-13'	Strong
7	28-33	Strong Wind	13-20'	Strong
8	34-40	Near Gale	13-20'	Gale
9	41-47	Strong Gale	13-20'	Gale
10	48-55	Storm	20-30'	Whole Gale
11	56-65	Violent Storm	30-45'	Whole Gale
12	65+	Hurricane	over 45'	Hurricane

When you hear the Weather Service prediction, the important thing to remember is that the winds in the channels will be stronger. The sea height given for each category of wind speed in the Beaufort Scale is for the seas in the open ocean. When moderate, fresh, or strong trade winds blow, the seas in the channels will often be higher than those in the open ocean. Also, the waves in the channels are typically short and steep rather than the long swells we find in the open ocean.

WIND STRENGTH

During the summer months, when most boaters are cruising the Islands, the trades dominate. But the rosy view that trades blow 15 knots day after day is incorrect. In fact, a more typical pattern is for strong trades to blow for a few days, often 20-30 knots, and then for moderate trades to blow for another week. After the moderate winds blow, the winds might go back to strong trades, or they might become light and variable.

Squall over the Pacific

When winds are light and variable, the conditions are typically about the same in the channels as along the coasts of the islands. However, in moderate-to-heavy trades the velocities increase in the channels as these winds are squeezed between the islands. For example, in moderate trades of 15 knots, the winds are typically light and gusty on the leeward coasts, 15 knots on the windward coasts, but 20-25 in the channels.

In these moderate-to-heavy trade winds, most sailors try to avoid crossing channels upwind and do not even consider visiting the anchorages on the windward coasts of the islands.

KONA WINDS

When the winds reverse and come out of the southwest or west, these leeward winds are called *kona* winds. A wind blowing from this leeward direction catches many people off guard, especially boaters. Also, *kona* winds are often strong and bring rain. These winds rarely hit the Islands, and they almost never hit except during the winter months. But even that is not a certainty.

Because of the excellent weather reports in the state, careful boaters do not get caught by *kona* storms. If you listen to weather reports every day, you will usually have two or three days to prepare for the arrival of *kona* storms, ample time to get to a safe harbor.

SWELLS

Although surfers love the swells, the relationship between boaters and swells is not much of a love affair. Try anchoring in a south-facing anchorage when a south swell is running and you will quickly discover the definition of "uncomfortable."

Swells can come from any direction. Generally, however, storms in the southern hemisphere produce summer swells in Hawai'i. Most of these are not dangerous; they simply make boats anchored in bays with southern exposures roll uncomfortably. When such swells become excessively large—a rare occurrence—boaters generally move to a more comfortable anchorage.

The islands are small enough that you can easily get around to another shore or even to another island, in some instances. If you're enjoying the anchorages along the southwest coast of Lāna'i when an uncomfortable south swell rolls in, you can move around to Mānele Bay for a day or two or head for one of the harbors with better protection on Moloka'i, such as Kamalō or Pūko'o.

The swells that come from the north during the winter months are larger and have a greater impact on boaters. Storms in the North Pacific generate more serious swells because these storms are closer to the Islands. From late October to April, north swells make anchorages along the north shore of all the islands unusable much of the time. These high swells become breakers as they reach shallow water, and they can be dangerous. One storm about 30 years ago produced 50-foot-high breakers that caused massive destruction to the north shores of all the islands.

Although these high swells are dangerous, you shouldn't have to worry about them if you monitor the weather forecasts. High surf advisories will interrupt regular programming on NOAA Weather Radio whenever a high surf is expected. With data coming in from far-ranging weather buoys and satellites, the Weather Service can normally warn boaters many hours before swells reach the Islands. Even without advanced warnings, you can detect an increasing swell before it becomes dangerous, and you will have time to get to the safe southern shore of the island. While few boaters visit even the most beautiful north shore anchorages, such as Hanalei Bay, in the late fall, winter, and early spring, those who do watch the weather continuously.

Similarly, the large swells associated with a *kona* storm or a hurricane make entering even the largest and most accessible small boat harbors, such as the Ala Wai, questionable or entirely out of the question. Again, because of the excellent weather reports, few boaters get into trouble with the swells or storms.

STORMS

The hurricane season in Hawai'i is generally between May and November, though in fact few hurricanes hit the Islands directly. Those that threaten Hawai'i originate along the West Coast of Mexico and head across the Pacific every year, but few arrive here. They either break up along the way or pass offshore.

Nevertheless, two hurricanes have hit Kaua'i directly in recent history—'Iwa in November 1982 (illustrating that November can no longer be considered a hurricane-free month) and 'Iniki in September 1992. Both hurricanes devastated Kaua'i and did considerable damage to boats on other Hawaiian islands, providing startling evidence that, despite their rare occurrence, hurricanes can hit the Islands with force. Thus boaters and residents alike should have emergency plans in place.

Because most hurricanes that threaten the Islands originate 2,500 miles away, the Weather Service has several days to track each storm's progress and estimate its intensity. NOAA radio then broadcasts warning bulletins 24 hours a day on KBA-99 and VHF 1 and 2. Those boaters who monitor these weather reports will have plenty of time to find a safe place for their boats.

To experience a hurricane is to develop respect for its power. When Hurricane 'Iwa came through in 1982, our boat was at a dock in Ke'ehi Lagoon on O'ahu. The winds on Kaua'i were clocked with gusts up to 117 mph. At the dock in Ke'ehi, they reached a maximum of only 78 mph, but even that was enough to do considerable damage.

Boats at sea fared well during Hurricane 'Iwa. On one boat en route from the south to Kaua'i when Hurricane 'Iwa came through, the crew members had not been monitoring weather and were caught by surprise. The hurricane went directly over the boat. Although the crew had a rough ride, both crew and boat survived unscathed.

Boats in some harbors did not fare so well when 'Iwa hit. In Port Allen, the harbor on the south of Kaua'i, the breakwater failed. The waves and swell washed virtually all the boats in the small boat harbor up on the shore, destroying many of them. By contrast, almost all the boats in Nāwiliwili Small Boat Harbor, only a few miles away, survived. The difference is location. Because the storm approached from the south, Port Allen and the entire south coast of the island

NOAA-11
9/11/92
1400 UTC
Thermal
Data

Hurricane
Iniki

20 N

15 N

Kauai

Hawaii

Hurricane 'Iniki, 1992

felt the full force of the 117-knot winds, while Nāwiliwili, on the eastern shore, was protected at least somewhat by the hills to the south, east and west.

When a hurricane is predicted, you should certainly not keep your boat in any anchorages facing the direction from which the hurricane is expected. And you might also consider moving the boat out of any harbor open to that direction when the forecast calls for a direct hit by a hurricane. Port Allen on Kaua'i, Mānele Bay and Kaumalapau on Lāna'i, Kaunakakai and Lono on Moloka'i, and Lahaina and Mā'alaea on Maui, for instance, could all be unsafe in a hurricane approaching from the south.

While none of us wants to ride out a hurricane at sea, we and our boats will in some instances be much safer there than in a harbor that is directly in the path of a hurricane. Even though the center of Hurricane 'Iwa was never closer than about 100 miles from Ke'ehi Lagoon, where we were docked, a number of boats in the lagoon did not survive. A 30-foot ketch anchored near our boat sank when the planks in the wood hull opened. A wood-hulled World War II PT boat disintegrated after it was repeatedly slammed into the dock to which it was tied. A 55-foot schooner in the anchorage dragged anchor and was destroyed when it washed ashore.

Fortunately, these lost boats were exceptions. Of the 500 boats docked and 200 anchored at Ke'ehi, the majority came through the storm undamaged. If you don't plan to ride a hurricane out at sea, make haste to the safest harbor you can find before the storm arrives. What is and is not a safe harbor depends in part on the direction and strength of the hurricane, but most boaters agree that Nāwiliwili on Kaua'i; Ala Wai, Kāne'ohe, Ko Olina, and Ke'ehi on O'ahu; Kahului on Maui; and Honokōhau and Hilo on Hawai'i would provide the best protection in most storms. Despite the fact that these harbors generally have no vacant slips, the harbormasters try to find a place for everyone when a hurricane is forecast.

Before the storm hits, you should store below decks everything on deck that can be removed. The strong winds will often manage to unroll roller furling headsails enough so that the sails are reduced to a few scraps of sailcloth. All other sails should be stored below to reduce windage and minimize the chance of damage. Even a dodger should be removed and stored below. Another frequent casualty when hurricanes hit is the tender. A hard dinghy may end up holed and submerged, and an inflatable may fly away when the painter fails.

Making sure the boat stays put when a hurricane blows requires some serious tackle. Boats at sea will probably do best lying to a sea anchor, a giant parachute-like device that many ocean cruisers carry for just such an emergency. The sea anchor works best for most boats because it forces the boat to keep its bow, its strongest part, headed into the waves. Some boaters prefer to use a drogue, however, which allows the boat to go downwind in front of the storm, but at a controlled rate of speed.

Boaters who ride out a hurricane at anchor or on a mooring in a harbor will want to use their largest ground tackle, of course. Multiple anchors are better than one when a hurricane hits. The same is true of mooring lines. And without chafing gear to protect all anchor or mooring lines, the lines will wear through in minutes.

Having said all this about hurricanes, we hasten to reiterate that hurricanes almost never hit the Hawaiian Islands, so the chance of your having to deal with one is remote. Nevertheless, you will want to have ready an emergency plan for that eventuality.

TSUNAMIS

Even though tsunamis present little threat to cruising boaters, residents of the Hawaiian Islands take them seriously. When a tsunami hits the Islands, a potential exists for major damage and loss of life. The most common causes of the tsunamis that hit the Islands are earthquakes, especially those occurring in Alaska or California. In addition, volcanic eruptions and even landslides can trigger tsunamis.

What most people find incredible about tsunamis is that they are essentially undetectable by boaters at sea. A 20-foot wall of water that reaches an island might have been a mere 2-foot wave mid-ocean. On the other hand, boats in a harbor are almost sure to be badly damaged or destroyed in a major tsunami. For this reason most boaters, even those who regularly keep their boats in the safest of harbors, such as the Ala Wai Small Boat Harbor, take their boats out to sea when the arrival of a tsunami is imminent.

Despite the great speeds at which tsunamis travel across the ocean—sometimes at an amazing 600 knots—the Pacific Tsunami Warning Center usually provides adequate warning so that boaters have time to move their boats out of harbor. When only 2 miles offshore, boats are almost guaranteed to suffer no damage. If the boat can't be moved for some reason, the best advice is to get everyone off the boat and up to high ground. Do not stay aboard a boat in a harbor when a tsunami is approaching.

All this talk about high surf, *kona* storms, hurricanes, and tsunamis may suggest that Hawai'i is a dangerous place to go boating, but remember that all these extreme weather conditions are just that: extreme and therefore rare. Our goal in spending this much time describing each of these potential threats is to assure that our readers don't get surprised.

Kewalo Basin

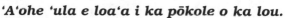

EQUIPMENT FOR THE HAWAI'I CRUISE

'A'ohe 'ula e loa'a i ka pōkole o ka lou.
("No breadfruit can be reached when the picking stick is too short.")

Any boat that is well built and competently handled can be a good cruising boat for Hawaiian waters. We have occasionally seen 176-foot yachts cruising Hawai'i, and just about as often we have seen 24-foot sloops. Generally, and not surprisingly, larger boats provide more comfort when crossing oceans and channels. But the equipment on a boat is the more important in determining how the boat handles, how safe it is, and, finally, how confident you are in a seaway.

Sailors will no doubt continue to debate among themselves the question of which pieces of equipment are, indeed, essential for the handling and safety of a cruising boat in Hawai'i. In this section we list alphabetically and briefly describe the equipment commonly seen on cruising boats in the Islands, some of it required by law, some strongly recommended for the safety of the boat and crew, and some recommended for the added comfort.

ANCHORING AND MOORING EQUIPMENT

MOORING

While cruising the Hawaiian Islands, you'll find yourself in one of three situations every night: tied up in a small boat harbor, tied to a mooring buoy, or anchored. Each of these requires specific equipment if the boat is to be secure.

Although the State of Hawai'i has a critical shortage of marina space, occasionally you will be able to get your boat into a slip or on a dock, tied Tahiti-style, for a night or two. If you plan to try to obtain one of these accommodations, you must be prepared with enough lines and, in some cases, an anchor. In some small boat harbors—for example,

Whitecaps in Lahaina Roadstead

Honokōhau on the Big Island, Kaunakakai on Moloka'i, and Lahaina and Mā'alaea on Maui—you can expect to tie one end of your boat to a buoy and the other end to cleats on the seawall. To tie to the seawall in Hilo's Radio Bay, you'll have to drop an anchor (or two) and then pull the boat up to the seawall and tie it to cleats. In these harbors you'll need lines of various lengths, and, for some harbors, stronger than usual lines to combat the tremendous surge.

In other harbors, such as Kahului, Mānele Bay, Kāne'ohe Yacht Club, He'eia Kea, Hale'iwa, Wai'anae, Ke'ehi, Ala Wai, Nāwiliwili, and Port Allen, you'll most often tie to a fixed pier rather than to a floating pier. At a fixed pier, you'll need to tie fore and aft, of course, but you'll also need to set spring lines and, if possible, lines to a piling to keep your boat from banging against the pier. Some of these small boat harbors have tremendous surge, especially Mā'alaea, Wai'anae, Hale'iwa, and Port Allen, so you may need to use as many as six mooring lines to secure your boat. In addition, large, sturdy fenders are necessary to avoid getting horrendous black marks on the sides of your boat from the tires used as bumpers on the piers.

At a few destinations, moorings are sometimes available for visiting boats. To tie to a mooring, you'll typically need only a single line, but it should be a heavy one if you plan to go ashore or to stay overnight. In some cases the buoys for these moorings are on the surface of the water; in others they are 6 feet or more below the surface and will necessitate your diving down to tie to them. Some of these buoys will have a pennant attached to them that you can simply bring up to the bow or stern cleat of your boat. Others will require that you slip one of your lines through a large shackle or ring and take the line back to your boat.

ANCHORS

Despite the clear appeal of tying to a seawall or a mooring, you'll find few opportunities to do so around Hawai'i. Of the 68 cruising destinations identified in this guide, only 14 have such facilities. In short, if you are going to explore many of these destinations, you can expect to use ground tackle far more frequently than mooring lines, and this ground tackle should be the best you can buy.

The basic component of your ground tackle is your anchor. Every cruiser has a favorite, so you'll hear conflicting opinions about the best anchor. In deciding on the right anchor for cruising Hawai'i, talk to as many people as you can, preferably people who have spent a lot of time cruising.

Anchoring conditions vary greatly from anchorage to anchorage in Hawai'i; consequently, the best hook is the most versatile one. For example, the bottom in Kaunakakai Harbor is mud so sticky it will challenge you to retrieve your anchor; you will rarely worry about dragging anchor there if your anchor is adequately sized. Other anchorages have rocks on the bottom or a bottom so hard that almost no anchor will set. The Lahaina Roadstead and the dredged basin behind the reef at Pūko'o come to mind. Even with the largest hook available, we would not want to spend a night anchored in either if strong winds were blowing.

Wind conditions in the Islands are yet another variable to consider. Because all the anchorages and harbors can have strong and gusty winds blowing through them, we recommend your bow anchor be at least one size larger than the manufacturer recommends for your boat's size.

The anchor most common on cruising boats in Hawai'i is the CQR. This anchor performs well in these waters, provided it is larger than the recommended size. One reason the CQR is good for Hawai'i cruising is its robust construction. Although we all try to drop our anchors in sand, all too often boulders or lava rock will be what stops our anchors' movements across the bottom, especially when strong winds are blowing. Some of the rocky bottoms in Hawaiian anchorages, such as those at Māhukona, Keauhou, and Okoe Bay on the Big Island, will test the strength of any anchor.

Another anchor that performs well in Hawai'i is the Bruce. On our heavy Hardin 45 ketch, we use a 66-pound Bruce for our primary. We rarely have trouble setting it, though it doesn't do well in two circumstances: when the bottom is a thin layer of sand over lava rock or dead coral, as at the Lahaina Roadstead, Māla Wharf, or Keauhou Bay, and when the bottom is boulders, as at Māhukona. On the whole, though, in Hawaiian anchorages the Bruce works better for our boat than our old CQR.

Some boaters in the Islands give high marks to their fluke-type anchors. The Danforth, the West Marine Performance, and the Fortress all do well in sand or mud, the most common material on the bottoms of anchorages in the Islands. Because these anchors are easy to stow in the bottom of a locker, many people who go cruising only a week or two a year can keep their anchors out of the way the remainder of the time. Some boaters have found, however, that the flukes bend badly when these anchors are used in anchorages with boulders or lava bottoms.

The Delta receives unconditional praise from boaters who've replaced their other anchors with it. It has all the best attributes of the CQR and the Bruce. We've had one on our boat for almost ten years now. Yet we still prefer the Bruce, perhaps because it has been so dependable over the past twelve years.

Although we might prefer the Bruce, all the other anchors listed above will work equally well for some boats in some conditions. Every anchor, if large enough and well set, has merit in certain conditions. Where you anticipate doing most of your anchoring should help you determine your choice of a primary anchor

ANCHOR RODES AND WINDLASSES

Once you've chosen an anchor, you'll need to select a rode, either an all-chain or a nylon and chain rode. The all-chain rode is best for Hawaiian waters. Even though we try to drop our anchors only in sand or mud, we will end up with the rode over coral at one time or another. During the night when the wind drops to zero and then changes direction a number of times, nylon rode will wrap around a piece of coral. When the winds come up again the next day and begin to move the boat around, the coral will cut into and sometimes sever the nylon rode. For this reason alone, most cruising boaters in Hawai'i equip their boats with all-chain rodes.

Carol bringing in the anchor with the electric windlass

Having said that all-chain rodes are best, we nevertheless recognize its disadvantages that may make it prohibitive for some boats and boaters. First, an all-chain rode is expensive, about $1,000 for a 300-foot rode of HT chain. Second, it is heavy. A 300-foot rode of 3/8 HT chain weighs close to 500 pounds. In the chain locker in the bow of a boat, that much weight will often cause the boat to "hobby horse" when going to weather in rough water.

The weight of an all-chain rode is also a problem when you weigh anchor. Having hauled our chain and 66-pound Bruce aboard using back power a few times when our windlass failed, we can assure you that you'll not want to bring in the all-chain rode by hand as a rule. If you put an all-chain rode aboard, you'll almost certainly have to install a windlass. We know some cruisers with boats under 30 feet with one-quarter inch chain who pull their anchors up without a windlass, but they are the exception. And they have strong backs.

If you decide you need a windlass for your boat, you can choose between an electric or a hand-powered model. Bringing in 150 feet of chain with an electric windlass takes far less time and effort than with a manual windlass, but the hand-powered models are, of course, less expensive. Not only is the initial purchase price of the electric windlass about twice that of the manual; the parts necessary for the installation of the electric windlass include, at the least, two heavy battery cables (often as long as 35 feet), a solenoid, and a foot-operated switch.

For some boaters who cruise the Islands, the weight and expense convince them to go with the chain and nylon rode. Then they anchor carefully.

DODGERS

A dodger for your boat does exactly the same thing as clothing does for your body: it shields the cockpit from the flying water and from the sun. Dodgers come in all shapes and sizes. Some small ones do little more than provide protection for the crew members as they come on deck through the companionway hatch. The advantages of these smaller dodgers are that they don't destroy the aesthetic lines of the boat and that they are relatively inexpensive.

Other dodgers, like the one on our center-cockpit boat, completely enclose the cockpit area, enabling the crew to sail in rainy weather without getting wet. In addition, larger dodgers protect the crew from the heat and harmful effects of the sun. These larger dodgers turn the cockpits into all-weather rooms. The primary disadvantages of these larger dodgers are that they change the lines of the boat and that they are much more expensive than the smaller ones.

A new concept in dodgers is catching on quickly: hard dodgers that look like soft dodgers. The most significant advantages of the hard dodgers are that you can stand on top of them to reef or furl the sail, they don't deteriorate in the sun as the fabric ones do, and they offer a more secure place to hold onto in rough weather.

ELECTRICAL AND MECHANICAL DEVICES

For cruising Hawai'i, you need but a few of the electronic marvels on the market.

•**A depth sounder** belongs at the top of the list because it will give you much needed information as you're entering an anchorage or negotiating a channel through a reef. With a depth sounder, you can also determine how much scope you need on your anchor rode. In addition to these two critically important uses, you can use your depth sounder as a navigation aid. By comparing readings on the depth sounder to those on a navigation chart, you can estimate how far from a shoreline you are when traveling along a coastline.

Many cruising boaters have installed the new generation of forward-viewing depth sounders because they like the idea of being able to see the depths ahead of their boats. Some of these new depth sounders can scan the bottom 120 feet ahead of the boat. Such a feature would be extremely useful for a boater looking for the best route when crossing reefs such as those at Kamalō, Pūko'o, or Pauwalu on Moloka'i.

Some boaters have purchased one of the portable depth sounders to use when they are exploring with the dinghy, thinking that the same unit could be used as a back-up depth sounder should their primary units aboard their cruising boats fail.

•**A VHF radio** is the second important piece of electronic equipment that should be aboard every cruising boat in Hawai'i. Even though few harbormasters monitor VHF, the VHF radio still provides an important link in case of emergency because the Coast Guard monitors VHF 16 at all times. In addition, the Weather Service broadcasts information continuously on WX1 and WX2, providing cruising boaters with advanced warnings of potentially dangerous weather.

Most fishing boats have CB, but not VHF, radios aboard. For this reason, some harbormasters monitor CB channels used by local fishermen rather than VHF. Another peculiarity about sailing Hawai'i is that many harbormasters, yacht clubs, and even vessel assist companies monitor neither VHF nor CB. Instead, they assume local boaters will contact them by cell phone. Although we haven't used our cell phone offshore in Hawai'i, other boaters have told us they have good coverage when sailing around Oahu and Maui. We have no reports regarding how well cell phones work in the more remote areas of Kaua'i and the Big Island.

•**The GPS** has become an almost indispensable electronic device for boaters who cruise Hawai'i. These units help boaters locate anchorages, especially those that have few distinguishable landmarks. Without local knowledge, finding anchorages such as Pūko'o or Pauwalu harbors on Moloka'i once was so difficult that few cruising boaters ever visited them. Now, however, with the GPS anyone can find and enter these harbors.

In addition, these little navigational wonders make trip planning easy. By keying in the coordinates of each destination you would like to visit on a cruise, you can have instant and reliable information about distances. And while on the cruise, you have continual assistance from the GPS regarding course, speed, distance, and time.

•**Autopilots and wind vanes** are hardly essential, but they certainly make cruising more comfortable. When making passages between islands, Hawaiian boaters often choose to cross the channels during the night, when the winds have less strength than during the day. When we've gone from O'ahu to Kaua'i, from O'ahu to Hawai'i non-stop, or even from Maui to Hawai'i when the winds were blowing, we've made the trips overnight. On these night passages particularly, self-steering is a welcome relief. Whoever is on watch can then move about the cockpit or step out on deck to check a line.

During the day, self-steering is almost as welcome, for it allows both of us to enjoy the scenery more fully, go out on deck to take photographs, write in our journals and logs, or read about the places we're passing on shore.

In general, we use the autopilot when we're on the motor and the wind vane when we're under sail. The vane is especially useful on long passages, when we don't want to run the auto-pilot and deplete our batteries.

•**Radars** are certainly not essential equipment, but almost all cruising boats now have them. The reasons given for putting a radar on a boat are many; most fall into the category of safety. When you're approaching a harbor after dark, even if you've previously been in that harbor, a radar will make the night entrance safer. The radar will show the locations of the buoys, breakwaters, and any other objects around the harbor clearly.

Radar is also good when you're cruising along a coastline. Radar can show you the locations of other boats and ships within range and can track the movements of those other vessels for you. It can also show you the location and distance of rocks and exposed reefs along the coast. In such a situation, you can check radar occasionally, adjusting your course as needed.

We also use radar to check on squalls. When we see one that looks particularly intense, we change course or shorten sail accordingly.

•**Knotmeter and log** combinations are on most boats cruising the Islands, and while they are not absolutely essential, they are close to it. The log is especially important on boats that don't have a GPS. By showing how far the boat has gone, the knotmeter aids the boater in estimating the distance to the next landfall. Even though we have a GPS, as a back-up we carefully measure the distance from one point to the next on a chart before we depart so that we can tell when we are approaching our destination by checking the log.

•**EPIRB** (Emergency Position Indicating Radio Beacon) units may not be essential equipment on all cruising boats in Hawai'i, but they should be aboard all boats making long ocean passages. When we talk to Coast Guard personnel about making passages between Hawai'i and Midway Atoll, for instance, they invariably inquire if we have a 406 EPIRB aboard. From their perspective, a 406 EPIRB means they can find a boat that is in trouble in a matter of hours rather than days.

For cruising only around the major Hawaiian islands, an EPIRB may not seem worth the expense to many boaters.

SAFETY EQUIPMENT

When the winds blow strongly and the waves bounce the boat around, boaters are only one moment of carelessness or one equipment failure removed from the water at any instant. You want to be especially careful that neither you nor anyone else falls overboard when crossing the channels between the islands. In heavy channel weather, turning a boat around and finding a person overboard is extremely difficult during the day and almost impossible at night.

Whatever other provisions you make for boating in the Islands, set up your boat to minimize the risk of anyone's accidentally falling overboard. Check lifelines and grab rails regularly, replacing anything that

Wind vane at work

looks even slightly suspect. You'll fall against the lifelines and hang onto the grab rails many times when making sail changes, and you must be confident they will keep you on the boat. To be reliable, stanchions must be through bolted with backing plates on the underside of the deck. In addition, seriously consider the following safety items, some of which are required by Coast

Guard regulations:

•**PFDs** (personal flotation devices) are required by the Coast Guard, and common sense also demands them. Regulations require that you have a Type I, II, III, or V personal flotation device for every person aboard if your boat is between 16 and 65 feet. These categories of PFDs, established by the Coast Guard, cover characteristics such as the amount of buoyancy and the construction. The Type I PFD gives the wearer the most support in the water; the others give adequate support. In addition to these wearable PFDs, you must have a device such as a LifeSling or a horseshoe ring to throw to a person in the water,

These Coast Guard categories—I, II, III, IV, and V—can be confusing to boaters. West Marine's newest categories make more sense because they describe the utility of each PFD. After studying these descriptions, sailors can then buy PFDs designed for their specific requirements. For instance, the least expensive PFDs, which many of us put on our boats in the past, are now clearly sold as "Near Shore Vests." Boaters planning to use their boats for ocean cruising or racing should purchase PFDs labeled "Offshore Sail" or "Offshore Power."

The PFDs on the market present the cruiser with many options. The least expensive are those of the traditional design of the original kapok vests but now with polyethylene foam flotation. These jackets come in a variety of sizes, styles, and prices. The less bulky PFDs with inflatable bladders and built-in safety harnesses are now common on many cruising boats. Their advantages are clear: their streamline design and inflatable buoyancy give greater comfort to the wearers. The only drawbacks are that these vests must be periodically checked and serviced and the expensive cartridges replaced each time the vests are inflated.

•**Safety harnesses** should be aboard every cruising boat. Although you'll not need to wear a harness every time you take your boat away from the dock, you should wear one whenever you're in heavy weather or working on deck at night. Too many cruisers go overboard from simple gear failures or mistakes. Since boaters who venture to distant locations—even those islands that are only 30 miles away—can get caught by heavy weather or darkness, safety harnesses, tethers, and jacklines are important safety items. These items should be mandatory for boats making long ocean passages.

•**Tethers** are just as important as safety harnesses. In fact, tethers and harnesses should be kept together in a location readily accessible from the cockpit. The most effective tether has a snap shackle on the end that attaches to the two D rings of the harness and a carabiner to attach to the jackline or pad eye.

•**Jacklines** should run from the bow to the stern along each side of the boat. Attach one end of the jacklines to a solid padeye at the bow and the other end to a padeye or cleat at the cockpit or stern of your boat. Ideally, you should be able to snap your tether onto the jackline as you get out of the cockpit and then be able to go from the cockpit to the bow, never having to disconnect your tether. Good jacklines are made of either nylon or dacron webbing or of the same covered wire used for lifelines. Jacklines made of webbing won't cause you to slip and fall if you step on them while working on deck as will the ones made of covered wire. The covered wire has a distinct advantage, however: it doesn't stretch as the webbing does.

Set up your jacklines before you depart if you expect even moderately heavy weather or if some or all of the passage will be made after dark. You'll not want to wait for either of these eventualities before rigging the lines.

•**Overboard rescue systems** have become increasingly popular with cruising sailors. The Lifesling is the most common rescue system. The Lifesling allows you to drag a line with an attached life-saving device to the person in the water and then to keep that person tethered to the boat until you can haul him or her aboard. All boaters who put these units aboard their boats would be well advised to practice using them before actual emergencies arise.

•**Life rafts** cause countless debates. Some boaters will not cruise Hawaiian waters without rafts aboard while other boaters have sailed around the Islands without rafts and consider them a needless expense. Since much of our cruising involves long-distance passages, we have a life raft aboard our boat, as do most bluewater cruisers we know.

•**Fire extinguishers** are required by the Coast Guard on all boats with enclosed spaces. Boats up to 26 feet with enclosed spaces must have at least one B-1 extinguisher. Boats between

26 and 40 feet must have two B-I extinguishers or one B-II. Boats between 40 and 65 feet must have three BI or one BI and one BII extinguisher. Several fire extinguishers strategically spaced throughout the boat are especially important for cruising sailors who will be cooking and using electrical devices out in remote anchorages. Make sure you can get to the extinguishers from every part of the boat. Don't just have one by the galley or in the engine room.

•**Flares** are required on all boats. These may seem superfluous on boats that cruise only around one island, but Coast Guard boarding parties will check for flares as routinely as they check for PFDs. The Coast Guard requires a minimum of three flares of any of the various types. For long ocean passages we recommend you carry more flares than this minimum specified; that is, carry at least six red meteor flares, six red handheld flares, three parachute flares, and one smoke signal.

•**Radar reflectors** enhance your chances of being seen by ships and boats around the Islands, especially important if you are still under way after dark or if you get caught in a heavy squall. However, don't assume your boat will show up on the radar screens of large ships. Radar operators on these ships have reported they can't always see small boats, even if those boats have reflectors. You must always take responsibility for spotting the ship.

TENDERS

If you cruise only to marinas in Hawai'i and tie up to a dock every time out, you obviously won't need a tender. However, you also won't have many choices of destinations. In fact, you may find that anchorages such as Pōka'ī Bay, Hanalei Bay, or Māla Wharf are the most appealing destinations around the Hawaiian Islands. In that case, you'll need a tender to explore, to get ashore, or to go over to see friends on another boat. If you decide to get a tender, you will have three basic types from which to choose.

The tender used by boaters for centuries is the **hard dinghy**. The hard dinghy has one outstanding characteristic: it rows well. Many boaters have gone to the hard dinghy after trying to row an inflatable in windy conditions. People also choose hard dinghies because with them they can quietly explore an anchorage or a coastline without disturbing wildlife or other boaters. Hard dinghies have a couple of disadvantages that keep them from being widely used: they are difficult to get aboard and stow, and they are unstable when being loaded or unloaded.

For convenience and safety, most cruising boaters have inflatable dinghies or sport boats aboard. Those cruisers wanting to save money often equip their boats with **inflatable, or soft, dinghies** such as some models made by Achilles and Zodiac These dinghies generally come with soft floors. Wood floors are available for soft dinghies, but they are rare because they make the dinghy expensive and heavy. The primary advantage of the soft dinghy is its weight: without wood floors it typically weighs well under 100 pounds. Although most inflatable manufacturing companies made these inflatable dinghies at one time, many have discontinued them recently.

The disadvantages of these inflatable dinghies are several. They are difficult to row in winds over 10 knots and almost uncontrollable when the winds reach 15 knots. Although many boaters buy small outboards for their soft dinghies to make them more usable when winds blow, the cruisers we've spoken with who use them almost universally complain that the inflatable dinghies are still too slow. Even when powered by an outboard, they will not make more than 5 or 6 knots.

In addition, these inflatable dinghies have serious loading limitations because of the soft floors. Anything heavy aboard one of these tenders, such as a scuba tank, is in danger of falling through the bottom. Furthermore, the soft bottom precludes your standing in the dinghy as you load or unload it, a serious disadvantage.

As serviceable as the hard dinghies and soft-bottomed dinghies are, their limitations are so pronounced that **sport boats** have taken over the market. While their most noteworthy feature may be their load-carrying capacity, sport boats also get high marks for their speed. With a 10-hp outboard on the transom, the 10-foot sport boat with two or three people aboard can easily plane and travel at almost 20 knots.

Their speed makes long distance travel quite comfortable. We regularly range up to 5 miles from our anchored sailboat in our sport boat. When we were at Midway Island, we used our sport boat to explore the reef on the far side of the atoll from the anchorage. In order to make the trip, we had to travel at least 6 miles. The shallow depths would have prevented us from exploring these areas in our sailboat, even if we could have gotten permission to take it.

If you use a motor on any kind of tender, you should always take the motor off and bring it aboard when you move from one anchorage or marina to the next. In many instances cruisers have lost their outboards when the tenders flipped over in the heavy waves around the Islands. Many sailors tow their tenders after taking off the motors, but even that practice is not always to be advised in the Islands. The winds here can pick up unexpectedly, causing tremendous pressure on and sometimes breaking the tow painters.

Hawaiian children enjoying a sport boat ride

PROVISIONING AND OTHER CONSIDERATIONS

I ola no ke kino i ka mā'ona o ka 'ōpū.
("The body enjoys health when the stomach is well filled.")

PROVISIONING

In crossing the Pacific Ocean in a sailboat from anywhere along the west coast of North America to Hawai'i, you should plan on being at sea for approximately three weeks. To ensure ample food and supplies, plan for a minimum of four weeks—and then add whatever else you have room for.

While you'll be eager to find the warmer Pacific waters after you leave the coast, your fresh foods will be entirely happy with the cool weather that you'll be in for a good two-thirds of the voyage. You'll try to use the most fragile of the fruits and vegetables within the first week or so, but common foods such as potatoes and yams, winter squash, cabbage, cauliflower, carrots, onions, apples, bananas (purchased green, on a stalk), oranges, grapefruits, and lemons will last well beyond that first week. With planning, you can have some fresh foods every day of the passage.

Eggs that have not previously been refrigerated will last several weeks when stored in a cool, dry place. Other dairy foods that last well in the refrigerator are yogurt, sour cream, cream cheese, and all kinds of hard cheese. For that time when the fresh milk runs out, carry along vacuum-packed cartons. These "bricks" are excellent for passages because they don't need to be refrigerated until after you have opened them. Regular and skimmed milk are available in these cartons as well as plain and flavored soy and rice milk.

Plan to bring with you not only the meat and chicken you'll want but also the fish. You'll probably catch little on your hook once you're in the deep water of the ocean. Once you are within two or three days of the Islands, your luck with fishing may improve, though you shouldn't count on fishing to supplement your diet.

To summarize, provisioning for this particular passage is relatively trouble-free because of the cool weather for so much of the trip.

Bob cleaning a *mahimahi*

Provisioning for a cruise around the Hawaiian Islands is even less challenging. Once you get to any of the larger towns—Hilo, Kailua-Kona, Kahului, Lahaina, Kaunakakai, Honolulu, Kāne'ohe, and Hale'iwa—you'll find most of the foods common in markets on the Mainland. Kailua-Kona, Kahului, and Honolulu even have Costco wholesale stores, which have essentially the same items on the shelves as in the Mainland Costco stores. A few differences between shopping for food in the Islands and on the Mainland, though, may be instructive as you plan what to store aboard your boat before you leave the Mainland.

One of the differences you'll note when you first shop on one of the Islands is the prices. The Islands produce little of the food sold in the supermarkets. Most of the canned, bottled, and packaged foods and beverages are shipped from the Mainland and are naturally going to be more expensive because of the shipping, but you may be surprised at how much more expensive.

Surprisingly, for a location with soil as rich as that of the Islands, many of the fresh fruits and vegetables in the markets also come from elsewhere: the Mainland, Mexico, South America, and other countries around the Pacific Basin.

But even the food produced here is more expensive in the supermarkets than its equivalent on the Mainland. Fruits and vegetables grown in the Islands are costlier in supermarkets here than in many other parts of the United States. Around the Islands grow abundant crops of delicious fruits, the popular pineapples, apple bananas, mangos, papayas, oranges, and avocados, as well as the lesser known cheramoyas, guavas, passion fruit, and many others, Abundant, too, are purple, yellow, orange, and white sweet potatoes and the starchy breadfruit. Increasingly, vegetables such as tomatoes, cucumbers, green beans, and broccoli are being grown locally. Maui onions, Kahuku watermelon, Waimanalo corn, Mānoa lettuce, and Kīlauea corn from Kaua'i are justifiably treasured. Yet all these fresh foods, even when grown on the Islands, are expensive when you buy them in the supermarkets.

To have a healthful diet while in Hawai'i, you'll not always be able to avoid simply paying the price at the supermarket. However, you can do a couple of things that may help. The first depends on how much storage space you have on your boat and on how long you plan to cruise. That is, bring as much of the canned and bottled food and beverages with you as your boat can accommodate. All alcoholic beverages are especially expensive, even if you can get to Costco to purchase them. Canned fruits, vegetables, soups, and any other canned goods won't take quite such a bite out of your budget, but this is another place where you can save by bringing as much as you can from the Mainland. Packaged goods present the same problem, but you'll not want to bring such large quantities of some items, such as crackers and cookies, that you'll lose from spoilage whatever savings you might have gained.

Saturday Market, Hilo

With regard to fresh goods, storing enough aboard and keeping it for the duration of the approximately three-week passage will be enough of a challenge. Additionally, the Hawai'i Department of Agriculture prohibits your bringing into the state any fresh produce. But you can save on the cost of buying produce in the Islands by finding farmers' markets and local produce stands. (Be careful about the produce stands on the highways frequented by tourists. Here, food is often more, not less, expensive than it is in the supermarkets. What you're looking for are the places where the locals shop.) You'll often find the quality as well as the price is better in these markets. Naturally, you can expect that most if not all of the produce is grown in the Islands.

Another difference is more promising for keeping the water line of your boat from being an *under*water line. The supermarkets and the many small ethnic markets throughout the Islands have a fascinating variety of ethnic foods that you'll want to try, and the prices in the small markets, for example, in Chinatown, Honolulu, are often competitive with comparative products on the Mainland. Go to an Asian noodle shop and buy fresh noodles for a fraction of what you'd pay for packaged pasta at the market; buy inexpensive *chesa,* a fruit eaten raw that tastes like the best yam you can imagine, and plantain, the delicious cooking banana, at a Filipino market; pick up *manapua,* a pork-stuffed Chinese bun, and *manju,* a small Japanese pastry traditionally stuffed with sweet bean paste, at almost any corner market. The prices in these local markets are but a small part of the pleasure of trying out the many foods of Hawai'i.

OTHER CONSIDERATIONS

Ako ʻe hale a paʻa, a i ke komo ana mai o ka hoʻoilo.
("Thatch the house beforehand so when winter comes it will not leak in the shower of Hilinehu.")

•**Clothing.** To be comfortable on the passage to or from Hawaiʻi, you'll need both warm and cool clothing, no matter what time of year. When you leave the northern coasts of the continent, you'll be on a cool ocean from the beginning of the passage. You should be prepared for this weather with long underwear, long pants, sweaters, jackets, caps, and gloves, as well as foul weather gear and boots. Within a week you'll begin to notice a warming trend, but you probably won't be ready to switch entirely to your tropical wear before the end of the second week. Then it's shorts and T-shirts weather until you're on your way back to the continent.

In Hawaiʻi the dress is even more informal than on the mainland West Coast, if you can imagine that. Shorts, T-shirts, and sandals are *de rigueur* for everything except job interviews, symphony concerts, and church. You may occasionally want to dress up by wearing a shirt with a collar rather than a T-shirt, Even in Honolulu, the only place that seems to be a bit less casual, you'll find few restaurants where you'll feel out of place in good shorts and sandals.

Hawaiʻi does have a few cool evenings in the winter months, evenings when long pants and a light jacket or sweater will feel good. You may also want to join in the fun of "Aloha Dress," when the men wear long pants, often khaki or white, and a colorful tropical print shirt and the women wear a colorful long or mid-calf-length dress. While these long dresses are generally all put into the category of the *muʻumuʻu,* many of them are far more becoming than the "Mother Hubbards" the missionaries introduced.

To keep whatever clothing you're wearing dry when you must walk in the rain, bring an umbrella or two. Often, any kind of raincoat is simply too warm.

•**Fishing Equipment.** For those of you who enjoy catching and/or eating fish, some fishing equipment is a must. Few cruising boaters invest in expensive poles and reels, preferring to drag fishing lines. Our lines are made up of 100 feet of 200-pound monofilament line with a lure, usually a plastic squid, on one end and a 2-foot bungee cord on the other to serve as a shock absorber when a fish strikes.

We don't shorten sail when we get a fish on; we simply drag the fish through the water until it gets tired before trying to pull it aboard. The disadvantage of using drag lines is that we lose some fish because we can't let out more line or stop the boat while we play the fish. In fact, on our trip to Midway Atoll, we lost many rigs because the fish that hit were so large they broke the 200-pound monofilament. But the most exciting moment of your day may be when you've just pulled a 2-5-foot *mahimahi,* striped marlin, or *ono* aboard. Nothing is more pleasing to the palate than a meal of fish caught less than an hour earlier.

•**Roll Stabilizers.** Because Hawaiian anchorages are often exposed to swells, boats at anchor frequently develop an uncomfortable roll. In some particularly windless anchorages such as Lahaina or Kailua-Kona, your boat will end up beam-on to the swell. Anchorages such as these have much to offer, so to be able to enjoy them, use roll stabilizers. In some anchorages, you'll need a roll stabilizer on each side of your boat, though in most one will be sufficient. These amazingly effective devices are sold under a variety of names, such as Flopper Stopper, Rock 'n' Roll Boat Stabilizer, Roll Control, and Rocker Stopper. These are best deployed from the end of a spinnaker or whisker pole hoisted on a masthead halyard or from the end of the main boom.

•**Snorkel and Dive Equipment.** When you get to the Islands, you'll want a mask, a snorkel, and fins. The water in the Islands is remarkably clear and is teeming with fish and luxuriant stands of coral. You'll also want snorkel equipment to get into the water to check your anchor or to pick up a mooring.

Whether you take the scuba equipment may be based on how much space you have on your boat. While scuba equipment can enhance your underwater sightseeing capabilities, you may also find that in the lucid and relatively calm waters off the shores of the Hawaiian Islands, you can see enough as you snorkel on the surface.

•**Solar Showers.** Solar showers are synonymous with cruising. While many boats have showers below decks, few have hot water after the first day under sail. If you're among the large group of boaters who don't care for cold showers (except on the hottest of days), put a solar shower aboard your boat. You can fill the shower with 2.5 gallons of fresh water every 2 or 3 days, put it in the sun for a couple of hours, and enjoy a hot shower for 2 or 3 people. How often you shower depends on how much water your boat carries and if it has a watermaker. Another alternative is to use salt water to bathe in and then rinse with fresh water.

•**Spare Fuel and Water.** Although some boats have enough tankage for normal cruising, boaters making the trip to and from Hawai'i frequently carry spare fuel and water on deck to extend their range. On the trip to Hawai'i, you should need little extra fuel since calms are rare, but on the return trip, you may be glad to have extra fuel on deck, especially if you get close to the Pacific High. Spare fuel jugs are also helpful if you need to carry fuel to your boat from a service station. (Marine fuel docks are rare in the Islands.) Most cruising boaters also carry at least one spare water container, whether it is called the emergency water supply or the water transportation device.

•**Ventilation.** Since the weather in Hawai'i is often quite warm, especially in the summer and early fall, consider installing small fans. Depending on the size of your boat, you'll need 1-4 fans usually. The most popular fans among cruisers are the little Hella fans. They are inexpensive, use a small amount of battery power, and take up little space. Have at least one for each bunk that will be used, one for the galley, and one in each head.

Boaters who spend much time cruising the Hawaiian Islands usually use a sun awning. Sun awnings can reduce the heat on deck and below decks by several degrees. In Hawai'i they also are useful when it rains, for with them in place you can keep your hatches and ports open in all but the windiest of rain storms without worry that the rain will come in. Generally, the favorite anchorages are on the leeward sides of the Islands, where you will find more breezes than winds, but in the windier anchorages such as Kaunakakai or Kamalō on Moloka'i, you won't need to put up the awnings because the air will move through your boat to keep it cool.

You can't have too many opening ports and hatches on a boat when you're in Hawai'i. If your boat has only fixed portlights, consider replacing some with opening ports.

Available on the market are many products that hang in the rigging above your hatches to funnel air into your boat. Some brands commonly seen are the Wind Scoop and the Down the Hatch Ventilating Sail. These devices are particularly welcome on those days when you'll be in an anchorage briefly and won't want to take the time to rig a large awning. These are also better for the windier anchorages because they usually won't come loose or tear when gusts of 20 knots or more come through the anchorage.

Vickie Buck taking a solar shower

MEDICINES AND FIRST AIDS

Poʻohū ka lae kahi i ka pōhue.
("When the forehead lumps, rub it with a gourd.")

Many boaters who are planning for a cruise in the Hawaiian Islands will be from the Mainland or foreign countries. If you fit into that category, preparations to assure the health of yourself and your crew should begin several months in advance of your departure. Those of you who live in Hawaiʻi should also have good first aid kits aboard and have first aid training before you go cruising in the Islands, since you will often be some distance and several hours from medical help.

If you regularly take any medicines or rely on any medical aids that you should not be without, stock up on plenty of spares. For example, get all your regular prescriptions filled in quantities to last you for the duration of the cruise plus an additional month or two to preclude a crisis if some of the medication is lost or damaged or if by the grace of some kindly fate you don't have to return home as early as you had thought. One reassuring fact is that in Hawaiʻi you can find a drug store or at least a store with some over-the-counter drugs on all the major islands, though these stores are not always easily accessible for

Ed the caretaker giving us a gourd

boaters. Additionally, you have the problem of having to spend an inordinate amount of your precious cruising time taking care of the chore.

One other prescription to have filled before leaving the dock to head out to sea is that for the Transderm scopolamine patches if you, your crew, or anyone else you expect to join you for part of the cruise is susceptible to seasickness. (These patches are once again available by prescription.) To be effective, these patches need to be applied the night before departure. Some people experience some side effects such as a dry mouth, an unpleasant metallic taste in the mouth, drowsiness and lethargy, and stomach discomfort, but anyone who usually gets seasick will probably exchange that awful feeling for one or more of these relatively minor side effects.

A less invasive preventive is Dramamine, available without prescription, but for most people not as effective in preventing motion sickness as are the patches. We keep both the patches and Dramamine aboard, the patches for the seriously at-risk sailors and the Dramamine for those who just want to be cautious. The Dramamine is also useful to give to someone who is beginning to experience the ill effects of the boat's motion on the ocean. Though its full preventive powers come only with its ingestion before the sailor feels these ill effects, it may still have some salubrious effect after the onset of the illness. The side effect of Dramamine can be extreme drowsiness.

Another precautionary drug to have along is one for diarrhea. Lomotil and Imodium, the latter available without prescription, are both recommended by doctors. While the likelihood of needing this remedy is no greater around the Hawaiian Islands than on the Mainland, one of these drugs should be aboard a boat that may be hours or days removed from medical care.

The warm, moist climate of Hawaiʻi makes an ideal breeding ground for some insects. Mosquitoes can be a problem, especially when you go exploring up rivers and streams in your dinghy or hiking on mountain trails, so have along a good repellent such as Cutters or Avon. We found clouds of mosquitoes when we traveled up the Hulē'ia Stream at Nāwiliwili. Since we had applied Avon Skin-So-Soft (which comes in a handy spray bottle), we had no problems. Be sure to have a small container of insect repellent to take along when you go out for hikes in case you get wet and need to reapply.

Because we all have our own favorite remedies for minor ailments or accidents, your home medicine cabinet is your best source of reference for other incidentals to add to your cruising medicine chest. Do you regularly keep such remedies as hydrogen peroxide, rubbing alcohol, antacids, laxatives, and cough drops on hand? A thermometer and a jar of Vaseline are useful items to include as well. If you're a contact lens wearer, take along enough cleaning and wetting solutions to last throughout the cruise. You may not always be able to find the particular brands you use.

While not exactly medicines, eyeglasses and contact lenses are essential for many of us. If you wear either glasses or lenses regularly, take along a back-up pair, either an old pair that you can get by with or a new pair you have to spring for. Eyeglasses are easily lost or broken in rough weather at sea or during a beach landing in the sport boat. Contact lenses have a way of popping out at the most inopportune times. Neither of these items do you want to be without during the time you may need to find an ophthalmologist, optometrist, or optician.

If you must replace your lost or broken eye wear, you'll save yourself both time and money if you have along with you a copy of your prescription.

Have extra pairs of sunglasses also. Your eyes will need more protection than usual in the brilliant sun of Hawai'i. Sunglasses have an even greater propensity for getting lost than do regular glasses or contact lenses. We keep several pairs of old non-prescription sunglasses on the boat for both ourselves and our visitors.

Once you and your crew have provided yourselves with medicines and aids to see you through the cruise, think of preparing for medical emergencies that may arise from illnesses or accidents. A cruise around the Islands, unlike a trans-oceanic cruise, will not generally put you far from medical assistance in an emergency. Nevertheless, locating that assistance and traveling to it will often require several hours. Hence you and your crew must be prepared to respond quickly and ably to a variety of kinds of emergencies. Your goal will be, in most cases, to stabilize the injured or sick person's medical condition until you can obtain qualified medical assistance.

The Anahulu Stream bridge

The first step in preparing for medical emergencies is for all members of the permanent crew to take a CPR and a first aid course before embarking on an ocean passage. The minimum goal will be for all to obtain the skills necessary to respond immediately and appropriately to an acute life-threatening illness or accident. Check with your local office of the American Red Cross for its schedule of available CPR and first aid classes.

The next step, and one that you should initiate several weeks before your scheduled departure on this cruise, is to obtain a first aid book with detailed illustrations and to study that book thoroughly. A good choice is *The American Medical Association Handbook of First Aid and Emergency Care* (Random House 2000). This book is organized like an encyclopedia, with injuries and illnesses arranged alphabetically. It also includes sketches, though neither as numerous nor as detailed as those in the *First Aid Book*.

Another good choice is *First Aid Afloat,* by Peter F. Eastman, M. D., out in 1993 in a 4th edition from Cornell Maritime Press. This book's advantage is Eastman's having designed it specifically for cruising sailors. It is about the same length as the first book. Where it differs significantly from both, in addition to its appeal to cruising sailors, is in the complexity of some of the treatments explained. For example, Eastman introduces a lesson on amputation by starting with a gangrenous toe, about which procedure he says, "Anyone can amputate a finger or toe." In the next paragraph he goes on to assure the reader, "If a foot and leg below the knee are involved you can likely amputate successfully." For a cruise around the Hawaiian Islands, you're unlikely to need to prove (or disprove!) his optimistic words. This book has some illustrations, though not so many as either of the other two books. You will like its medical lore from the cruising sailors' world.

Besides reinforcing the information you've mastered from the CPR and first aid courses you've taken, this study of the first aid book will familiarize you with the organization of the book so you can readily turn to the desired section. From the CPR and first aid courses you'll have mastered the three life-saving basics: restore breathing, restore circulation, and stop excessive bleeding. In almost any medical emergency, your ability to act quickly and appropriately will be important, but if the injured or ill person is breathing and is not losing great amounts of blood, you can take time to refresh your memory about the appropriate treatment. Know your first aid book well enough so you can simply review the recommended treatment rather than have to study it for an hour before taking any helpful measures.

Next, begin assembling your first-aid kit. Dr. Thom Macpherson, physician and surgeon as well as cruising sailor, has given us three lists of medical aids he believes all cruising boats should carry. The aids in the first list, in addition to those we've already discussed, you can administer or apply with no particular expertise. To use those in the second list, you may need to consult your first aid book. The third list of aids consists of those you would use only under the direction of a medical professional when the patient's life is endangered; in other words, carry these aids but do not attempt to use them unless you are in voice contact by VHF, ham, or single sideband radio with a professional who can direct you step by step and can monitor the patient's symptoms and reactions.

List One

    Oral antibiotics obtained from your physician before the trip
    Benadryl, an antihistamine and a sleep remedy (25 mg. X 50)
    Compazine, either suppository or oral, for nausea (25 mg. X 20)
    Motrin, 800 mg., anti-inflammatory and analgesic
    Tylenol #3
    Robitussin DM, for respiratory tract congestion
    Silvadene ointment, for burns
    Neosporin or polysporin ointment, for open wounds
    Hydrocortisone cream, 1%, for skin ailments
    Benzoin tincture, a sticky substance to help Steri-Strips adhere to a wound
    Afrin nasal spray
    Ammonia spirits, for reviving an unconscious person or for treating jellyfish stings
    Bee sting kit, for people allergic to the sting of bees or other insects
    Gauze pads, 4" x 4", for cleaning or dressing wounds
    Kerlix or Kling gauze roll dressings, assorted sizes, for securing large dressings or splints (x 5)
    Steri-Strips (butterfly-shaped), assorted sizes, to close small lacerations
    Sterile eye pads (x 2)
    Aluminum finger splints
    Wrist splints
    Ace wrap, 4" (x 2)
    Q-tips
List Two
    Betadine soap, to clean large and dirty lacerations (may be obtained in a scrub brush
        or E-Z Scrub Hibiclens form with soap instilled)
    Tweezers or surgical forceps
    Curved hemostat, to clamp a large blood vessel that pressure alone will not control
    Disposable prep razor, for removing hair around a wound
    Surgical staples, to close large lacerations (x 30)
    Adaptic dressing, 3" x 3", a non-stick, clear dressing impregnated with salve (x 10)

Tegaderm, a clear covering both sticky and breathable, to cover abrasions, cuts, blisters, etc.
Foam tape, 2", to apply pressure to wounds
Web roll, 3", for cast padding (x 4)
Fiberglass cast material to be used for splints (also comes in handy for stopping leaks in engine
    hoses)

List Three

(Dr. Macpherson stresses that, unless you are medically trained, you'll not use the aids in this list except under the direction of a physician; hence we've not listed their use. Dr. Macpherson recommends that you have them available for critical emergencies when a physician can direct their use.)

Assorted syringes and needles, including a 10 cc. syringe and 18-gauge and 25-gauge needles
Epinephrine, intravenous, 1 amp. 1:1000
Calcium chloride and gluconate, 1 amp.
Morphine, 50 mg. vial
1/4% marcaine, 30 cc.
Nitroglycerin tablets
Digoxine, 0.5 mg.
Atropine, 0.4 mg = 1 amp.
Demerol injection, 100 mg.
Temozysom, 30 mg., #30
Diphenhydromine, 50 mg./ml. injection
Prochlorpecozine, 5 mg./ml, injectable I.M.
Lidocaine, 100 mg., injectable
Amenophylline, 200 mg./10 ml.
Injectable local anesthetic

You may have difficulty obtaining these medical aids in List Three, since their purchase requires a doctor's prescription in the U.S. Additionally, those of you who live in Hawai'i may believe you need not be prepared for these kinds of major emergencies because you'll always be close to shore and to trained assistance. Those of you who will be crossing the Pacific Ocean to get to Hawai'i, however, should have an extensive medical kit similar to that suggested by Dr. Macpherson.

Often you'll use the sport boat to take you several miles from where you've anchored your sail or motor boat. Just as often you'll be many more miles from a town or village where you could get first aid treatment. Be prepared with a waterproof kit that becomes part of your standard apparatus to be put into the sport boat whenever you take it ashore in remote regions. In this kit include a small bottle of alcohol or hydrogen peroxide for disinfecting, medicated powder, Neosporin cream, tweezers, Band-Aids and gauze pads, moleskin, adhesive tape, a bee-sting kit, and a disposable scalpel. Keep this kit at the ready; then, as you're leaving the mother ship, add to it your hand-held VHF and your Swiss army knife or Leatherman.

When you get ashore, you'll want to carry the kit with you in your fanny pack if you're planning to hike some distance from the boat, so keep it compact.

An ideal cruise, from a medical standpoint, would be one from which the cruisers return without ever having opened their first aid kits. And we're sure many, if not most, cruisers to Hawai'i can count their medical emergencies on the fingers of one hand. A few other cruisers, however, have painful memories of accidents and illnesses during their cruises, the pain of those memories lessened in some cases because of the application of prompt and appropriate medical care on the spot.

Arch rock on south coast of Maui

Jon Petersen fishing at Midway

THE PASSAGE TO AND FROM THE ISLANDS

'Au i ke kai me he manu ala.
("Cross the sea as a bird.")

For a number of cruising boaters everywhere, the passage to a destination promises challenge but also as much pleasure as the destination itself. Certainly that is no more true than among sailors who have crossed the Pacific Ocean to come to Hawai'i. Cruising boaters come from around the world to cruise in these Islands, but, as one would expect, the largest single group of non-resident cruising boaters in Hawai'i are those from the Mainland. Hence we will focus our attention on the trip from the Mainland.

Preparing for a passage from the Mainland to the Hawaiian Islands is the beginning of the challenges. For the trip across the Pacific to be pleasurable for all aboard, the boat must be well equipped for safety and navigation. In addition, the navigator should become competent and confident enough about using charts and navigational instruments so that everyone on board will be able to relax. Even the provisioning is a challenge. Deciding what and how much food and drink the crew will need to be happy will keep someone busy for a long while. And that does not even begin to consider the task of stowing the provisions, invariably as challenging a task as deciding what to buy.

Wing and wing across the Pacific

THE TIME OF YEAR TO GO TO HAWAI'I

Though the consensus is that some months are preferable to others for making the trip to Hawai'i, cruising sailboats make this trip during virtually all months of the year. We've made the trip from California to Hawai'i in three different months: February, June, and August. Our most recent trip, a February crossing, was no more difficult a passage than any of the others, although it was different in some inconsequential ways.

In planning the date and the course for your trip, you should take into account the different locations of the Pacific High throughout the year. This high pressure area moves across the Pacific Ocean between the Mainland and Hawai'i. Not only does it move, but it also increases in size at various times of the year. You want to stay clear of the Pacific High because the winds inside this high will be light and variable. Boaters who have inadvertently sailed into it and stayed near the center of its circle for a week or two refer to it as "The Great Pacific Parking Lot."

But the High is not without its positive effects for the passage to and from Hawai'i. Because of the Coriolis Effect, the winds in the High rotate in a clockwise direction in the Northern Hemisphere. Boats enroute to Hawai'i can get a boost in winds by skirting along the southern edge of the High. Similarly, boaters returning to the Mainland from Hawai'i can get a boost by skirting the northern edge of the High. To take advantage of this boost from the High, you will need to monitor its position carefully to avoid inadvertently sailing into its near calm center and parking for a long while.

In the summer months, the High usually prevails between the 35N and 40N latitudes, leaving a wide path for boaters wanting to make good time sailing to Hawai'i. In the winter months, the high pushes below 30N latitude. But the high moves back and forth from east to

A lone albatross, our only companion in mid-ocean

west, as well. In mid-summer it is often centered near 150W longitude, while in winter months its center is closer to 130W longitude.

To predict the position of the high in any given month, look closely at the *Pilot Chart of the North Pacific Ocean* for that month. In the inset in the upper right corner of the chart is the barometric pressure in various parts of the Pacific Ocean. In September, for example, the predicted high pressure area is huge, but its western edge lies far to the north of the Hawaiian Islands. September, then, is a good month to make the trip from California to the Islands, for the course would be far below the southern edge of the High. Departing from Oregon or Washington, you would need to go south a little before changing course for the Islands to avoid a potential encounter with the High. Knowing the location of the High can make the difference between an enjoyable, quick trip and a long, tedious trip.

Crossings from the Mainland to Hawai'i are more common in the summer months than in any other season. This schedule has much to recommend it. Boaters making the trip during June, July, and August can cruise the Islands and then return to their home ports in the late summer or early fall, ahead of the rough late fall and winter weather that begins in October in the North Pacific Ocean. (Because of the shortage of slips in Hawai'i, you cannot count on being able to leave your boat in the Islands over the winter and return for it later.)

Another reason to choose the summer months is the weather on the southern route between the Mainland and Hawai'i. Although you can safely make this trip any month of the year, during a summer crossing you'll run almost no risk of encountering a gale. The frequency of gales during these months drops to almost zero. In fact, though the number of gales reported during the winter for the same area is also surprisingly low, not more than two or three days of gales per month. Nevertheless, if given a choice of making a trip with the likelihood of no days of gale winds or one with two or three days of gale weather, we would all certainly take the trip with no gales.

Although few boaters sail to Hawai'i during the spring months, a spring crossing also has much to recommend it. The frequency of gales is still low, and the weather in the Islands may be at its best for cruising because the winds are consistent and the temperature is a bit cooler than in the summer. In addition, crossing during the spring allows plenty of time to explore the Islands before making the trip back to the Mainland. If you arrive in late April, for example, you will be able to spend four months cruising around the Islands before heading back in early September, the month many consider best for making the return trip.

Fall and winter crossings to the Islands can also be safe and comfortable, of course, but a major consideration here is the duration of your cruise. If you are going to cruise for only a month or two, you will have created a dilemma. You won't want to make a return trip through the North Pacific before May; otherwise, you risk running into storms that come down out of the Gulf of Alaska during the late fall, the winter and the early spring. On the other hand, you may not be able to find a place where you can legally and safely leave your boat. You should probably consider making the trip to Hawai'i in the fall and winter only if you can spend a long, relaxing time cruising the Islands or if you expect to go on from Hawai'i to the South Pacific in time for the summer cruising season there.

THE SUGGESTED COURSE FOR BOATS SAILING TO THE ISLANDS

Departing from any harbor on the California coast during the summer months, you can follow a straight line to Hawai'i if you choose. More commonly, however, boaters drop south to avoid contact with the capricious North Pacific High. By making a curve south, you can also get to the warm weather and trade winds more quickly. This southern curve makes the trip to Hawai'i longer in miles, and will likely take an additional day or two, but the trade-off is better winds and warmer weather.

If you'll be enroute to Hawai'i from Oregon and Washington, you won't have the option of sailing straight to the Islands if you wish to avoid the High. Instead, you will need to follow the coastline until you are at least as far south as San Francisco. (Many Northwest boaters include in their agenda a few days or weeks exploring San Francisco before jumping off for Hawai'i.)

TYPICAL WEATHER EN ROUTE TO THE ISLANDS

You may be surprised by the number of light air days on the southern route from the West Coast to Hawai'i. Only 200 miles or so offshore, light winds are far more common than heavy winds. Even non-racing boaters begin digging out every light air sail on the boat to get some speed up. A spinnaker may become your favorite sail, if you have one aboard. (When you're using a self-steering device, you probably won't want to fly a spinnaker. On most boats, wind vanes and autopilots work better with some other sail configuration).

These light air days and nights are, of course, punctuated by squalls. Some boaters put up

Pōka'i Anchorage

light air sails and run with them day and night until a squall forces them to change sails. Others prefer to run under spinnakers or other light air sails until dark and then put up smaller sails, choosing not to get caught by a squall at night with all the light air sails flying. Other more conservative boaters run working sails day and night.

While the winds along the coast vary greatly in strength, the winds at sea are more consistent. What does vary from one part of the ocean to another is the wind direction. Along the Pacific Coast and out a few hundred miles, the winds generally blow from the northwest or north, often with gusto. Below the 30th parallel of latitude, however, the winds come almost exclusively from the east or northeast and with less force. These are the fabled trade winds. Although the *Pilot Chart of the North Pacific Ocean* suggests that you will find 11-16 knot winds most of the time once in the area of trade winds, cruising boaters regularly tell of never encountering any winds stronger than 10 knots, except when a squall hits.

And boaters making the passage to Hawai'i will experience squalls. In the summer months, you'll get hit by fewer squalls than in the winter, but squalls are common along the route at any time of the year. Although squalls can be vicious, most of them pack relatively modest winds. On our last passage from San Francisco to Honolulu, a February trip, we saw far more squalls than on our June and August trips combined. But these were not the fearsome squalls of the movies; the winds in these squalls rarely exceeded 30 knots.

As you near the Islands, you might find the winds increasing. If strong trades are blowing near the Islands, wind strength may jump from 10 knots to 20 knots, providing an exhilarating ride for the last day or so. And then, of course, you will almost certainly have good winds as you transit the Kaiwi Channel if your first stop is Honolulu.

THE LENGTH OF THE STAY IN THE ISLANDS

Some cruisers to Hawai'i spend many months wandering around the Islands. At the other extreme, one boater we know spent a mere two days in the Islands before setting sail for the Mainland once again. His entire purpose in making the trip was to enhance his skills at making ocean passages.

The Hawaiian Islands will recompense you generously whatever the length of your stay, but, if you have at least seven or eight weeks, you can come in the spring or summer, return in the late summer or early fall, and have time in the interim to sample anchorages and harbors on all the major Islands.

One workable schedule for a seven-to-eight-week cruise of the Islands is to leave the Mainland in May or June, sailing directly to Hilo, on the Big Island. After spending a week or two in some of the anchorages and harbors around the Big Island, you have a downwind sail to Maui. Then you can cruise around Maui, Lāna'i, and Moloka'i for two to three weeks before another downwind sail to O'ahu.

On O'ahu, in addition to enjoying the harbors and anchorages, you'll have access to the most complete range of parts and facilities for effecting repairs to your boat. Here, too, you can most completely provision for the return trip to the Mainland. After two or three weeks on O'ahu, sail to Kaua'i, visiting some of this island's beautiful anchorages and harbors before heading north and then east to the Mainland.

Nā Pali, Kaua'i

Some boaters have gotten to Hawai'i and for one reason or another want to leave their boats in the Islands until the following year. If you're one of these boaters, you'll discover that finding a secure place to leave your boat is difficult. All the slips in the state harbors and private marinas are typically rented, with long waiting lists for some sizes of vessels. You'll want to have other options in mind.

Slips for lease are sometimes available at Makani Kai, a condominium development with resident docks, in Kāne'ohe Bay. Some of these docks are empty because not all the residents have boats. In that case, the manager of the facility will rent spaces to non-residents. No one may stay overnight on a boat moored in Makani Kai.

While storing their boats on the hard is the preferred choice for many sailors, such storage is rarely available in the Hawaiian Islands. Ke'ehi Marine Center, in Honolulu, no longer has long-term storage on the hard, and the 300 spaces on the hard at Gentry Marine, in Honokōhau, on the Big Island, are generally filled. However, the perpetual waiting list at Gentry, from which available spaces are filled, is sometimes a short one.

THE RETURN TRIP TO THE MAINLAND

The trip from Hawai'i to the Mainland contrasts sharply with the trip to the Islands. Some people have a good time on the trip from Hawai'i to the Mainland; others hate everything about it.

Whereas on the trip to the Islands, you'll experience winds coming over the transom most of the time, on the return your boat will be close-hauled most of the time until you alter course at about the 40th parallel of latitude. From that point on the boat will generally be on a broad or beam reach.

After the first few days, the sunny, warm days grow colder and colder until everyone aboard digs out thermal underwear and foul weather gear. Unlike the trip to Hawai'i, where squalls are the norm, boaters generally encounter few squalls on the return trip. Instead, the rains that come don't pass through quickly as the squalls usually do; they may last for days. In addition, the starry nights of the trip to the Islands become overcast nights on the return.

Though these conditions probably aren't as appealing as the promise of ever warmer and balmier weather on the trip to Hawai'i, they need not result in a miserable passage. The return trip can, in fact, be downright pleasurable if you choose the best time and the optimum course and your boat is prepared.

The major concern is, of course, weather. Although accurately predicting the weather is beyond most mortals, an examination of the *Pilot Chart of the North Pacific Ocean* suggests that some months are far better than others for the return trip. July, for example, is the month when the North Pacific has the lowest incidence of gale force winds. Even two months later, the picture changes. The chart for September shows the chance in most areas of the North Pacific has increased from 0 percent in July to 4 or 5 percent. By the time January and February arrive, the chance of encountering gale force winds in most areas north of the 30th parallel of latitude reaches 10 percent. The months with the least risk of gale weather, then, are June, July, and August.

As with the trip to Hawai'i, you will have a more pleasant passage if you can avoid the Pacific High. However, a close look at the *Pilot Chart* reveals a problem. During the summer, the time with the fewest days of gale force winds, the High is at its most northwesterly position, forcing you to go far north to get around it. As a consequence, the distance you'll have to travel on this northern route will be substantially greater than the southern route. The 2100-mile passage straight from Honolulu to San Francisco becomes closer to 2500 miles on the return trip. If you make the trip to the Mainland in June, July, or August, the best months for avoiding gales, you'll probably have to spend three or four extra days at sea in order to get around the Pacific High.

Some boaters who make the trip back to the Mainland during the summer decide to power through the High. To ensure that they won't become stuck for weeks in "The Great Pacific Parking Lot," these boaters load extra fuel on deck in jerry jugs or even 55-gallon drums. If you choose this option, load enough fuel aboard to give you an 800-1,000-mile range under power.

Though this option sounds ideal, you'll still want to sail north for the first few days, until you pass the 30th parallel of latitude or until the trades slacken. You won't want to motor directly into the trade winds.

We know one couple, however, who got southeast winds when they were only about one day north of O'ahu. They headed for San Francisco at that point, assuming they would have to fall off and head north when the east or northeast winds filled in again. But they never had to change course and arrived in San Francisco 16 days later, having motored only two or three days.

If you examine the suggested routes chart, you can see the dramatic difference between the routes in winter and spring compared to the summer. The northern summer route to the Mainland is a good distance farther than the southern winter route, but the incidence of gales is negligible in June, July, and August.

May and September are borderline. The Pacific High will not usually be as far north as it is in the summer, and gales are not as frequent as they are in the winter. If these months are the only months that fit your schedule for returning to the Mainland, you should still have a reasonably comfortable and safe trip. Many cruising boaters choose to return in September because that best fits their cruising schedules in Hawai'i.

Few cruising boaters would attempt a midwinter passage from Hawai'i to the Mainland. Delivery skippers make the trip because they are paid to go even though the weather is almost sure to make the trip miserable.

The other variable is one boaters have complete control over: preparation of the boat for the return passage. Before leaving the Islands, provision as carefully as you did before leaving the Mainland. The trip time for sailing a boat back to the Mainland varies greatly. As we said, we know one couple who made the trip back in 16 days, but they are the exception. Most return trips take between 21 and 30 days, depending primarily on the time of year, the boat, and how hard the crew chooses to push the boat.

You should have enough provisions aboard for at least 45 days, allowing for ample food for at least 30 days and for spoilage. Stories abound in the cruising community about boats

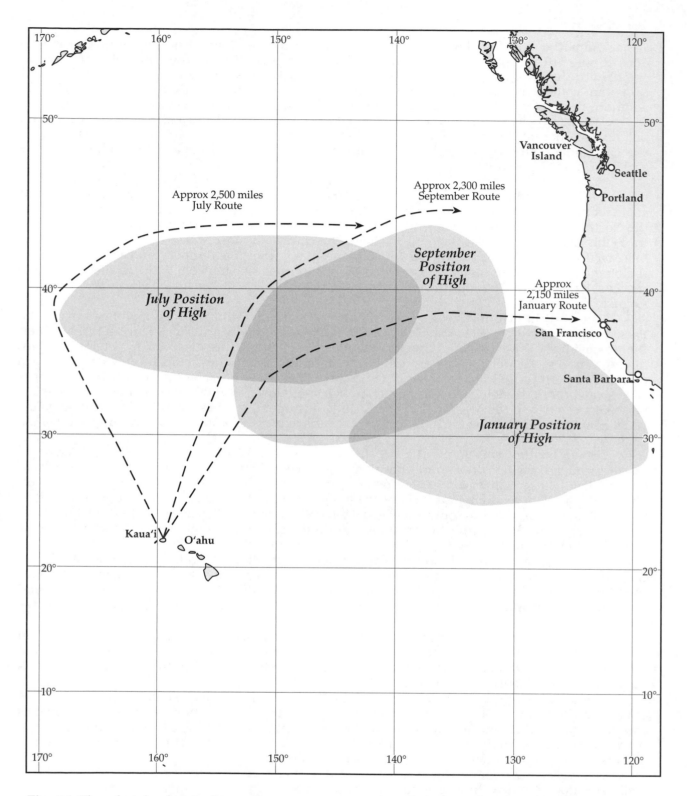

Fig. 7.1 The sketch above shows the average positions of the Pacific High for the months of January, July, and September (taken from the current *Pilot Charts*). Although the High is continually in motion, the locations during these three months generally fall within the areas shown on the sketch. Using the sketch, you can see what your routes should be as you depart Kauai for the Mainland. Suggested routes shown here are only hypothetical and may vary, depending on the exact position of the High, the strength and direction of the wind, and the hull and sail configuration of your boat.

arriving at a Mainland destination with no food left aboard. We have one good friend who crewed on such a boat. When the boat arrived at its destination, the only food left to eat was a piece of fish they had caught the day before. Although no one died of starvation on that trip, no one had much fun either.

Because the trip back to the Mainland will almost certainly put greater stresses on the equipment, you'll also want to examine and replace, or at least have spares for, any equipment that is most likely to fail. Pay particular attention to the rigging and sails. They must be strong. Be sure someone who is qualified goes aloft to check the rigging carefully and replace anything that looks suspect.

One other consideration, and perhaps one you should entertain before you make the trip to Hawai'i, is the seaworthiness of the boat itself. An axiom among sailors familiar with the passages to and from Hawai'i is that any boat can sail to Hawai'i, but only a good sailboat can make the trip back to the Mainland. While this axiom may be a bit of a generalization, it contains more than a grain of truth.

A small, lightly built boat may, in fact, get you back to the West Coast, but only after a long, miserable trip. One couple who departed from Hawai'i on just such a boat spent three days of banging into waves, until they were too tired to continue. They sailed back to Honolulu, sold their boat, and flew home.

Many boaters have made the trip back to the Mainland in small, light boats and lived to tell about it. After all, small race boats are sailed to the Islands and back every year the Pacific Cup is held. If you have such a boat and want to make the trip over and back on it, prepare yourself for a less-than-pleasant return passage.

If your boat is small and light and you aren't confident making the trip back to the Mainland, consider the barge/ship solution. We met two men on Kaua'i this year who had sailed their Norsea 27 to the Islands from San Francisco. After sailing around the Islands for two months, they took the mast down and put the boat on a barge in Nāwiliwili Harbor. The barge took the boat to Honolulu, where it was loaded on a ship for transport back to California. Although many boaters would argue that the Norsea 27 would easily handle the rigors of a trip from Kaua'i to San Francisco, the two men aboard chose not to make the trip by boat. (Small boats can be shipped to the Mainland West Coast for approximately $5000. Ship service to Los Angeles, Oakland, and Seattle is provided by Matson Lines, 808-848-1211.)

Other boaters have shipped their larger boats home on freighters, too, but the price goes up significantly. To ship a 73-foot race boat California costs the owner $90,000.

Some cruising boats are returned as cargo on barges. This means of transportation is somewhat cheaper than a ship, but not much. The charge for shipping a 35-foot cruising boat to Seattle, for instance, is about $9,000. (Barge service to Seattle is provided by Aloha Cargo, 808-536-7033.)

ENTERING THE ISLANDS

Mai hahaki ʻoe i ka ʻōhelo o punia i ka ua noe.
("Do not pluck the ʻōhelo berries lest we be surrounded by rain and fog.")

All boaters entering the State of Hawaiʻi must check in with the appropriate agencies. Depending on the boat owner's nationality and last port of call, various agencies will need to be notified.

•U. S. CITIZENS ON VESSELS ARRIVING FROM MAINLAND U. S. A.

U. S. citizens who have departed from the United States and arrived in the Hawaiian Islands without having stopped en route at a foreign port may enter the State of Hawaiʻi at any harbor. If every person on the boat is a U. S citizen, these boaters must contact only one governmental agency, the Hawaiʻi Department of Agriculture (808-483-7154), as soon as they go ashore for the first time on any island in the State. (Many U.S. boaters choose to make one of the designated Ports of Entry their first destination in Hawaiʻi. These ports are Honolulu, on Oʻahu; Kahului, on Maui; Nāwiliwili, on Kauaʻi; and Hilo, on the Island of Hawaiʻi.)

The Agriculture Department has but one requirement for visiting boaters who are U.S. citizens: they may not bring in any prohibited animals, plants, or insects. In the past, large numbers of harmful insects, animals, and plants were introduced accidentally by visitors. The mosquito, for example, was an alien species accidentally introduced in 1826 by sailors from the *Wellington,* a ship that brought the larvae from San Blas, Mexico. Today, Hawaiʻi is doing everything it can to prevent the introduction of other pests, such as the brown tree snake that has ravaged the island of Guam, and diseases carried by animals and insects, such as rabies. To prevent the introduction of such pests, the State of Hawaiʻi requires every boat entering the Hawaiian Islands to call the Department of Agriculture immediately upon arrival. Most cruising boats will have none of the prohibited species aboard, so the inspection, if even required, is simple.

•U. S. AND FOREIGN CITIZENS ON VESSELS ARRIVING FROM A FOREIGN PORT

In addition to notifying the Hawaiʻi Department of Agricultural (see above) all boaters who have departed from a foreign port, including citizens of the United States as well as of a foreign county, must make their first destination in Hawaiʻi one of the designated Ports of Entry (see above). The same requirement applies if a U.S. boat coming directly to Hawaiʻi from the Mainland has aboard a person or persons of foreign citizenry. Within 48 hours of arrival in any of these Ports of Entry, these boaters must call U.S. Customs (808-522-8012 or 808-522-8001). No one other than the skipper, who may go ashore to call Customs, may leave the boat until a Customs officer has been on board. Nor may anyone else board the vessel before this officer visits.

Customs charges $25 for clearing a vessel, but the boater has to pay this fee only once a year. Additional charges are levied for all inspections requested after normal working hours, 0800-1630 M-F, or on weekends.

Boaters on vessels arriving from a foreign port must have clearance from the port of departure. All boaters must also obtain a clearance from U.S. Customs before leaving Hawaiʻi for foreign destinations.

All boaters must declare everything being brought from a foreign country. U.S. citizens as well as foreign citizens will be charged duty for items in excess of the normal allowance.

All boaters arriving from a foreign port must also notify Immigration (808-532-4600). U.S. citizens and citizens from North America will need to have proof of citizenship. Citizens of any other foreign country must have obtained visas prior to their arrival and must have a passport that is valid for at least six months.

•FOREIGN CITIZENS ON VESSELS ARRIVING IN HAWAIʻI

Foreign citizens arriving in Hawaiʻi, whether their last port was in the United States or a foreign country, must meet other Customs and Immigrations requirements in addition to those in the previous section.

First, with the exception of citizens of some exempt countries, foreign citizens must clear with Customs at the Port of Entry for each island they visit. For all Customs clearances, they must report within 48 hours and must show (1) clearances from previous ports, (2) Ships Stores Declarations, and (3) Crew's Effects Declarations.

Foreign citizens must also obtain a Cruising Permit ($19 for 60 days, plus a live-aboard fee of $2 a person/a day). The permits are good for 60 days only.

PETS

When a boat arrives in Hawai'i with a pet aboard, the pet's owner must notify the Hawai'i Department of Agriculture (808-483-7154) or the Animal Quarantine Station (808-837-8413). No pets may leave the boat until an official from one of these two agencies comes aboard for an inspection. To keep the State free of diseases carried by pets, especially rabies, all pets entering the State will be quarantined for 120 days in the Quarantine Station unless the owner has contacted one of these agencies before departing from Mainland, U. S. A. and obtained a health form for each pet aboard. Pet owners will also need a health record card from a certified veterinarian, preferably one in the U.S.

Pets on boats having last departed from ports other than those on the U.S. Mainland will be subject to more stringent requirements. In some cases, they will automatically be quarantined for 120 days. The owners of these pets should call one of the agencies, Agriculture or Quarantine, well in advance to ascertain the specific regulations that apply to them.

FIREARMS

Those boaters who have guns aboard must take them to the local police department where they enter and register them. Only firearms designed and intended to be used for hunting or sporting purposes may be brought into the state. Failure to register any firearms may cause serious problems in the event a Coast Guard boarding party finds them aboard the boat.

Clipper Ship in Ke'ehi Lagoon

GETTING AROUND IN ISLAND WATERS

Hiki mai ka mālie, a hiki mai no ka 'ino.
("Good weather comes, and bad weather comes too.")

Hawai'i is an ideal cruising destination for boaters who are willing to concede that the weather is all-powerful. Cruising boaters generally say that they respect the forces of nature; cruising in the Hawaiian Islands is bound to increase that respect. Cruisers here must always consider the weather before departing for their next destination, and they must be willing to alter their plans to go to a particular anchorage or harbor when the weather is not right.

Hawai'i's reputation as a cruising destination has suffered recently for a variety of reasons. Two of the most pervasive are the myths that the weather is often not conducive to cruising and that the Islands have few good anchorages. Both of these criticisms will seem valid to the cruiser who wants to be able to go to any anchorage or harbor any day of the year. This cruiser will soon grow disenchanted with these enchanted isles because, when the wind or swell is up, from any direction, some place on each island is a place you'll not want to be on a boat at anchor.

Because these are islands, one side will be protected and one side fully exposed, no matter from which direction the weather comes. If the trades are blowing from the northeast or east, the anchorages on the southeast or west are protected. When *kona* winds blow (from the southwest or west), the north and east shores are protected.

In this cruising guide, we describe 68 anchorages and harbors. Each one can be a comfortable and secure destination in certain conditions; at another time, these same destinations may be untenable. Depending on wind direction, the destinations vary from day to day or week to week. Generally, however, the trade winds blow from the east or northeast during the summer months, as much as 90 percent of the time. For boaters who cruise the Islands during the summer months, then, some of the beautiful anchorages on the windward side of the Islands are difficult to visit.

Some local cruisers, in fact, rarely take their boats out during the summer because they can't visit their favorite anchorages then. Instead, they prefer the fall and winter months, when they can visit anchorages on the north sides of the Islands. If you can spend enough time here, you can, of course, wait for the right weather and visit them all.

CHARTS AND NAVIGATION

Charts are the road maps of the oceans. As such, they will help you get to your destination safely. You should have aboard a chart of all the Hawaiian Islands as well as an individual chart of each island you plan to visit. We have used the following 8 charts most frequently:

19004 Hawaiian Islands
19320 Island of Hawai'i
19340 Hawai'i to O'ahu
19347 Channels between Moloka'i, Maui, & Lāna'i
19351 Channels between O'ahu, Moloka'i, & Lāna'i
19357 Island of O'ahu
19380 O'ahu to Ni'ihau
19381 Island of Kaua'i

NOAA (National Oceanic and Atmospheric Administration) puts out lists of charts and publications. The NOAA free catalog #2, covering the Pacific Coast, including the Hawaiian, Mariana, and Sāmoa islands, lists 48 charts that would be useful to boaters cruising the Hawaiian Islands.

Since charts currently cost about $18 each, the price of the 48 charts covering the Islands totals over $800. Rather than buy individual charts of every harbor and bay to supplement your basic charts, you may want to invest instead in a CD copy of the charts of Hawai'i if you have a computer aboard and a program such as Cap'n or Nobeltec to drive it. As do many other cruisers, we use our paper charts for ocean passages and channel crossings, but for identifying harbors we prefer electronic charts with our laptop connected to a GPS.

In addition to charts of the Islands, you should also have aboard a copy of the *Light List, Vol. VI, Pacific Coast and Pacific Islands*. When you're approaching an island or a harbor at night, you'll depend on the lights you see to help you make sense of the approach. Be sure your *Light List* is up to date; the lights change from year to year.

Another useful book to have aboard is the *U. S. Coast Pilot #7*, which covers the Pacific Coast and the Hawaiian Islands. This volume contains extensive information about all of the Islands, including the channels between the Islands and all the harbors on each island.

When making passages between the Islands, your primary tools will be your charts and your compass. If you don't have current charts and an accurate compass, you can easily get into trouble since you will not be able to see the island you are heading for in many instances.

Before you depart for a destination, draw a line on your chart between your last point of land on the island you are leaving and the point of land you wish to go to. Use your parallel rules to find the compass course of that line; write the course on your chart. Next, use your dividers to find the distance between the two points, and write this distance on your chart near the course you are going to follow. Make sure that everyone aboard knows the course and the distance.

Use your distance to establish an ETA (estimated time of arrival) at the desired point, and share this with all hands. For example, if you are making a passage from Lono Harbor on Moloka'i to Ala Wai Harbor on O'ahu, your last point of land on Moloka'i is Lā'au Point. The first point of land that you will pass close to on O'ahu is Diamond Head, a distance of approximately 30 miles. If your boat averages 5 knots under these conditions, you can plan on a total of about 6 hours from Lā'au Point to Diamond Head. You don't need to write this time on your chart, but you should inform the other people on your boat so they can relax, knowing about when the boat should arrive.

Another navigation technique many cruising boaters use is periodically to mark their position and the time on the chart so they will know where they are if darkness falls before they get to their destination or if a squall reduces visibility. This position may be from dead reckoning derived from the boat's course and speed, but it will more commonly be a position taken from a GPS at regular intervals.

As the price of GPS units has dropped significantly, more and more boaters have begun using them for channel crossings. By entering the coordinates of a point of land, a buoy, or a harbor, boaters can have continual information displayed on the screen about the course and distance to that point, the speed, and the course made good. When used in conjunction with a chart, this information makes navigation easy. By plotting a position every hour or two, you can see how accurately you are following the desired course you established on your chart before you departed. If you encounter a strong cross current that pushes you significantly off course, you can recognize the problem quickly and make a course correction.

GPS units are also a tremendous

Spinner dolphins off the Big Island

help in finding the entrances into anchorages and harbors. Before we depart from one anchorage, we enter the coordinates of our next destination into our GPS. By monitoring the GPS, we know when the destination is near.

Although GPS units have made navigation easy, they have also created a potentially dangerous dependence. Some boaters sail across channels and even across oceans without ever making any notations on their charts. What happens then when the GPS unit fails, whether because of an internal malfunction, a power failure on the boat, or a weak satellite signal? If darkness falls about the same time as the GPS fails, boaters have no way of knowing their position. The solution to this potential problem is easy: plot a position every hour or two on the chart.

VISITING ANCHORAGES ON LEEWARD COASTLINES

Kāne'ohe Bay, protected by the reef

Most of the frequently visited anchorages in the Hawaiian Islands are located on leeward shores during normal trade wind conditions. (Because trade winds are the overwhelmingly dominant winds in Hawai'i, these leeward shores are generally called "leeward," even when an unusual wind makes them windward.) In summer months boaters can visit these anchorages almost any day and be confident that the boat will be safe and the crew comfortable. Each island has a number of them.

Eleven of the 12 anchorages and harbors we visited on the Big Island are leeward anchorages. Essentially every anchorage on the Kona Coast enjoys the protection of the island whenever trade winds blow. Similarly, on Lāna'i all 4 tenable anchorages and harbors are on the leeward side of the island. Even when strong trades are blowing, the anchorages on Lāna'i, like those on the Big Island, are safe, even though the waters might not be flat calm.

Maui has 12 anchorages that you can visit when trade winds are blowing. Some will be rolly when strong trade winds blow, and others will be calm, but all are safe.

Moloka'i has 6 anchorages on the leeward side (including the anchorage in Kaunakakai Harbor). All of them except 'Īlio Point (Pāpōhaku Roadstead) provide a safe and comfortable anchorage even when strong trades blow. 'Īlio Point is an excellent anchorage when light or moderate trades blow, but it becomes a little too rolly to be classified as comfortable when strong trades blow. Still, even with the roll, fishing boats anchor there regularly even in strong trade winds.

On the island of O'ahu, only 3 anchorages are on the leeward side, but Kāne'ohe Bay has such great protection behind the reef that it is as good as a leeward anchorage. Many people also consider the anchorage outside Hale'iwa Harbor and the one at Waimea Bay to be excellent destinations in the summer months when trades are blowing.

Kaua'i has 5 leeward anchorages. Ni'ihau and Midway each have one.

All totaled, Hawai'i has over 40 leeward anchorages, each different in terms of scenery and weather.

The reason cruising boaters don't visit more of these beautiful leeward anchorages has more to do with getting there than with the anchorages themselves. To get from one of these anchorages to the next one, you often have to cross a channel; more about that problem later.

VISITING ANCHORAGES ON WINDWARD COASTLINES

To get the most pleasure out of the anchorages on the so-called "windward" side, that is, the northeast and east sides of the Islands, wait until the trade winds change or drop to light and variable. Yes, you can visit Hāna or any of the eastern Maui anchorages when the trade winds are blowing, but you'll be too busy hanging on to your boat to enjoy the anchorage. When the trades slacken, however, these anchorages are comfortable. The same is true with the North Shore anchorages on Moloka'i.

CROSSING CHANNELS BETWEEN THE ISLANDS

Crossing the channels between Islands is, for too many cruisers, the greatest impediment to visiting more of the splendid and varied destinations throughout this chain of Islands.

Some channel crossings require little planning; others require maximum planning. For example, the 'Au'au Channel, between Lahaina and Lāna'i, presents few problems anytime trades are blowing, even strong trades. By contrast, the Pailolo Channel between the west end of Maui and Moloka'i, has some of the roughest water in the Islands. The most remarkable part about these contrasting channels is that they are adja-

Three generations crossing the channel in light airs

cent; in fact, the winds from the Pailolo become the winds in the 'Au'au.

Before making any channel crossing, consider the geography of the channel. If a channel begins at the Pacific Ocean, it requires special consideration. Only four of the channels fit this description: the 'Alenuihāhā, the Pailolo, the Kaiwi, and the Kaua'i. The winds that travel across the Pacific are funneled down as they come through the channels, increasing in strength. Often when 20-knot trade winds are blowing at sea, the winds in the channels will be blowing at 30 knots.

Even more significant, perhaps, is the size of the waves in the channels. Wave size increases as the wind strength increases. When winds of less than 10 knots are blowing, the seas in the channels will usually be 4 feet or less. When moderate winds (16-20 knots) are blowing, however, the seas in the channels will generally be in the range of 8-12 feet. And when strong trades are blowing, the seas will normally be 12-18 feet or greater.

Only under extraordinary circumstances should you attempt to cross any of these four channels open to the Pacific Ocean when strong trades are blowing. When boaters do occasionally make such a trip going downwind, they and their boats get bounced around, and sometimes worse. One local boater who crossed the Kaiwi Channel recently when strong trades were blowing had his boat pooped twice. Needless to say, being pooped leaves the crew in the cockpit wet and the boat vulnerable when the next large wave comes through.

If going downwind through the channels in strong trades is challenging, going upwind appeals only to race boat sailors and masochists. "Uncomfortable" is far from adequate to describe the pounding the crew and boat would take; indeed, such a crossing should properly be classified as a gear-breaking experience. Even the ocean-going tugs that pull barges between the Islands have trouble when these strong trades blow. Normally traveling at 11 knots, these tugs must slow to 4-5 knots when the wind and seas are this large. Otherwise, they can sustain serious damage. One tug captain told us of having the wheelhouse on his 60-foot steel tug torn completely off by a wave in the 'Alenuihāhā Channel.

After listening to this and other stories, we have chosen to make channel crossings only in light or moderate trades, never when strong trades are forecast. And if the crossing is to be upwind, we try to wait for light trades. We may have to use the motor to make good progress, but motoring across a channel is preferable to pounding across it, risking harm to both crew and boat.

Another way to make channel crossings comfortable is to choose the angle across the channel based on the direction of the wind and swells and the protection afforded by the islands nearby. This route will invariably be longer than if you simply punched straight across from one island to the next, but you'll greatly increase the likelihood of having an enjoyable, safe passage.

The following are some suggested routes:

•HONOLULU TO NĀWILIWILI OR TO HANALEI BAY ON KAUA'I

Make the passage more comfortable by following the west O'ahu coastline to Pōka'ī Bay or Mākua Anchorage. Wait there for the right time to depart so you can sail overnight, arriving just after dawn. This plan works well when light or moderate trades blow. The same tactic works well when returning from Kaua'i. Depart from Hanalei on the North Shore holding a course for Pōka'ī Bay and fall off for Barbers Point or farther south if you must. However, don't make the return crossing in strong trades.

•HONOLULU TO MOLOKA'I, LĀNA'I, MAUI, OR THE BIG ISLAND.

Since this trip requires you to sail to weather across the Kaiwi Channel, you would do well to follow one of two approaches. The first is to follow the coastline around Diamond Head and Koko Head to Makapu'u Point, staying as close as possible to the shore without getting dangerously close. Even though this route makes the trip to Moloka'i slightly longer, it reduces the time spent in the channel, and it allows you to fall off slightly as you sail across the channel. On this course you may be able to sail directly from Makapu'u Point to Pāpōhaku Roadstead in the lee of 'Īlio Point on Moloka'i if you're making a daylight passage when light trades are blowing and you wish to run your engine to supplement your sails.

A second approach to crossing the Kaiwi is to set a course for Palaoa, the south point on Lāna'i, as soon as possible after passing Diamond Head. You almost certainly won't be able to hold this course immediately after passing Diamond Head because the wind will be bending around Koko Head and in your face until you're about 10 miles south of the Diamond Head buoy. After you're about half way across the channel, the winds usually will allow you to hold a course for Palaoa. After you round the south end of Lāna'i, you can stop at Mānele Bay, go around the island and across the 'Au'au Channel to Lahaina, or continue on to the Big Island.

•KAUNAKAKAI OR LONO HARBOR TO LAHAINA OR MĀLA WHARF.

Although the distance between Kaunakakai and Lahaina is only 24 miles, avoid going directly when moderate or strong trades blow. Most boaters who know the Kalohi well say that you'll rarely find calm or light winds there during the summer months. The Kalohi Channel is almost as difficult to cross as are the channels that border directly on the Pacific Ocean. A far better route will take you in a southerly direction across the Kalohi around the island of Lāna'i to Lahaina. Taking this route will require you to travel some 46 miles, almost twice as far as the more direct route, but you'll find the trip much more relaxing.

•MĀLA WHARF OR LAHAINA TO MOLOKA'I.

When departing from either Lahaina or Māla Wharf, you can easily sail down the Kalohi Channel directly to Moloka'i when light winds blow, but the same trip can be challenging when moderate winds are blowing through the Pailolo Channel, making the weather in the Kalohi unappealing. This trip in strong trades is downright ugly.

For example, the ideal way to make a trip from Lahaina to Kamalō on Moloka'i is to follow the West Maui coastline around as far as Kahana or even Hāwea Point before changing course and entering the Pailolo Channel. Although this course will add 5 miles to the trip, it will change the direction of the winds and waves hitting your boat. From Hāwea Point to Kamalō, you'll be on a broad reach; from Lahaina to Kamalō, on the other hand, will be a close reach that will almost surely be wet and rough. Of course, if the winds are light, the trip from Lahaina to Kamalō is an easy trip, so establish what level of wind strength is expected before you depart for the crossing.

·LA PEROUSE, MAUI, TO THE KONA COAST.

The 'Alenuihāhā Channel has the reputation of being one of the world's worst channels; thus, you should plan any crossing of it carefully. If you're coming to the channel from the west, you can stop at La Perouse, near the southeast corner of Maui, and wait for the best time to depart. When light or moderate winds are blowing, hug Maui's east shoreline as long as possible after leaving La Perouse, perhaps until you're abeam of Nu'u Landing or Mamalu Bay. This course makes the trip slightly longer, but it also puts the winds and waves on the beam rather than on the bow. If you set a course directly for Māhukona or Kawaihae as you depart from La Perouse, you will almost certainly get pushed off course if moderate trades are blowing, and you will probably end up at Kailua-Kona.

Some boaters prefer to depart for the Kona Coast from Mānele Bay on Lāna'i, making the 100-mile passage an overnighter. From Mānele, they lay a course for one of the most southerly bays on the Kona Coast, such as Okoe Bay or Honomalino, passing close to the southwest corner of Kaho'olawe. They then cross the 'Alenuihāhā Channel 50 miles south of the ocean's entrance into the channel, where the strength of the winds and the height of the waves are markedly decreased from what they are at the upper end or middle of the channel.

On the return trip from the Kona Coast, most boaters go as far north as practicable, usually to Nishimura Bay or farther, before turning toward La Perouse Bay. We generally drop anchor for the night at Nishimura before we cross the 'Alenuihāhā. We then get up and set sail just before dawn to arrive at La Perouse before noon. The following illustration from our last trip across the 'Alenuihāhā shows the wind and seas at various times and distances. (Winds were forecast to be in the moderate range on that particular day.)

	DISTANCE FROM NISHIMURA BAY	WIND	SEAS
Time	(in miles)	(in knots)	(in feet)
0530	0 (at Nishimura)	1	flat
0615	4	9	3
0630	5	11	5
0730	10	12	6
0830	16	15	6
0930	22	15	6
1015	28	20	7
1130	37 (at La Perouse Bay	16	2

The winds that were blowing 20 knots by 1015 were probably blowing well above 25 knots and the seas were probably 12 feet or more by mid-afternoon in that location.

Yet another important variable when making channel crossings is the time of day. After the sun sets, the winds and the seas in the channels decrease. The next day the winds and seas increase, reaching their maximums by early afternoon and sustaining those maximums until just before dark, when they begin to drop again. For this reason, we prefer to make all channel crossings at night if we are going to weather and the weather forecast calls for anything greater than light and variable winds. Going downwind when moderate winds are blowing is comfortable for us, provided we can get underway before dawn.

SAILING AROUND THE ISLANDS WHEN STRONG TRADE WINDS ARE BLOWING

If you are not going to cross channels when strong trades blow, where do you go then? To one of the many magnificent anchorages in the lee of the island where you are.

Since the strong trade wind conditions typically last only for three or four days at a time, you can extend for a few days the time you had allotted for a given area. While we were anchored in Kaunakakai for what we thought would be a day or two, the winds came up to 30 knots in the Kaiwi Channel, with 18-24-foot seas. We stayed put for five more days, not wanting to subject ourselves and our boat to these conditions.

Charter boat operators can provide many good ideas about where to go when strong trades are blowing. These boaters have to go out, regardless of the weather, so in strong trades they find protected places to take their customers. The Lahaina charter boater skippers take their charters to the south or west coast of Lāna'i when the winds pipe up. On days when winds are particularly strong, they anchor their boats off Mānele Bay, Palaoa Point, Pali Kaholo, or Nānāhoa. Similarly, the charter boaters from Mā'alaea Harbor avoid many of their favorite haunts, particularly Molokini Island, in strong trades. Instead, they take their customers to places such as Coral Gardens or Olowalu. Watch what these skippers do to make their customers happy, and you'll know what to do to make life more pleasant aboard your boat.

SAILING THE ISLANDS WHEN OTHER THAN TRADES ARE BLOWING

Though trade winds are the prevailing winds around Hawai'i, they do not blow all the time. During some months, in fact, trades kick in only about 50 percent of the time. These months, usually late fall and winter, will present you with an opportunity to explore anchorages inaccessible during the summer. But even in the spring and summer, when trades blow with remarkable consistency, you still will get opportunities to explore new areas. Occasionally those trades do give way to winds out of the south, west, or north.

If you remain flexible, you can seize the opportunity to visit new areas when trades die. By listening to the weather reports every day, you'll know sometimes almost a week in advance what the weather pattern will likely be. Then, when a forecast calls for light south winds during the late spring, summer, or early fall, for example, you can make a quick run to the lush North Shore of Moloka'i and explore the anchorages there. When the winds shift back to trades a few days later, it is time to head for the south coast of Moloka'i or some other protected area.

Just as the North Shore of Moloka'i is a wonderful destination when light *kona* winds kick in, the east coastline of Maui becomes a nearly perfect destination when southwest or west winds blow. When we heard the forecast calling for southwest winds, we sailed to Hāna. Two days later the winds began clocking around and were soon blowing out of the north, creating an uncomfortable motion in Hāna Bay. We immediately weighed anchor and sailed along the southeastern coast of Maui for the next few days, exploring anchorages rarely accessible when trade winds blow because they are open to the east. When the north winds blow, these anchorages are then on the protected side of the island.

Another concern to cruising boaters exploring any of the rarely visited north shore anchorages on any of the Islands is the north swell. Although the north swell is a relatively small threat in the spring and summer, it can present a serious problem in late fall or winter. If you visit any of the Islands' north shore anchorages between late October and April, be prepared to get out if the north swell develops. The weather forecast gives plenty of warning, so remember to listen regularly to the reports. When a north swell of more than 6 feet sets in, commonly in the fall and winter, you don't want to be anchored on a north shore.

WHEN STRONG WINDS BLOW FROM AN UNEXPECTED DIRECTION

Most of the strong winds during the late spring, summer and early fall are from the east or northeast. These are the famous trade winds. But not all strong winds are trades. In fact, the strong winds that play havoc with boaters in the Islands are usually the *kona* winds. Since trades blow most commonly, boaters prepare for them and know how to cope with them. In *kona* winds, however, anchorages that are normally safe are suddenly on the weather side of the island. Boaters who don't get out of these anchorages when such a wind kicks in may very well find their boats on the beach.

Coping with these atypical winds requires immediate action. When strong *kona* winds begin to blow, all boats in southwest-facing anchorages should be moved to a north shore anchorage or a protected harbor. When a strong *kona* wind blew through the Islands last year three boats moored or anchored off Sugar Beach, on Maui, broke loose or dragged their moorings, ending up on the beach. Other boaters who sailed around to the north side of Moloka'i or Maui had a rough ride, but their boats suffered no damage.

When a strong *kona* is predicted, check with the nearest harbormaster to see if room will be available at that harbor in the event of a serious storm. Most harbormasters will accommodate all of the boats they can.

ANCHORING

Anchoring in Hawai'i requires a few special considerations. First, boaters should consider the bottom they will be dropping their anchors onto. Often the bottom in Hawai'i will be a sand bottom, but many anchorages have lava, coral, or boulders on the bottom. Although we all attempt to avoid dropping our anchors on lava, coral, or boulders, sometimes we inadvertently do so.

Most of the anchors on the market hold well when the bottom is sand, but some hold poorly when dropped on anything else. Some of the fluke-type anchors bend or break when dropped on lava or boulders; some of the plough-type anchors lodge themselves firmly when dropped among boulders, requiring someone to dive down and remove them by hand.

Coral grows beautifully in the Hawaiian Islands. Most anchorages are home to some coral. Try as we might, we sometimes end up with our anchors near the coral. Even when we drop in a sand patch that appears to be large enough so that we won't break up the coral, our anchors drag a little while we are setting them, or the sand patch is smaller than we originally thought, and, although our anchor is in the sand, our anchor rode stretches across the coral.

If you're using a nylon rode with a short piece of chain connecting it to the anchor, your rode is at risk. When a nylon rode wraps around a piece of coral, the coral will begin cutting the nylon almost immediately. In the course of a day or two, coral can render a nylon rode worthless. For this reason most boaters cruising the Islands equip their boats with all-chain rodes. But don't despair if your boat is equipped with a nylon/chain rode; just be extremely cautious.

Just as coral presents a special problem for boaters, so too does the depth of anchorages in Hawai'i. In some anchorages, you will drop your hook in 10-20 feet of water, but in others you will have to drop in 50 feet. The problem this creates is with the amount of scope you must let out. It is all too easy to get in the habit of letting out 50-60 feet of chain when you're dropping in shallow anchorages regularly. That 50-60 feet of chain that you customarily let out may barely touch bottom in the deeper anchorage, and it certainly won't hold if a little wind begins to blow. Always check the depth in an anchorage and deliberately compute the amount of scope you will need.

We recommend strongly that you meet or exceed the long-held standards for scope on your anchor rode: use a 7-1 scope for nylon rode and a 4-1 scope for all-chain rode. When you drop in one of those anchorages that is 50-feet deep, you must let out at least 200 feet of chain to be safe. If you're using a chain/nylon rode, you must let out over 300 feet of rode. Don't tell yourself that you don't need to let out that much scope because the winds are light; the winds may pick up just after dark, and you'll then have to worry about dragging all night long.

After your anchor is down and the appropriate amount of scope has been let out, use your motor to set your anchor. Put the boat in reverse and increase engine speed to about one-half of the engine's normal cruising RPM. Keep the boat in reverse and the engine straining against the anchor for a full minute to indicate whether your anchor will drag if the wind picks up. If the anchor does drag while you're backing down, be glad you found out before the middle of the night when the wind picks up.

If your boat doesn't have an engine, set your anchor using your sails by dropping anchor while the boat is still slowly sailing forward into the anchorage. After letting out the proper amount of anchor rode, snub off, and let the boat come up against the end of the rode. Picking out a good sand patch in which to drop is a bit more challenging when you're anchoring under sail.

A good procedure used by many experienced boaters in Hawai'i is to get in the water with mask, fins, and snorkel after the anchor is down and check to be sure it is going to hold. The water is clear enough in most anchorages in Hawai'i so that you will be able to see your anchor and rode easily. Although you'll usually be comforted by what you see, at other times you'll not like the scene at all. When we last cruised the Kona Coast, we anchored at Māhukona Harbor. When we got in the water to check the anchor, we saw a bottom littered with boulders, old tires, old machinery from the now-defunct sugar operation, and coral. Our anchor had dragged a little among the boulders, coming to a stop up against a large boulder. We were so unimpressed with what we saw that we immediately hoisted anchor and moved to Nishimura Bay.

REGULATIONS ON ANCHORING

The Department of Land and Natural Resources (DLNR) has established rules that all boaters in the Hawaiian Islands must follow.

The first rule to remember is that you can anchor in any anchorage for 72 hours without checking in. The one exception is that you must check in immediately whenever you enter a harbor with a harbormaster on site, such as Ala Wai, Ke'ehi, Wai'anae, Hale'iwa, He'eia Kea, Kaunakakai, Hilo, Honokōhau, Lahaina, Mā'alaea, Mānele, Kahului, Nāwiliwili, or Port Allen. After the first 72 hours is up, boaters are required to move to another anchorage or even to another part of the same anchorage.

The exceptions to this right to anchor in any anchorage for 72 hours are the areas that are part of a Marine Conservation District or Natural Area. All or parts of some bays have been placed in Conservation Districts because the heavy traffic and the delicate ecosystem on the bottom of the bay required intervention on the part of the State of Hawai'i. Boaters may not anchor in part or all of the following bays:

> Hā'ena Bay—boats may not anchor inside the reef overnight
> Hanauma Bay—no boats allowed in this bay
> Hulopo'e Bay—no boats allowed in the bay
> Kealakekua Bay—boats may not anchor in Subzone A
> La Perouse Bay—boats may not anchor in the western half of the bay
> Waikīkī Anchorage—no boats allowed within .4 mile of the beach.

When boaters visit small boat harbors in Hawai'i, they must obtain a permit from the harbormaster and pay a daily fee, as is the case in harbors anywhere. The difference here is that the facilities are not the plush ones some boaters might be accustomed to elsewhere. Although some might complain about the facilities, the low daily rate charged to visiting boaters more than makes up for any shortage in facilities.

AVOIDING COLLISIONS

Perhaps no other aspect of seamanship deserves as much attention as avoiding collisions with other vessels. When two sailboats collide sailing along Waikīkī, of course, the risk to people on the boats is slight because the boats are generally traveling at less than five knots. If two fast-moving powerboats collide, however, people can be seriously injured. And if either a sailboat or a powerboat collides with a ship, the results can be disastrous. The ship will usually

Barge being towed across the 'Alenuihāhā Channel

not sustain any damage; in fact, the crew members of a huge ship that collides with a pleasure boat are often unaware that the ship has been involved in a collision.

Few areas around the Hawaiian Islands have heavy ship traffic. And that may create a serious danger. Boaters come to feel alone and secure as they sail around the Islands. But cruising boaters are not alone when making passages in the Islands. Although few ships are around the Islands, tugs with barges in tow are common. We have rarely made a passage from one island to another during which we failed to see at least one tug and barge. To make matters even more serious, the number of barges increases at night. Any time you see lights at sea at night, look carefully to see if you are encountering a tug and barge. If it is a tug, it will have three vertical white lights on its mast, indicating a tug with a tow. Whenever you see three white lights showing one above the other, be extremely careful. Assume that the tug captain can't see you, and get your boat out of the way immediately.

The greatest danger may be your inadvertently cutting between a tug and the barge in tow. While tugs normally tow barges on a cable 2,000-2,400 feet long, the tug and barge will generally be closer to .25 mile apart. The weight of this cable causes it to sag in the water so that when the tug is at normal operating speed, the cable will be at least 100 feet below the surface of the water. (With the cable this deep, tug captains generally avoid areas with water under 100 feet deep.)

You can be confident that a professional captain is aboard any tug moving around the Islands. These professionals have years of experience and know the channels and weather. But in typical channel weather a small boat is hard to see from the wheelhouse of a tug. Remember, too, that these large tugs and barges can't stop for you. A tug pulling a barge can barely begin to slow down or turn in less than a mile. If you get in front of one that is traveling at 8.5-10 knots, the typical speed, all the pilot can do is sound the horn to warn you, if he can even see you.

The chart below shows the routes commercial tugs with barges commonly use in the Hawaiian Islands:

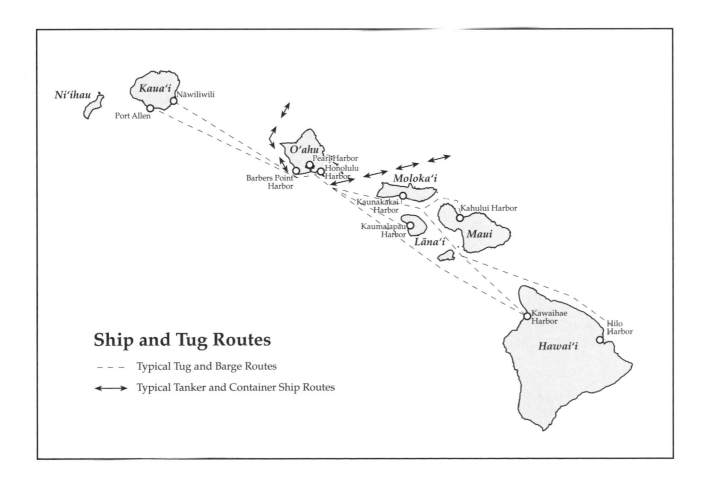

Ship and Tug Routes

- - - Typical Tug and Barge Routes

←—→ Typical Tanker and Container Ship Routes

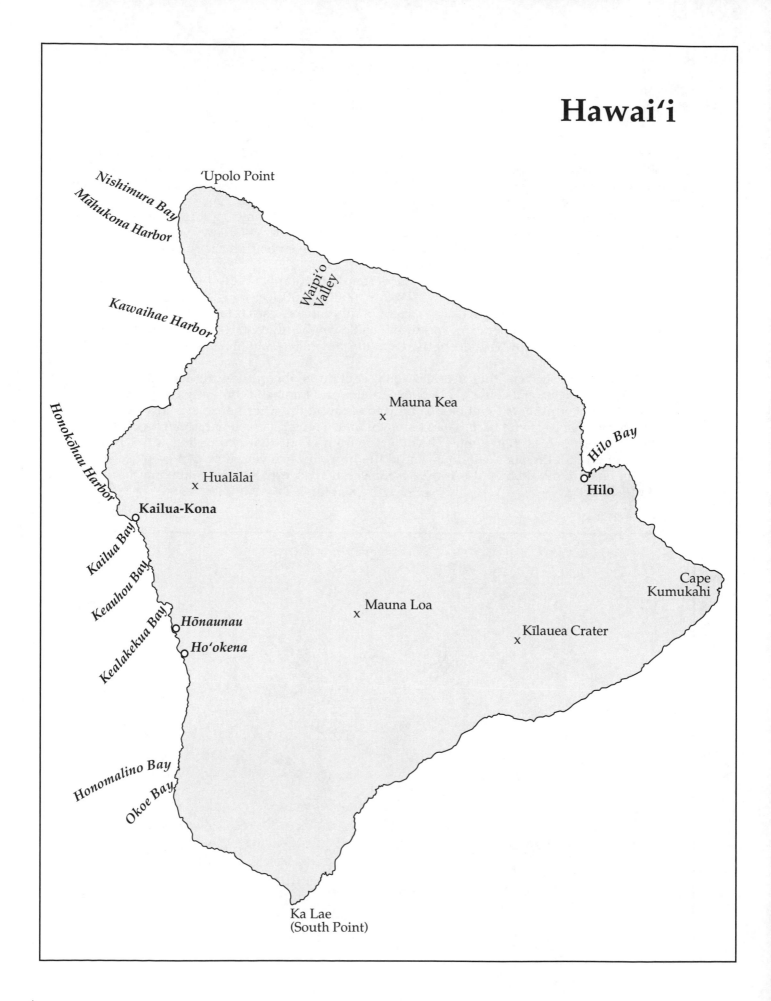

Hawai'i

Nishimura Bay

Māhukona Harbor

'Upolo Point

Kawaihae Harbor

Waipi'o Valley

Honokōhau Harbor

Mauna Kea
x

Hilo Bay

x Hualālai

Kailua-Kona

Hilo

Kailua Bay

Keauhou Bay

Cape Kumukahi

Kealakekua Bay

Hōnaunau

Mauna Loa
x

Ho'okena

Kīlauea Crater
x

Honomalino Bay

Okoe Bay

Ka Lae
(South Point)

THE ISLAND OF HAWAI‘I

THE ORCHID ISLE

Twilight at Honokōhau Harbor and Hualālai Volcano

"Ku ka‘apa ia Hawai‘i, he moku nui."
("Hawai‘i should lead forth, for she is the largest.")

THE ISLAND OF HAWAI'I

With approximately 250 miles of coastline, the island of Hawai'i deserves its nickname of "the Big Island." This southernmost island in the Hawaiian chain is almost twice as large as all the other islands in the state combined. But this island is not only large in size; it also offers big challenges and big rewards for cruising sailors.

This youngest of the islands in the chain, formed by five volcanoes, the Big Island is the only one of the islands to have experienced volcanic eruptions in the past two hundred years. Because of the eruptions of Mauna Loa ("long mountain") and Kīlauea ("spewing"), it is still a growing island, destined to become an even bigger Big Island. When Pele, the goddess of Kīlauea, is in one of her particularly fiery moods, boaters at sea can watch the molten lava flow into the ocean, though sometimes only the steam rising hundreds of feet into the air as the hot lava meets the cool Pacific is visible. Kīlauea began its current period of more or less continuous eruptions in 1983; Mauna Loa last erupted in 1984, for 22 days.

This island also has the greatest variety of terrain to enthrall and entertain cruising boaters. It has the highest peaks in the Islands, Mauna Kea ("white mountain") at 13,795 feet the tallest mountain in the Pacific and, if measured from its base on the ocean floor, the tallest mountain in the world. The high elevation of Mauna Kea has created a sub-arctic climatic zone, making possible snowfall sufficient for skiing. Atop Mauna Kea, with its clear air and proximity to the equator, are the world's largest and most sophisticated observatories.

Mauna Loa ("long mountain") is probably the more widely known of the two mountains because of its recent volcanic activity. Its peak is 13,679 feet above sea level and about 29,000 feet above its base on the ocean floor. It has not only phenomenal height but also enormous girth, covering half the island and probably is the largest single mountain mass on earth, having more mass than the entire Sierra Nevada range.

At the bases of the mountains, the tropic zone assures comfortable temperatures for swimming and other water sports year round. This island has more than 100 beaches, with a variety of colors: black, white, green, or golden sand. The newer beaches on this still growing island are rocky.

All along the coasts of South Kona and Ka'ū flows of black 'a'a lava mark the hillsides, especially dramatic when seen from the ocean. The beauty of this scene, though, has been lost on some viewers. Lt. James King, of the Captain Cook expedition, called the Ka'ū coast *"a prospect of the most horrid and dreary kind, the whole country*

Waterfall on the Hāmakāu Coast

appearing to have undergone a total change from the effects of some dreadful convulsion." Many more "dreadful convulsions" have added to the prospect in the 200 years since King judged it so harshly.

Too bad King didn't see the north coast of Hawai'i, where the high cliffs seem to have been carved by a giant's knife and billowy clouds boil up from their peaks. Deep green canyons disappear into even darker, thicker greens. Along the shore are black and white sand beaches at the mouths of some of the canyons, some with their own waterfalls. In other spots the waterfalls drop into unseen caverns or plunge into the ocean from a sheer sea cliff.

In the interior valleys are over a million acres of farm lands, producing coffee, macadamia nuts, papayas, tangerines, oranges, bananas, and guavas. Nursery products are also a major industry on the Big Island. In addition, it has a big ranch, the Parker Ranch, near Waimea (Kamuela), one of the largest privately owned ranches in the United States.

Another distinction of the Big Island is the historical one. Some Hawaiian historians ascribe to this island the site of the earliest Polynesian settlements in the Hawaiian Islands, believing the first immigrants to these islands were from the Marquesas, and may have arrived on this island as early as A. D. 0. (The date of the first migration continues to be pushed back as contemporary historians review both the physical evidence and Polynesian oral history.) These early voyagers perhaps landed at Ka Lae, the most southerly point in the islands, as well as in the United States.

Kamehameha I, the most powerful of the chiefs on the island of Hawai'i at the time of Captain James Cook's arrival in 1778, consolidated his power on the Big Island, and moved on to conquer all the other islands except Kaua'i and Ni'ihau to become the first king of the Hawaiian Islands in 1795. In 1810, by agreement, Kaua'i and Ni'ihau also came under his rule.

Though the Big Island is not the first site Cook discovered on his third historic Pacific voyage, one of its most beautiful and well-protected bays, Kealakekua, made it an island favored by Cook for its safe anchorages and the abundant supplies offered for trade by the islanders. At Kealakekua Bay, Cook

An offering to Captain Cook

also met his untimely death in a conflict with the Hawaiians over a stolen ship's boat.

Just as much of the history of the Hawaiian Islands begins here, so might your Hawaiian cruise. Hilo, on the east side, is closer to the Mainland than any of the other ports among the Islands, and it always seems to have space for a visiting boat either to moor or to anchor in Radio Bay. It's also a good place to provision. Hilo will give you the experience of a tropical rain forest, with its lush vegetation that gets an almost daily bath from the heavens. Another reason for beginning one's cruise with this island is that it is the upwind island; hence, passages to the other islands will, in the prevailing trades, be downwind. Crossing the 'Alenuihāhā from the Big Island always promises excitement. Why not make your virgin crossing with the excitement following you rather than meeting you head-on?

If you begin in Hilo and then continue on around the island counterclockwise, you'll come to the drier coast—and the coast with all the other tenable anchorages and harbors.

Nishimura and Māhukona are two small bays on the northwest coast, where you'll likely be the only cruising sailor around. They are both good places to stop before you cross the 'Alenuihāhā to the other islands. Kawaihae and Honokōhau are both harbors and, as one might expect, sites of fairly heavy boat traffic. Kawaihae is a commercial harbor for ships and barges; Honokōhau is home for over 200 commercial fishing boats. Both, however, have some facilities for pleasure craft.

Kailua Bay is the scene of the most activity on the Big Island these days, both on the water and the land. The roadstead here is not one of the most comfortable in the Islands, but it does put you near the action. Keauhou, the next anchorage to the south, is in a rich natural and historical setting. Unfortunately for visiting boaters, the private moorings take up most of the small anchorage.

Charter boats moor or drift in Ka'awaloa, the small bay on the northwest end of Kealakekua Bay, during the day, but, once they've gone, the entire bay may be yours except for an occasional fishing boat anchored for the night. Some of the bay is restricted to preserve the coral and other marine life. Hōnaunau Bay, too, is a destination popular with charter boats, and it also has coral areas you must avoid when anchoring, but this coral is one of the chief attractions for stopping here. The snorkeling may be even more outstanding than at Kealakekua. Hōnaunau is the site of the most completely restored place of refuge and *heiau* in the state.

   After Hōnaunau, you'll see no more charter boats—and probably no other pleasure craft— in the anchorages. Hoʻokena was once a busy little seaport, but now only a few outrigger canoes are occasionally launched here. The bay will likely be unoccupied except for a few snorkelers swimming with the spinner dolphins.   Honomalino and Okoe are even less used, neither having any permanent residents on its shores and both accessible by land only with 4-wheel drive vehicles.

A King of the Hawaiian Islands

"Why do you want to go there? All it does is rain."

Yes, it does rain in Hilo, more than 200 inches in a wet year but usually in the 150-inch range. But an ancient Hawaiian proverb calls it *"the lehua-sounding rain of Hilo."* (The lehua is the highly prized Hawai'i County flower.) The residents of Hilo appreciate all this rain, for it nourishes one of the prettiest, greenest sites in the islands.

The plentiful rain at Hilo, the county seat of the Big Island, is the reason for one of the county's nicknames, the "Orchid Island." Orchids, as well as anthuriums and numerous other varieties of tropical flowers and trees, grow abundantly in this moist environment. In fact, the primary cash crop in Hilo is flowers— orchids and anthuriums, in particular. To marvel at, too, are the mango trees, 50 feet tall, with lobes of fruit hanging from every limb, and the philodendron with leaves far larger than one could encircle with one's arms.

The Anchorage at Radio Bay, Hilo

A traditional *hula* chant says, *"When Hilo clears up, it is heavenly."* When the showers cease, the emerald hills sheltering Hilo Bay sparkle under sunny blue skies. Perhaps more important to cruising boaters is the fact that Radio Bay, the only designated mooring area for visiting cruising boats in Hilo Bay, is a remarkably secure harbor, safe in all but the extremely rare hurricane or tsunami. In both cases, ample warnings are usually given.

The dredging of the commercial harbor and the construction of Pier One between 1925 and 1930 created this nearly perfect bay between the pier and the breakwater. The United States Naval Radio Station that formerly was ashore of the bay gave it its name.

The historic business district of Hilo, beginning right on the bay on Kamehameha Avenue and extending inland for two blocks, borders on the funky, many of its weathered storefronts looking unchanged since the last tsunami. Other historic buildings, however, retain much of their former grandeur.

Between 1863 and 1890 a wharf at the foot of Waianuenue Avenue brought passengers and freight ashore from ships anchored in the bay. In the early 1900s another wharf was constructed in calmer water at the Waiākea end of the bay. Before the devastation of the 1946 tsunami, Hilo also had of a busy train depot on the bay side of the corner of Shipman and Kamehameha. Today this part of the city sleeps rather than bustles, but a very pleasant sleep it is for the cruising sailors who want to leave behind the frenetic pace of so many other regions.

Hilo has a long history of human habitation and boating. According to oral history, Hilo was settled as early as 1100 A. D. by migrant Polynesians who farmed, fished, and navigated inland on the Wailuku River to trade their goods.

While downtown, be sure to leave enough time to visit the Lyman Museum and Mission House, only three blocks from Kamehameha Avenue. The Mission House is worthwhile for the history of the Islands, and of Hilo particularly, after Western contact. Surprisingly, the Museum also has outstanding exhibits of seashells, rocks and minerals. On Wednesdays and Saturdays, Hilo has a produce and flower market unrivaled in the Islands. There, you'll see vegetables and fruits not seen elsewhere. If you don't want to shop for produce, go by the market simply to marvel at the floral displays or to talk with the friendly people. A pleasant taxi ride farther inland will take you to Nani Mau Gardens, a vast floral garden that includes almost every flower and tree found in the islands. It has a particularly large exhibit of orchids, featuring more varieties than most of us knew existed. The beauty of these gardens compares closely with the Butchart Gardens in Victoria, B. C.

On a day when you want to stay closer to the harbor, ride your bicycles or walk to Banyan Drive, a street that curves around Waiākea Peninsula. This street, perpetually shaded by a canopy of 100-year-old banyan trees, each named for a well-known American, is made more enchanting when the rain sends down a fresh shower of banyan leaves. At the west end of Banyan are the Lili'uokalani Gardens and Coconut Island, both remarkably beautiful vantage points for appreciating Hilo Bay.

Hilo also has one waterfall—Rainbow—within walking distance of downtown. You find it, and the Boiling Pots above it, by following the Wailuku River, the second longest river in the state, inland for about 3 miles.

After this or another long walk, you can come back to Coconut Island Park for a swim. Once a place of refuge, the island was called *Moku Ola*, meaning "healing island." Hawaiians came here to bathe in a natural spring; they also brought the umbilical cords of their infants here, burying them under rocks. The island today is a small, usually peaceful park with restrooms, a pavilion, and picnic areas. Watching the sunset from this island may convince you the healing spirit yet lives here.

Out the other direction, southeast of the harbor along Kalaniana'ole Avenue, are three county beach parks, where you'll be able to swim in more seclusion.

Wherever you go in Hilo and by whatever mode of transportation, you'll be glad if you have a poncho or an umbrella with you. A clear, sunny day can suddenly turn rainy, and, while the rain is warm, you may not always want to be soaked by it.

The Saturday open market in Hilo

APPROACH

Hilo is the only bay on the eastern side of the island of Hawai'i that offers good anchorage. All other anchorages are for day use only in calm weather.

If Hilo is your first stop after a long ocean crossing from Washington, Oregon, or California, you can enter the coordinates of Hilo into your GPS before you depart for the Islands. Then all you'll have to do as you close on the island is to miss Pepe'ekeo Point, 7.5 miles north of the breakwater in Hilo Bay.

If you're making a passage to Hilo from any of the other islands, you'll most likely approach Hilo from the north. The 61-mile passage from Ūpolu Point to Hilo is a good day's run

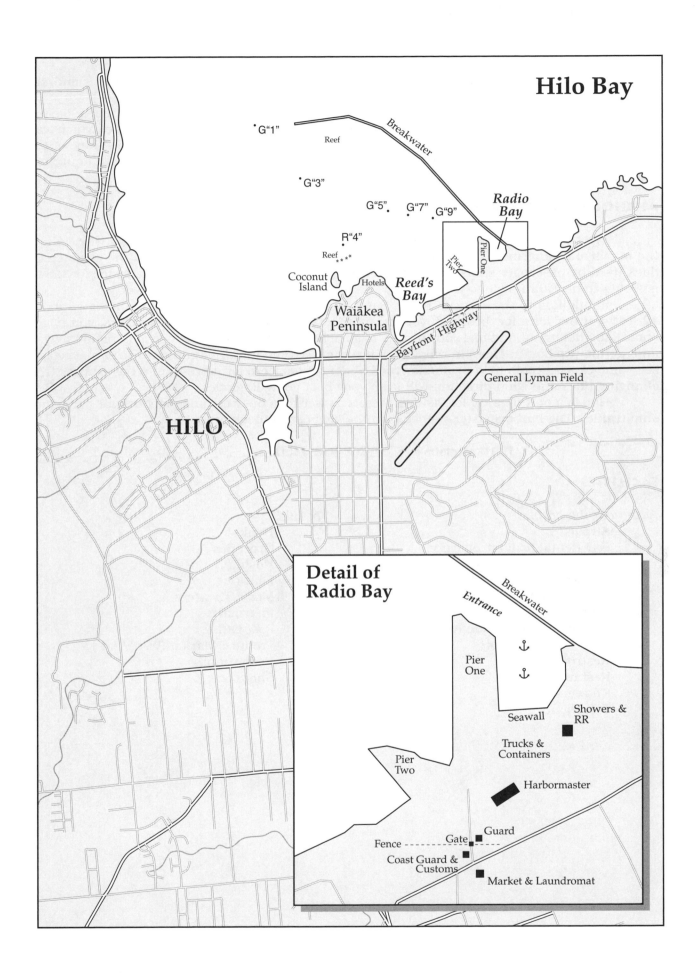

Hilo Bay

G"1"

Reef

Breakwater

G"3"

G"5" G"7" G"9"

Radio Bay

R"4"

Reef ****

Pier Two

Pier One

Coconut Island

Hotels

Reed's Bay

Waiākea Peninsula

Bayfront Highway

General Lyman Field

HILO

Detail of Radio Bay

Entrance

Breakwater

Pier One

Seawall

Showers & RR

Trucks & Containers

Pier Two

Harbormaster

Fence

Gate

Guard

Coast Guard & Customs

Market & Laundromat

for most cruising boats. We departed from Nishimura Bay, on the *kona* side of the island, an hour before dawn and arrived at Hilo just before dark that evening.

By contrast, the passage from South Point is 89 miles to Hilo, the extra 28 miles, mainly upwind, convincing most cruising boaters to approach from the north. Regardless of which way you decide to go to Hilo from one of the other islands, you'll almost certainly spend some of the distance working to weather; therefore, make the trip to Hilo when the winds are light or are not trades.

ANCHORAGE AND BERTHING

After passing the breakwater extending from the east shoreline of Hilo Bay, follow the buoys and rangemarks to Radio Bay, the small, protected inner bay behind the commercial dock used by passenger ships and container barges. Inside Radio Bay is ample space for ten or so boats to tie Tahiti-style to the seawall. Many more could squeeze in if necessary.

In addition to the seawall, Radio Bay has an anchorage area with good holding in about 12 feet of water for a few boats. If you expect to be in Radio Bay for only a few days, you might choose to anchor out and use your dinghy to go ashore to avoid the challenge of tying to the wall and setting two bow anchors in this bay of heavy surge even in calm weather. You can expect to see some classic knots in your anchor rode if you anchor here for more than a day or two. The changing tides and wind direction will keep your boat going in circles.

Hilo is a port of entry for visiting vessels as well as a busy commercial dock for barge and ship traffic. The harbormaster's office is in the commercial dock area.

Harbormaster   808-933-8850

FACILITIES

At or near the harbor:
- Airport
- Car Rental (call for delivery)
- Fuel (diesel by truck; gasoline by jerry jug)
- Laundromat (.5 mile)
- Mini-market and Deli (.5 mile)
- Propane
- Public Transportation (when a cruise ship is in harbor)
- Restrooms
- Restaurants
- Showers
- Telephone

In Hilo:
- Banks
- Groceries
- Hospital
- Library
- Movie Theaters
- Pharmacy
- Post Office
- Produce Market (Wed./Sat.)
- Restaurants
- Shops

NISHIMURA BAY
CHARTS #19320, 19329
LAT. N20° 10.980 LONG. W155 54.152 (ANCHORAGE)

The northernmost anchorage on the Kona side of the island of Hawai'i is one that isn't even named on charts or in the *Coast Pilot*. Not only do the NOAA charts not name this bay, but they also indicate it is fouled with rocks. Yet, in our view, this small bay, known to local sailors as Nishimura Bay, is a far superior anchorage than the better known Māhukona. It offers superior holding in sand with no apparent fouling, and it offers quiet and solitude away from the launching of fishing boats and personal water craft at Māhukona.

Although this bay is a good destination in its own right, it also affords cruising boaters an excellent overnight anchorage before they cross the 'Alenuihāhā Channel from the Big Island to Maui. The distance across the channel from Nishimura to La Perouse Bay, on the southeastern shore of Maui, is only about 36 miles. By departing from Nishimura before dawn, boaters can be across the dreaded 'Alenuihāhā well before noon, when, typically, the winds begin to gain force.

One of the pleasures of anchoring in this bay is the beauty of the water. When the anchor goes down in 30 feet of water, you can watch its progress all the way to the bottom. The patches of coral are equally distinct. Even on bright moonlit nights, you can easily see where the patches of coral are around the bay.

Beyond the points of lava rock protecting Nishimura Bay, the winds whip up whitecaps whenever the moderate or strong tradewinds blow. Safely anchored inside, you can watch the whitecaps march by this eastern edge of the 'Alenuihāhā and rejoice you aren't out there getting pounded.

Anchorage at Nishimura

Though this isolated cove has no beach on which to land the tender, we went ashore by clambering up the rocks in the cove on the southern end of the anchorage. If climbing up the rocks is not to your liking, take your tender around Maka o Hule Point to Māhukona Harbor. You can get ashore more comfortably at the old pier at the back of the harbor. Be careful not to block access to the crane on the pier where local boaters launch and retrieve their boats. Also, be cautious of the swell that surges into Māhukona. Don't get caught half in or half out of the tender when one comes in.

Ashore at Nishimura is a portion of the old railroad bed built in the late 19th century for a narrow-gauge railway running from Māhukona north to Niuli'i. The Kohala Sugar Company used this railway primarily to transport sugar cane and bagged sugar to the Māhukona docks for shipment, but the railway also carried some freight and passengers. The tsunami of 1946 destroyed three of the railroad bridges, as well as many other sections of the railroad, and put the railway company out of business. The railroad bed remains as an ideal hiking trail through thick stands of *kiawe* where cattle may wander out to gaze at you.

On a hill above the rock wall are the ruins of what is believed to have been an ancient Hawaiian navigational *heiau*. It may remind you of Stonehenge on a much smaller scale. One local sailor who has visited this observatory many times says he gets "chicken skin" every time he goes there, just from the aura of the place.

APPROACH

Nishimura is 5.5 miles south of 'Upolu Point and 9.5 miles north of Kawaihae Harbor. From either direction the best landmarks are the Māhukona Light on Kaoma Point and the buildings ashore at

Holo Moana, the navigational *heiau* above Nishimura

Māhukona. Once you've identified Māhukona, you can easily spot Nishimura immediately north of Maka o Hule Point, the northern shore of Māhukona Harbor. The two anchorages are a mere .25 mile apart.

The small Nishimura Bay is distinguishable by the rock wall on the face of the cliff on the north side of the anchorage. This wall was a part of the bed of the railroad used by the Kohala Sugar Company. From either direction, once you've identified this rock wall on the north side of the anchorage, proceed directly into the center of the bay, avoiding the rocks and reef off Maka o Hule Point on the south side of the bay.

ANCHORAGE

Inside the bay, you can readily identify the sand bottom, where you should drop anchor, by the lighter turquoise color of the water. At least two large sand patches are suitable for anchoring, one in the center of the bay and the other in the north part of the bay off the rock wall. Perhaps you can find even additional sand patches in this bay, but do take care to locate a sand patch before dropping the anchor to avoid the extensive areas of coral on the bottom.

We've anchored in Nishimura on four occasions and found excellent holding. Our favorite anchoring spot is approximately mid-way between the old rock wall at the north side of the bay and Maka o Hule Point to the south. We try to set our hook about 150-200 feet from the rocks on the east side of the bay. When we let out 120 feet of chain, we drift back to the west side of the bay when the trade winds are blowing, and, when a gentle southwest breeze picks up at night, we drift back to within 50 feet of the cliffs to the east. This is, indeed, a snug anchorage that can accommodate only two boats without crowding.

We've enjoyed a gentle boat motion every time we've been in Nishimura. However, strong *kona* winds (winds blowing out of the west) would make this anchorage, and virtually all others along the Kona Coast, most uncomfortable. When *kona* winds are blowing 20 knots or more, take refuge in Honokōhau or Kawaihae Harbor

Rock wall at Nishimura

or around on the eastern side of the island. As with all bays and harbors along the north coast of Hawai'i, winds are inconsistent at Nishimura Bay. During the afternoon, gusts will blow through the anchorage for a few minutes and then die out to almost nothing for a few. As soon as you've become accustomed to the quiet, the winds will kick in again. After the sun sets, the winds are usually negligible.

FACILITIES

At Nishimura:
　　None
At Māhukona:
　　Showers (cold water)
　　Restrooms

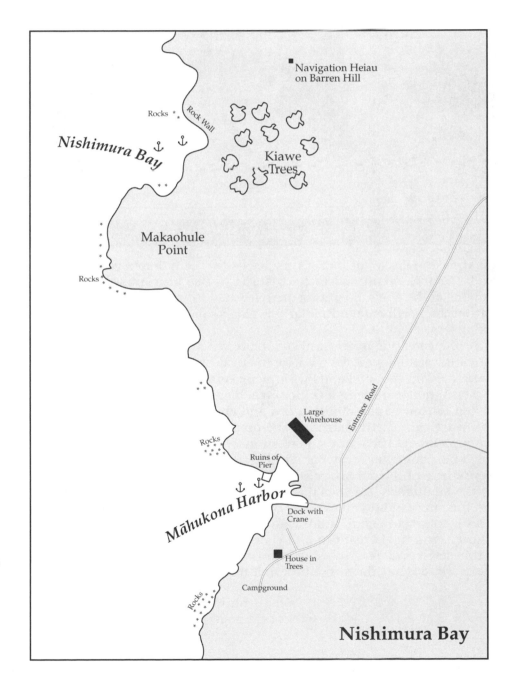

MĀHUKONA HARBOR
CHARTS #19320, 19329
LAT. N20° 10.987 LONG. W155° 54.155 (ANCHORAGE)

Māhukona ("leeward stream") was once an area where the Hawaiian kings built canoes and launched them. It was known as the "other Kona" and was popular because of the plentiful fresh water available here.

Tying the tender to the launch dock

Māhukona Harbor has a more current history dating back to the 1880s, when it was the harbor for the Kohala Sugar Company. A train brought sugar cane and bagged sugar to this harbor for shipment until the beginning of World War II. The U. S. government ordered its use discontinued for security reasons. The railway operation resumed following the war, but the company went out of business after the tsunami of 1946 destroyed sections of the railroad. Trucks continued to haul sugar to this once busy harbor until 1956. Today, all that remains of the sugar operation are a few buildings, the roadbed used by the train, and a decaying pier on the north side of the harbor, plus a fair amount of debris in the bay to attract snorkelers and divers.

The visiting boater will see the ruins, of course, but little at Māhukona today will remind one of its past glory days as a commercial harbor. This harbor is now a part of a busy county park, filled on the weekends with picnickers, campers, swimmers, hikers, and boaters.

A non-profit organization teaching the ways of the ancient Hawaiians, especially as related to Hawaiian sailing canoes and navigation, currently uses the old office building on the southeast side of the harbor. The organization's canoe, the *Makali'i*, which has made trips to many South Pacific islands, is often moored in Māhukona Harbor. If you anchor here, you may see young students studying voyaging and navigation on the boat and Hawaiian culture in or around one of the old sugar company buildings.

Māhukona is a good destination for its historical interest and the beauty of both the water and the surrounding hills, trees, and lava flows. Unlike many other anchorages, Māhukona has the added advantage of a dock on the seawall, where you can tie up your tender while you go ashore. (You might want to pull your tender up on the seawall if you plan to be ashore for more than a few minutes. Not only is this dock a busy place with boats and PWCs being launched and retrieved, but the surge here will throw your tender against the rough concrete seawall.)

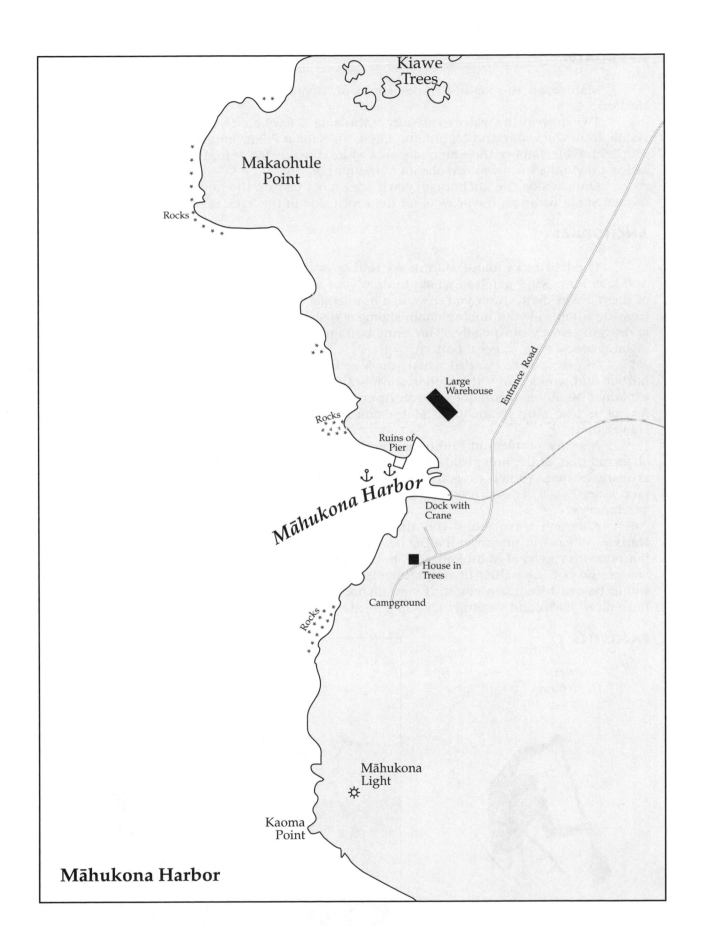

Kiawe
Trees

Makaohule
Point

Rocks

Rocks

Large
Warehouse

Entrance Road

Ruins of
Pier

⚓ ⚓

Māhukona Harbor

Dock with
Crane

House in
Trees

Campground

Rocks

Māhukona
Light
☼

Kaoma
Point

Māhukona Harbor

APPROACH

Māhukona Harbor is 6 miles south of 'Upolu Point and 10 miles north of Kawaihae Harbor.

Two noteworthy features identify Māhukona: a few houses and warehouses that are easily visible from the water and Māhukona Light, on Kaoma Point, immediately south of the harbor. The light, 64 feet above the water, sits on a white concrete tower that is 22 feet tall. Stay offshore at least one mile until you are abeam of the harbor.

Once inside the anchorage, you'll see an old pier on the north side and a crane used to launch small boats on the seawall on the south side in the back of the harbor.

ANCHORAGE

The bad news about Māhukona Harbor is the anchorage. If you come into the harbor and look for a sand patch in which to drop your anchor, you'll not be disappointed. A number of them are evident. After you've settled in to enjoy the anchorage, however, you'll hear the distressing rumble of your anchor chain sliding across rock. After awhile, you'll realize your anchor is dragging slowly but noisily. The "sand bottom" at Māhukona is, in many places, a thin layer of sand over a rock or coral bottom.

In case you're puzzled when you see the huge sailing canoe *Makali'i* at anchor in the harbor and wonder why its anchor stays set but yours won't, the sailing master of the canoe explained to us his technique: one of the crew always dives down and sets the anchor by hand. Any of us who want to anchor at Māhukona with confidence should follow the example of these Hawaiians.

Another problem at Māhukona is the debris scattered all over the bottom. One writer observed that all the industrial debris produces a good home for sea life but a bad anchorage for cruising boaters. When we got into the water to check our anchor that seemed to be dragging (and indeed was), we saw a bottom littered with old tires, pieces of pipe, and various parts of old machinery.

Although we've found the anchorage unsatisfactory, boaters do anchor at Māhukona Harbor. When en route from the Big Island to Maui, for instance, many boaters anchor for a few hours or overnight at Māhukona before they head out across the 'Alenuihāhā Channel. These boaters do not leave their boats unattended, however, while they are anchored here. And that would be our recommendation: If you anchor here, leave your boat unattended only after you have dived down and carefully chosen a good sand patch, then set your hook by hand.

FACILITIES

Showers
Restrooms

The double-hull sailing canoe *Makali'i*

KAWAIHAE HARBOR
CHARTS #19320, 19330
LAT. N20° 02.511 LONG. W155 50.402 (ENTRANCE BUOYS)

Kawaihae Harbor, one of the two deep-water commercial harbors on the Big Island, offers good protection in all weather. The breakwater that protects the harbor has an opening facing the northwest, one direction from which winds in this area rarely come. The breakwater is particularly effective in protecting against the potentially disastrous storms that occasionally come from the south or west.

The commercial dock at Kawaihae

Though Kawaihae was designed as a commercial harbor, it has room for about 20 private boats in the southeast portion at present. Virtually all the private boats in the harbor are on moorings, first, because the soft mud bottom in the harbor does not provide good holding at all. In fact, the harbor has been the scene of many a tragedy because of dragging anchors. The second reason the moorings are preferred is directly related to the first, and that is the strength of the wind, which, when coupled with the poor holding, puts boats anchored here at risk. Winds are often clocked at 50 knots in the harbor, and local boaters even tell of 80-knot winds. The damaging winds are not usually the result of storms but of strong trade winds funneling down the hills to the east.

Added to the poor holding and horrific winds is one other reason that makes Kawaihae Harbor an unsatisfactory anchorage: This commercial harbor lacks sufficient space for the tugs and barges to operate safely when pleasure boats fill the moorings. Because a number of boats moored here have been damaged by barges in the last few years, the State of Hawai'i plans to remove the moorings and designate Kawaihae a commercial harbor off limits to private boats.

A new small-boat harbor, located one mile south of the entrance to Kawaihae and tentatively named South Basin, is scheduled to be completed by mid-2006. The protective breakwater has already been constructed, and the legislature has appropriated money for the development of the facilities for boaters. At the time this edition went to press, the personnel of the Department of Land and Natural Resources (DLNR) had not yet decided on a plan for the facilities, so no one knew how many boats will be accommodated. All the people we asked agreed the 20 boats on moorings in the commercial harbor will be moved to facilities in South Basin so the moorings can be removed. Nancy Murphy, the Hawai'i District Manager for the DLNR, said that, if possible, accommodations for visiting boaters would be included in South Basin. The final number of slips in South Basin appears unlikely to meet even the needs of local boaters, however, because the Harbormaster has a long list of people who would like to have permanent places.

Until facilities in South Basin have been completed, check with the Harbormaster at Honokōhau, who is in charge of the moorings in the commercial harbor, before you set sail for Kawaihae. This Harbormaster will advise you whether to anchor in the basin or to go into the commercial harbor.

When you arrive, you must anchor your boat temporarily as close to the moored vessels as is prudent while you go ashore to call the Honokōhau Harbor Agent. If any moorings are temporarily empty, he will assign you to one. We have visited the harbor twice and found a temporary mooring both times. Accommodations for visiting boaters will, of course, change when South Basin opens, and Kawaihae commercial harbor is closed to pleasure boats.

The limited anchoring and mooring possibilities at Kawaihae are unfortunate, for the area around the harbor has outstanding attractions for visiting boaters. The waters offshore are among the most pristine in the state, excellent for snorkeling and diving. For deep-sea fishing, few places in the Hawaiian Islands rival this area.

Small boat harbor under construction

The village of Kawaihae, a fifteen-minute walk along the highway going north from the harbor, is not a major tourist attraction, though it does attract a few tourists to its restaurants because it is the nearest town to Pu'u Koholā Heiau and Lapakahi State Historical Park.

Located in one of the dry parts of the island, Kawaihae, which translates as "water of wrath," was named because the early people who lived here fought for the water from a fresh water pool. Despite the aridness, the surroundings of the harbor are picturesque. Beyond the beach are *kiawe* and *milo* trees covering the gently rising slopes

From the decks of your boat in the harbor, you can see one of the Hawaiian Island's best known historic spots, the Pu'u Koholā Heiau National Historic Site. It sits atop the hill Pu'u Koholā ("the hill of the whale") above the harbor, with a commanding view of the bay. Kamehameha I and his subjects completed this shrine in 1791 to honor his family war god, Kūkā'ilimoku, in response to the prophecy of a Kaua'i *kahuna* that such a shrine would result in Kamehameha's dominion over all the Hawaiian islands. A few years later, whether the result of the building of the *heiau* or of his determination, Kamehameha became the first ruler of all the islands, naming them after the island of his birth. The site now has a small museum and a walking path around the *heiau*.

At least two other *heiau* are known to have been nearby, the Mailekini and the Haleokapuni. John Young, advisor to Kamehameha I, converted the first to a fort, and storms and tidal waves leveled the remains of the latter.

For swimming and snorkeling, you'll find an excellent beach nearby, the Spencer Beach Park, though you can swim, as many of the local residents do, at the beach in the harbor.

If you want simply to relax on the deck of your boat, Kawaihae is a fine place to do so. Watching the comings and goings of the tugs and barges and the Army transport vessels is fascinating for many boaters. Yet the harbor is a peaceful place, with little traffic where the private boats are moored.

While the commercial docks and the Army launch area have little in their appearance to commend them, the bay itself is beautiful, its sparkling, clear water lapping a long, curving white sand beach. Fish jump around the boats, and large manta rays cruise through the harbor. Though the wind often blows ferociously through the rigging, the anchorage is generally calm. You could do much worse than spend a few days in Kawaihae.

APPROACH

From Māhukona south to Kawaihae Harbor is an easy 10-mile passage. If you're approaching from Honokōhau, you'll have a longer but an equally easy 27-mile passage. Rarely does the wind blow strongly enough to impede the progress of boats that move up or down the Kona Coast. Rather, the more common problem for sailboats along this coast is the lack of wind. Sailboaters must either swallow their pride and run the diesel or make long, slow passages. One problem with sailing along this coast is that the winds change direction often, and wind strength can be count-

Pu'ukoholā Heiau above the harbor

ed on to change just as frequently.

The large white warehouses and ship loading equipment in Kawaihae Harbor are visible from several miles away. Four large fuel tanks and a large round feed tank are also visible from at least 4 miles at sea. A growing number of metal warehouses have been built .25 mile north of the entrance to the harbor. All these buildings make Kawaihae easy to spot when you're approaching from the south or west. The harbor is a little more difficult to spot from the north because it is deeply inset into the northern corner of the bay.

Enter the commercial harbor on the north side, using the range marks and the two pairs of buoys. The entrance channel is 200 yards wide to accommodate commercial ships and barges.

You can readily find Kawaihae at night because of the lights. A lighthouse on the shore just opposite the north end of the breakwater has a 9-mile light atop a 59-foot structure. The channel entrance buoys are lighted, and two flashing red lights on 20-foot poles warn mariners of the breakwater. In the entrance channel, the lighted range marks are easy to see. If the dock crew is loading or unloading a barge at night, the entire dock area will be aglow.

If your destination is South Basin, enter approximately one mile south of the entrance to the commercial harbor.

ANCHORAGE AND BERTHING

Although the situation at Kawaihae will undoubtedly change in the near future, the current recommendation for visiting boaters is to anchor in South Basin until construction on the facilities there begins. (Once construction is under way in South Basin, visiting boaters should anchor inside the commercial harbor.) The depth in the Basin is 10-12 feet; however, the basin already has some shoaling which has reduced this depth in some areas to almost 0 feet. But we have had reports of a couple of boats anchoring there in the past few months, so getting in and out is clearly possible.

A red buoy marks the end of the outer breakwater of Kawaihae. For boaters coming from the north, this buoy is somewhat obscured by the breakwater. A light on the end of the inner breakwater marks the starboard side of the channel for boats entering South Basin.

A youth group has installed a private dock in the southeast corner of South Basin, but visitors are not allowed to use this dock. To go ashore, tie your dinghy instead to the breakwater until the new facilities are installed.

Immediately inside the breakwater on the northeast side of the commercial harbor is a small inner harbor used by local fishing boats. This area also has a launch ramp. But this tiny harbor is overcrowded, never having any open space for visiting boats.

The facilities for unloading ships and barges are on the east side, just south of the small boat harbor. In the southwestern corner of the harbor is a large launch ramp belonging to the U. S. Army and used by Army landing ships to transport troops and equipment to and from the island. Traffic in and out of the shipping dock and the Army launch ramp is almost constant, with frequently one or more barges at the shipping dock and an Army LST being filled with trucks, jeeps, and artillery.

In the commercial harbor, drop your anchor as close as possible to the moored private boats, making sure you are out of the way of both the tug and barge traffic and the Army traffic. The water depth in the harbor is between 30 and 35 feet As soon as your anchor is down, call the harbormaster at Honokōhau to see if you can use one of the moorings in the harbor. (The marine cargo coordinator at Kawaihae has authority over only the commercial dock.) Do not plan to remain on your hook overnight. A capable crew member must remain aboard the anchored boat at all times, even if only for the few minutes while you go ashore to make a call. Because the winds come from a variety of directions and the anchoring room is limited, a boat on an anchor may be a danger to itself and to other boats.

Another possibility to consider is the four Tahiti-style moorings at the southeast corner of the harbor, just north of the small pier used by private and commercial boaters in the harbor who need to take customers, fuel, and water aboard. While you're asking the harbormaster at Honokōhau about a place for your boat for a few days, you might ask about this possibility.

If you get a mooring or drop your hook in the commercial harbor, go ashore in the southeast corner of the anchorage, immediately south of the commercial docks, where tenders belonging to boaters in the area are in racks behind the seawall. A small dock extends out into the harbor, where you can get up onto the seawall. Local boaters use this small dock to load supplies and people onto their boats, so don't leave your dinghy in their way. We found it convenient to leave our tender tied bow and stern between the head of the dock and the seawall.

Honokōhau Harbormaster   808-329-4215

Kava Drinking

FACILITIES

Fuel (diesel by truck; diesel and gasoline by jerry jugs)
Fish Market
Mini-market and Deli
Post Office (limited hours and services)
Restaurants
Telephone
Water

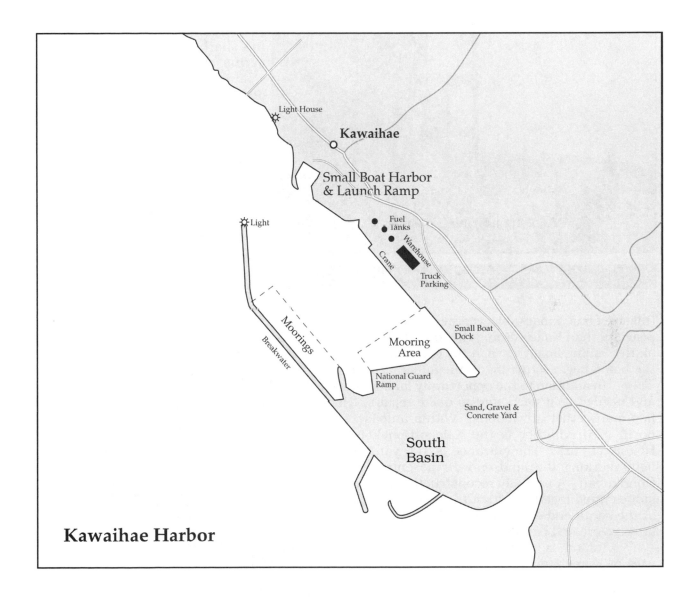

Kawaihae Harbor

HONOKŌHAU HARBOR
CHART #19327
LAT. N19° 40.260 LONG. W156° 01.950 (ENTRANCE BUOY)

Honokōhau ("bay drawing dew"), 27 miles south of Kawaihae, is one of the most important destinations for cruising sailors to the Big Island to know about. This harbor was blasted out of solid rock and is the safest place on the Big Island to moor a boat during heavy weather.

But Honokōhau is more than just a safe harbor. Honokōhau has the only haul-out facilities on the island and the only fuel dock. As were most of the other harbors in the islands, however, it was designed primarily for fishing or commercial boats, not for cruising boats. As a consequence, this harbor has neither transient berths nor adequate facilities for visiting boaters. For example, the docks have no electrical hookups for boats, and the restrooms and showers are deplorable. When we questioned the harbormaster about this lack of accommodations, he told us bluntly that the harbor needs no additional facilities because the harbor regulations prohibit living aboard vessels moored there.

Stand for offerings at the *heiau*

Still, Honokōhau Harbor serves those cruising boaters who need to haul out or to get boat parts better than any other destination on the island of Hawai'i. In addition, this area has remarkable weather, which makes a stay here most pleasant. It is also much more peaceful than Kailua-Kona, the tourist hot spot on the island 4 miles south of Honokōhau. Once all the fishing boats leave in the early morning, the docks at Honokōhau are often deserted until the boats begin returning in the late afternoon.

In addition to the opportunity for boaters to get fuel and needed boat parts and to make repairs, Honokōhau has many other attractions. Within an easy walk to the north of the harbor is the Kaloko-Honokōhau National Historical Park. The entrance is 100 yards north of the light marking the land end of the entrance channel to Honokōhau. A partially reconstructed *heiau* of black lava stones fitted together without mortar sits out on the point at the south end of the beach. North along the beach is a large re-created canoe hut with thatched roof.

Inland is the Queen's Bath, where the favorite wife of Kamehameha I, Queen Ka'ahumanu, bathed in spring-fed waters. A trail winds along the edge of the old 'Aimakapā fishpond, which today is most valued as a waterfowl habitat, providing a home for black-crowned night-herons (*'auku'u*), Hawaiian ducks (*koloa maoli*), Hawaiian coots (*'alae ke'oke'o*) and pied-billed grebes, the grebe nesting no place else except this pond. To get to the pond, walk along the shoreline for about .75 mile from the entrance to the park.

Kaloko Pond is, according to legend, the site of a secret underwater cave where the bones of Kamehameha

On the King's Highway

I were secretly hidden. Hawaiians customarily hid the bones of Hawaiian chiefs to secure them from ill use by the enemies.

At the north end of the beach, where the road from the highway comes down to the beach, are restrooms. If you take the road toward the highway, winding through an *'a'a* lava field, you'll come to a portion of the ancient "King's Highway" that has been beautifully restored. In one direction it goes back toward the ocean; in the other, it ends in a large parking lot.

This park reportedly also has a number of petroglyphs. If you want to find them, you might need to have a local resident show you where they are, or at least draw you a map. If you are going to explore the entire park, plan to spend a half day, perhaps ending with a swim back at the long sand beach curving between the *heiau* on one end and the road on the other. These waters are also excellent for snorkeling.

Fuel dock at Honokōhau

The other swimming beach is a tiny cove on the south side of the harbor, where many of the local children come to play in the shallow water near the shore.

On at least one of your days at Honokōhau, be back at the weigh-station at the south end of the fuel dock by 1600, where you can watch as the fishing boats bring in huge bill fish for weighing, measuring, photographing, and then transporting to market.

At the end of the day, the deck of your boat sitting in Honokōhau Harbor is an ideal spot for viewing the waning light shining on one of the Big Island's five volcanoes, Hualālai, last erupting in 1800-1801. After sunset watch the black-crowned night-herons flying one by one over the harbor, as they make their nightly migration to fishing grounds to the south. (If you're up early the next morning, you can watch their return.)

For a human rather than nature experience, check out the restaurant and bar in the harbor. It's a favorite hang-out for boaters in the harbor, a place where you can probably hear some salty tales of the sea.

APPROACH

The entrance into Honokōhau Harbor is 4 miles south of Keahole Point, an easily identified landmark because the airport is immediately inland from the point. From the south, Honokōhau Harbor is only 4 miles from Kailua-Kona.

You can safely enter Honokōhau Harbor at night if you have some knowledge of the harbor and a radar aboard. Lights are on each side of the opening in the rock wall at the entrance into the harbor. On the approach a light directly in front of you as you enter shows green when you stray to the port side too far, red when you stray to starboard, and white when you are in the center of the channel.

ANCHORAGE AND BERTHING

Honokōhau Harbor has no slips. Instead, it has 250 spaces where boaters tie one end of their craft to the seawall and the other to a buoy. Powerboats, mostly charter fishing boats, currently occupy over 200 of the available spaces, with fewer than 40 spaces being occupied by sailboats.

As is common among the harbors around the state, all the spaces in Honokōhau are assigned; none are reserved for boats in transit. Nevertheless, visitors can usually find a space for a few days. We came into the harbor for fuel and called the harbormaster from the fuel dock to ask for a space for a couple of days to make some minor repairs and to reprovision. He immediately granted our request, putting *Carricklee* in a space just vacated, where we spent four nights comfortably tucked in between two charter fishing boats. More good news follows: we paid $6.50 per night for our space. By the way, don't be offended if someone off a neighboring boat questions you about your being in that space. The permanent residents watch out for one another's spaces.

The best plan would be to call ahead from another harbor to see if space is available for your boat. If that is not practical, and it often isn't for cruising boats, you can stop by the fuel dock and fuel up. While one person from the boat handles the fueling, another can call the harbor office. If a space is available, the harbormaster will probably ask you to come to the office, leaving your boat temporarily at the fuel dock, to get a space assignment. Try to arrive at the fuel dock at some time other than around 1200 or between 1600-1800 hours, when fishing boats flock to the dock for fuel.

By the way, expect a new experience when you stop here for fuel. Rather than tie alongside the fuel dock, you must pull directly in, catching a stern buoy as you go by, or back in,

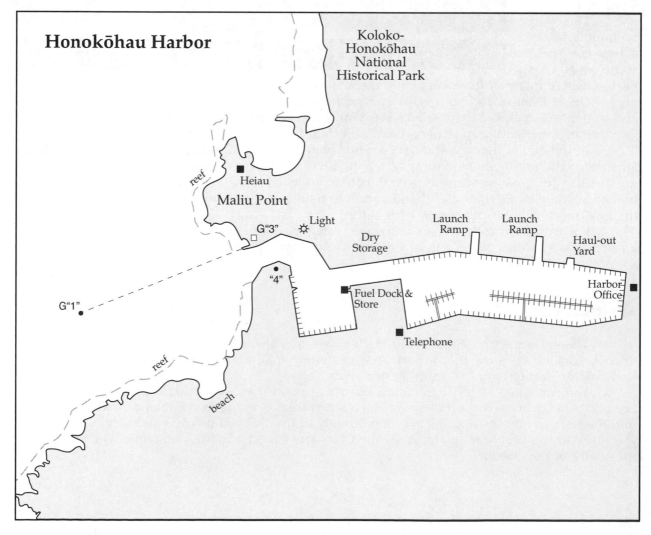

Honokōhau Harbor

Koloko-Honokōhau National Historical Park

reef

Heiau

Maliu Point

G"3"   ☼ Light

Dry Storage

Launch Ramp   Launch Ramp

Haul-out Yard

"4"

G"1"

Fuel Dock & Store

Harbor Office

Telephone

reef

beach

securing the bow to a buoy as you go by. When the cross winds are blowing, this method of tying to the fuel dock can be a challenge, especially for some sailboats with much windage.

Many areas in the harbor have depths in the 6-7-foot range, so proceed slowly in the harbor if you draw more than 7 feet.

If you need a dock to tie to for a day, see the office staff at Kona Marine, which is also Gentry Boatyard. The boatyard has two floating docks in the northeast corner of the harbor, one on either side of the haul-out ramp and Travelift. If space is available, the boatyard will rent you a slip for $1.00 per foot of boat length per day. Gentry Marine (Kona Marine) also has the only dry storage facility for pleasure boats in the Hawaiian Islands. Although it has space for 300 boats, all those spaces are typically leased, but check with the facility (808-329-7896) if you wish to leave your boat on the hard; the waiting list is sometimes relatively short.

If, when you check in with the Honokohau harbormaster, you find the harbor is full, you can anchor outside the harbor entrance, just north of the entrance channel. Anchor about 200 feet north of the channel and about 100 yards from Maliu Point, in 25-30 feet of water. Select a good sand patch to drop your anchor; coral patches are plentiful here. You will be limited to a 72-hour stay, so don't get too comfortable.

Honokohau Harbormaster   808-329-4215

FACILITIES

Boat Repairs (including a marine diesel engine repair shop)
Fuel (diesel and gasoline)
Haul-out
Mini-market
Restaurant
Restrooms
Telephone

Other facilities are available in Kailua-Kona, approximately 3.5 miles south by land. Unfortunately, no buses run between the harbor and the town. Taxi service is available, or you can ride bicycles. The bicycle lanes along the highway into Kailua are wide, and the hills are not too steep.

Kailua ("two seas, or currents"), perhaps the busiest and most rapidly growing town on the island of Hawai'i, is both the most modern and the most historic town on the island. Much of its former ambiance is lost in the crowds of tourists arriving here daily, but its temperate weather, its natural beauty, and its history make it worth exploring. Because of the pleasant weather, several members of the early royal families of Hawai'i spent much of their time here. You'll find much to delight and interest you in Kailua, so don't pass by without stopping.

Among the richest historical sites in all the Islands, Kailua was the last home of Kamehameha I, who died here in 1819 at his court called *Kamakahonu* ("the turtle eye"), where the King Kamehameha Hotel is today. Kamakahonu was also the place where, shortly after the death of Kamehameha, his son King Liholiho sat down to dine with two of Kamehameha's widows, Keōpūolani and Ka'ahumanu. This breaking of the ancient *kapu* forbidding men and women to eat together effectively destroyed the *kapu* system that had governed virtually every aspect of the lives of the ancient Hawaiians.

Steeple of Moku'aikaua Church

Besides its function as a hotel, the King Kamehameha is also a mini-museum, housing Hawaiian artifacts, portraits of the royal family, a display of the medicinal herbs of old Hawai'i, and a mounted 1,200-pound marlin. Next to the hotel is the restored Ahu'ena Heiau, dedicated to the god of fertility, Lono, and first rebuilt by Kamehameha. Unlike many other *heiau* that Kamehameha built or restored that were dedicated to war, Ahu'ena ("red-hot heap") was dedicated to peace and prosperity.

Later members of the royal family had a vacation home here, the Hulihe'e Palace. Completed in 1838 for the first governor of Hawai'i, John Kuakini, this Victorian house is now a small museum with furniture and artifacts of members of the royal family who spent time here, as well as spears and a stone exercise ball weighing 200 pounds believed to have belonged to King Kamehameha I.

In 1820, the first Christian missionaries to Hawai'i landed in Kailua to obtain permission from Kamehameha II to build a church here. He ceded them land in Kailua, where they built the first Christian church in the Hawaiian Islands in 1823. The present building, the Moku'aikaua Church, named for the forest above Kailua where the timber to build the church was cut, was completed in 1836 to replace the original church destroyed by fire. Two exhibits in the church that are of particular interest to sailors are a model of the *Thaddeus*, the brigantine that brought the first missionaries to Hawai'i, and a Micronesian navigation stick chart, its intricate design representing the ocean conditions for a particular region of the Pacific.

In the early 1800s planters found that coffee plants thrived on the often cloudy slopes of Hualālai, the volcano behind Kailua. In 1845 they harvested the first crop of coffee beans. Kona coffee continues to be a popular gourmet—and expensive—coffee.

Before tourism became its primary industry, Kailua was a major port for the cattle ranches on the Big Island. The cattle were brought to the pier, unloaded, and driven into the water by the *paniolos* to swim out to a steamer anchored offshore. When the deep-draft harbor at Kawaihae opened in the 1950s, the ranchers began to use that harbor instead of Kailua because they could load the cattle directly onto barges.

While Kailua doesn't have one of the island's premier beaches, it does have a small beach right in town, the Kamakahonu, between the pier and the King Kamehameha Kona Beach Hotel. The Ironman Triathlon World Championship, a yearly event held each October, starts at this beach.

In the late afternoon, arrange to be on the pier as the charter fishing boats begin returning with their catches for the day. At the weighing station you'll usually see huge blue marlins on the scales, some perhaps weighing more than 1,000 pounds. The Kona Coast reputedly has among the best marlin fishing grounds in the world; Kailua hosts the annual Hawaiian International Billfish Tournament.

Above all the current bustle of Kailua-Kona placidly sits the majestic Hualālai Mountain, one of the five volcanoes of the Big Island. Quiet since 1801, when, according to legend, Kamehameha I offered sacrifices to Pele and stopped the flow, this volcano is merely dormant, not extinct, and is deemed by some who study volcanoes to be ready to erupt at any time.

Distinctive architecture of the Royal Kona Resort

With all this town has to offer, the bay would be crowded with visiting boats except for the wind and the waves often coming from different directions, making this one of the most consistently uncomfortable anchorages in the islands. You can easily find a spot to anchor because most boaters tend to move on rather quickly.

APPROACH

Traveling south from Honokōhau Harbor to Kailua Bay, round Kaiwi Point and go about 2.0 miles southeast. Past Kaiwi Point, you'll begin to see the buildings of Kailua-Kona. Approaching from the south, you'll find Kailua Bay about 50 miles northwest of Ka Lae, the south end of the island. As you approach from either direction, you'll recognize Kailua Bay first by the Royal Kona Resort, noteworthy for its layered architecture, each floor above smaller than the one below it. The hotel is south of the pier on a striking bed of black lava. The other prominent features are the busy pier in the northernmost part of the bay and, east of the pier, the white spire of the Moku'aikaua Church, built in 1836 on the site of the first church in the Hawaiian Islands. You'll also see about 20 boats on moorings .30 mile south of the pier.

At night the light on Kūkā'ilimoku Point, .30 mile west of the pier, visible for 10 miles, and the bright lights of the hotels, restaurants, and shops ashore make Kailua-Kona easily recognizable.

ANCHORAGE

Kailua Bay, like much of the Kona Coast, has some healthy but fragile coral growth. Before dropping a hook here, be sure to select a sandy place where your anchor and chain won't damage the coral.

The best way to avoid damaging the irreplaceable coral is to tie up to one of the moorings in Kailua Bay. Before doing so, however, check with the harbormaster in Honokōhau, if possible from another harbor. A better possibility for cruising boaters who do not always have access to a telephone is to check with one of the working boaters if one is present in the anchorage when you arrive. These boaters generally keep track of which moorings are being used and which are not, and they are eager to assist visiting boaters avoid dropping their anchors in coral patches.

Whenever you tie to a vacant mooring at Kailua-Kona, or anywhere else in the Islands, you should dive on it to assure it is strong enough to hold your boat. If you tie your 45-foot cruising boat to a mooring designed for a 22-foot fishing boat, for example, your boat and the mooring may be elsewhere when you return from a trip ashore.

Because Kailua is so rolly, we've found the only way to be comfortable here is to put out a roll stabilizer. Two roll stabilizers, one on either side of the boat, could be an even better idea.

Although you'll want to end up tied to a mooring eventually, if possible, you may need to drop a hook until you can find an empty mooring. The best anchorage is south of the Kailua pier about .25 mile, in a sand patch just north of the moorings west of the Royal Kona Resort. You can also find good anchorage 250 yards southwest of the pier 100 yards off the shore in 15-20 feet of water. Take your time and look at the bottom carefully before you drop the anchor.

In Kailua Bay, you can anchor out for the first 72 hours without checking in with the harbormaster. After that, be sure to call the Honokōhau harbormaster.

When you want to go ashore, you may tie your tender on the west side of the Kailua pier. You'll find a large number of sport boats already there; just squeeze yours in among the crowd.

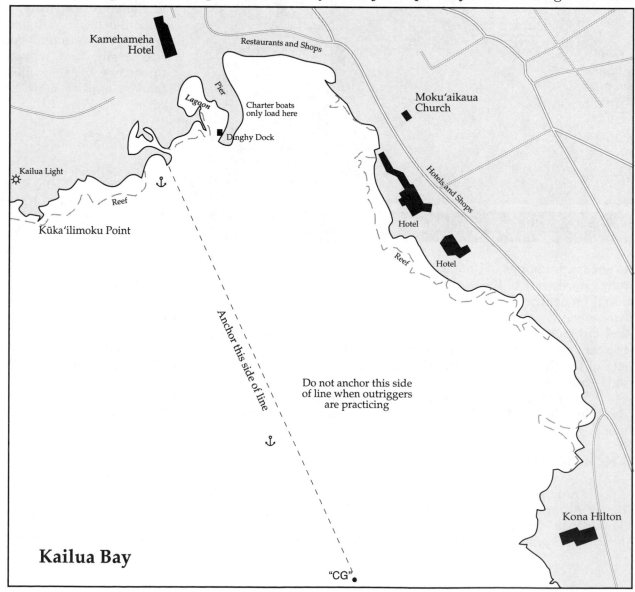

Kailua Bay

Honokōhau Harbormaster   808-329-4215

FACILITIES

Airport
Banks
Car Rental
Clinic/Hospital
Fuel (diesel and gasoline by jerry jug)
Grocery Stores
Laundromat

Library
Pharmacy
Post Office
Public Transportation
Restaurants
Restrooms
Water

KEAUHOU BAY
CHART #19327
LAT. N19° 33.494 LONG. W155° 58.567 (ENTRANCE)

Keauhou ("the new era"), a small, secure bay in a lovely setting 5 miles south of Kailua-Kona, is a choice anchorage except for one problem: the number of boats permanently moored in this bay, so many that visiting boaters can find no secure place to drop an anchor. While only approximately 15 boats have moorings at Keauhou, that number is a full house for this tiny bay.

On first entering the bay, you will see what you think are suitable anchoring spots on the ocean side of the moorings. But when you drop your hook, you'll discover that the bottom of the bay is rock with a thin layer of sand over it. You can see the sand, but after you've dropped your hook and backed down on it, it will rumble across the rocky bottom. Another problem is the narrowness of Keauhou Bay. In trying to find a place to anchor, you must carefully stay outside the traffic channel in the middle of this busy bay. Because of these problems, we can't recommend this destination.

Keauhou Anchorage

Probably the main attraction to Keauhou is its natural environment. Despite the development, this little bay retains much of its intimate ambiance because of the many trees and shrubs along the shore and by the flows of black lava embracing the entrance. The snorkeling is excellent on the coral reef on the north point, with clear, calm water on most days.

The historical significance of Keauhou is also rich. Near the bay is a boulder that is marked with a bronze plaque as the Kauikeaouli Stone. In 1814, Keōpūolani, the wife of Kamehameha I with the highest lineage, gave birth to a stillborn son in a house near the boulder.

A *kahuna* took the baby out to the boulder and revived it. Such was the legendary beginning of the man who ruled Hawai'i as Kamehameha III from 1825 to 1854.

At the Keauhou Hotel you can take a self-guided walking tour of the hotel's historic grounds, most notably the remains of three *heiau*—Kapuanoni, Hāpai-ali'i, and Ke'eki. This rich historic site also has a fish pond, fishing shrines and a few petroglyphs on the shore and underwater south of Ke'eki Heiau.

One-quarter mile south of Keauhou is the Kuamo'o battlefield, where King Liholiho's forces defeated Kekuo'okalani, a nephew of Kamehameha I who was fighting to preserve the *kapu* system. Some petroglyphs have been carved into a *pāhoehoe* lava rise on the battlefield.

APPROACH

From Kailua Pier, Keauhou Bay is 5 miles south; it is 5 miles north of Kealakekua Bay and 45 miles northwest of Ka Lae, the southernmost point on the island of Hawai'i.

Picking out Keauhou Bay as one moves along the coastline is not easy without a GPS unit. Two identifying features are the condominiums on the north point of the bay and the Kona Surf Hotel on the south point of the bay. But these are but two of the many developments on this popular Kona shoreline between Kailua and Keahou.

Probably the best way to spot Keauhou Bay is to look for the cluster of boats moored there and the small, busy pier on the south side of the bay, where charter boats load and unload passengers and equipment.

ANCHORAGE

A tri-color light on a pole is at the back of Keauhou Bay. Keauhou Light is at the top of the 35-foot pole; the entrance light is 10 feet below the Keauhou Light. The center part of the entrance light is white, signifying the entrance channel; you may not anchor anywhere the white light is visible to you. The channel here is busy much of the time, for not only do the 15 or so moored boats use it, but so do a number of charter boats that load at the pier and the private boats coming into and out of the launch ramp.

The green light on the port side of the pole is visible from the north part of the bay. This area has a reef, coral heads, and boulders on the bottom, so it does not offer good anchorage. The red light shows when you are on the south side of the bay. The moorings take up most of the space on the south side, but it is the only place where you might find good anchoring ground. The depths in the bay are generally between 12 and 15 feet.

Given the permanent moorings filling the bay, the best remaining space to drop an anchor is at the outer edge of the bay, a somewhat exposed location. Although others have told us they anchored there, we have never been able to find a place where our anchor would hold at Keauhou.

Another possibility is to call the harbormaster at Honokōhau Harbor (808-329-4215) and ask if a mooring is empty for a night or two. Having your boat secured to a mooring would make for a far more comfortable visit; you would then feel secure enough to go ashore and see the attractions of Keauhou Bay.

FACILITIES

At Keauhou Bay:
  Launch Ramp
  Restaurants
  Restrooms
  Telephone

At Keauhou Shopping Center:
  Bank
  Fuel (gasoline)
  Grocery Stores
  Hardware
  Pharmacy
  Post Office
  Shops

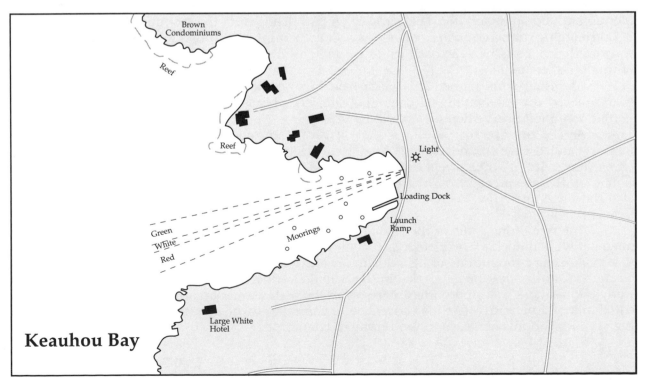

Keauhou Bay

Kealakekua Bay is best known as the place where Captain James Cook was killed in 1779, his death commemorated by a large monument in Ka'awaloa Cove, in the northwest corner of the Bay. Long before Cook anchored in these protected waters to trade for food and water, Kealakekua Bay was well-known for its security for boats. Thousands of Hawaiians lived around the bay, growing taro on the slopes and fishing in the waters rich with marine life.

Captain Cook Monument in Ka'awaloa Bay

Today, charter boats bring their customers to the bay to snorkel, and a fishing boat or two will be moored off the hamlet of Nāpō'opo'o. Otherwise, the boating is generally limited to a few kayakers paddling across the bay between Nāpō'opo'o Beach County Park and Ka'awaloa Cove.

The major attraction for most who come here today is the Marine Conservation District in Ka'awaloa Cove, the northwest part of the bay. Here, visitors can swim over one of the healthiest and most varied stands of corals in all the Islands and among the most friendly and abundant of tropical fish. Moray eels hide in crevices in the coral, and red pencil and jet black urchins add accent to the already colorful coral heads. In addition, dolphins and manta rays feed regularly in these nutrient-rich waters. You may even hear a humpback whale blowing alongside your boat, especially at night.

You can tie your tender to the remains of a dock at the base of the Captain Cook Monument and go ashore for a closer look. A path leads from the monument through a tunnel of overhanging branches, where mongooses slide themselves through impossibly small passageways in the rocks. Then the path winds through an *a'a* lava field to the coast on the other side of this little peninsula.

The Hawaiians named this place Kealakekua, meaning "pathway of the god," because they believed the gods often slid down the cliff here to cross the bay quickly. One god, in particular, left a footprint when he slid down.

Across the bay to the east is the village of Nāpō'opo'o, with a small swimming beach, formerly called Black Sand Beach. Now, local residents refer to it as Boulder Beach because Hurricane 'Iniki, in 1992, swept away all the sand, leaving behind only the bare boulders. About a mile up the steep road from the village is a coffee mill, where you can sample the coffee and visit the small museum. You can also purchase some freshly roasted coffee and other local products.

The remaining walls of the Hikiau Heiau, a *luakini* (a place where human sacrifices were made) of Kamehameha I, overlooks the bay from the southeast corner of the beach. Here, on his first visit, Cook brought one of his seaman for a Christian burial, the *heiau* now commemorated as the site of the first such service in the Islands. Hikiau Heiau is also remembered because Henry Opukahaia was apprenticed here before he sailed away on an American boat to be educated in New England. After his conversion to Christianity, he successfully argued for the sending of American missionaries to the Hawaiian Islands.

This *heiau* seems to embody the cultural upheavals that followed. In a bit of historical irony, it looks directly across the bay to the Cook Monument, erected by "some of his fellow countrymen" near the spot where Cook, one of the greatest navigators of all times, was killed in a sad cultural misunderstanding.

Numerous burial caves in the cliffs rising immediately from the water's edge add to the mystique of this beautiful bay, where events unfolded that changed Hawai'i and the Hawaiians forever.

APPROACH

Boaters traveling south will notice a distinct difference between the terrain north of Keauhou and that to the south. From Kailua-Kona to Keauhou the shore appears covered with houses, hotels, apartments, and condominiums. South of Keauhou few structures are visible near the water. The few houses to be seen are those near the highway, some 1-2 miles high on the mountain behind the shoreline. The distance south from Keauhou to Kealakekua Bay is only 5.0 miles. For boaters traveling north from Ka Lae, Kealakekua Bay is about 40 miles away.

A light on Cook Point (27 feet high, 7-mile range) marks the north boundary of the entrance to the bay. The distance between Cook Point and the village of Nāpō'opo'o to the east is approximately 1.0 mile. Swing wide as you round Cook Point because of the reef and rocks extending southeast from the point. Water breaks on the reef here in all but the calmest conditions, so you will have adequate warning of the location of the reef.

As you come into the bay, you'll see in the northwest corner the 25-foot high, white concrete shaft of the memorial to Captain Cook. The north boundary of the bay is a vertical 400-600-foot high cliff that extends from the Cook Monument to Nāpō'opo'o village and beyond. In the extreme eastern corner of the bay is the village of Nāpō'opo'o, recognizable by the

Fishing and swimming off the dock at Nāpō'opo'o

red-roofed white church steeple rising above the trees. Lying in the middle of all this is what many people call the most beautiful water in Hawai'i.

ANCHORAGE

Kealakekua Bay, a Marine Life Conservation District, is divided into two areas: Subzone A and Subzone B. Subzone A includes all the bay inside a line drawn from Cook Point to the beach just north of the village of Nāpō'opo'o. No boat may be anchored inside Subzone A, and no one may fish inside this area.

The small corner in the northwest side of Kealakekua Bay where Cook's Monument is located is identified on your charts as Ka'awaloa Cove. You may not anchor here, but you will see a large catamaran, the *Fairwind*, bring snorkelers into the cove every morning at 0830 and every afternoon at 1330, departing for the day at 1630. (The boat occasionally returns with passengers for a night snorkel.)

Subzone B is just south of Subzone A. It extends from Cook Point to Manini Beach Point and includes all of the water from this line to Subzone A. No one may fish in this area, but boats may be anchored here. However, the Hawai'i regulation for this Marine Life Conservation District (MLCD) states: "Anchoring of boats is prohibited in Subzone A. In Subzone B anchors may only be dropped onto sand, or in such a way as to avoid damage to coral."

The anchorage off Nāpō'opo'o village is in Subzone B and is the only area in the MLCD that has water shallow enough to anchor. The bottom close to the village is generally sand that provides good holding, but look closely to avoid the areas of coral that are, in some instances, extensive. You can expect to drop anchor in 25-40 feet of water This area is one of the best anchorages on the island because the bay indents far into the coastline, providing good protection.

Two moorings lie directly off the village. Do not tie up to either of these moorings; they are privately owned and constantly monitored by members of the Leslie family, long-time residents of this bay. Some visiting boaters have been challenged by local residents when they anchored too close to the coral or too near the buoys off Nāpo'opo'o village, so be especially careful where you anchor.

If you're going south when you depart from the anchorage off Nāpō'opo'o village, don't cut the corner at Palemano Point, some .75 mile to the southwest. A reef extends out 300 yards.

FACILITIES

Landing dock for tenders	Shower
Restrooms	Telephone

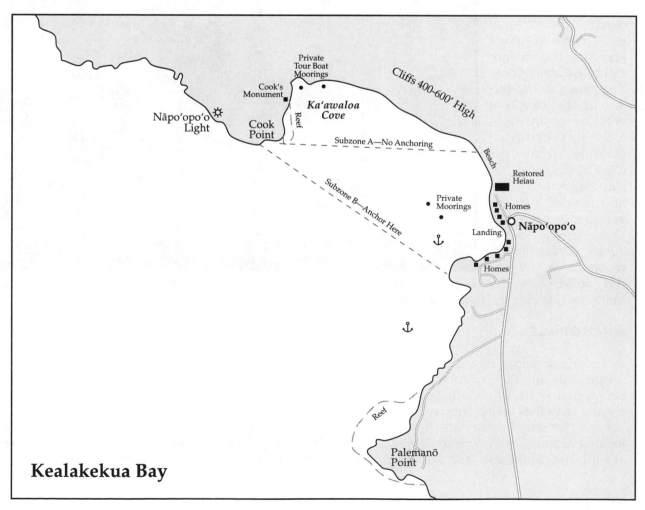

Kealakekua Bay

HŌNAUNAU BAY (PU'UHONUA O HŌNAUNAU)
CHART #19327
LAT. N19° 25.600 LONG. W155° 55.000 (ANCHORAGE)

Hōnaunau Bay has a unique history. The point of land just south of Hōnaunau Bay was the site of Pu'uhonua O Hōnaunau, ("the place of refuge at Hōnaunau"), the largest place of refuge in all the Hawaiian Islands.

In the days of the ancient Hawaiians, defeated warriors and ordinary people who broke a *kapu* ("rule") could be put to death instantly, even for violating a *kapu* as seemingly minor as failing to prostrate oneself when an *ali'i* passed by. If a *kapu*-breaker could get to Pu'uhonua O Hōnaunau (or any other place of refuge) before being apprehended, however, he or she could not be put to death. No matter what the offense, the *kahuna* ("priest") in charge of the place of refuge had to accept and protect anyone who reached a place of refuge.

The best known recipient of this protection was one of the wives (some say the favorite wife) of Kamehameha I, Ka'ahumanu, who had broken the *kapu* Kamehameha had put on her not to have sexual relations with any other man. The British Captain and confidante of Kamehameha George Vancouver persuaded the couple to reconcile their differences.

Hōnaunau has been a sanctuary for Hawaiians in trouble since at least the 16th century, and perhaps for many years before that. Early Hawaiians believed the place gained even more *mana* ("divine power") because a number of high chiefs were buried here over the centuries of the existence of the refuge.

Restored carefully to reflect the condition of the facility in the late 18th century, Pu'uhonua O Hōnaunau, now a national historic park, is one of the most complete and faithful reconstructions of a historical site in the islands. A 1,000-foot long wall, 10 feet high and 17 feet wide,

Place of Refuge at Hōnaunau

Humpback whale near the bay

justifiably called "the Great Wall," separates the refuge from the village. The wall, like the original built in the 1500s, was constructed of dry-stone masonry. In the compound are also the Hale o Keawe Heiau and the grounds of the royal residence for the ruling chiefs of the area.

A self-guided tour takes you through this window into the past, where you'll see not only a reconstructed refuge and *heiau* but many other representations of early Hawaiian life. Most imposing are the enormous 'ōhi'a logs carved into figures representing Hawaiian gods. Taped messages at the various sites, colorful murals, and artifacts of everyday life fill in more details about this rich culture.

Despite the richness of the cultural environment here, many visitors come for the rich marine life in Hōnaunau Bay. Around the reef are turtles and tropical fish in profusion, and humpback whales, the Hawai'i state marine mammal, frequent the waters off the southern shores of the bay

Hōnaunau Bay is small, only about 500 yards wide and 500 yards deep. A swimming zone is in the northwestern part of the bay. For most boaters, however, this swimming zone, where boats may not anchor, will not interfere with their plans. The central, eastern, and southern parts of the bay are still available for boaters to anchor in, provided, of course, they avoid dropping their anchors in coral.

APPROACH

Hōnaunau Bay is 3.4 miles south of Kealakekua Bay and 37 miles northwest of Ka Lae Point. When coming from the south, you will pass many areas giving evidence of volcanic flows coming downslope. Generally, the terrain between Ka Lae and Hōnaunau is dry, with sparse vegetation. Only a few villages between Ka Lae and Hōnaunau indicate any human habitation.

To identify Hōnaunau Bay, you can use Pu'uhonua O Hōnaunau, atop black stone walls 10-12 feet high, on the south point of the bay. The royal palms soaring above the site serve as beacons for those approaching by land or sea. As you near the entrance to the bay, you'll see a thatched building out on the point. At the eastern edge of the bay, among the trees, is the small village of Hōnaunau, little of which you'll see from the water. In the southeastern corner of the bay behind a natural breakwater is a small bay with a launch ramp. A reef extends from the eastern side of the bay all the way around to the south point, Pu'uhonua, and beyond. Local fishing boats with a shallow draft enter the area behind the breakwater by going carefully over the reef.

Hōnaunau Bay has neither lights nor other navigational aids to assist boaters.

ANCHORING

When entering the bay, be on the lookout for people in the water. Because this bay offers such remarkable sight-seeing and snorkeling opportunities, snorkel boat companies, most using inflatable RIB boats, bring large numbers of tourists to Hōnaunau. Tourists also flock to the bay by car to snorkel in the remarkably clear water of the bay. These swimmers should be in the swimming area in the northwest corner of the bay, but they often scatter across the entire bay. As with all destinations in Hawai'i, be careful not to drop your anchor in the coral. And, as in many other areas, finding a spot with sand rather than coral on the bottom can be a challenge. The first time we stopped by this lovely bay, the sky was overcast, and we couldn't see the bottom well enough to distinguish between a sand bottom and a coral bottom. In frustration, we went on to another anchorage rather than risk dropping in the coral. The second time we visited, we could see the bottom quite clearly but had to look long and hard to find a large sand patch for our anchor.

The best place to begin your search for a place to drop a hook is 100-150 yards north of the south shore of the anchorage, which puts your boat just slightly south of the center of the bay. You should be anchoring in water 25-40 feet deep. Holding in the bay is good, that is, if you can find a large enough sand patch to drop your anchor in so that your rode and anchor do not damage the surrounding coral. Be prepared to go on to another anchorage if you can't find that patch of sand.

To go ashore, you can land your tender in the southeast corner of the bay and take the short walk to the place of refuge.

We must warn you about a potential ugly situation that may develop at Hōnaunau Bay. Some residents who have become frustrated by the influx of tourists are threatening rebellion and trying everything they can think of to stop the flow. They can do nothing to stop people from coming in by private car, and they've been unable to do anything to stop the RIB boat tours that bring in 150 or more snorkelers a day. The charter companies that operate the RIB Zodiacs are there only a short time and don't anchor. One person stays in the boat while a crewperson takes the snorkelers for a swim. However, when visiting boaters drop a hook in the bay, they may find themselves the objects of harassment from some of the townspeople. If you are threatened by anyone while you are anchored here, call the Coast Guard, 808-522-6458.

FACILITIES

Launch Ramp (for shallow-draft vessels only)

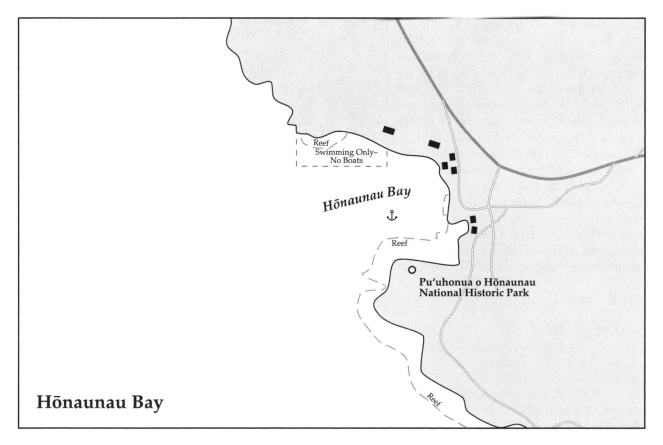

Hōnaunau Bay

HO'OKENA ANCHORAGE (KAUHAKO BAY)
CHART #19320
LAT. N19° 22.623 LONG. W155° 53.799 (ANCHORAGE)

The tiny fishing village of Ho'okena ("to satisfy thirst") was the main port in South Kona in the past because it had a good bay, Kauhakō, and a wharf from which farmers of the entire area could ship their produce. Just before World War II, however, the state completed the road connecting the Kona Coast to Hilo, and the wharf was no longer used to ship produce to market. After that, the town slipped into the status of a small fishing village. When storms destroyed the wharf, no one bothered to rebuild it. A few pilings remain to mark the passing of the village's prominence.

Ho'okena also drew well-known visitors in the days when it was a major port. In 1889 Robert Louis Stevenson came to this village to spend a short time so he could write and clear his mind of the confusion caused by living in Honolulu. He described the scene that greeted him at Ho'okena:

On the immediate foreshore, under a low cliff, there stood some score of houses, trellised and verandaed, set in narrow gardens, and painted gaudily in green and white; the whole surrounded and shaded by a grove of coco palms and fruit trees, springing (as by some miracle) from the bare lava. In front the population of the neighborhood were gathered for the weekly incident, the passage of the steamer, sixty to eighty strong. . . . .

He could undoubtedly find the same peace today that he found then—but not the "sixty to eighty" residents. But certainly the natural beauty of the place remains.

The long gray-sand beach sweeps from the *pali* on the east end to a black lava reef on the northwest corner of the bay. Behind the beach are tall palm trees offering a shady respite from the sun. A much smaller beach at the foot of the *pali* is excellent for body surfing, and all along this eastern shore is good snorkeling in exceptionally clear water. A pod of spinner dolphins makes its home in Kauhako Bay, providing a daily acrobatic show of spins, flips, and dives.

Beach at Ho'okena

The attitude of the local residents toward visiting boaters here will uplift your spirits, especially if you've just come from Hōnaunau. As you enter the bay, you can see in the northwestern corner a long white rock wall on which large black letters spell "HOOKENA ALOHA." When we entered the anchorage with our boat, local children playing in the surf reiterated that sentiment. They stopped what they were doing long enough to wave and yell repeatedly, "Aloha! Aloha! Aloha!"

APPROACH

Kauhakō Bay is 2.9 miles south of Hōnaunau. Approaching from the north, shortly before arriving at the cove, you'll pass the village, a small collection of houses. A reef extends a short distance from the point immediately south of town, but water breaks on it, giving good warning to boaters.

When you've passed the village of Ho'okena and the reef, you can look into Kauhakō Bay and see a red-roofed building in the trees and the "HOOKENA ALOHA" sign on the rock wall behind the rock outcropping on the northwest corner of the bay.

From Hōnaunau Bay, the coastline is quite low all the way until Ho'okena Bay, where the *pali* rises almost 100 feet from the water's edge on the east shore.

The beach itself is a good landmark. It is a south-facing beach of gray sand with a restroom and a sometime snack bar prominent on the west end. On the beach, too, are a grove of palm trees and a few canoes.

Welcoming sign

Approaching from the south, you'll have few clear waypoints, other than Ka Lae, 34.5 miles to the southeast. The same warning about the reef at the corner of the bay applies to those coming up from the south: Rocks extend out from the south point of Kauhakō.

ANCHORAGE

Kauhakō Bay, at Ho'okena, is small, about .25 mile deep and .50 mile wide, but it can easily accommodate 5 or 6 boats. Some south swell enters the cove, but boats anchored here have protection from north and east swell. The lack of protection from westerly winds and swells in the cove will rarely be a problem since the island experiences few west winds.

The best anchorage in the cove is near the cliffs on the east side. We have anchored about 150 feet from the cliffs, midway between the beach to the north and the southern extreme of the cove in about 20 feet of water. The sand bottom provides excellent holding. The water is so clear we watched our anchor go down and dig in. This is a textbook perfect anchorage.

FACILITIES

Restrooms
Showers (fee)

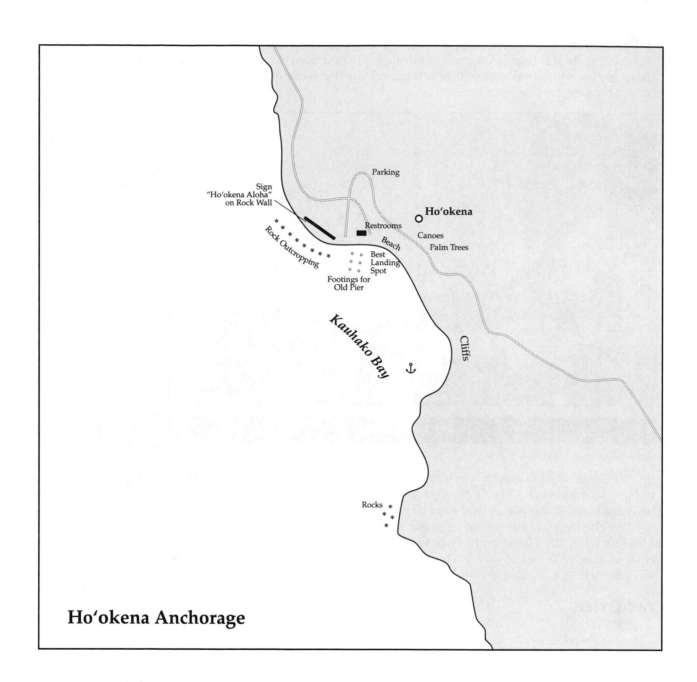

Parking

Sign
"Ho'okena Aloha"
on Rock Wall

Ho'okena

Restrooms

Rock Outcropping

Beach

Canoes
Palm Trees

Best
Landing
Spot

Footings for
Old Pier

Kauhako Bay

Cliffs

Rocks

Ho'okena Anchorage

HONOMALINO BAY
CHART #19320
LAT. N19° 10.242 LONG. W155° 54.491 (ANCHORAGE)

Honomalino Bay is one of the great destinations for cruising boaters in Hawai'i. It has it all: isolation, great sand bottom for anchoring, protection from the waves that sweep into other anchorages, lovely coral bottom for snorkeling, large, private beach, and dramatic, clear water. What more could any boater ask for?

The charts show this isolated bay between Miloli'i and Okoe but fail to give it a name. Similarly, the *Coast Pilot* ignores it completely. As a result, we've found only one other boater who has even heard of it, much less anchored in it.

This now mostly deserted bay was once the site of a fishing and farming community. Near the bay and along the gulch are numerous sites from centuries past.

Quiet anchorages lead to contemplation.

The setting here is perfect. The black sand beach (more of a dark gray than black) sweeps in a long crescent from lava flows at either end defining the north side of the bay. Behind the beach is a large grove of coco palms, with a number of vacation homes tucked among the trees. When we visited this bay, boards covered the windows of all the homes, and we could see little sign of recent habitation. Access to this beach (other than by boat) is along a 5-mile road through chunky, grinding 'a'a lava; hence it has not become one of the "hot spots" on the coast. If you anchor here, you might see a few visitors on the weekend, but during the week you're likely to have both the anchorage and the beach entirely to yourself.

You can take your tender ashore at the northwest corner of the beach, where the slight swell will almost certainly result in a dry landing. Ashore you will enjoy the beach and maybe even a little hike along the road that wanders off from the east side of the anchorage up through the lava flows.

At some point during your stay at Honomalino Bay, you should get into the water with mask, fins, and snorkel to enjoy fish and coral between your anchored boat and the beach and the wall to the east. The water clarity here is so good that you'll have 50 feet of visibility almost every day of the year.

At night, the only lights visible from Honomalino Bay come from many miles away, on the highway high on the mountain above. The "vog" (a haze that forms when the volcano is active) sometimes drifts over this part of the Kona Coast, making for a dramatic sun show late in the afternoon. From about 1600 until it sets, the sun is a brilliant coral red disk, sharply outlined through the haze. At sundown, the full western sky glows coral and scarlet. Then the vog disappears, leaving a clear sky in which the stars blaze.

APPROACH

Approaching from the north, you can use the town of Miloli'i to help identify Honomalino. Numerous homes ascend the slopes at Miloli'i. A small pier extends from the black sand beach, and a few mooring buoys float seaward of the pier. From Miloli'i, Honomalino Bay lies only 1.0 mile south. To avoid the rocks at the north entrance, swing wide and enter the center of the bay.

From Ka Lae Point, Honomalino is 22 miles northwest. For boaters coming from the south, the best landmark is the one put there by the volcano many years ago: the lava flow that extends out into the ocean .25 mile from the shoreline, forming Hanamalo and Mokunai'ā points. Honomalino is exactly 1.0 mile north of Hanamalo Point, the southern edge of that lava flow. As you come around the lava flow, you will see Honomalino.

Two bright red-roofed buildings sit among the palm trees growing north of the beach, making the bay easy to distinguish. Seaward of the buildings, water breaks on the many rocks and boulders of Kapulau Point, which protects this anchorage from any north swell.

ANCHORAGE

Once inside the bay, which has a width of nearly .30 mile, head north toward the beach. Watch the bottom carefully so you drop your anchor in sand rather than in the rocks. Though the clarity of the water here is remarkable, the sand bottom is a little more difficult than normal to recognize since it's a black (or gray) sand bottom. The rocks with their generous covering of coral, however, are easily distinguished, even in low light.

Generally speaking, rocks and coral cover the bottom within 150 yards of the beach. The remainder of the bay has primarily a sand bottom that provides excellent holding. Anchor in 20-25 feet of water.

The configuration of this bay assures boaters good protection from winds from the north, south, or east. The boat motion is mild, but a flopper stopper is a good idea since boats tend to lie beam-on to the waves after the winds die out during the night. The boats anchored closest to the beach will have the most comfortable motion because they are most protected by the point on the northwest corner of the anchorage.

Honomalino is large enough for 5 or 6 boats to anchor safely.

FACILITIES

None

'A'a lava and black sand beach

Honomalino Bay

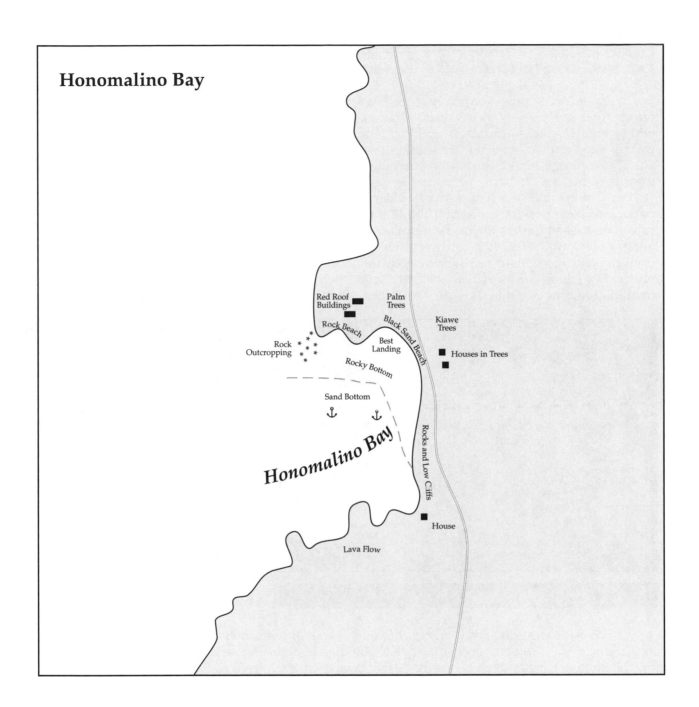

Red Roof
Buildings

Palm
Trees

Kiawe
Trees

Rock Beach

Black Sand Beach

Rock
Outcropping

Best
Landing

Houses in Trees

Rocky Bottom

Sand Bottom

Honomalino Bay

Rocks and Low Cliffs

House

Lava Flow

OKOE BAY
CHART #19320
LAT. N19° 09.270 LONG. W155 54.980 (ANCHORAGE)

Okoe is the most southerly of the bays along the west coast of Hawai'i that can be counted on as good anchorages. This minute bay has a stark beauty typical of the South Kona Coast, with a small black sand beach and low lava and reefs deepened to a jet black by the breaking water. *Kiawe* trees between the sand and the lava add contrast.

The huge boulders scattered on the bottom near the beach have healthy stands of coral growing on them. In some areas these coral heads are less than 6 feet deep.

Unfortunately, these same boulders and the shallow water that make great snorkeling make less than perfect anchoring. Still, it can be a good destination. Although cruising boaters rarely visit Okoe Bay, some of the more adventuresome Hawaiian boaters go back to anchor here again and again. They like to travel from Mānele Bay, on Lāna'i, or some similar stopover, and then make an overnight passage directly to Okoe. From this bay, the southernmost anchorage on the Big Island for most boaters, they begin their cruise of the Kona Coast. Some sportfishermen also anchor at Okoe Bay now and then when they are returning late from a fishing trip to Ka Lae.

Carricklee anchored at Okoe

Okoe is another good place to snorkel along the Kona Coast. The beautiful coral here is unusual in that it is atop large boulders.

To go ashore, the best beach landing is at the west end of the 200-yard beach. At the east end of the beach in the *kiawe* trees is a nicely kept yellow house, apparently a vacation cottage. A sandy road in front of the yellow house leads to a rocky road through the lava flow, probably not a road that will stimulate you to go far, though it is interesting to look at. The road bed is nothing but graded 'a'a lava.

APPROACH

If you're traveling south along the coast, you can use Miloli'i village as a point of reference for finding Okoe. You can recognize Miloli"i by the large number of houses atop the low cliffs and up the slopes, the small pier, and the few mooring buoys. From Miloli'i, Hanamalo Point, a bed of black 'a'a lava jutting out into the ocean, is 1.75 miles. Okoe Bay is tucked under the south side of Hanamalo Point, .25 mile east.

Okoe Bay is 20 miles northwest of Ka Lae. Okoe is somewhat difficult to find from this direction, though you can use as a landmark Hanamalo Point, the prominent lava flow on the north. But, since lava flows are common along this coast, you may discover using a GPS to be the best way to find Okoe. Another feature of this bay that may help you locate it is that, unlike virtually all the other harbors and bays to the south, Okoe Bay faces south rather than west.

ANCHORAGE

The anchorage is off the black sand beach in front of the *kiawe* trees, at the point where the coastline changes from an east-west orientation to a southerly direction. If you look closely, you can see a yellow house in the *kiawe* trees.

The anchorage is relatively shallow, less than 10 feet in some areas, so don't be in a hurry as you enter. Also, shallow-lying rocks foul the western side of the anchorage. Enter the anchorage from the south rather than hugging the north shore as you round Hanamalo Point.

If you enter Okoe Bay from a point directly south and proceed slowly, you'll see some small sand patches about 200 yards off the beach, most of them too small for comfortable anchoring. Close to the beach, several large sea mounts rise to within 6 feet of the surface. You may want to come back to these to snorkel after you've anchored your boat elsewhere.

However, "elsewhere" does not mean a place where you can avoid the rocks altogether, for the bottom here is fairly well covered with rocks. Because the sand patches are so small, your anchor and chain will almost surely drag across or hook around a few rocks, both while you're setting the anchor and when your boat swings. By staying at least 200 yards out from the beach, you can find depths of 15-25 feet, where you can drop your anchor without harm to the coral. For anchoring at Okoe, a Bruce, a Delta, or a CQR anchor will do better on this rocky bottom than a fluke-style anchor.

Kiawe trees behind the beach at Okoe

When we anchored at Okoe, we did drop our anchor in a sand patch, but that anchor did, in fact, come up against a rock before it was thoroughly dug in. Needless to say, we didn't move the large rock, and we didn't drag anchor. We just stopped. When we pulled up our anchor to leave, we were careful to use the motor to move ahead so that we were forward of the position of our anchor before we lifted it. By doing so, we assured ourselves the anchor would not become lodged permanently behind the rock.

In Okoe you can expect to have a comfortable motion on the boat in most weather conditions. With the lava flow on the north side of the anchorage extending .25 mile to the west, the normal northerly swell is blocked completely, leaving the water in the anchorage calm. Clearly, though, this anchorage would not be comfortable if a south wind or swell set in. If the forecast calls for south winds or swell, don't go to Okoe; if you hear such a forecast when you're anchored at Okoe, get out.

Okoe Bay is a small bay, with room for only a few boats. If other boats are anchored at Okoe when you arrive, go around the corner to Honomalino Bay. In fact, if you have trouble finding a good sand patch you might want to explore Okoe during the day and move around the corner to Honomalino for the night. You'll sleep better.

FACILITIES

None

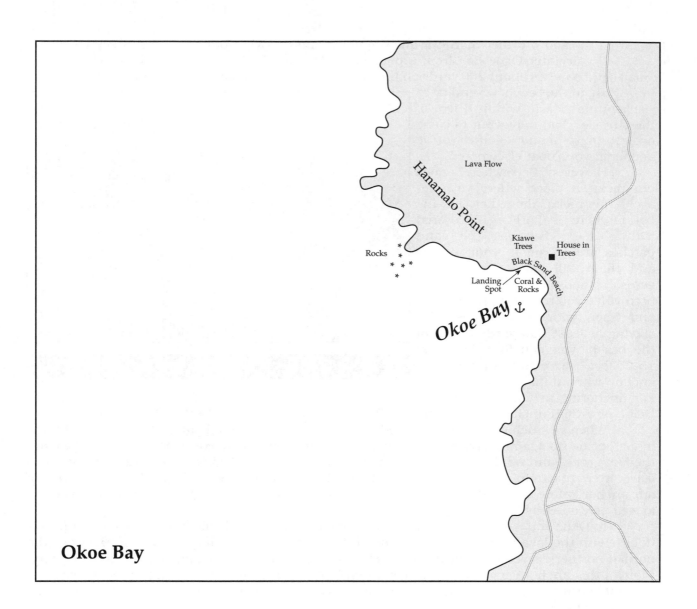

Lava Flow

Hanamalo Point

Kiawe
Trees

House in
Trees

Rocks

Black Sand Beach

Landing
Spot

Coral &
Rocks

Okoe Bay

Okoe Bay

THE ISLAND OF MAUI

THE VALLEY ISLE

Looking toward Lahaina Roadstead

Ua puni 'o Maui me ka nani, 'a'ohe mea like aku.
("Maui is surrounded by beauty, and there is none to equal it.")

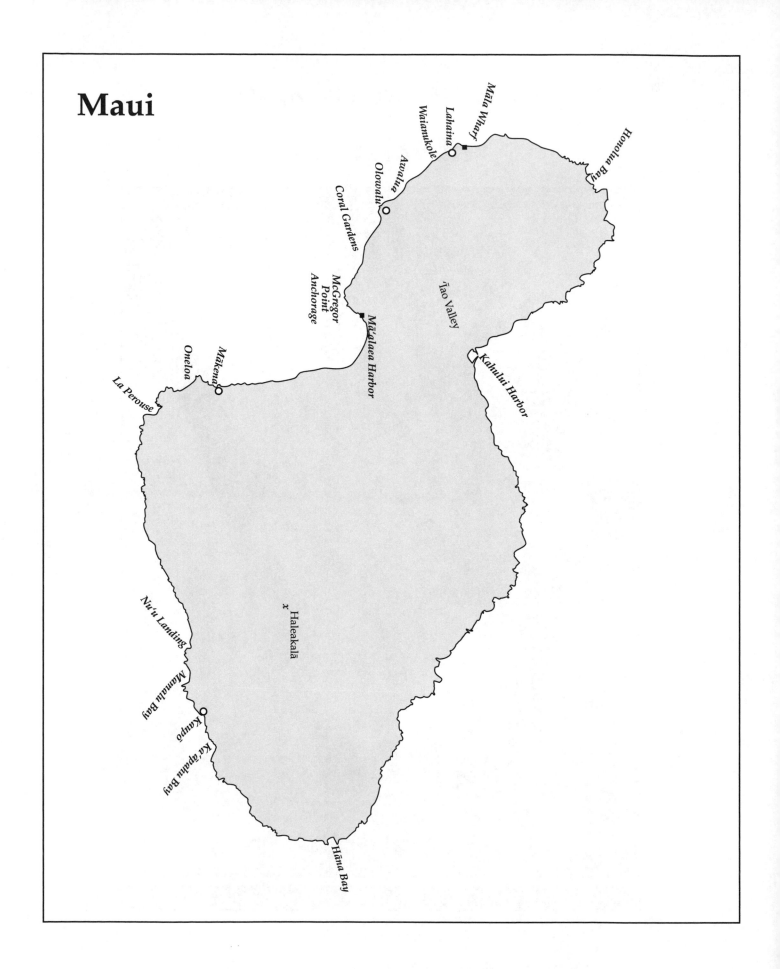

Maui

Honolua Bay

Maʻla Wharf

Lahaina

Waiamukole

Awalua

Olowalu

Coral Gardens

McGregor Point Anchorage

Māʻalaea Harbor

ʻĪao Valley

Kahului Harbor

Oneloa

Mākena

La Perouse

Nuʻu Landing

Manula Bay

Kaupō

Kaʻāpāhu Bay

Haleakalā
x

Hāna Bay

In the oral history of Hawai'i, Māui, the trickster demigod, was born of a human mother, Hina-a-ke-ahi ("Hina of the fire"), His father was in some chants a human, in others a god. In at least one chant Māui had no father at all; Hina conceived him even though, "She had not lived with a man." He was, in some legends, the creator of all the Islands, fishing them up from the bottom of the ocean. Continuing to provide for the people of Hawai'i, he secured fire from a mudhen for them and gained for them more hours of daylight by lassoing the genitals of the sun god and forcing him to slow down, He is also credited with lifting the sky so the people would no longer have to crawl but could walk upright. A trickster of legendary proportions, his final trick proved to be the fatal one. When he crawled into the vagina of the powerful goddess Hina while she was sleeping, the laughing of the birds around him awoke her, and she angrily squeezed him to death inside her.

Though his delight in pulling pranks led to an undignified death, this fun-loving spirit is surely one of the reasons the Hawaiians loved him enough to name an island in his honor. In fact, Maui is the only island in the Hawaiian Chain to be given the name of a god.

Maui, the Valley Island, would surely do honor to any deity. Along the coasts are beaches of every size and color: the long white sand beach that is more or less continuous along the coast of West Maui; the black and red and green sand beaches around Hāna on the east side; the curving white beaches on the north shore near Pa'ia, where the surf breaks over the reefs in stupendous bursts of white and aquamarine. Ashore are distinct lava rivers, hundreds of steep cliffs eroded by wind and water, fields of sugar cane, tropical jungles, historic small towns, and mysterious gorges disappearing into the white clouds.

The Upcountry of Maui is a different kind of treat, with its rolling green pastures dotted with cattle and horses and an occasional *paniolo* (cowboy); here, the biggest and best known rodeo in the state, the Makawao Rodeo, celebrates Independence Day. Narrow roads wind past purple-blossomed jacaranda trees; lantana, with its tidy little blossoms of orange and yellow, curls along the roadside and under the wire cattle fences. Capping it all, majestic Haleakalā, the "house of the sun" presides, its highest peak, Pu'u'ula'ula (10,023 feet), sometimes showing itself through the clouds, sometimes not.

Maui, in the heart of the state of Hawai'i, may well become the center of your cruise in the Islands. It has more anchorages and harbors than any of the other islands.

'Īao Needle

Tug and barge in Kahului Harbor

The four islands comprising Maui County—Kahoʻolawe, Lānaʻi, Molokaʻi, and Maui—were, geologists believe, once connected. The sea inundated the connections after the last ice age, leaving exposed the four islands (or five, if you count little Molokini). They form a rough circle, creating a kind of large ocean lake, the favorite calving and breeding grounds of the humpback whales that annually migrate from Alaska and the Arctic.

Boaters can often cross this "lake" without deterrence from the weather. Too, the distances from Maui to some anchorages and harbors on Molokaʻi and Lānaʻi are short. Consequently, a cruising sailor could use Maui as a base from which to make day or weekend trips to both islands, as local sailors do.

The four harbors on Maui—Kahului, Hāna, Māʻalaea, and Lahaina—are about as different from one another as they can be and still be on the same island.

Kahului is the only deep-water commercial harbor on the island, where barges and ships bring in food, manufactured goods, and building materials to supply the entire island and take out the island's produce: beef, sugar, pineapple, vegetables and flowers. The city of Kahului, while small by mainland standards, is the island's largest, made even more so by its much smaller twin city, Wailuku, the county seat of Maui County. In Kahului, you'll have the best access on the island to boat parts, supplies, or provisions.

View from Haleakalā

Hāna is the most remote of the harbors, the most picturesque, and the least used. It still has standing the old commercial dock that has not been in use commercially for a number of years, but a few trailerable fishing boats are launched at the ramp behind the dock each day. You may well be the only cruising boat in Hāna.

Ashore is a lush tropical forest that climbs the mountain behind the town to the rain clouds above. The town is small—you can walk all the city streets in an hour or so. No commercial charter boats operate out of Hāna. The tourists come here to play golf or simply to get away from the crowds elsewhere. Some even come merely to be able to boast, "I survived the road to Hāna." But you'll not encounter many of these tourists on the beaches nor in the two small markets. Walking around town, you may encounter no one! What you will find is a seclusion and quietude wholly unlike the other harbors.

Māʻalaea and Lahaina have a bit more in common: they are both on the leeward side of the island, have long stretches of white sand beach, and are essentially warm and dry. For these reasons, both harbors have thriving fishing, diving and snorkeling, and whale-watching charter operations. The differences are nonetheless great.

Māʻalaea Bay, sitting on the southwest corner of the flat, narrow isthmus that joins West Maui and East Maui, has little more than a small harbor with a handful of restaurants ashore and a few hotels and condominiums spread along the beach. However, it is also the site of a splendid new tropical aquarium, the Maui Ocean Center, and in the bay is the Māʻalaea Pipeline, with the fastest breaking surf in the Islands.

On the other hand, Lahaina, once reported to be the whaling capital of the world, has been for several hundred years a busy place of habitation and trade. Its city front, a combination of both old and new buildings, enhances the beauty of the roadstead. Symmetrical cane fields frame the triangular residential area on two sides, and, beyond the fields, the West Maui Mountains rise in steep green splendor until they disappear into the puffy white cotton. The surf breaking along the reef on either side of the channel into the harbor repeats the white of the clouds, and its turquoise combines the green of the hills and the blue of the sky.

The roadsteads and anchorages on Maui range, with some frequency, up and down the southern and eastern coasts of the island, a few giving boaters access to villages but most not; many with fine sand beaches, others with rocks and gravel; some with close-up views of lava flows, others with views of weathered cliffs and gulches; but all featuring some kind of spectacular water world. Some will be comfortable and safe in northerly winds, others, only in southerlies.

This great variety in harbors, roadsteads, and anchorages results from the geological history of Maui, after Hawai'i the youngest of the islands. Like all the other Hawaiian Islands, it, too, is the result of volcanic activity millions of years ago. As do the others, it has the varied features of a small continent, with mountains, plains, sandy beaches and reefs, desert-like south and west sides, and a tropical rain forest on the east.

Maui began as two separate shield volcanoes, one now called the West Maui Mountains, about two millions years old, and the second, Haleakalā, about a million years younger. The two volcanoes created two islands that have during the last million years become one. A narrow isthmus joined the two shield volcanoes, giving the resulting one island the appearance of the carved granite bust of a woman, tipped over and about to fall on tiny Kaho'olawe. The head of the bust is West Maui, and the chest is East Maui. On either side of the isthmus–low, flat, and sandy–are the two major working harbors on the island, Kahului on the north and Mā'alaea on the south.

Sandy beaches, primarily along the eastern and southern shores, have resulted from erosion of the lava cliffs or from the alluvial deposits of streams. The cliffs and the gorges of the volcanic coasts of both East and West Maui show the effects of erosion on the originally sloped lava flows.

While a youngster among the islands geologically, Maui lays claim to a long cultural history. Before the arrival of the first colonizing Polynesians, the legendary demi-god Māui cast his snare to slow down the sun, some claimed from atop Haleakalā, others, from Ka'uiki Head, at Hāna. Hāna's further claim to historical significance is as the birth site of Ka'ahumanu, the favorite wife of Kamehameha. After Kamehameha's death in 1819, Ka'ahumanu persuaded the irresolute son of the king, Liholiho, to begin abandoning the ancient system of *kapu* that had so restricted the lives of the Hawaiians, especially the women.

By this time, Lahaina had already become a major shipping port for the exportation of the sandalwood once covering many of the slopes of these islands. It was also a primary target for the zeal of New England missionaries, who began arriving in Lahaina in 1823. In the 1820s, also, the town began its evolution (the missionaries would claim *devolution*) into the whaling capital of the world, for the whalers, with their drinking and womanizing, turned the town into a dissolute port.

The rich soil of the isthmus and lower mountain slopes has made this island a significant agricultural center, from the fruits and vegetables supplied to the early explorer and whaling vessels to the sugar and pineapple plantations that prospered in the 19th and early 20th centuries. In the latter half of the 20th Century, Maui vegetables and flowers have become much prized throughout the Islands.

A seat of government for Maui royalty from the 16th century on, in 1819 Lahaina became the center of the Hawaiian government when Kamehameha II assumed the throne, and it remained so until 1845. Thus, Lahaina is where modern Hawaiian government began.

Maui is second among the Hawaiian Islands, after O'ahu, in attracting tourists, to most cruising sailors probably a dubious distinction. For what boaters seek usually is to get away from the crowds. Most of these tourists, however, do not come by boat, nor will you find them in most anchorages. They frequent the towns, where the hotels, restaurants, and shops are, though some do, of course, visit sites of cultural and natural interest. You can find plenty of spots to anchor for a day or two or three and not see another boat in the anchorage nor even anyone on the beach. Fortunately, too, though, the towns are there to provide you with the opportunity to shop for provisions, to take on fuel and water, and to visit stimulating sites ashore.

KAHULUI HARBOR
CHARTS #19342, 19347
LAT. N20° 55.910 LONG. W156° 28.500 (ENTRANCE BUOY)

Of all the major harbors in the Hawaiian Islands, Kahului is in many ways the most logical first stop for the cruising boater. It is a port of entry, but more than that, it has the closest complete shopping of any harbor in the Islands. Except for boat repairs and maintenance, the facilities at Kahului are more convenient to the harbor than even those of Honolulu. And the harbormaster and his staff, friendly and helpful, welcome visiting boaters.

A cruise ship entering Kahului

Kahului does not, in fact, appear on the itineraries of most cruising boaters because of its location and because of its reputation as a strictly commercial harbor. Located on the windward side of the island of Maui, it does not beckon to visitors the way Lahaina does. While boaters anchored here can bask in sunshine and light winds many days, especially during the summer months, strong tradewinds can howl in Kahului any month of the year, a daunting prospect to some boaters, who might otherwise consider a stop here.

If you are dissuaded from a stop here for those reasons, though, you'll be missing one of the cleanest, best run harbors in the state in terms of facilities for handling ships and barges. Although a commercial harbor with a large volume of ship and barge traffic, Kahului seems neither crowded nor overly busy because of its size, about 0.5 mile deep and 0.75 miles wide. The ships and barges have exclusive use of Piers 1, 2, and 3, on the east side of the harbor. The west side of the harbor, where the launch ramp is located, is too shallow for all but trailerable boats to navigate. In the center of the harbor at the extreme south section, between the turning basin and the beach, is a small anchorage area that will accommodate six or eight cruising boats.

Because of its breakwater, Kahului is an excellent all-weather harbor. Boats sit comfortably at anchor here even when strong tradewinds whistle through the rigging.

Visiting boaters are allowed to anchor three days at Kahului Harbor before being required to move on to another anchorage.

The town of Kahului is immediately south of the harbor, with three shopping centers not more than a mile away. In addition to the shopping centers, boaters can find just about any service desired, including rental cars to go sightseeing and an international airport. Though over a million visitors a year come through this airport, few of them tarry in Kahului, hardly a tourist mecca. Kahului lacks much of what visitors expect to find when they come to Hawai'i. Its twin, Wailuku, 3 miles northwest, has most of the preserved historical sites around Kahului Bay. Hāna has the isolation and beauty of a tropical jungle. The West Coast has the more temperate weather and inviting beaches.

From the anchorage area at this large harbor, you'll have no doubt you're in an urban environment. Ships and tugs with barges lie up daily to the piers in Kahului, airplanes take off regularly from the airport to the east, and cars and trucks create a fairly steady stream along the highway to the west. Yet the anchorage is distant enough from all these potential sources of bothersome noise that, on a boat at anchor, you can still feel isolated. After all, you'll probably have the whole place to yourself except for the occasional sea kayaker, canoeist, or swimmer.

Kahului, despite the lack of pre-contact sites to attract visitors, has its place in Hawaiian history. In the last decade of the 18th century, Kamehameha I landed his war canoes from the Big Island at Kahului Bay to continue his campaign to

Dinner from Kahului Bay

conquer Maui. From the bay, he went on to what is now called Wailuku and engaged the warriors of the Maui chief Kalanikūpule in a battle that continued up into the 'Īao Valley and that Kamehameha won decisively. (Wailuku and Kahului may have gained their names after this battle; Wailuku means "water of destruction," signifying that the 'Īao Stream flowing into the sea was red with the blood of the slain warriors, and Kahului means "the winning." Both names, however, may have earlier origins.)

In 1900 the bubonic plague was the invader, resulting in the town's deliberately being burned to the ground to halt the spread of the disease. It has risen, if not beautifully at least prosperously, from the ashes.

On January 1, 1942, the most contemporary invasion of Kahului occurred. Japanese submarines shelled the bay but inflicted little damage.

The growth of Kahului began after the war with the development in 1949 of the subdivision Hale Koa, with modestly priced houses, affordable for the pineapple and sugar workers. Parks, commercial and industrial centers and a hospital soon followed.

Kahului Harbor has a narrow beach that is adequate for swimming, but the water hasn't the sparkling clarity of that of either Hāna or of West Maui. You'll probably see more fishermen,

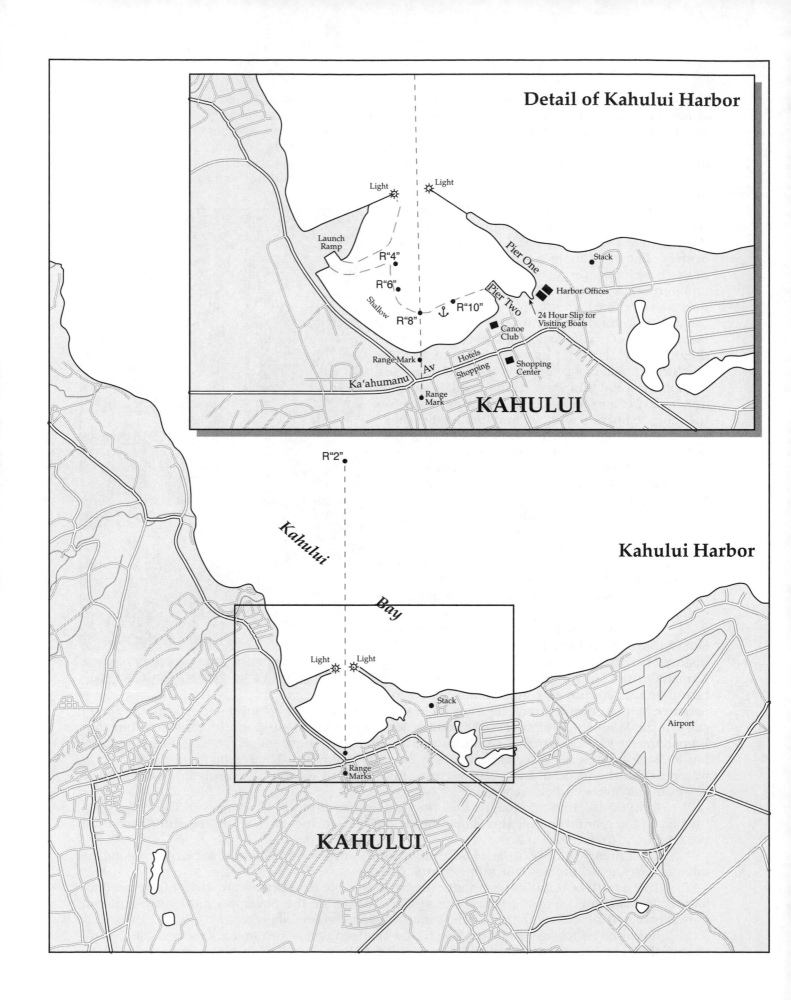

Detail of Kahului Harbor

Light

Light

Launch
Ramp

Pier One

Stack

R"4"

R"6"

R"10"

Pier Two

Harbor Offices

Shallow

R"8"

24 Hour Slip for
Visiting Boats

Canoe
Club

Range Mark

Av

Hotels

Shopping

Shopping
Center

Ka'ahumanu

Range
Mark

KAHULUI

R"2"

Kahului

Kahului Harbor

Bay

Light

Light

Stack

Airport

Range
Marks

KAHULUI

boaters, and *limu* (seaweed) pickers than swimmers in this harbor. The Kanahā Beach Park is a much better choice for water sports, having a good beach, light but steady winds for the beginning surfboarder, and a picnic area. Unfortunately, it's slightly over 2 miles from the anchorage.

For a viewing of nature, go to the Kanahā Pond Waterfowl Sanctuary, not quite so far away from the harbor. This sanctuary provides a suitable habitat for two endangered species of indigenous birds, the Hawaiian stilt and the Hawaiian coot. For this reason, it is one of the most important bird sanctuaries in all the Islands

However ideal Kahului might appear from the previous description, one problem keeps this harbor from becoming a perfect destination: its location on the windward side of Maui. Whenever strong trades are blowing, the winds and waves are fearsome in the area. Boaters who want to visit Kahului should plan to do so only when moderate or light winds are blowing.

APPROACH

If you plan to make Kahului Harbor your first landfall in the Islands after an ocean crossing from the Mainland, you will be approaching from the northeast. As you near Maui, the island will appear as two separate islands until you are within 4-5 miles. Then you'll be able to see the isthmus connecting the mountains of West Maui and Haleakalā to the east. Although the clouds may obscure the peaks of the mountains, you should be able to see the town of Kahului at the base of the West Maui Mountains.

The first landmark you see will be the smoke stack on the Kahului Power Plant, adjacent to the east end of the harbor. Next, identify the R"2" buoy 1.6 miles from the harbor breakwater. After passing this buoy, locate the range marks south of the harbor. The bearing from the buoy to the entrance is approximately 166° magnetic (177° true).

From other harbors in Hawaii, you will almost certainly approach from the west. When coming from the south side of Maui and around the west end, most boaters spend a night at Honolua. Then they leave early the next day in order to be well underway before the winds build, expecting to complete the 16-mile passage from Honolua to Kahului before noon.

Boaters from islands west of Maui often stop for a night at one of the eastern harbors on Moloka'i, such as Kamalō or Pūko'o, and then begin the crossing of the Pailolo Channel at dawn in order to be in Kahului shortly after noon. These boaters sometimes work their way up the east shore of Moloka'i as far as Cape Hālawa before heading across the Pailolo. From Hālawa to Kahului is only slightly more than 20 miles.

ANCHORAGE AND BERTHING

Kahului Harbor is a busy, well-run harbor, clean and attractive. As many as three or four tugs with barges in tow will arrive on a single day, and at least one cruise ship arrives each week. You must be careful to anchor where your boat is clear of the turning basin.

Once inside the breakwater, continue south until you get to the R "8" buoy. Do not go beyond the "8" buoy as the bottom shallows up quickly there. Rather, turn immediately to port, and proceed toward the R "10" buoy. Anchor south of an imaginary line drawn between those two buoys. The best anchorage, where a sand bottom will provide excellent holding, is about 100 feet south of the line between these two buoys. Anchor in 10-18 feet of water.

Once anchored, check in with the harbormaster. The harbor office, open weekdays from 0745 to 1600, is across the road at the east end of the harbor.

At the present time, Kahului Harbor offers no convenient place to leave your tender. The best option we found is to take the tender ashore and ask permission to leave it on the grounds of one of the two canoe clubs 200 yards to the east of the anchorage area. This option has two fairly serious drawbacks: one, you may not find anyone around the canoe clubs to give you permission to leave your tender ashore there, and, two, thefts have been reported in this area, apparently committed by the street people hanging around the beach near one of the canoe clubs.

Beach and canoe club

Kahului Harbormaster 808-873-3350

FACILITIES

At the harbor:
    Telephone
In Kahului:
    Airport
    Banks
    Car Rental
    Fuel (gasoline & diesel, by jerry jugs)
    Grocery Stores
    Hardware Stores (with some boat parts)
    Hospital

    Laundromat
    Library
    Movie Theaters
    Post Office
    Propane
    Restaurants
    Shops

HONOLUA BAY
CHART #19347
LAT. N21° 00.905 LONG. W156° 38.417 (ANCHORAGE)

Honolua ("two bays") is part of a Marine Life Conservation District that includes the second of the "two bays," now called Mokulē'ia Bay. Honolua has long been a favorite anchorage of cruising boaters in the Islands. One reason is the excellent protection in the anchorage. Līpoa Point juts far out into the channel and protects the bay from north and east winds; the island, of course, protects it from the east and south. Thus, boats sit comfortably here, with no more than a gentle motion to remind those aboard that they're lucky enough to be on a boat.

Too, Honolua has a beauty unique among Hawaiian anchorages. As in many other anchorages in Hawai'i, in Honolua rocky cliffs of lava and boulders rise immediately from the water's edge, in a cozy embrace of the bay. But these steep cliffs rise not to more rocks and boulders

Pineapple pickers

but to tropical vegetation of deep emerald green. Behind the beach at the head of the bay, this emerald color also extends down the hill and across the narrow valley formed by the Honolua River. Above all this green, the West Maui Mountains add another layer of color that sometimes touches the clouds.

The trees and plants are almost the last vestiges of the headquarters, homes, and businesses associated with the Honolua Ranch. Cattle hides and coffee went out from a pier on lighters to waiting steamers. The ranch began planting pineapple in 1914 and gradually phased out the cattle operation. In 1915 the owners of the Honolua Ranch moved everything to Honokahua, inland of the bay. The 1946 tsunami destroyed what was left of the old landing.

In 1976 the history-making voyage of a replica of the double-hulled canoes believed to have brought the first Polynesians, the original settlers of the Hawaiian Islands, began at Honolua. With no modern navigational aids, not even the sextant, the crew of the replica, the *Hokule'a*, successfully sailed to Tahiti in 34 days.

Though the beach at Honolua is not much for sunbathing or walking, it's pretty enough to look at from the water. At the head of the bay—to the east—is a stand of palm trees and the old, unused concrete launch ramp. The beach itself is nothing more than a small, narrow strip of rocks between the water and the vegetation 100 feet from the water's edge.

To many boaters, and most tourists, the primary attraction to Honolua is the underwater world. In the crystalline water grow healthy stands of coral, with a profusion of tropical fish, sea turtles, and moray and spotted eels. Because this bay has also long been a Marine Life Conservation Area, some species of fish here have little fear of their human observers. Underwater photographic opportunities abound, as the fish often continue what they're doing even when approached closely.

Another attraction to the waters around Honolua is the surfing. Some surfers regard the breakers off Līpoa Point to the north or Mokulēʻia Bay to the south as the best on Maui and among the best in the world. As a boater, you'll be relieved to learn that the water inside the bay itself is far too calm for that particular activity.

Some boaters complain that its beauty has been its undoing, that the hundreds of snorkelers and divers who visit Honolua every day make it an unpleasant place to anchor. Fortunately, however, the bay is large enough so that the snorkelers who enter the water from the beach rarely swim as far offshore as the anchored boats. And the snorkelers off the charter boats are in the water for such a short time they're no problem either. Surprisingly for a place with such a splendid underwater world, Honolua does not appear to be overcrowded.

Besides, all the charter boats and most of the visitors on the shoreline leave long before dark. Then the sailors have the bay all to themselves. This is a beautiful bay at night, too. An occasional car light will glow on the highway skirting the cliffs to the north, but you'll not hear much noise from the road at night. (The one exception to the general quiet at Honolua is the sound of the trucks hauling pineapples down this road during the day. The drivers of these laden trucks use the engine brakes to slow on the sharp curve at Honolua and sound their trucks' air horns to warn of their approach on this narrow stretch of the Honoapiʻilani Highway.)

You might think this beautiful bay will usually be crowded with cruising boats, but, despite the number of local boaters who profess to love this spot, yours will likely be the only boat left in the anchorage once the charter boats have gone for the day.

APPROACH

Honolua Bay is on the northwest corner of Maui. If you're approaching from the north and west, use Līpoa Point, only .65 mile north of Honolua, for a landmark. From the south, Honolua is about 10.0 miles from Lahaina. Coming to the bay from Lānaʻi, you can use the westernmost point of land on Maui, Kekaʻa Point, for a landfall. From this point to Honolua is 6.5 miles northeast. Farther north along the coast is Hāwea Point, 1.5 miles from Honolua. When you pass Hāwea Point, you can see into Honolua Bay.

Typically, when boaters approach Honolua, white caps and large waves fill the Pailolo Channel. Inside the bay, however, the motion stops, and the pleasure begins.

As you enter the bay, don't hug the shoreline; it has rocks near the surface along both the north and south sides.

ANCHORAGE

The best anchorage in the bay is in the center. The shorelines to the north and south have rocks and reefs. The sand patch in the center, easily 100 yards wide in places, extends from a point about 500 yards from shore to a point about 150 yards from shore. In addition to the large sand patch in the middle of the bay, you can find smaller ones in various other areas. With a bit of a search, you'll find one that suits you perfectly. Seeing the areas of sand is easy when the sun is high, but they're more difficult to spot after 1600.

Be on the lookout for snorkelers and swimmers in the water as you enter the bay.

Water depths in Honolua vary. Expect to drop in 35 feet of water in the center of the bay and less if you go closer to shore. The sand bottom provides excellent holding.

The winds will come from a variety of directions while you're anchored at Honolua. They'll come predominantly over the beach, out of the east, but they also may shift often and come out of the north. In either case, Honolua is well protected. However, when winds come out of the northwest or even the west, this anchorage can be quite uncomfortable. Honolua is best as a tradewinds anchorage, during the summer and fall.

FACILITIES

None

Honolua Bay

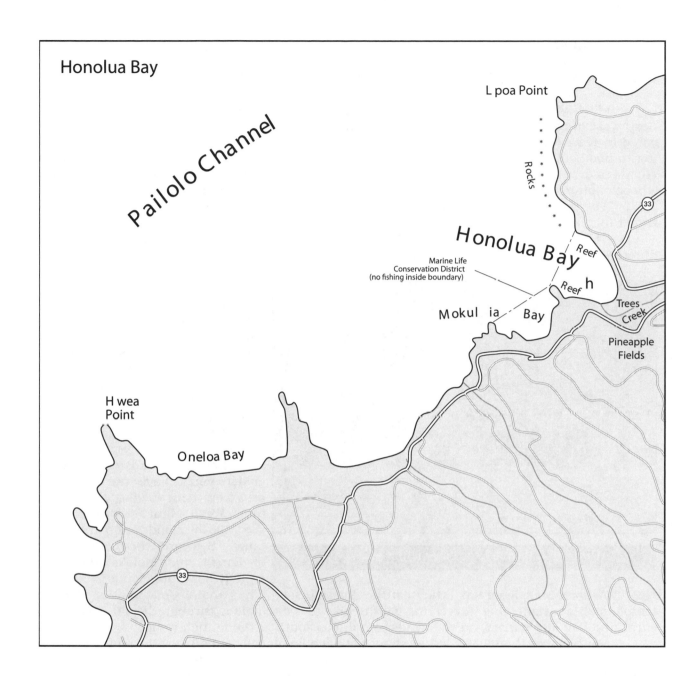

Honolua Bay

Pailolo Channel

L poa Point

Rocks

Honolua Bay

Reef

Marine Life
Conservation District
(no fishing inside boundary)

Reef h

Mokul ia Bay

Trees
Creek

Pineapple
Fields

33

H wea
Point

Oneloa Bay

33

MĀLA WHARF ANCHORAGE
CHART #19340, #19347, OR #19348
LATITUDE N20° 53.350 LONGITUDE W156° 41.420 (ANCHORAGE)

Māla Wharf has fallen down. What was once a beautiful pier extending into deep water northwest of Lahaina is now a mass of crumbling concrete. However, this beautiful pier, dedicated in 1922, was ill-conceived. This wharf was planned to eliminate the inconvenience of having to use lighters to load and unload steamers anchored in Lahaina Roadstead. Yet only two steamers ever landed here successfully. Strong currents and heavy surf damaged many others whose captains attempted to tie up at Māla. The state closed the wharf in 1950.

The protected indentation in the coastline at Māla is the site of a busy launch ramp for trailerable boats.

The tiny, quiet community of Māla is but a mile from busy Lahaina, but it has a wholly different ambiance. The sidewalks that line this roadway do not have the streams of tourists that one encounters in Lahaina, nor does the anchorage bustle with charter boats in and out, day and night. Yet the anchorage is close enough to Lahaina for you to avail yourself of the services and goods there, though the new Cannery Shopping Center, almost directly across the highway from the wharf, will have almost everything you'll need.

Buddhist Temple and sugar mill stack

The view of Māla lacks the beauty of Front Street, Lahaina, as seen from the roadstead, but otherwise you'll have the same view of green cane fields, the precipitous West Maui Mountains, and the billowy clouds atop the mountains. Seaward, the mountain tops of Lāna'i and Moloka'i sit under equally beautiful clouds.

Ashore, Māla itself has little to attract the sightseer. The Lahaina Jodo Mission Buddhist temple merits a visit. One interesting path to take to the temple is through the old Asian graveyard, desolate and barren, on the windswept dunes south of the launch ramp.

For boaters, though, Māla has some distinct advantages. Because of the reef to the south of the anchorage and the sharp indentation of the coastline between Hanaka'ō'ō and Pu'unoa points, boats moored or anchored at Māla do not roll as badly as do those at the Lahaina Roadstead. This indentation also results in much less current at Māla than at Lahaina, where the current often keeps boats beam-on to the winds. The winds at Māla, particularly if they're from the north, will be stronger than those at Lahaina, but these winds will more often than not be welcome to keep your boat cool.

The relevance of these comparisons between Māla Wharf and the Lahaina Roadstead is that the two are your choices of anchorages for seeing the sites in the town of Lahaina. The land division called *Māla* is at the northern end of Lahaina.

The one-mile walk into the heart of the activity on Front Steet in Lahaina is a pretty one, past houses with lush tropical gardens and then along the waterfront, where the wind has permanently bent the tall palm trees lining the shore. As you near the town, you'll have a fine view of the Lahaina Roadstead and, at the dock, the *Carthaginian II,* a replica of the square riggers that once carried freight across the seas.

Some boaters who speak Spanish think *māla* must mean "bad," this translation supported by the fact that in south or west winds Māla Wharf is a dangerous anchorage and one you should avoid—or vacate, if you are already here. North winds are far more common here than either south or west winds, but, because they're offshore, they present little danger for anchored boats. The majority of the time Māla Wharf is certainly not bad.

Launch ramp at Māla

In fact, what *māla* means in the Hawaiian language is "plantation or garden." The slopes above Māla remain a garden today, the green fields of sugar cane and pineapples nestled right up to the foot of the West Maui Mountains.

If the Māla Wharf anchorage area has a serious disadvantage, it is simply that Māla has become too popular. Private moorings monopolize most of the good anchoring area, leaving only marginally protected areas available for visiting boats. Some of the owners of the moored boats are aware of the problem and will generally offer assistance to visiting boaters looking for a suitable anchoring spot.

APPROACH

Māla Wharf anchorage is easy to identify on an approach from any direction. Ashore are many houses and a large apartment building, Lahaina Roads Vacation Rentals, immediately east of the anchorage. Palm trees stand out above the houses. Between the trees and the base of the West Maui Mountains are cane and pineapple fields.

Perhaps the most prominent of the landmarks is the stack of the old Pioneer sugar mill at Lahaina. This stack rises above all the other landmarks in the southeast corner of the anchorage.

To the south of the anchorage on Pu'unoa Point, the spire of the Lahaina Jodo Mission Buddhist Temple rises above the *kiawe* and palm trees. Near the Buddhist Temple on the south side of the anchorage is the crumbling Māla Wharf, which has a northwest-southeast orientation, and the launch ramp, built in 1979. Three or four pairs of channel markers outline the limits of the channel leading to the launch ramp.

From any direction, you'll also see from some distance away the many masts of the 20 or so sailboats anchored or moored here.

Coming from Honolua on the north, you'll pass numerous beaches, tiny coves, and large hotels and condominiums stretched along the coast. After the last hotel at Hanaka'ō'ō Point, the shoreline opens up, giving you a view of the cane and pineapple fields and then the houses and the apartment building east of the anchorage at Māla Wharf.

The Māla Wharf anchorage is 1.5 miles north of the Lahaina entrance buoy. If you travel to Māla from Lahaina, swing out around the reef at Pu'unoa Point; it extends 300 yards out from the shore. Water breaks over the reef in all but the calmest weather, so you'll have little difficulty avoiding it during daylight hours. Be especially careful at night, however.

ANCHORAGE

Because the moorings at Māla are so close together, you'll not be able to find a place to anchor close to shore or to the launch ramp. The best anchorage is seaward of the moored boats, where, typically, a few boats ride at anchor. Anchor in 40-50 feet of water.

The holding at Māla is good in places and not good in others. The sand bottom near the entrance of the channel leading to the launch ramp is only a thin layer on top of the old coral bottom. When the winds are blowing through the anchorage, your anchor will not hold in this area. The north side of the anchorage area has much better holding.

Another good reason not to anchor near the channel entrance at Māla is the large number of boats entering and exiting the channel, particularly in the morning and evening. Many of these boats transit the channel at high speeds.

If you wish to go ashore, you can either go to Lahaina Harbor, a rather long run even if you have a high speed sport boat, or tie alongside the Māla launch ramp. Those people on boats in the Māla anchorage usually tie the sterns of their tenders to the piers on the side of the launch ramp and the bows to the rocks on the breakwater. Getting out of or aboard the dinghy can be a challenge when the surge is particularly nasty.

FACILITIES

Bank
Grocery Store
Pharmacy

Restrooms
Shopping Center
Telephone

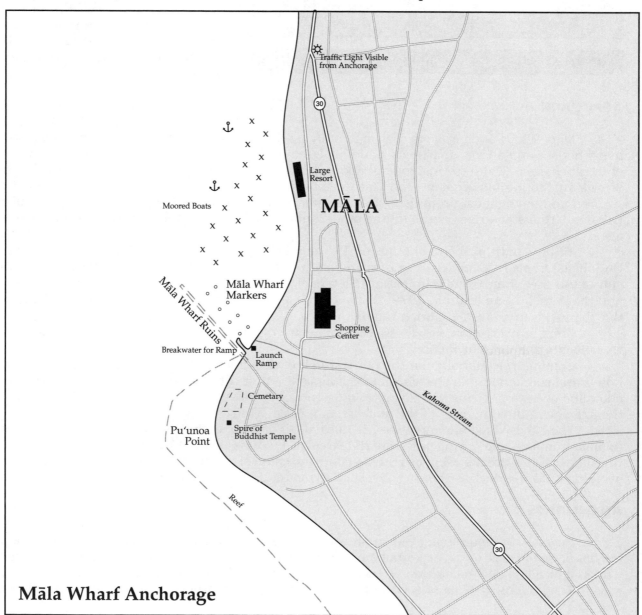

Māla Wharf Anchorage

LAHAINA HARBOR AND ANCHORAGE
CHART #19340, #19347, AND #19348
LATITUDE N20° 52.050 LONGITUDE W156° 41.000 (ENTRANCE BUOY)

Lahaina harbor and anchorage is one of the most popular destinations in the Hawaiian Islands. The weather here is better than at almost any other place in the state. Lahaina, which means "merciless sun" in Hawaiian, is indeed the sunny spot of the island. but the sun is "merciless" only in the sense that it shines daily, from season to season, year to year.

Located in the lowland lee of the island, Lahaina gets an average of only 14 inches of rain annually, most of that resulting from winter storms. The thunderheads that build over the West Maui Mountains year round rarely come down off the hill to the shore, giving Lahaina endless days of sunshine, summer and winter. Yet the daytime temperature even in the warmest months—from May to October— rarely rises above the upper 80s because of the cooling tradewinds. In the winter months the average temperature is in the lower 80s. In both summer and winter the nighttime temperature runs about 20 degrees cooler than that of the day. For this reason, Lahaina has long been the favored site on Maui.

Old sailing ship

Kahekili, the warrior king, the last ruler of the independent kingdom of Maui before Kamehameha I brought all the islands in the chain under his rule, lived at Lahaina, as had all the rulers of Maui since the 16th century. From this power base Kahekili at one time controlled O'ahu, Moloka'i, and Lāna'i, as well. After Kahekili's defeat by Kamehameha I and the subsequent unification of the Hawaiian Islands, Lahaina became the governmental center for all the Islands, remaining so until 1845, when Kamehameha III moved to Honolulu. This town continued to lure the vacationing royalty, all of whom had second homes here during their reigns.

The Lahaina Roadstead does not have the most protected waters along this west coast of Maui; it nevertheless became one of the two primary anchorages for the hundreds of whaling ships that came to Hawai'i to hunt sperm and humpback whales, beginning in 1819. This ample roadstead can accommodate at least a hundred boats.

The missionaries came to Lahaina shortly after the whalers, at the request of Queen Keōpūolani, who was one of the most powerful widows of the deceased Kamehameha I. The grog shops and prostitution that flourished with all the whalers ashore so alarmed the Christian queen that she invited the missionaries to come and save the town from sin. Many of the historical sites preserved in Old Lahaina Town date from the missionary era.

What finally makes Lahaina a fascinating place for sailors to visit is its pleasing combination of the old and the new, its sedate charm blended with a jazzy contemporaneity.

During the day, the historic sites are the chief attraction, though judging by the number of shoppers crowding the narrow sidewalks of Front Street, some tourists might argue with that evaluation. The first site you see as you approach the breakwater is the *Cathaginian II*, a replica of the freighters that sailed to Lahaina in the whaling era. Converted from a German two-masted schooner, this square-rigged ship is now a whale and whaling museum.

Across Wharf Street from the square-rigger is the Pioneer Inn (1901), its green and white French Colonial exterior invitingly cool and exotic. An open air bar on the veranda adjacent

Old Lahaina Town

to the indoor bar, where a honky tonk piano player plunks away, is an ideal spot for a drink and/or a light meal while you acquaint yourself with the bustle of Lahaina.

Directly across Hotel Street are the restored courthouse (1850), now housing the Visitors' Center and a small art museum, and the famed Banyan Tree, planted in 1873 to celebrate the centennial of the Congregationalist Mission. Under the shelter of this magnificent tree is a large, cool park where children play, musicians jam for an afternoon, and visitors stroll by in wonderment at the girth of this one tree.

West of the Banyan Tree on Front Street is the Baldwin Home (1834), an excellent introduction to the lives of the missionaries whose presence left lasting marks on these Islands. Besides being a religious leader, Dwight Baldwin, the original owner of the house, was also a teacher and the first doctor and dentist in Hawai'i.

Other sites are more distant from the docks but still within walking distance and worth a visit for those interested in the history of Maui and of Hawai'i generally. The Pioneer Mill Company, processing sugar cane since 1860, remains on Lahainaluna Street. On up the hill is the Lahainaluna School (1831), the oldest school west of the Rockies, and today a public high school. On its campus is Hale Pa'i, where the first newspaper in the Islands was printed in 1834. The present Waine'e Church has been rebuilt on the site where the first Christian services in the Islands were held in 1823; members of the Maui royal family are buried in the adjoining cemetery.

Other historic buildings are the Hale Pa'ahao, the prison (1850s); Maria Lanakila Church, built on the site where the first Roman Catholic Mass in Lahaina was celebrated in 1841; and Seamen's Cemetery, where the dead off the ships in the Lahaina Roadstead were buried.

While the citizens of Lahaina have vigorously maintained its historical sites, at the same time the town also seems assured of a prosperous future. After several years as a sleepy sugar plantation town, Lahaina rarely sleeps now. For night life in the Islands, only Honolulu outdoes this otherwise modest little town. Good music, good food, and good vibes abound on Front Street, where it's party time every night. You stay-at-homes of an evening will be able to hear some of the musicians from your boat in the roadstead.

For a break from the city lights, Lahaina has a swimming and snorkeling beach at Malu' 'Ulu o Lele Park at the southeastern end of town as well as another, Lahaina Beach, northwest of town near Māla Wharf. Surfboarders ride the waves that come in beside the harbor office.

If you're among those lucky cruising sailors who have extra cash on hand, consider one or more of the many commercial excursions out of Lahaina. Numerous charter boats leave the dock daily for scuba diving, snorkeling, submarine trips, and whale watching (in season). Or you can catch the Lāna'i Express for a quick trip over to this neighboring island, where one of the Islands' most beautiful beaches, Hulopo'e Beach, is near where the Express docks. *Mauka* (as you will learn to call the direction away from the sea, *mauka* being "mountain"), you can choose the Sugar Cane Train to tour a sugar plantation near Lahaina. More distant excursions are those to Haleakalā Crater (by bus or by helicopter), Hāna, and the Upcountry.

Unless you plan to stay here for several weeks, you'll not run out of places to go and things to do in Lahaina. It's one of the most popular tourist destinations on all the Islands, and thus it has many attractions for tourists, whether they come by plane or by boat.

APPROACH

Approaching Lahaina from the north, you curve around the West Maui shoreline for about 9.0 miles after passing Hāwea Point, going by pineapple and cane fields and hotels and condominiums. The last significant landmark when approaching from the north is the *Mala* Wharf anchorage, 1.5 miles north of the Lahaina Roadstead.

From the southwest, you will probably be coming from Lāna'i. The last significant point of departure is Mānele Bay on the southeast corner of the island. The distance from Mānele to Lahaina is approximately 13.5 miles.

From the southeast, the most significant point of departure is Molokini Island, 17.5 miles away.

Perhaps the stack of the old Pioneer Mill on Lahainaluna Street, visible from 5 miles or more out at sea, is the best landmark for Lahaina. You'll also see boats anchored or moored outside Lahaina long before you arrive.

The harbormaster at Lahaina requests that visiting boaters call on VHF 16 before entering the harbor, including coming in by dinghy. In addition, since the Homeland Security Act was implemented, no one may enter the harbor area from either the land or water side without security clearance when a cruise ship is in the anchorage.

If you're trying to enter the harbor at night, an unlikely event unless you've made prior arrangements and know a slip is available for your boat, proceed with extreme caution. The lights of the town surround the two green range lights, making them difficult to discern. Move toward the harbor from the channel entrance buoy only after you've located both green lights and you have them directly in line. The three pairs of buoys marking the entrance channel into Lahaina are lighted at night, although they, too, might be difficult to see because of the lights of the town in the background.

ANCHORAGE AND BERTHING

The 99 dock spaces in the Lahaina marina are permanently leased, and the marina has no guest berthing. The harbormaster will try to find a space on the dock for a day or more for boats needing repairs.

Generally, though, boaters who visit Lahaina anchor or pick up a mooring in the Lahaina Roadstead. Anchoring should be your second choice. The bottom in the anchorage area has a thin layer of sand over a base of long dead coral. When we first visited Lahaina, we dropped our 66-pound Bruce anchor and 200 feet of chain, then listened in amazement as it dragged noisily across the bottom for 500 feet before it finally found enough sand to bury itself in.

The better choice is to tie to one of the eight moorings the Lahaina Yacht Club has set in the roadstead. The club's moorings are marked with heavy plastic orange balls, each marked with the letters "LYC" and the number of the mooring (1 to 8). Before leaving your boat on one of these moorings, get into the water and check the security of the mooring. After you've settled in, go ashore and check in with the business office of the yacht club, located on Front Street. While you are at the club, you can have a drink and enjoy the view of your boat at anchor just outside the club's back deck.

Another disadvantage of the anchorage at Lahaina is the rolling that every boat does here, whether it's at anchor or on a mooring. Most of us have the mistaken notion that boats head into the wind and swell when at anchor. However, you'll learn at Lahaina that current is stronger than wind in determining the direction a boat points, and, when the strong current here holds your boat abeam to the wind and swell, the result is a rolling boat. When we anchor or tie to a mooring at Lahaina, we set a roll stabilizer (and sometimes two) as a matter of course.

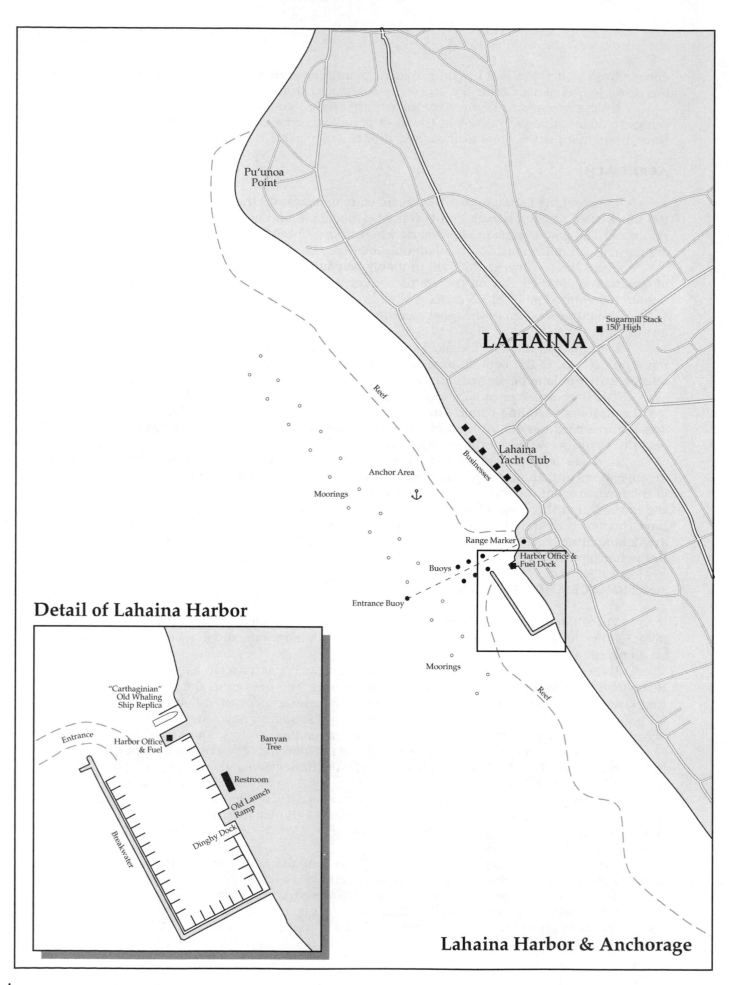

Pu'unoa
Point

Sugarmill Stack
150' High

LAHAINA

Reef

Businesses

Lahaina
Yacht Club

Anchor Area

Moorings

Range Marker

Harbor Office &
Fuel Dock

Buoys

Entrance Buoy

Moorings

Reef

Detail of Lahaina Harbor

"Carthaginian"
Old Whaling
Ship Replica

Entrance

Harbor Office
& Fuel

Banyan
Tree

Restroom

Old Launch
Ramp

Dinghy Dock

Breakwater

Lahaina Harbor & Anchorage

(See the sections on Māla Wharf and Waianukole for two other anchorage options when you visit Lahaina.)

To go ashore, land your tender at the dinghy dock halfway along the city side of the marina. The marina charges a small daily fee for the use of this dock.

Lahaina Harbormaster	808-662-4060
Lahaina Yacht Club	808-661-0191

FACILITIES

Banks
Car Rental
Dinghy Dock (fee)
Fuel (diesel and gasoline)*
Grocery Stores
Laundromat
Library

Movie Theaters
Post Office
Propane (by taxi or truck)
Restaurants
Shopping Centers
Taxis
Water**

*Gas and diesel are available at the dock at Lahaina, but you can't simply pull up to the dock and take on fuel. The company with the fuel concession at this marina has no attendant on site; rather, each user must have a fuel card from the company. (Neither an ATM nor a charge card is usable.) If you want to fuel at Lahaina, you first must go to the Lahaina Yacht Club office, about three blocks north of the dock on Front Street, for the card.   The office hours of the yacht club are Monday through Friday, 0830 1700. You'll be required to leave a deposit that you'll get back when you return with the card. After you've fueled up, take the receipt for the fuel back to the yacht club office so the secretary there can record how much you took on and collect the amount charged.

A related problem with the fueling at Lahaina is the 30-minute time limit at the dock, necessitated by the large number of boats, primarily commercial, using the dock. The fueling alone can take 30 minutes. A solution is to go ashore by dinghy at 0830 to borrow the yacht club card, then go back out and bring the boat into the fuel dock, leaving the sport boat on the mooring to reserve it.

**Again, because of the heavy traffic, the harbor staff has had to restrict boaters where water is concerned. To fill up with water or wash off your boat, make arrangements with the harbor office and pay a small fee. The small fee serves to make boaters aware that Lahaina is on the dry side of the island and does not have unlimited flows of water.

Fuel dock at Lahaina

WAIANUKOLE ANCHORAGE (LAHAINA EAST)
CHART #19340, #19347, OR #19348
LATTITUDE N20° 50.600 LONGITUDE W156° 39.750 (ANCHORAGE)

The large beach catamarans use Waianukole Anchorage when the north winds blow strongly enough to prevent them from taking their customers to snorkel sites along the Kāʻanapali Coast. Boaters with boats normally moored or anchored in Māla Wharf and Lahaina Roadstead also move their boats to Waianukole when the north winds make those anchorages uncomfortable or unsafe.

Like Lahaina Roadstead, Waianukole is not in a cove or bay; it is simply a place to anchor where you can get good protection from north winds. This anchorage is also an option when the Māla Wharf and Lahaina Roadstead areas are so crowded that anchoring or mooring at either place is undesirable. Unlike both of these other anchorages, Waianukole has excellent holding in a sand and silt bottom.

In addition to its advantage as an anchorage, especially in some weather conditions, Waianukole has at least one other advantage. It's close enough to Lahaina Town for you to enjoy all the "city life" you want but away from the noise and lights. You can watch surfboarders ride the waves off the small beach. The charter submarine from Lahaina brings its customers here to look at the marine world on the bottom.

APPROACH

To reach the Waianukole Anchorage, go 1.5 miles southeast along the coastline beyond the Lahaina entrance buoy. From Mākila Point, identified by Puamana Beach County Park at the southeast edge of Lahaina town) to the anchorage is .50 mile. Another small white sand beach is between Honoapiʻilani Highway and the sea, and to both port and starboard of the beach are rock and concrete seawalls used to stabilize the highway. In the cane fields across the highway from the anchorage area are large mounds of rocks, five mounds to port, one in the middle, and another five or so to starboard. The high West Maui Mountains rise sharply beyond the cane fields.

ANCHORAGE

Much of the area between Mākila Point and Launiupoko Point, 2.0 miles farther east, would serve as a good anchorage in north or tradewind conditions. However, the popular anchorage is off the second small beach. Anchor in 20-25 feet of water, 200 yards off the beach between the two seawalls, with your bow pointed directly at the center rock mound in the cane fields. The surf breaks 150 yards seaward of the seawalls. Because the bottom is red silt mixed with sand, you'll not be able to see any features on the bottom, but reportedly all this anchorage has good holding.

You can land a tender on the small beach directly north of the anchorage or at the Puamana Beach Park, though legally you may not leave a boat on the beach itself but must pull it above the vegetation line. If you plan to leave the beach area, a better idea is to take the tender to the the dinghy dock in

Rock mounds identify the anchorage.

Lahaina Harbor, where it will be safe. When you take your tender into Lahaina Harbor, check in at the harbormaster's office, and pay a small fee for the use of the dinghy dock.

FACILITIES

None

**Waianukole
(Lahaina East)
Anchorage**

Lahaina and sugar cane fields

Kaupō Landing

AWALUA BEACH ANCHORAGE
CHARTS #19340, 19347, OR 19348
LATTITUDE N20° 49.571 W156° 38.150 (ANCHORAGE)

Awalua ("double harbor") Beach Anchorage shares its one major attraction with most of the other anchorages on West Maui: the sapphire and aquamarine water sparkles in the sun that shines here every day, and the white water breaking on the reef and the shore dazzles the eye. Yours will usually be the only boat in the anchorage. Surfboarders will provide passive entertainment, but you'll not be able to resist for long the water's lapping call.

The other great attraction of Awalua is its excellent protection from the north winds. When north winds become threatening to the anchorages at Lahaina and Māla, local boaters often head for the safety of these anchorages southeast of Lahaina. The West Maui Mountains, to the northeast of the anchorage, shelter Awalua Beach from the tradewinds and even heavy north winds. This anchorage has no protection, however, from west or south wind and swell and only minimal protection from heavy trades.

You can swim, snorkel, and dive in the quiet, crystalline water, but the somewhat steep, rocky shore is not one you'll want to land a tender on.

APPROACH

The Awalua Beach anchorage is 4.0 miles southeast of Lahaina Harbor and 1.0 mile northwest of the Olowalu pier at Hekili Point. Little distinguishes it from the surrounding coastline, but it does have a small, bushy patch of green in the east corner.

ANCHORAGE

Anchor at least 400 yards off the beach. The bottom has good holding in 35 feet of water if you are careful to drop in sand. Closer to shore, the holding is poor because the bottom is old coral with a little sand covering it. Drop anchor just west of the bushy trees growing on the beach.

FACILITIES

None

Early Hawaiian dancers

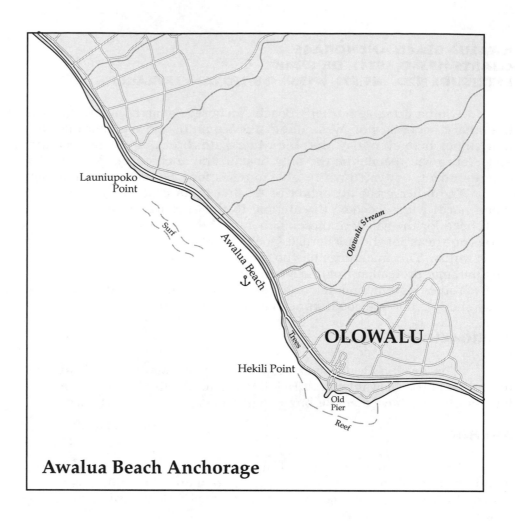

Awalua Beach Anchorage

OLOWALU ANCHORAGE
CHARTS #19340 OR #19347
LATITUDE N20° 48.190 LONGITUDE W156° 36.780 (ANCHORAGE)

Dive and snorkel charter boats use this anchorage during the daytime because of the well-developed reef around Olowalu Wharf and Hekili Point. Once these boats leave in the late afternoon, you'll almost surely be alone in this quiet anchorage seeming so far away from the busy traffic and hectic pace of the Lahaina area.

In addition to the underwater world to be explored here, Olowalu Anchorage is as near as you can get by boat to one of the most intriguing petroglyph sites on Maui. You'll have to be fairly determined, though, first, to take the long hike to the site and, second, to find it.

The landing beach is to the north of the anchorage, immediately east of a large house with a red roof. Carefully cross the reef between the anchorage and the beach. Unless a south swell is running, the landing on the beach is easy.

After landing the tender, walk about .25 mile west to the Chez Paul Restaurant and the Olowalu Store (these two comprise the "town" of Olowalu). On the northwest side of the store is an old house, alongside which a dirt road leads to an old highway, approximately 100 yards north-

east of the main highway. Turn left onto this old road, and travel on it for about 100 yards. Then turn right on the first dirt and gravel road you come to. This road leads through the cane fields for about 1.0 mile. At the pump house on the right, begin to look on the right for the petroglyphs—families, sails, animals—carved on the boulders for the next 0.25 mile. Some of

Petroglyphs at Olowalu

these carvings on the vertical faces of the boulders are near the road. Many others are some distance above the road. Take along a pair of binoculars to see the petroglyphs. You'll also want to have with you some insect repellent for the mosquitoes.

Though nothing remains ashore to commemorate it, Olowalu is also the location of the infamous Olowalu Massacre. Simon Metcalfe, captain of the American merchant ship *Eleanora*, avenged the theft of one of his small boats and the killing of one of his crew by making a truce with the Hawaiians, luring them out to his anchored ship, and then slaughtering more than one hundred of them.

Even if you don't choose to go ashore here, Olowalu ("many hills") is a good spot to stop. The mountains of Maui protect the anchorage in tradewind and in north wind conditions, and, because of the reef and Hekili Point, it is even a comfortable anchorage when west winds are blowing.

APPROACH

Getting into Olowalu Anchorage is a matter of first identifying Olowalu Wharf, 5.0 miles along the coastline southeast of Lahaina Harbor. An easily identifiable reef extends out from the shore beginning about .50 mile west of the wharf to a point slightly beyond Hekili Point, which is some .25 mile east of the wharf. Across the highway from the anchorage is a lush stand of sugar cane, the field forming a triangle whose apex disappears into the mouth of a narrow valley in the West Maui Mountains.

From the east, Olowalu is about 7.0 miles westward from Māʻalaea Harbor.

ANCHORAGE

Olowalu Anchorage is .75 mile east of the old wharf. Go around the reef, and then go north .30 mile. Be alert to the reef at all times as you enter this anchorage. Anchor in 25 feet of water.   The bottom has patches of sand, so be sure to select your spot carefully.

Some of the charter boat companies have set moorings in the anchorage, difficult to locate because the mooring buoys are at least 10 feet below the surface. Nevertheless, be on the look-out for them to avoid dropping on top of one.

FACILITIES

Mini-market
Restaurant
Telephone

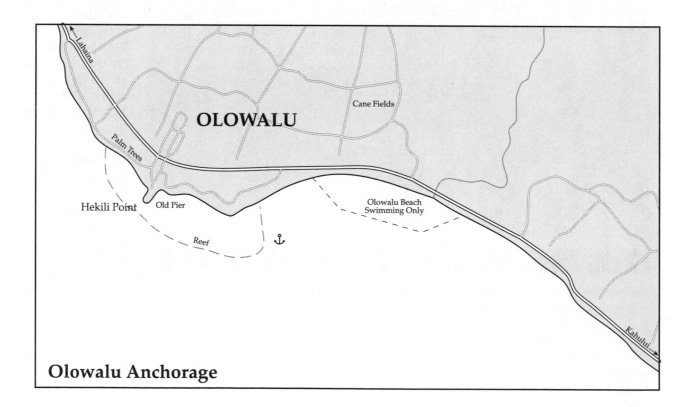

Olowalu Anchorage

CORAL GARDENS ANCHORAGE
CHARTS #19340 OR #19347
LAT. N20° 47.175 LONG. W156° 33.690 (ANCHORAGE)

On those days when the winds are blowing too hard for the dive/snorkel charter boats to take their customers out to the island of Molokini, they are anchored at Olowalu or Coral Gardens. The underwater scenery at Coral Gardens rivals that found at Molokini. Molokini is more dramatic only because it is the rim of a crater left from a blown-out volcano.

Coral Gardens offers great holding and superior protection from north winds and unusually strong tradewinds. Once the charter boats have gone—if, in fact, any have been anchored there—you'll almost assuredly have the splendor of this anchorage to yourself. The steep cliffs drop straight down to the rocky shore. As darkness settles over the anchorage, the glimmering lights on East Maui begin to appear across the water to the southeast.

Mending fishing nets

APPROACH

Coral Gardens Anchorage is 9.0 miles southeast of Lahaina Harbor and about 1.50 miles west of Papawai Point. The best landmark is the Honoapiʻilini highway, the major roadway that traces much of the West Maui coastline. The highway is close to and at almost the same elevation as the coast from Lahaina to Coral Gardens, where it abruptly rises in elevation just before the anchorage. If you look closely, you can see the tunnel where the highway cuts through the mountain. The anchorage is about halfway between the mouth of this tunnel and the point at which the highway begins to rise from water level.

A second way to identify the anchorage is to watch the reef that fringes the coast all of the way from Olowalu to a point .25 mile northwest of Coral Gardens. The water inside the reef is far lighter in color than the water outside. Often surfers will be riding the waves that break on the reef. Along the reef, the water is shallow at least .50 mile out from the beach. At Coral Gardens, the water depths increase; you can anchor within 100 yards of the beach in most areas.

ANCHORAGE

The charter boat companies have sunk four moorings in the choice anchorage just east of the first cutaway on the highway, where the road begins to rise. The buoys attached to these moorings are about 10 feet below the water's surface and are visible only when you are directly over them You will also be able to estimate this prime location by noting the position of a speed sign on the highway east of the first cut in the hillside. When your boat is perfectly located, the sign should be off your port bow.

You can anchor anywhere along the coast from the tunnel westward for about one-half mile. Most of the sandy spots are about 100 yards off the shoreline in 30-40 feet of water. If the winds are light, the south swell here may give your boat an uncomfortable roll. In that case, you might want to anchor bow and stern to keep your bow pointed into the waves. An alternate plan, of course, is to set a roll stabilizer.

This anchorage is good only in calm conditions or in tradewinds or north winds. If you decide to spend the night at Coral Gardens, monitor the weather closely to avoid getting caught here in a *kona* wind or a strong east wind.

FACILITIES

None

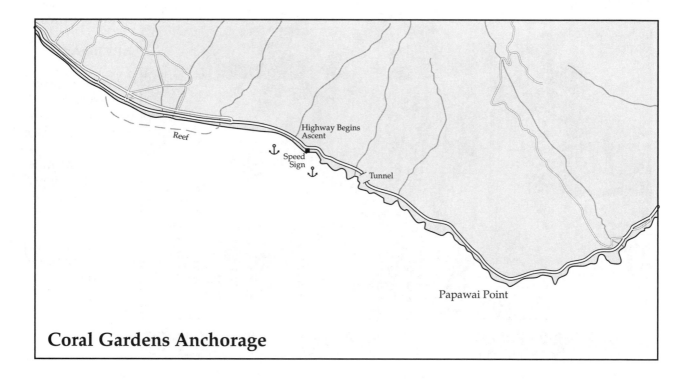

Coral Gardens Anchorage

MCGREGOR LANDING
CHART #19340, 19347, 19350
LAT. N20° 46.603 LONG. W156° 31.490 (ANCHORAGE)

The story told of McGregor Landing is a novel one, and perhaps more legend than fact. Somewhere around the 1870s, Captain Daniel McGregor, who ran interisland trading ships, was enroute to Māʻalaea Landing. While sailing into the Bay during the night, his ship encountered heavy winds and rain. Knowing he could not anchor in his usual spot in Māʻalaea, Capt. McGregor had three men go forward with lead lines to sound the water ahead while he searched for a less exposed anchorage. When the wind seemed to diminish and the water became significantly more shallow and calm, he ordered the anchor dropped. The captain awoke the next day to find he'd discovered, quite by accident, a wonderfully protected little cove. The protecting point and the cove bear his name.

Boy fishing

Soon captains of other ships began to anchor at McGregor Point, and eventually a wharf was built here for for the use of interisland steamers and other ships.

Today, Māʻalaea Harbor attracts most of the boaters on this part of the coast because of the small boat harbor there. Boats rarely anchor at McGregor Landing, although it is a much more comfortable place than Māʻalaea.

While McGregor Landing is a good anchorage, the landing is not appealing. The steep, rocky shoreline at McGregor makes landing, except on the calmest of days, almost certainly a wet experience. You can have a much more pleasant experience in the water if you simply jump over the side to swim and snorkel in the wonderfully clear waters of this bay.

If you're content to stay aboard and merely look at the rocky shore, you'll appreciate the beauty of the place. Many of the boulders have tumbled out into the cove, where water breaks over them in foaming bursts of white and turquoise. A local fisherman or woman may be out on one of the boulders above the breaking water, giving the appearance of his or her flirting with a salt water bath.

One of the pleasures of being anchored at McGregor is to sit on your boat in this protected bay and smugly watch the whitecaps racing by outside the anchorage no more than 200 yards away. Winds inside the cove tend to be gusty, but the gusts rarely exceed 15 knots and the sustained winds are more likely to be about 10-12 when winds at Māʻalaea are 25 knots.

Another kind of pleasure is found in watching the humpback whales that have migrated from Alaska and the Arctic region. They remain around the Islands between November and April to calve, nurse their young, and breed. Some of them seem to favor the relatively calm waters in the lee of the sea cliffs along this shore.

APPROACH

From Lahaina Harbor, McGregor Landing lies about 11.0 miles southeast. McGregor is only 1.0 mile before Māʻalaea Harbor. From the south, McGregor is 9.0 miles directly north of Molokini.

McGregor Light is on the point immediately northeast of the anchorage.

ANCHORAGE

Anchor in the center of the cove, about 300 yards from McGregor Light. Drop anchor about 150 feet from the beach in 20-30 feet of water.

The bottom is rocky but with considerable sand to give good holding.

FACILITIES

None

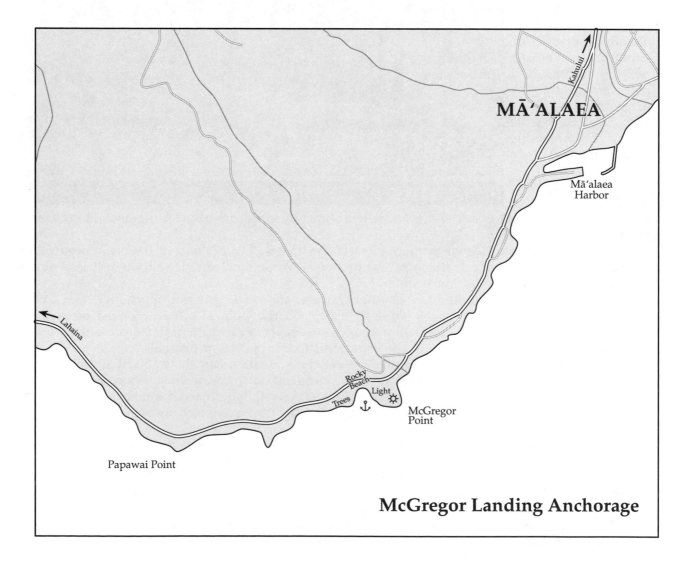

McGregor Landing Anchorage

MĀʻALAEA HARBOR
CHARTS #19347, 19350
LAT. N20° 47.580 LONG. W156° 30.610 (ENTRANCE)

An old Hawaiian proverb says, "When the Moaʻe wind blows, the dust of Kahoʻolawe goes toward Māʻalaea." Some local sailors who keep boats in this harbor would agree that all the dust blowing onto their boats couldn't come from only the shores of Māʻalaea Bay. Māʻalaea Harbor has the reputation of being the windiest spot in the Islands. When trade winds blow, the slopes of Haleakalā and the West Maui Mountains funnel the winds across the isthmus between Kahului on the north and Māʻalaea. These winds pick up speed as they go so that by afternoon, they often exceed 30 knots, carrying dirt from the surrounding cane fields over the harbor. The Māʻalaea

harbormaster says the winds are occasionally so strong they blow the head off his anemometer atop the harbor office. When strong trades are blowing, the winds at Māʻalaea often exceed 50 knots.

. . . and a reef runs through it.

Another unusual feature of Māʻalaea Harbor is the reef that runs through the middle of it. Many harbors have a reef outside or one that boaters must cross to get into the harbor, but Māʻalaea Harbor has a reef that runs almost exactly east-west down the middle. Local boaters seem to have adjusted to this unusual arrangement and rarely have a reef encounter.

In addition to the reef, boaters here must contend with the surge. When the weather is benign, the surge is heavy enough to break small lines. When the weather turns sour, the ferocious surge in this harbor will break heavy lines and chain. The likelihood of the state making any changes to the harbor entrance to eliminate or reduce the surge is slight; any substantial changes to the entrance would also mean unwelcome changes to a favorite surfing spot that surfers have used for years.

Māʻalaea Harbor, built in 1952, has no guest slips, but occasionally the harbormaster will put a guest boat in a space vacated by its regular owner for a day or two. Most of the 100 or so boats permanently docked at Māʻalaea are charter boats. The few pleasure boats in the harbor seem out of place. Boats here must be tied Tahiti-style. Only the crews on visiting boats may stay aboard their boats overnight; none of the permanent boats may be liveaboards.

Māʻalaea does have genuine attractions. The people, both in the harbor office and on the boats, are exceptionally friendly and helpful. The aquarium, restaurants, and small shops at Maʻalaea make this a busy harbor. Māʻalaea Bay is a prime location for watching humpback whales that come here between November and May to calve and breed. These whales have been observed to give birth in Māʻalaea Bay. In the course of the next several months, many of the parents and calves swim north past Lahaina before turning west to Molokaʻi and Lānaʻi. In the spring they return to Māʻalaea by way of Kahoʻolawe before beginning their migration to Alaska and the Arctic regions for the summer.

The beach east of the harbor is a favorite among surfers. Sometimes the water off this beach is clear enough for good snorkeling and diving. Māʻalaea reportedly has a large number of species of mollusks growing on the rocks and reefs.

Nevertheless, we cannot wholeheartedly recommend Māʻalaea as a cruising destination. Because of the heavy wind and accompanying dust and dirt, the heavy surge, and the congested harbor, you may experience so much tension you can't enjoy your stay.

APPROACH

Mā'alaea Harbor is in the northwest corner of Mā'alaea Bay, approximately 12.0 miles southeast of Lahaina and 9.5 miles north of the island of Molokini. McGregor Point Light (72 feet above the water, with a 7-mile range) is about 1.0 mile southwest of the Mā'alaea Harbor entrance. A pair of buoys mark the channel into the harbor, with range marks behind the entrance. All in all, Mā'alaea Harbor is easy to locate.

ANCHORAGE AND BERTHING

Mā'alaea Harbor has no anchorage area. The nearest anchorages are at McGregor Landing, 1.0 mile to the southwest, and at Sugar Beach (Kīhei), 2.5 miles to the east.

Entrance at Mā'alaea

To get a temporary slip inside the harbor, contact the harbormaster. When possible, call ahead and tell the harbormaster what time you expect to arrive. If you can't call ahead, pull up to the loading dock in the northeast corner of the harbor and walk around the harbor to the harbor office. (The surge at the loading dock is probably the worst in the harbor; when a south swell is running, it may well be the worst in the state.) If you leave your boat here, leave someone aboard to move fenders around to protect your boat from the tires on the side of the seawall.

When the Coast Guard cutter is in the harbor, the crew puts out an anchor amidships to hold the cutter off the pier. If the harbormaster instructs you to tie up at the loading dock for more than a few minutes, you, too, should put out a midship's anchor.

Depths in the harbor are about 7 feet at best, but because of the construction adjacent to the harbor, some silting/shoaling problems are occurring.

Mā'alaea Harbormaster   808-243-5818

FACILITIES

Boat Parts*   Mini-mart and Deli
Fuel (diesel only)**   Restaurants
Haul-out Facility***   Restrooms
Launch Ramp   Telephone

*The small market and deli on the street north of the harbor has some boat parts.
**Diesel is regularly delivered to the harbor on Monday, Wednesday, and Friday. Contact either the harbormaster or Maui Oil, the distributor. Boaters who are only in the harbor to get fuel and need it immediately can get service almost any day. As with most harbors, the minumum fuel order is 100 gallons, so boaters regularly get together and share the order.
***The haul-out facility, though primitive, can handle boats up to 50 feet in length.

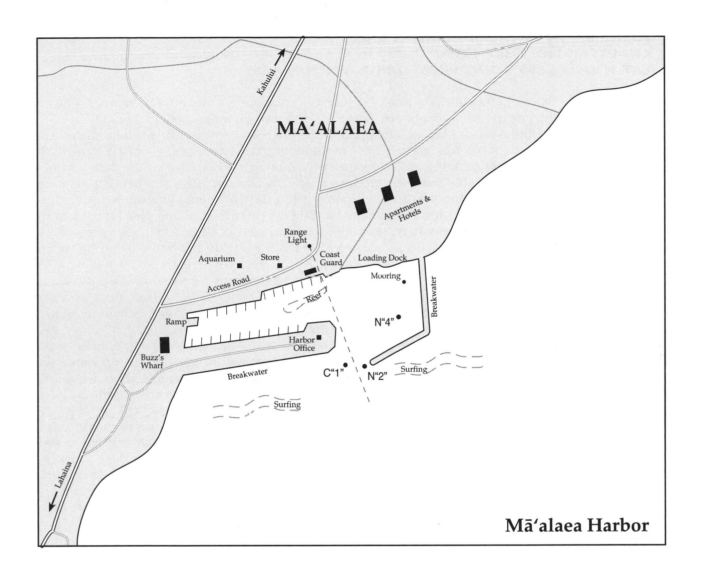

MĀʻALAEA

Kahului

Range
Light

Aquarium   Store   Coast
Guard

Access Road

Loading Dock

Apartments &
Hotels

Mooring

Breakwater

Reef

Ramp

N"4"

Harbor
Office

Buzz's
Wharf

Breakwater

C"1"   N"2"

Surfing

Lahaina

Surfing

Māʻalaea Harbor

SUGAR BEACH ANCHORAGE (KĪHEI ANCHORAGE)
CHARTS #19340, 19347, 19350
LAT. N20° 46.889 LONG. W156° 28.112 (ANCHORAGE)

Sugar Beach is in Māʻalaea Bay, 2.5 miles east of the entrance to Māʻalaea Small Boat Harbor. Usually a dozen or so boats are moored in this rather wide-open anchorage.

In ancient times, Hawaiian warriors pulled their canoes ashore at this beach. Later, Capt. George Vancouver anchored his boats here; a monument marks the spot where he landed. The footings for the Old Kīhei Landing, a 200-foot pier built around 1890, are on the east end of the anchorage. The Islanders shipped their produce from this landing; steamers brought in freight. Shoaling became an increasing problem so that by 1915 the steamers could no longer get in to the wharf. Local boaters continued to use the landing for their fishing and pleasure boats until 1952, when the state closed the wharf. In 1959, what was left of the wooden pier burned.

For the boaters who want to go ashore at Māʻalaea but do not want to be in Māʻalaea Harbor, Sugar Beach Anchorage is the best alternative. The winds here are about half what they are at Māʻalaea, the surge is minimal by comparison, and the air is clean. And what remarkable weather Sugar has, with an abundance of sunny days and clear nights. This quiet anchorage away from all the lights of a busy harbor is a fine place for star-gazing. Yet it is close enough for you to take your tender into Māʻalaea Harbor if you wish to go ashore.

You can make a landing on Sugar Beach on the west side of the old wharf to go ashore, but you should do so early in the day because by noon the south swell and wind make going ashore a little too challenging. This beach is, in fact, better for swimming than for landing. However, the advantage of going ashore here rather than at Māʻalaea is the proximity of this beach to some facilities and services in Kīhei.

Nothing can be all good, of course. Sugar Beach has been the scene of many nautical disasters. Accordingly to one local resident, every time the wind blows strongly out of the south, boats wash ashore here. Local boaters attribute many of the beached boats to the carelessness of their owners, who put their boats on moorings and forgot about them, failing to check the moorings regularly. When the inevitable south swell builds, the boats snap their moorings and are ashore in minutes. If you anchor here, let out plenty of scope, and, if a south swell sets in, leave so yours isn't one of the boats that wash ashore.

APPROACH

Sugar Beach is 2.5 miles east of the entrance to Māʻalaea Harbor. If you approach Sugar from the west, just follow the northern shoreline of Māʻalaea Bay. It will take you directly there.

Boaters approaching from the south can best begin measuring at Cape Kīnaʻu, the south corner of Maui that is closest to Molokini Island. Sugar Beach is 11.0 miles northward along the coast.

The boats moored at Sugar Beach will help you identify the anchorage. In addition to sailboats and fishing boats, large fishing boats regularly use the anchorage when prevailing winds are blowing. On the shore to the northeast of the anchorage is the old Kīhei wharf. Mai Poina ʻOe Iāʻu County Park begins immediately south of the old pier and the Sugar Beach Anchorage. The Vancouver monument is in this park.

Perhaps most easily recognizable of all are the four high-rise resort hotels and condominiums just behind the beach north of the anchorage.

ANCHORAGE

Anchor between the Kīhei wharf and the two most westerly of the resort hotels. Drop your hook about 300 yards off the beach in 30-35-foot depths. You'll have better boat motion here than if you anchor closer to shore, where the refracted waves bounce off the shoreline.

Early in the day the winds at Sugar Beach are light, often from the south or west. After noon, however, the winds increase and most often come from the north or east.

The bottom at Sugar Beach is a mixture of sand and rocks. When you drop the anchor, you may hear the anchor or anchor chain rumble across a few rocks, before it stops moving suddenly and then stays put. Some boaters claim the bottom at Sugar Beach has more rocks than sand, so you might be well advised to move to another location if your anchor fails to dig in. We had no trouble getting an anchor to hold the first time, but we may have simply chosen the best spot accidentally.

FACILITIES

Grocery Store
Produce Stand
Restrooms
Showers (cold)
Telephone

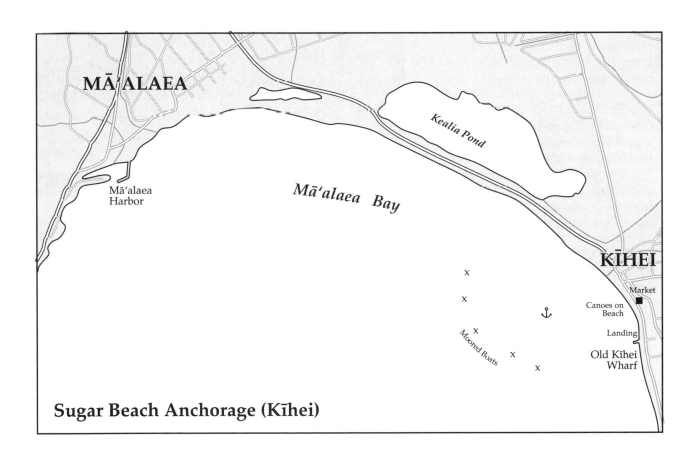

Sugar Beach Anchorage (Kīhei)

MĀKENA ANCHORAGE
CHARTS #19320, #19340, OR #19347
LAT. N20° 38.533 LONG. W156° 26.925 (ANCHORAGE)

Mākena ("abundance") Anchorage, north of Puʻu Ōlaʻi, the large red-brown hill that juts out from the shore 10.0 miles southeast of Māʻalaea Harbor, provides boaters with an excellent place to drop a hook. The south swell that makes boats roll uncomfortably in so many anchorages on this coast is generally absent at Mākena, thanks to Puʻu ʻŌlaʻi. This lack of swell also makes landing a dinghy on the beach much easier than at most beaches on this shore. And Puʻu Ōlaʻi also protects this anchorage from the south winds that occasionally blow up this coast and make anchorages such as Oneloa uncomfortable.

Although boaters here will have to share the anchorage with charter boats that bring snorkelers into the anchorage, the problem is small since the snorkelers are concentrated on the reef 500 yards NE of the best anchorage area. By mid-afternoon the charter boats will be gone, and you'll probably have the anchorage all to yourself.

This bay was once a much busier place. The Makee Sugar Company opened a mill in the Upcountry near ʻUlupalakua Ranch in 1878, and interisland vessels carrying sugar, freight, and passengers used this anchorage. Mākena even had its own light, which was taken

Puʻu Ōlaʻi

out of service in 1918 with the inauguration of the light at Cape Hanamanioa. Nothing remains to mark the landing except the Mākena Landing County Park at Nāhuna Point.

The historical site of interest ashore is the Keawalaiʻi Congregational Church, established in 1832 and restored in 1952. Parts of the weekly Sunday services here are in the Hawaiian language.

The long stretch of beach from the village of Mākena to Cape Kīnaʻu has long been a favorite for swimming, snorkeling, and bodysurfing. In the '60s and '70s, it was a place where the free spirited congregated, its pristine beaches not yet lined with hotels and condominiums. Though development has begun here, the relaxed atmosphere of the bay continues relatively undiminished.

Some boaters take their sport boats and go about 1.5 miles north along the shoreline to what is called "Turtle Town," where a few turtles reportedly still lay their eggs on the beach. To locate the area, go in toward shore when you are about midway between the mansion on the point and the building with the bright red roof.

APPROACH

In approaching from any direction, locate the Mākena Anchorage by first identifying Puʻu Ōlaʻi. A mile or two before reaching Puʻu ʻŌlaʻi, you'll be able to see the Mākena Golf Course north of the point and immediately behind the anchorage. One mile to the north of Puʻu ʻŌlaʻi is the village of Mākena, easily recognizable because of the red roofs on some of the buildings.

A reef extends 200 yards out from shore .30 mile northeast from Puʻu ʻŌlaʻi. The best anchorage area is located between that reef and Puʻu ʻŌlaʻi. The anchorage area has a black sand beach behind it.

ANCHORAGE

For anchoring, select a spot as close to Pu'u Ōla'i and the black sand beach as you can. Anchor in 25-35 feet of water, being careful to select a sand patch in which to drop your anchor. In order to protect the coral, the charter boats that come in here put a crew member in the water with snorkel and fins to look for the sand patch. If you have trouble seeing a good sand patch, you might have to do the same.

You can also anchor north of the reef, closer to the village of Mākena. The only problem with this part of the anchorage is that the water close to shore is shallow, forcing you to anchor far enough out to make a long trip to shore.

FACILITIES

Restrooms
Showers
Sundries (at the hotel)
Telephone (at the hotel)

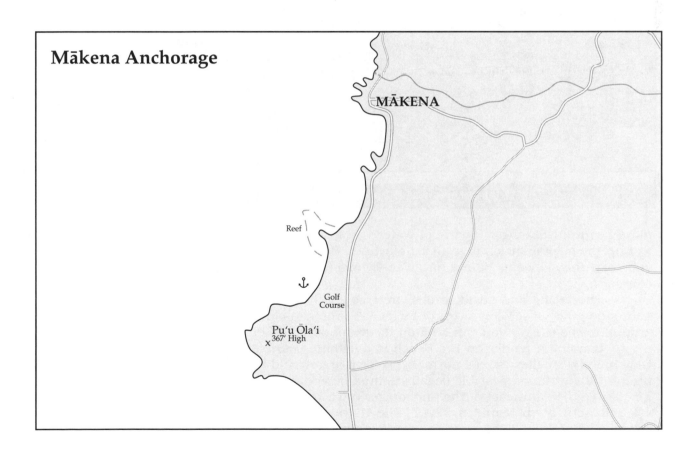

Mākena Anchorage

MĀKENA

Reef

Golf Course

Pu'u Ōla'i
x 367' High

ONELOA BEACH ANCHORAGE (BIG BEACH)
CHARTS #19320, #19340, OR #19347
LAT. N20° 37.729 LONG. W156° 26.920 (ANCHORAGE)

When tradewinds are blowing strongly, one of the best places to anchor your boat is along the 12-mile stretch of the Maui coastline between Māʻalaea Harbor and La Perouse Bay. Oneloa ("long sand") Beach, also called Mākena Big Beach, may well be the most secure of the anchorages along this stretch. When strong north winds blow, the prominent Puʻu Ōlaʻi ("earthquake hill"), a 367-foot reddish brown cinder cone extending out .50 mile from the shore, shields this anchorage from the north.

Oneloa Beach and Puʻu Ōlaʻi

You won't want to be in Māʻalaea Harbor itself, for the winds funnel through the isthmus, gaining velocity and churning up tons of dust along the way, then fairly scream through the marina. Farther east beyond La Perouse Bay, the many beautiful anchorages between Pākōwai Point and Hāna become uncomfortable and even unsafe in the trades.

Oneloa promises you more than security. It is called "long sand" by the Hawaiians and, more recently, "Big Beach" for a reason. The half mile of wide, white sand makes it indeed long and big—and surely one of the world's more beautiful beaches. Swirls of water rise in turquoise mounds, break, and then wash 50 feet up the sloping beach in scallops of white. Behind the beach is a thick forest of *kiawe* trees and then the slopes of Haleakalā. The swimming and beach-walking here are magnificent, of course.

Snorkeling and surfboarding are also excellent at Oneloa. One of the best snorkeling sites along the coast is just west of Puʻu Ōlaʻi. You can land your tender on Big Beach and walk around to the site, or you can land on the small beach off Puʻu Ōlaʻi.

Landing a tender on Big Beach is a definite possibility. The beach directly below Puʻu Ōlaʻi has the smallest swells normally, so that area would be preferable. Drag the tender as far up from the water as possible (legally it must be above the vegetation line).

To the southeast of the anchorage, you'll have a close-up view of the results of the last volcanic activity on Maui, in 1790. The Hawaiians call this flow *Paea* because, in Hawaiian legend, the source of the volcano was Pele's wrath as she destroyed a young man, Paea, who rejected her overtures. Scientists believe the flow from Kalua o Lapa cone resulted from a pocket of lava remaining long after the source became dormant. This flow formed Cape Kīnaʻu ("flaw"), now part of the ʻAhihi-Kīnaʻu Natural Area Reserve, and covered the coastline around this southwest tip of Maui with black *aʻa* lava.

APPROACH

Oneloa Anchorage is immediately south of Puʻu Ōlaʻi, the large cinder cone 10.0 miles southeast of Māʻalaea Harbor.

If you're coming from the south or east, Oneloa is 2.0 miles north of Cape Kīnaʻu. When you round Nukuʻele Point, you'll see Puʻu Ōlaʻi and, soon thereafter, the long white sands of Oneloa. Behind the beach are *kiawe* trees. At the south end are a few houses and palm trees. Another landmark for identifying Oneloa is Molokini Island, 2.5 miles west of the anchorage.

ANCHORAGE

Choosing a spot to anchor at Oneloa Anchorage is easy. Because the bottom shallows quite a distance from the beach, slowly work your way in behind Puʻu Olaʻi as far as you can to gain maximum protection from the wind and swell. You can safely anchor in 20-25 feet of water and still be 250 yards from the beach. Avoid anchoring too close to the beach; otherwise, your boat will roll in the same swells the nearby surfers are riding. The bottom at Oneloa is generally sand, but watch carefully as you drop anchor because some areas have rocks and coral.

FACILITIES

None

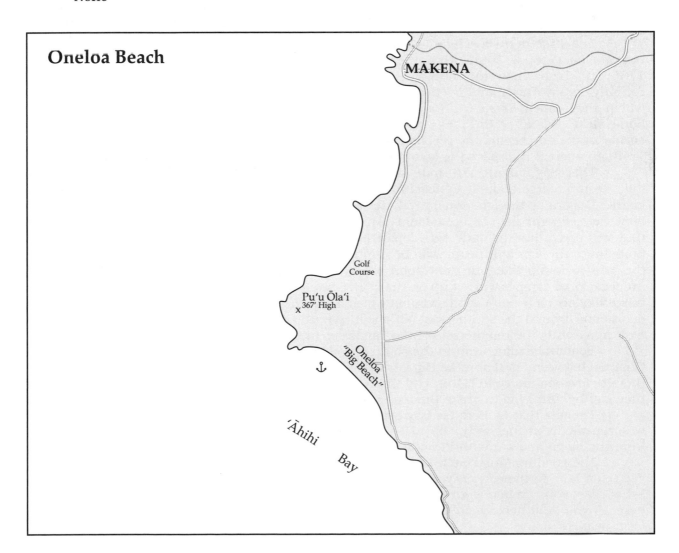

Oneloa Beach

MĀKENA

Golf Course

Puʻu Ōlaʻi
x 367' High

Oneloa "Big Beach"

ʻĀhihi Bay

LA PEROUSE BAY
CHARTS #19320, #19340, OR #19347
LAT. N20° 35.550 LONG. W156° 25.069 (ANCHORAGE)

La Perouse Bay, formed by two fingers (more like fists) of ʻaʻa lava from the most recent eruption on Maui, in 1790, has beauty, solitude and good protection to entice the cruising sailor. Cape Kīnaʻu to the northwest and Cape Hanamanioa on the southeast are black and rugged and starkly beautiful, with white water breaking at their rocky feet.

On the beach near the anchorage white lava rocks top the black-cinder beach, looking like marshmallows from this vantage point (though we know they wouldn't feel like marshmallows if we stepped on them). At one end of the beach, a large stand of beach naupaka separates the black cinders from the jumbles of large boulders that form the east boundary of La Perouse Bay.

Anchored in this bay, you can see clearly its recent geological history. The bay lies between the two bumpy black trails of lava that in 1790 erupted from the Kalua o Lapa cone and tumbled down the sloping hillside, covering the older exposed layers of smooth *pāhoehoe* lava and falling into the ocean.

The first non-Hawaiian to land on Maui, Captain La Pérouse, found this sheltered bay in 1786, and the bay has since borne his name. Until recently, many Hawaiians lived around this bay, which they called *Keoneʻōʻio* ("sandy [place with] bonefish"). Inland of the rocks at the southeast corner of the bay begins the reconstructed Hoapili Trail, an ancient trail paved of lava rocks.

This bay, about .70 mile wide and .50 mile deep, is large enough to accommodate many boats. Generally, though, you'll rarely see another boat here, except for the occasional fishing boat that will arrive just at dark and depart at dawn. Sometimes three or four people will be fishing from the lava rocks on the southeast point of the bay. An occasional camper will set up on the beach, but

Beach with camper at La Perouse

this rocky beach is not a good swimming beach and therefore doesn't get much day use. Though snorkeling around the south coast of Cape Kīnaʻu (the west boundary of La Perouse Bay) is excellent, apparently the remoteness of the bay keeps most of the snorkeling enthusiasts away.

Boaters heading around the south end of Maui to Hāna or those crossing the ʻAlenuihāhā Channel between Maui and the Big Island might use this bay as a stopover for the night. In fact, though, few boaters go to Hāna, and those crossing to the Big Island do not usually stop; rather, they sail by, hurrying to make this passage as quickly as possible.

The fact that La Perouse Bay gets few visitors is precisely its appeal for those few boaters who repeatedly anchor in the bay. It's a spacious, quiet bay with the only light at night coming from the moon and stars and the flicker of a lantern from the occasional campsite ashore.

The good landing beach here is in the northwest corner of the bay; unfortunately, when you're on land in the corner, you're behind a fence and on posted private property. In the calmest of seas, you can take your tender ashore at the center of the beach. Kayakers regularly go in here. If you land here, you'll be able to walk up to the Hoapili Trail or out on the points where local people fish.

This bay is also a favorite of spinner dolphins, which feed in large pods throughout the bay. Because it faces southwest, La Perouse Bay provides good protection from both trade winds and north winds. When *kona* winds blow, however, boaters looking for an anchorage should go elsewhere.

APPROACH

Coming to La Perouse from the west or north, you'll see the anchorage as soon as you round Kanahena Point on Cape Kīnaʻu. Turn wide as you round the point to head into the anchorage; many rocks lie offshore here. Approaching La Perouse from the south, you can use the light on Cape Hanamanioa as a landmark.

From the east, set a course for Cape Hanamanioa, the point with a light on the east side of the bay. Another helpful landmark from this direction is the island of Kahoʻolawe, just across the ʻAlalākeiki Channel from La Perouse Bay. When approaching from the east, stand out to avoid the shallow water and offshore rocks along the shoreline east of Cape Hanamanioa.

ANCHORAGE

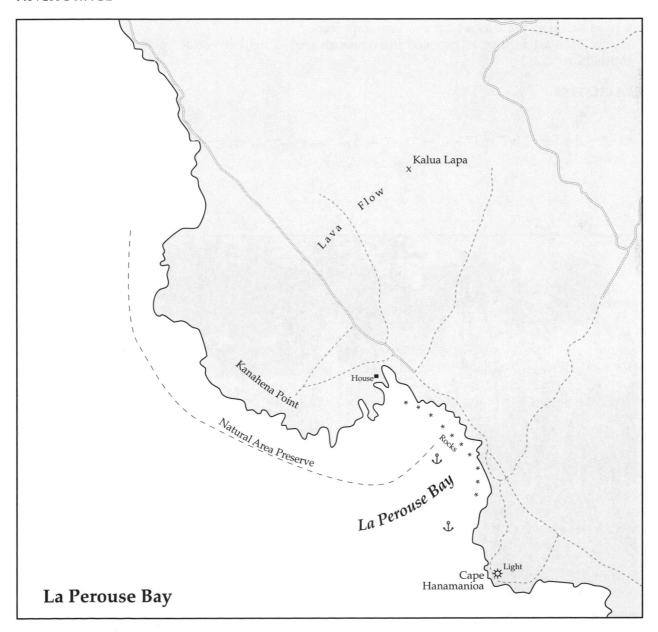

La Perouse Bay

The western half of La Perouse Bay is part of a nature preserve, so you may not anchor in that area. This restriction does not affect boaters much, however, since they are primarily interested in protection from trades blowing down the east side of the island and therefore will most commonly anchor in the middle or against the cliffs on the east side of the bay.

On the east side of the bay, anchor in 35-40 feet, approximately 100-150 yards from the cliffs. Look closely before you drop your hook to find one of the sand patches, where you'll find good holding. Whenever a southerly swell is entering the bay, a roll stabilizer will make the boat more comfortable.

When trades are blowing, the motion in the middle of the bay is little different from that in the east side of the anchorage. In strong north winds, anchoring in the middle, where you can get your boat farther back into the bay, becomes preferable. In the middle, drop your anchor in 40-50 feet of water. Again, look closely to find a good sand patch, carefully staying clear of the extensive coral on the bottom. Since the water is normally crystal clear here, you can easily see where the sand patches are.

Those who wish to anchor near the northeastern shore of the bay in the center can find a large sand patch in about 45 feet of water some 200 yards from the shore just to the right of a pass through the rocks that sea kayakers use.

This anchorage is exposed to the south and is neither comfortable nor safe when *kona* winds blow.

FACILITIES

None

Grass House

NU'U LANDING
CHARTS #19320 OR #19340
LAT. N20° 37.500 LONG. W156° 10.740 (ANCHORAGE)

Nu'u Bay is something of an oasis after the long desert of lava covering the south coast of East Maui past Cape Hanamanioa. A few miles west of Nu'u, the jagged black flows of lava give way to a more sloping terrain, with deep gulches sliced by streams, the sources of the streams hidden in the clouds typically shielding Haleakalā. Along the shore at Nu'u grows the first thick stand of *kiawe* trees you'll see after rounding the cape. The beach here is fine black sand, rather than the lava rocks lining the coast for miles before, and is probably the best swimming beach on this coast.

The sand beach makes a dry landing in your tender possible in calm weather.

Eroded landscape west of Nu'u Landing

Ashore are two historical sites, the remains of the Nu'u Salt Pond and the Koa Heiau. Not much that distinguishes the pond remains except a pool of water, and the *heiau* is behind a locked gate, so the only compelling reason to go ashore is to walk on or swim off the beach.

The Hawaiians may have given Nu'u its name, which means "height," because one of their gods lived on the protected ledges on the steep mountains high above. Near this bay was a large fishing village, and the bay was a well-known canoe landing. In the late 19th Century, a pier was constructed, from which the large Kaupō Ranch shipped its cattle to market.

From this bay you have exceptional views of Haleakalā when the clouds part and, across the 'Alenuihāhā Channel, of the island of Hawai'i.

Boaters making the trip to or from Hāna along this south coast can put in at Nu'u Landing to wait for the seas to moderate a little more before going on. One Park Service Ranger we spoke with told us that he thinks Nu'u Landing is the best anchorage on the south coast of East Maui; it offers reasonable protection from the uncomfortable seas that build up after the trades have been blowing for a few days.

When north winds are blowing or when the winds are calm, Nu'u Landing is an excellent anchorage. Few boaters choose Nu'u as a destination; however, if you want solitude and quiet, with spectacular views of Haleakalā and the north shore of the Big Island, consider this oasis in the lava.

APPROACH

From the west, the anchorage is about 14.5 miles from La Perouse Bay. The easiest way to identify the anchorage is to use the Pi'ilani Highway, which begins to run along the shoreline about 2.5 miles west of Nuʻu Landing. When you get closer, you can identify Nuʻu Bay and the anchorage by the volcanic outcropping that extends from shore .25 mile to define the eastern extreme of the anchorage.

From the east, use the changing topography and vegetation on shore as an indicator. Nuʻu Landing marks the eastern edge of the lava flows; this change is easy to see from the water. The landscape to the west is primarily barren lava rock, with a few small bushes and patches of grass growing around spires and turrets of lava; to the east it is lush and green. Also, a farm house and some outbuildings in the cove just to the east of Nuʻu Landing will let you know when you're getting close to the anchorage. Nuʻu Landing is 15.0 miles from Kaʻuiki Head at Hāna Bay.

Campers and fishermen often set up camp on the shore, especially up on the lava flow at the back of the cove. You'll be able to see their vehicles from the anchorage.

ANCHORAGE

When you're inside Nuʻu Bay, you will see the obvious lava flow forming the eastern edge of the bay and a black sand beach to the north. The best anchorage is in the waters protected from the swells coming down the eastern coastline of Maui by the lava outcropping.

Anchor in 30-40 feet of water, about 150 yards from the beach and 100 yards from the lava flow. The sand and gravel bottom offers good holding.

The best landing for your tender is in the northeast corner of the cove, close to the lava outcropping.

FACILITIES

None

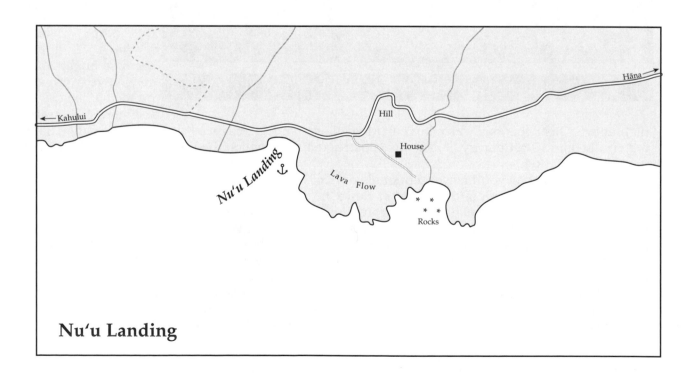

Nuʻu Landing

MAMALU BAY
CHARTS #19320 OR #19340
LAT. N20° 37.500 LONG. W156° 08.910 (ANCHORAGE)

Dramatic cliffs over 100 feet high protect the bay to the north and east. Graceful white tropic birds soar along these red-brown cliffs topped with green grass. Beyond, the green slopes climb to Haleakalā, the "house of the sun" that usually has its roof in the clouds.

As with all the anchorages along the south coast of East Maui, Mamalu Bay will almost certainly be empty when you arrive and when you leave. At night you will see no lights except for an occasional glimmer on the northwest coast of the Big Island some 20 miles to the southeast.

The snorkeling is excellent here, particularly in the northeast corner where a small reef provides a habitat for many tropical fish. This bay lacks a beach suitable either for walking or for landing a tender.

Mamalu is comfortable in north, calm, or light trade conditions, but it is not a place to go when heavy trades or *kona* winds are blowing.

Mamalu Bay

APPROACH

Mamalu Bay is 16.0 miles east from Cape Hanamanioa at La Perouse Bay and 13.5 miles southwest from Ka'uiki Head. When arriving at Mamalu Bay from the west, continue 1.5 miles eastward beyond Nu'u Landing. The red-brown cliffs forming the north and east boundaries of the anchorage stand out. Coming along the coast from the west, you'll also note a distinct difference in the vegetation at about Nu'u Landing or Mamalu Bay; whereas the terrain is volcanic flows and sparse vegetation to the west of these two anchorages, it turns to deep green here.

From the east, the most distinctive landmark is Ka'īlio Point, 2.2 miles past Huialoha Church, a small white church with a russet-colored roof at Kaupō. This church sits on the water's edge where several small rock islands lie offshore.

The two shacks on Ka'īlio Point are easy to spot from 2 miles out. Turn into the anchorage .50 mile west of the point. Another way to identify Ka'īlio Point is to use St. Joseph Church. This large white church, which looks like a barn from the water, sits high up on the mountainside some 2 miles inland from Ka'īlio Point.

ANCHORAGE

Anchoring at Mamalu Bay will challenge you. The first challenge is deciding where to anchor in this large bay. In north wind conditions, you can anchor anywhere along the bluffs to the north of the bay. In east wind conditions, anchor under the cliffs to the east.

But the bigger problem at Mamalu is picking a good sand patch in which to anchor. In much of the bay, the sand patches are quite small and therefore hard to hit with your anchor. The anchorage has large boulders in the northern part of the bay close to the cliffs. And the coral stands are luxuriant in much of the bay. Look for a sand patch in at least 40 feet of water because those areas with shallower water typically have excessive boulders and coral.

FACILITIES

None

Shacks on Kaʻīlio Point, east of Mamalu

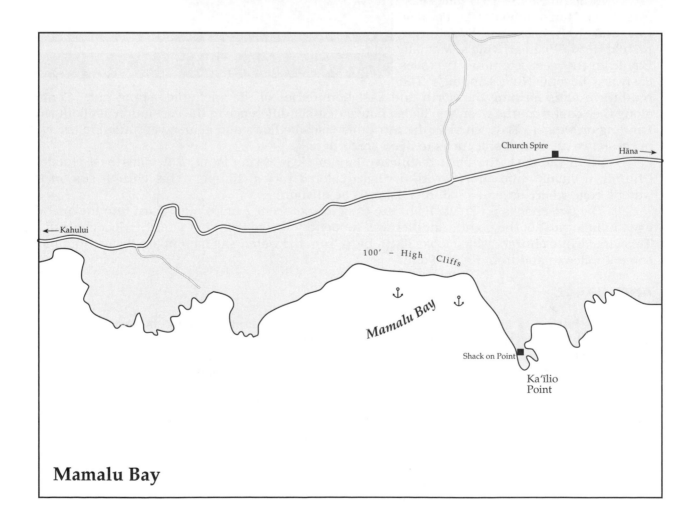

Church Spire

Hāna →

← Kahului

100ʹ – High Cliffs

Mamalu Bay

Shack on Point

Kaʻīlio
Point

Mamalu Bay

KAUPŌ LANDING
CHARTS #19320 OR #19340
LAT. N20° 38.502 LONG. W156° 06.690 (ANCHORAGE)

Kaupō was an ancient *ahupua'a* ("land division") between Pākōwai and Mokuia points, extending, as did *ahupua'a* typically, from the sea to the mountains. Near Kaupō Landing was a large and well-established fishing village of ancient Hawaiians. Hawaiian chants recall the residents of this village for their great fondness for *loli* ("sea slugs or cucumbers"). One of the legendary chiefs of Kaupō was said to have been so fond of *loli* that he had a special *imu* ("oven") constructed for roasting them, and his *imu* was famous throughout the Islands.

In one of the many attacks on this island from one of the chiefs on the Big Island, Kalani'ōpu'u, the most powerful chief of the Big Island when Cook arrived, landed his warriors at Kaupō, near Kalaeo'īlio Point. In a bloody battle and after many fatalities among the people of Kaupō, Kalani'ōpu'u and his forces withdrew, unable to overcome the warriors of the Maui chief Kahekili.

According to legend, Kaupō Landing was also the site of numerous fatal shark attacks that finally caused all the residents to move away. One of the hungry sharks then lamented, *"Onia Kaupō"* ("Barren is Kaupō"). The remains of three *heiau* nearby are testimony to the numbers of Hawaiians who once lived along this shore.

In the last century the Kaupō Ranch revived the village of Kaupō. The small bay protected by the tiny islands of Moku Lau served as a landing for transporting cattle from the ranch. Two churches survive from that era, St. Joseph Church, built in 1861, and tiny Huialoha (1859), visible from the anchorage.

The village of Kaupō has little else left except the churches and the remains of the *heiau*. Instead of a

Kaupō Landing, Huialoha Church, and campers

village, temporary fish camps often cover the flat spaces on the point between Huialoha Church and the water.

Kaupō Landing is another of the seldom used anchorages on Maui. The only boaters who regularly use this anchorage are fishermen. While Kaupō Landing is not a wonderfully comfortable anchorage, it is picturesque and remote, two attributes appealing to many cruising boaters.

If the winds are light or from the north, you can make a beach landing between Moku Lau (the small rocky islands) and the beach just below the Huialoha Church. In calm weather you can snorkel or dive around the rocky islands. Fishing is good here.

APPROACH

Kaupō Landing is 18.0 miles east of Cape Hanamanioa. Approaching Kaupō Landing from the west, you may find the anchorage somewhat difficult to spot. Huialoha Church is the best identifying mark, though you probably won't see it until you're directly abeam of it. If you cruise along the coast about a mile off shore until you see the church, you can turn directly into the anchorage, thus avoiding Moku Lau, the offshore rocky islets extending from the bay directly to the east of the church.

From the east, Kaupō is 12 miles southwest of Ka'uiki Head. You will be able to see the Huialoha Church after you pass Mokuia Point. The white walls and red-brown roof stand out clearly.

ANCHORAGE

The anchorage at Kaupō is deep; plan to anchor in 45-50 feet of water. Drop your anchor inside the cove, but not so far in as to be in the surf line. The sand bottom provides excellent holding. When you have your hook down, you should be about mid-way between the rock islands and Haleki'i Point.

FACILITIES

Restrooms
Shower (cold)

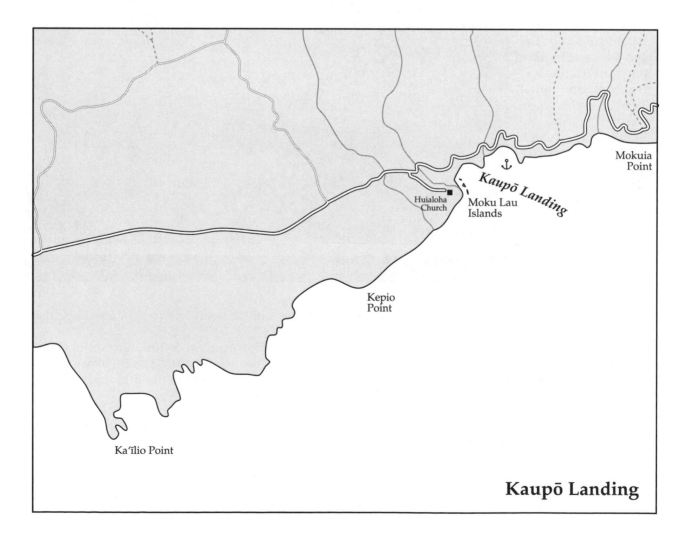

Kaupō Landing

KAʻĀPAHU BAY
CHARTS # 19320 OR #19340
LAT. N20° 38.906 LONG. W156° 04.595 (ANCHORAGE)

The anchorage at Kaʻāpahu Bay, also called Lelekea Bay, is quite similar in appearance to Hāna Bay. Both are nestled in close to high mountains covered with lush growth. The primary difference between the two is that boaters who anchor at Hāna can go ashore and enjoy the town, but those who anchor at Kaʻāpahu will have no place to go, except the beach, if they do go ashore (a questionable proposition except in the calmest of weather).

Despite this limitation, the beauty and isolation of Kaʻāpahu ("the truncation") make it an inviting anchorage. The green cliffs and gulches coming down from Haleakalā tower over the anchorage, and in the northeast corner is a small waterfall. The water in the bay will tempt you to jump in and enjoy snorkeling.

Not only are you unlikely to see other boats anchored in Kaʻāpahu Bay, but you'll also see few cars on the single-lane dirt road that runs along the shoreline here. It goes to Hāna, but few cars travel this bumpy, dusty road.

As is so much of this once widely populated coastline of Maui, this bay is rich in lore. At Kīpahulu, the *ahupuaʻa* (a land division) surrounding the bay, a woman left her husband and children to live on Oʻahu with another man. The aggrieved husband consulted a *kahuna*, who advised the man to find a container with a lid and talk into it, telling of his great love and longing for his wife. Then the *kahuna* chanted into the container and cast it into the sea, where it drifted to the woman while she was out fishing. After hearing the love song of her husband, she realized he was her true love, and she returned to Kīpahulu.

This anchorage, like all the others on Maui's south coast, is good in calm weather or north wind conditions. Do not plan to stop here if strong trades or south winds are blowing. Kaʻāpahu would be a dangerous anchorage in such conditions.

In calm weather you can land your tender on the small beach in the southwest corner of the bay.

Old dock footing west of anchorage

APPROACH

Ka'āpahu is 19.5 miles east of Cape Hanamanioa. You may have a difficult time identifying Ka'āpahu Bay, for the terrain along this rugged coastline all looks much the same. Perhaps the easiest way if you're coming from the west is to identify the old Huialoha Church at Kaupō and then travel 1.75 miles farther northeast to Ka'āpahu. When you've arrived at the anchorage, you can see the dirt road winding along the shoreline. West of the anchorage is an old concrete footing, which one local fisherman told us was once part of a pier.

If you approach from the east, you'll see farms and residences along the coastline until you arrive at Ka'āpahu. Nine miles southwest along the coastline from Ka'uiki Head is Āhole Rock, a low, barren, flat-topped rock about 200 yards off shore; Ka'āpahu Bay is 1.3 miles west of this rock. Two houses sit out on the point between Āhole Rock and Ka'āpahu. Stand out from shore as you approach Ka'āpahu because of the numerous rocks lying offshore along the coastline in the area.

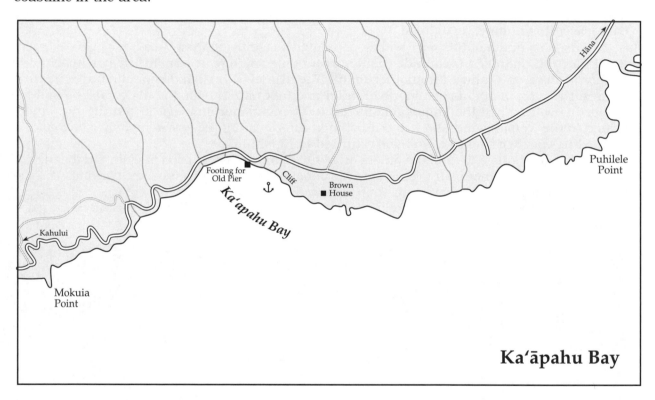

Ka'āpahu Bay

ANCHORAGE

If a north or trade wind is blowing, anchor in the northern part of the bay about 100 yards off the beach and 150 yards from the northeast edge of the bay. You'll see a small waterfall off your bow if your boat is facing northeast and a brown house on the point to the east.

This anchorage has good holding in easily located sand patches. Anchor in 30-40 feet of water.

The *Coast Pilot* observes that Ka'āpahu "can be used for small-boat anchorage in trade-wind weather; there are depths of 4 fathoms about 200 yards off the pebble beach." We found the depths 200 yards off the beach to be deeper, but we may have measured depths in a different area of the bay.

FACILITIES

None

HĀNA BAY
CHARTS #19320 OR 19341
LATITUDE N 20° 55.750 LONGITUDE W 155° 58.360 (ENTRANCE)

On the island of Maui, which has more than its share of beautiful anchorages, "heavenly Hāna" stands out. On the windward side of the island, Hāna has the luxuriant tropical vegetation to show for its more than 75 inches of average annual rainfall. Clouds form on the slopes of Haleakalā and then drift down to engulf Hāna, giving Hāna, according to an old Hawaiian proverb, the "Rain-of-the-low-sky."

The approach to Hāna by sea from either direction furnishes part of the appeal of this destination, for Hāna Bay sits in the middle of a long stretch of coastline of emerald cliffs and gulches, waterfalls, and deep, mysterious caverns. When you enter the bay, you may feel as if you've entered a velvety green Fabergé egg, the inside an even richer treasure than the outside.

The stories of Hāna, formerly called Kapueokahi, or "the single owl," are as ancient as those of the demigod Māui, whose favorite site, in some legends, was Hāna. Māui turned his daughter's lover into Ka'uiki Head, the heavily forested crater that stands 390 feet tall on the south side of the bay.

Ka'uiki Head, a natural fortress for the defense of the bay, was the site of many fiercely contested battles between invaders from the Big Island and the defenders of Maui. Queen Ka'ahumanu, reputed to have been the favorite wife of Kamehameha I, was born to exiled *ali'i* in a cave on this headland, at a spot now marked with a small plaque.

Beached canoes at Hāna

In 1860 the first sugar was planted in the Hāna area. Soon, the Ka'elekū Sugar Company drew Hawaiians, Filipinos, Portuguese, Japanese, and Chinese to Hāna to work in the fields. After the demise of the sugar industry in the 1930s, Paul Fagan, an American industrialist, established a cattle ranch which survives today. The large cross atop Pu'u o Kahaula, 545 feet above Hāna, is a memorial to Fagan.

One of the beauties of Hāna is that you can walk to the many sites of historical interest. The Hāna Cultural Center is only a few blocks from the harbor and, though modest, exhibits artifacts from both the pre- and post-contact eras of Hawai'i. On the grounds are what must be one of the tiniest jails and courthouses in the country and a reconstructed Hawaiian hut. On the main street is the Wānanalua Church, built atop an old *heiau*.

Going ashore at Hāna is particularly easy on the beach south of the old 300-foot pier which stands forlorn in the south corner. Behind the pier is a ramp used for launching small fishing boats. From here, you can walk around to Ka'ahumanu's birth site, up the hill to town, to the Fagan memorial, or to one of the other beaches of Hāna Bay.

The white sand beach in the bay is a fine swimming beach, where local children swim and play in outrigger canoes. With somewhat more lengthy walks, you can visit the black sand beach, Waikaloa ("long waters"), in the west corner of the bay, and Red Sand Beach (Kaihālulu to the Hawaiians, meaning "roaring sea"), which lies south of Ka'uiki Head. This latter cinder beach, created from the erosion of Ka'uiki, is both black and red, but the red predominates. It was a famous canoe-landing site in the past.

To enjoy this bay, you really have to do little more than sit in the cockpit of your boat and savor the ambiance. The water is calm, not even rippled by the little traffic of fishing boats in and out of the bay. The rainy periods are just frequent enough to encourage you to get your reading done.

With such a lovely spot to attract boaters, one might suppose the bay would be filled at all times with anchored boats. Not so. The reason Hāna rarely gets included in cruising plans is simple: the weather. Regardless of how you approach Hāna, you must consider the winds.

Moored near the Hāna pier

You should make a trip to Hāna only when the winds are blowing out of the south or when they are light. Both the trip to Hāna and the anchorage become extremely uncomfortable when trades are blowing strongly.

APPROACH

The approach to Hāna Bay is straightforward. The bay is on the extreme eastern end of the island of Maui. Regardless of the direction you approach from, identify Ka'uiki Head first. Shortly thereafter you should be able to identify Ka'uiki Head Light, which is not on Ka'uiki Head at all but on Pu'uki'i Island, a small island just seaward of Ka'uiki.

When you have the light in sight, look for Twin Rocks (sometimes called "Two Rocks,") the bare rocks about 300 yards northeast of the light. Then identify Nānu'alele Point, which marks

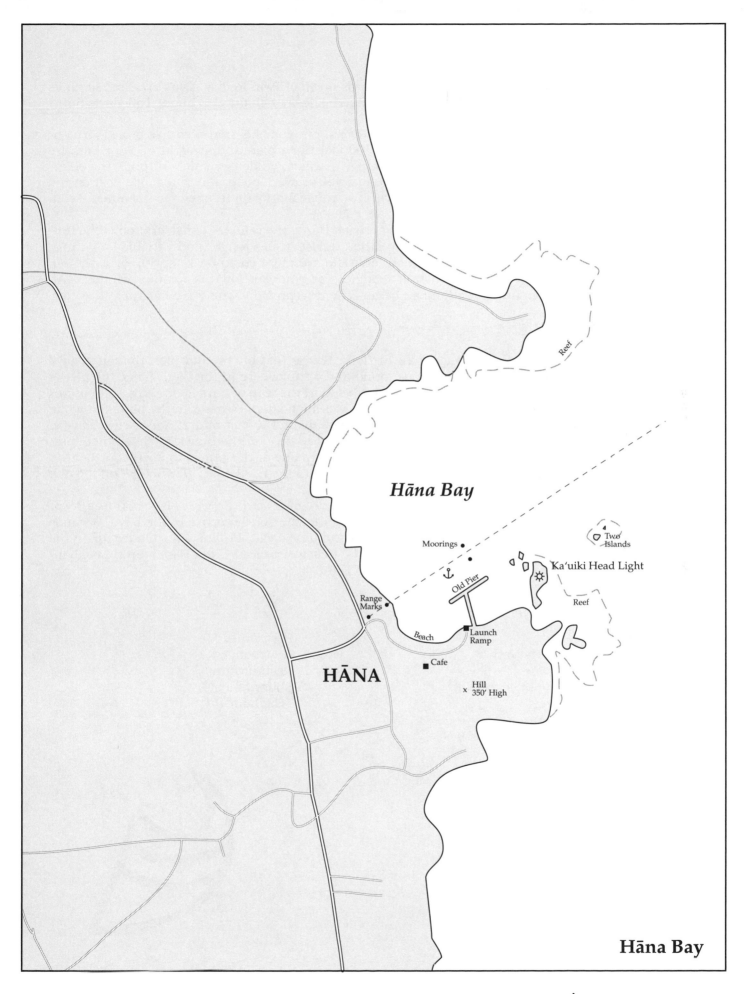

Hāna Bay

Moorings

Two Islands

Kaʻuiki Head Light

Reef

Range Marks

Old Pier

Beach

Launch Ramp

Cafe

Hill 350' High

HĀNA

Reef

Hāna Bay

the northern extreme of Hāna Bay, about 800 yards north of Twin Rocks. Seas break at all times over the rocks extending seaward from this point. The desired channel is about 150 yards north of Twin Rocks.

Once you're positioned outside of Twin Rocks, put your boat on a course of 241° true or 230° magnetic. Off your port bow will be the 300-foot Hāna pier, and straight off your bow are the range marks—but don't depend on these range marks to guide you safely through the channel. These range marks may be the most unusual you've ever encountered: a single post on the sea wall in the southeast corner of the bay with two range marks on it, one over the other. From Twin Rocks to the pier is a distance of only .25 miles.

No matter from which direction you approach Hāna, the primary consideration is the timing, based on the weather. Wait until the Weather Service issues a light and variable long-range forecast before setting sail for Hāna. Such forecasts are more common in spring or early fall. You will need to be in a state of constant readiness as you wait for this weather window. An approach to Hāna from any direction can be an easy trip, provided you have favorable weather.

ANCHORAGE

The recommended anchorage area in Hāna Bay is just off the old pier, though a local boater told us that good anchorage can be found almost anywhere in the bay. Since the pier is no longer in use, you won't have to worry about being in the way of barges or ships coming in.

A white sign on the end of the pier advises visiting boaters to moor to the blue and white buoys just off the pier. The two buoys are positioned about 150 feet and 225 feet, respectively, north of the seaward end of the pier. If you don't want to dive on the buoys to check them out, you can drop your bow hook and then tie a stern line to one of the buoys to keep your boat in line with the swell that usually comes into the harbor from the northeast. (Do not get on the old, unstable pier for any reason.)

The bottom near the pier and buoys is sand and mud, and the water is 25-30 feet deep.

You can easily land your dinghy on the beach in the south corner of the bay. Because the pier gives some protection, only small waves get to the beach. Pulling your tender up on the soft sand beach is easy. To the two small markets, Hasegawa's and Hāna Ranch Store, is about a 15-minute walk through the residential area of Hāna.

FACILITIES

Airport	Post Office
Bank (limited hours)	Restrooms
Car Rental	Restaurants
Fuel (gasoline by jerry jug)	Showers (cold)
Grocery Stores	Telephone
Library	Water
Medical Center	

THE ISLAND OF MOLOKINI

Sunset over Molokini

Molokini ka ʻiewe o Kahoʻolawe
("Molokini is the navel-string of Kahoʻolawe.")

MOLOKINI ISLAND
CHARTS #19320, #19340, OR #19347
LAT. N20° 38.020 LONG. W156° 29.650 (ANCHORAGE)

Pele's dream lover, Lohi'au, who was living at Mā'alaea, Maui, took for his wife a *mo'o* (a lizard) from Kaho'olawe. In anger Pele ripped the *mo'o* in half, the tail becoming Pu'u Ōla'i Hill at Mākena, Maui, and the head, Molokini Island. (Ironically, Molokini means "many ties.")

Of course, geologists have another tale to tell. Molokini, they say, is the southern rim of an extinct volcanic crater that was once connected to Maui, Kaho'olawe, Lāna'i, and Moloka'i and then was partly submerged after the last ice age. The shallow cove inside the rim is above the submerged floor of the crater. The geologists probably have it right, but even the early storytellers had some part of the truth, their myth iterating the ancient connectedness between Maui and Molokini.

Because only half the rim remains, Molokini presents boaters with a unique experience: taking their boats inside a crater. The highest part of the remaining rim is 156 feet above the water. From tip to tip, the island is .30 mile long, encircling an anchorage where as many as 15 boats can moor or anchor.

This rocky islet has neither water nor vegetation on it and shows no evidence of ever having been occupied. Now, the islet is a state seabird sanctuary; therefore, you may not go ashore. The waters surrounding Molokini to a depth of 30 fathoms are designated a Marine Life Conservation District. Snorkelers and divers can revel in the aquarium of tropical fish and many varieties of coral inside the protected cove. The diversity of fish and other marine life in the cove makes Molokini one of the best snorkeling sites in the entire state. Some varieties of fish will let you approach to within a few feet before they casually turn tail. Humpback whales have been seen in the cove during their breeding and calving season—between November and April.

The back, or southern, side of Molokini has a steep face that drops off more than 200 feet in places. Coral on this face and the many fish swimming around the outcroppings and through the crevices make this side of the islet a favorite dive site. Black coral was once abundant in the deep waters here, but unrestricted harvesting destroyed almost all the stands. A few small colonies are making a comeback on this back wall.

The island was once used as a target by U. S. military aircraft and ships. In past years divers reported unexploded ordnance on the bottom near the island, but none of the thousands of snorkelers and divers to the island have reported any such hazards.

Molokini is an ideal day sail from the southwest coast of Maui or a stopover for cruisers gunkholing along the Maui coast. Boaters can even make a round trip from Lahaina in one day because Molokini is only 17.5 miles from the harbor entrance.

APPROACH

Molokini is located between the island of Kaho'olawe and Pu'u Ōla'i, on the island of Maui (4 miles from Kaho'olawe and 2.5 miles from Pu'u Ōla'i). Enter the crater from the north. If you're approaching from the south or west, be cautious of the reef that extends northward from the northwest end of the island.

ANCHORAGE

Anchoring in Molokini is not recommended because of the extremely poor holding and because of the potential further damage to the coral. Rather, pick up one of the dozen or so moorings the state has installed for anyone to use on a first-come, first-served basis. However, they were not designed for overnight use. In fact, all boaters—whether private or commercial— are expected to limit themselves to a maximum of 3 hours on a mooring.

Picking up a mooring at Molokini may challenge you. Most of the mooring buoys are 6 feet below the surface of the water, and, though their faded pink color makes them easy to see in the clear water, you will have to dive down and pick up the mooring line hanging below the buoy.

By contrast, the state moorings have the new stainless steel pinion system that assures much more security. Whichever mooring you tie to, however, check the mooring line and anchor carefully once you're in the water.

All the buoys are located about 200 feet offshore of the crescent formed by the crater and the reef that extends northward from the NW corner.

FACILITIES

None (Landing on Molokini is prohibited.)

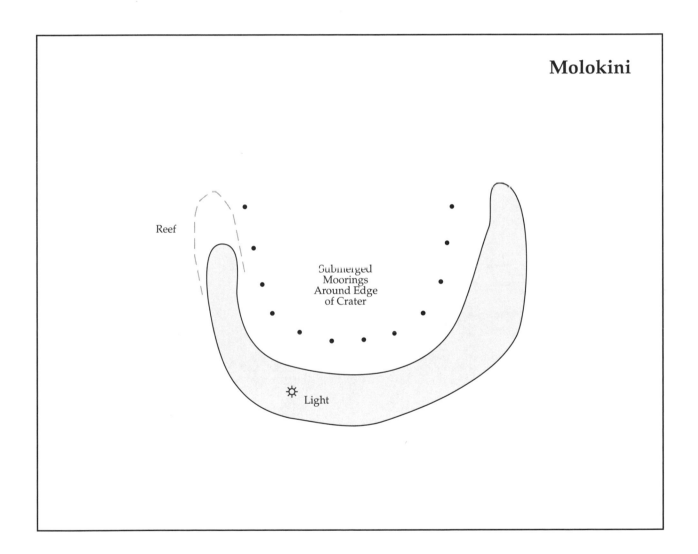

Lāna'i

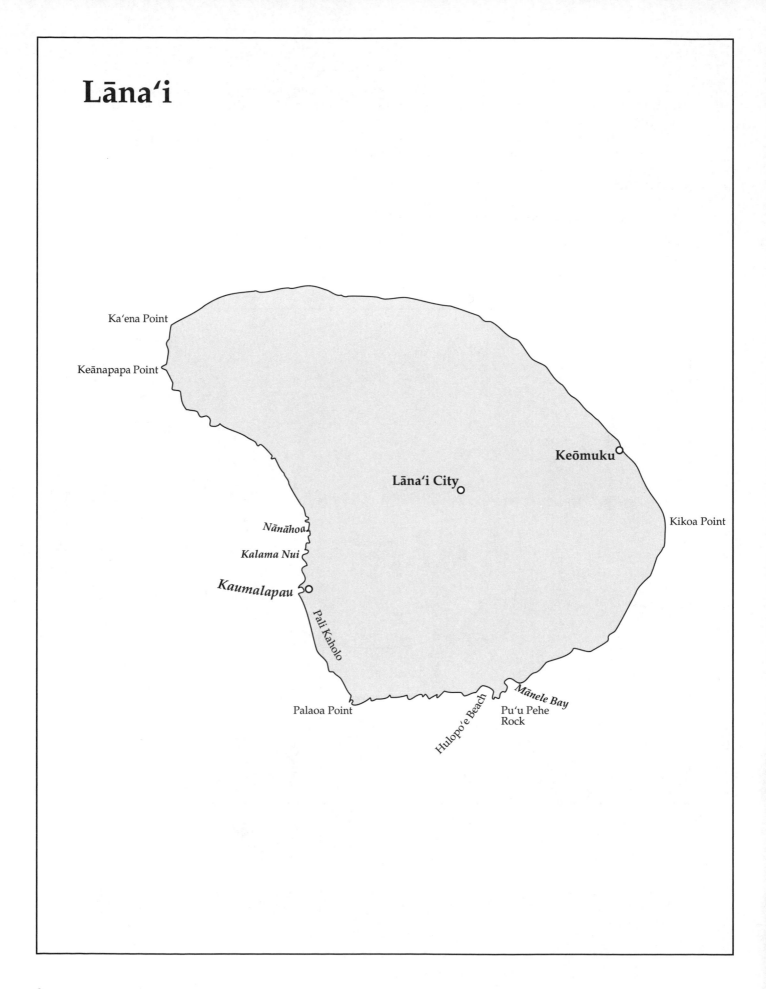

Ka'ena Point

Keānapapa Point

Keōmuku

Lāna'i City

Kikoa Point

Nānāhoa

Kalama Nui

Kaumalapau

Pali Kaholo

Palaoa Point

Mānele Bay

Pu'u Pehe
Rock

Hulopó'e Beach

THE ISLAND OF LĀNA'I

THE PINEAPPLE ISLE

Hulopo'e Beach (Mānele)

Lāna'i ke 'ehu o ke kai.
("Lāna'i stands among the sea sprays.")

THE ISLAND OF LĀNA'I

Lāna'i, with only 139.5 square miles of land, is geographically the smallest of the main Hawaiian islands, and, for the cruising boater, it offers fewer destinations than any of the other main islands. Nevertheless, cruising sailors should not overlook it, for each of its destinations—two harbors and two anchorages—is abundantly attractive.

Formed by a single shield volcano, the Pālāwai, it has a rounded hump-like shape. In the lee of the West Maui Mountains, Lāna'i receives sparse rainfall and hence is not a dot of green on the horizon as the other islands are. It does have a heavily forested area in the higher elevations around Lāna'ihale, at 3,370 feet the highest point on the island.

History seems sometimes to have forgotten little Lāna'i. The first inhabitants of this island may have arrived as late as the 1400s. According to Hawaiian legends, man-eating spirits occupied Lāna'i before that time. Depending on which legend one follows, either the prophet Lanikāula drove the spirits from the island or the unruly Maui prince Kaululā'au accomplished that heroic feat.

The more popular myth is that the mischievous Kaululā'au pulled up every breadfruit tree he could find on Maui. Finally his father, Chief Kaka'alaneo, had to banish him to Lāna'i, expecting him not to survive in that hostile place. However, Kaululā'au was able to outwit the spirits and drive them from the island. The chief looked across the channel from Maui and saw that his son's fire continued to burn nightly on the shore, and he sent a canoe to Lāna'i to bring the prince, redeemed by his courage and his cleverness, back home to Maui. True to himself, Kaululā'au had, in the meantime, pulled up all the breadfruit trees on Lāna'i, accounting for the lack of breadfruit on the island.

The name *Lāna'i* is of uncertain origin, but the island has historically been called *Lāna'i o Kaululā'au*; one theory is that the phrase means "day of conquest of Kaululā'au."

The first people to migrate here, most likely from Maui and Moloka'i, probably established fishing villages along the coast initially but later branched out into the interior, where they raised taro in the fertile volcanic soil. During most of those years, Maui chiefs held dominion over Lāna'i (even today Lāna'i is part of the County of Maui), but apparently the Maui leaders primarily left the people of Lāna'i to their own devices. However, the warriors of the powerful chief Kalaniopu'u of the Big Island invaded the island of Lāna'i in 1778, killing most of the people and destroying their villages.

When Kamehameha I established his summer home in Kaunolū, above the shimmering bay west of Palaoa Point, Lāna'i revived somewhat. Then foreigners began to arrive to try their hand at farming in this sometimes hostile landscape, where the most obvious "man-eating spirit" remaining was the lack of sufficient water.

A Chinese man brought sugarcane to Lāna'i in 1802 but failed in his attempt to cultivate it successfully. Then in 1854 a band of Mormons established a colony in the fertile Pālāwai Basin, only to be disbanded when their leader was discovered to be purchasing land for himself rather than for the church.

In 1922 James Dole bought the island for $1.1 million from the Baldwins, a prominent missionary family that got its start in Lahaina. Dole turned the island into one grand pineapple plantation, at the time the largest in the world. He built a town and stocked the island with wild game and fowl for hunting.

The Dole Company built the only town on the island, Lāna'i City, for its pineapple plantation workers. This town of approximately 2,500 people today (essentially, all the people on the island) sits almost exactly in the center of Lana'i and, at 1,600 feet elevation, is high enough to be in the clouds much of the time. Hence, it is cool and moist. The imported Norfolk pines thrive here and give the town a distinctly un-Hawaiian look.

The workers who came here early in the 20th century to work in the pineapple fields were of various nationalities—Japanese, Chinese, Hawaiian, Caucasian. But the majority were Filipinos, and Lāna'i is unique among the islands in having 50-60 per cent of its permanent residents of Filipino descent.

The Murdoch Company owns most of the island today and has brought great changes to what was once an island of pineapple fields. Today, the island produces only enough pineapple for the residents and the guests of the two luxury resort hotels on the island. One, the Lodge at Kō'ele, is near Lāna'i City, and the other, Mānele Bay Hotel, is near Hulopo'e Bay, each with a golf course as well as other sport facilities. The new airport has several flights a day between Lāna'i and the other islands, most of the passengers coming as guests to one of the large hotels.

But Lāna'i remains largely uninhabited, and certainly uncrowded. You'll not have to search for a free space on one of the many beautiful beaches on the north and south coasts of the island. No traffic jams will delay you if you rent a car to see more of the island than you can see from the dock, nor will you encounter lines of tourists as you stop to visit the many sites of interest.

Though Lāna'i has few harbors and tenable anchorages, it has much to offer visiting boaters, nevertheless. Of the four possible destinations, only Mānele Bay is busy. It is the only destination with any facilities and the only one from which you can readily gain access to some of the sites of interest ashore. From Mānele you can walk to the twin bay, Hulopo'e, or catch a ride into Lāna'i City to see the town that Dole built.

In Lāna'i City, you can rent a vehicle to visit some of the many historical sites on this fascinating island. At the top of our list are the remains of the village of Kaunolū; the Munro Trail, a ridge road climbing to Lana'ihale, the highest point on Lāna'i, Lāna'ihale; the petroglyphs and the nearby Shipwreck Beach; and the remains of Keōmuku village.

Plantation houses at Lāna'i City

The adventure of finding Kaunolū as you wind through the now defunct pineapple fields enhances the adventure of seeing the remains of this once important village on the cliffs overlooking the southwest point of Lāna'i, Palaoa Point. The lava rock foundations of dwellings, a canoe shed and fish shrine, and a large *heiau* are part of the most complete archaeological site of its type in Hawai'i. Above the water of the cove is the legendary Kahekili's Leap. For Kamehameha's warriors, this leap from a cliff 62 feet into the water, missing a 15-foot ledge in the fall, became a test of courage and loyalty to the king.

George Munro, brought from New Zealand in 1911 to manage the Lāna'i Company Ranch, became the "Johnny Appleseed" of Lāna'i. He planted hundreds of trees and shrubs along the ridge of Lāna'ihale in an attempt to create a watershed. Munro was the first to bring in Norfolk pines from New Zealand, these imports later to become the signature trees of the island. The Munro Trail winds through the vegetation and into the clouds atop Lāna'ihale.

Off the northwest coast of Lāna'i, the rusting hull of a shipyard oil tanker that was under tow between the Mainland and Japan in the 1950s reminds sailors of why this long stretch of white sand is called "Shipwreck Beach." The trade winds that roar through the Pailolo Channel between Maui and Moloka'i and then funnel into the Kalohi Channel have driven many a ship onto the reef here, most of them wooden ships from the days when Lahaina was a busy roadstead.

On some rock faces in the Po'aiwa Gulch, southeast of Shipwreck Beach, are some fairly accessible petroglyphs (unlike so many others that are neither easily found nor easily reached.) Continuing southeast on the dirt road along the north coast, you'll find the remains of the village of Keōmuku. Some machinery from the Maunalei Sugar Company train still lies rusting in the brush. The ill-fated company, owned by the daughter of the Mormon leader Walter Gibson, folded after the second year when the sweet well water suddenly turned brackish. The Hawaiian version of what happened to the well water is that the sugar company was being punished for disturbing a *heiau* (a sacred temple) when building the track for the sugar train.

The better preserved site is the tiny wooden church, Ka Lanakila o Ka Mālamalama, in a coconut grove across the road from the train. The church has restored walls and a new roof, but the interior is seemingly unchanged from almost 100 years ago.

Many other sites remain for you to discover on Lāna'i. The island abounds with petro-glyphs, ancient *heiau,* abandoned villages, secluded beaches, and many other natural wonders. However, if you choose to limit your sightseeing to what you can see by foot, you'll still find much to entice you in and around Mānele Bay.

In Kaumalapau, the other harbor where you can anchor, and in the two anchorages, Nānāhoa and Kalama Nui Gulch, an occasional fishing boat anchored for the night is far more common than a cruising boat. Charter boats bringing snorkelers and divers over from Maui dart in and out of some of the nearby coves, but once they're gone, cruising boaters can have the entire coast from Keanapapa Point to Palaoa Point pretty much to themselves. So, if you're primarily after solitude and beauty, these three destinations are better choices than Mānele.

Shipwreck Beach has earned its name.

NĀNĀHOA (FIVE NEEDLES OR PINNACLES)
CHART #19340, #19347, OR #19351
LAT. N20° 49.680   LONG. W156° 59.720 (ANCHORAGE)

The anchorage at Nānāhoa is popular with cruising boaters and with charter boat captains, especially when the winds are light or blowing trades. The five large sea stacks ("five needles" or "pinnacles") lying off the western shoreline protect the anchorage. The largest of these is called Nānāhoa for a man who, according to legend, abused his wife. As punishment both were turned into phallic stones. The outermost of the rocks, said to be the female, is about .20 mile offshore.

The pinnacles give to this anchorage a stark aura and beauty. They are black projectiles seeming to have been shot straight up out of the water. Geologically, they are either the remains of a collapsed sea arch or the hard cores left after erosion of softer materials around them; but the Hawaiian legend lends a poignancy to the natural beauty. The water sparkles with clarity, then breaks foaming white on the pinnacles, a mist lingering about the rocks for a few seconds.

Sea stacks at Nānāhoa

No signs of civilization are evident from the anchorage, making this an especially appealing destination for boaters wanting to get away from the confusion and bustle of harbors. It's also a place that, one can imagine, looks as it did hundreds of years ago, when the ancient Hawaiians saw the handiwork of their deities.

The combination of rocks and pristine water at Nānāhoa makes it ideal for snorkeling or diving. The shore is rocky, with no good landing beaches for taking a tender ashore.

APPROACH

From the north or west, first identify Keanapapa Point (the northwest corner of Lāna'i). From there travel 4.8 miles southeast along the western shore of the island, staying about .50 mile offshore. Because the pinnacles at Nānāhoa are the same color as the cliffs behind them, the anchorage is difficult to pick out unless you stay close to the shoreline.

Approaching from the south, go 2.3 miles north of Kaumalapau Harbor, again staying .50 mile offshore when approaching from this direction; the pinnacles are equally difficult to distinguish from seaward.

As you get close to Nānāhoa, you can pick out the pinnacles because the outermost one, .20 mile offshore, rises 32 feet above the water. The pinnacle closer to shore stands some 120 feet above the water.

ANCHORAGE

The best anchorage area is to the north of the outer pinnacle rock. You can comfortably tuck back into the anchorage until you are quite near the rocks close to the cliff. Select a good sand patch, and drop your anchor in 25-30 feet of water. Expect some boat motion here: Nānāhoa is merely a roadstead.

Some boaters drop anchor to the south of the pinnacles, but we can't recommend doing so because the bottom in that area has many large boulders.

If you are anchored at Nānāhoa when a *kona* or west wind picks up, leave the anchorage. This anchorage is excellent only when trade winds blow or when the winds are exceptionally light.

FACILITIES

None

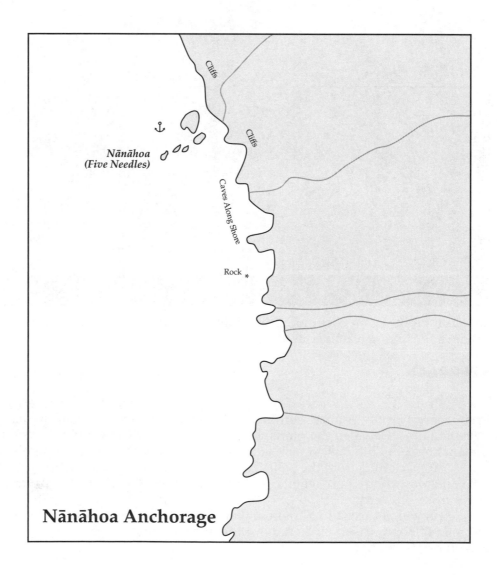

Nānāhoa Anchorage

KALAMA NUI ANCHORAGE
CHART# 19347
LAT. N20° 47.818 LONG. W156° 59.345 (ANCHORAGE)

The cove at the mouth of the steep Kalama Nui Gulch is another overlooked anchorage. Kalama Nui means "great Kalama" (Kalama is a family name and the name of the wife of Kamehameha III), and the gulch is indeed large. The cove, too, is large in comparison to the others along this coast. A long-time cruising boater around the Hawaiian Islands, Ben McCormick, told us this "secret anchorage" is his favorite on Lāna'i.

Tucked in between 100-foot walls of layered lava, with breaking water booming on the rocks, this cove gives one a sense of security and seclusion. The water here is so clear we could see our anchor 40 feet below the surface, its flukes buried in the fine black sand. In this clearest of water, too, we also saw dramatic sea mounts, luxuriant stands of coral, many varieties of tropical fish swimming around the mounts and the coral, and hawksbill turtles gliding about. Dolphins rest in the cove during the morning hours.

If you stop at Kalama Nui, you will almost certainly encounter no other cruising boats. During the middle of the day, however, you are likely to see one of the large rubber charter boats moored on the north side of the cove, with snorkelers in the water. You may want to wait until the snorkelers are out of the water before going in to anchor. We found it more comfortable to motor north about a half mile and have lunch while we drifted. When we saw the rubber boat leaving, we moved into the cove and dropped a hook.

Rock formations northwest of Kalama Nui

At night the view is unspoiled; you can't see a single light in any direction except for the moon and stars, and an occasional strobe light from an airplane taking off or landing at Lāna'i Airport. The moon glistening on the water as it races toward the western horizon dazzles the eyes of boaters anchored here.

Anchored in Kalama Nui, you'll have good protection from the trade winds. The high cliffs to the east produce an almost flat water condition in the cove. In the early morning hours, the winds are frequently out of the west, causing a little wave action, but a boat anchored in here will turn and face into the west wind, reducing the likelihood of rolling. Oftentimes in the afternoon, the heavy trades create heavy whitecaps just outside the cove, but inside, your boat will sit in water that is almost calm.

This is a snorkeler's paradise. The water is clear, and the sea life is friendly. You can land a tender on the beach at the back of the cove, but be careful if a swell is rolling into the anchorage. If your tender is a sport boat with a good-sized motor, consider a trip north along the coastline to look at the caves, especially Ana Puka, about 1.0 mile north from Kalama Nui.

We found the cave large enough to take our sport boat inside; unfortunately, we didn't take along a large flashlight to properly view the cave's interior but could see enough to appreciate the pinks and mauves and greens on the walls near the entrance. The interior of the cave is probably 50 feet deep, 90 feet wide, and 35 feet high.

Ashore between Kalama Nui and Nānāhoa are some rock formations unique in the Islands, looking like something belonging in a Utah desert.

APPROACH

En route to Kalama Nui Anchorage from the north, you'll likely be coming across the channel from Kaunakakai Harbor, an easy 17.0-mile trip in tradewind conditions. The best way to locate Kalama Nui is to stay within 1.0 mile of the coastline after passing Keanapapa Point. After passing Nānāhoa Anchorage ("Five Needles" or "Pinnacles"), travel another 1.9 miles. Long before arriving at Kalama, you can see the fuel tanks at Kaumalapau Harbor to the south. They appear remarkably close when you are at the entrance to the cove.

From the south, Kalama is .60 mile north of the barge harbor at Kaumalapau.

Whether coming from the north or south, you can recognize Kalama by its size. The width of the entrance into the cove is almost 500 yards, and the cove is at least 300 yards deep.

Arch rock south of Kalama Nui

Another helpful geological feature is the arch rock/cave rock at the point on the south side of the cove. It is visible from the ocean side, with difficulty, but easily visible from inside the anchorage.

When entering the cove from the north, do not cut the corner. A rock outcropping extends out from the point on the north side of the cove. The safe approach is to get lined up off the center of the cove before entering.

ANCHORAGE

Once inside, you will have 35-45 feet of water far back into the cove, IN MOST PLACES. On the north side of the cove are a reef that rises to within 3-4 feet of the surface, sea mounts only 3-5 feet deep, and numerous boulders and rocks. On the south side, the bottom is black sand, with sea mounts 10-15 feet below the surface, deeper than they look in this clear, clear water.

The only good holding at Kalama Nui is in this black sand in the southern half of the cove.

You will be able to tell the difference between the rock bottom and the black sand bottom quite easily. Coral is growing on the rocks, giving them a splotchy appearance. By contrast, when you are over the black sand, it appears uniformly dark. Your anchor will set well in the black sand. The water depth in the area with the black sand is 35-45 feet deep.

Although you wouldn't want to anchor here when west or south winds are blowing, the motion at Kalama Nui is comfortable when trade winds blow.

FACILITIES

None

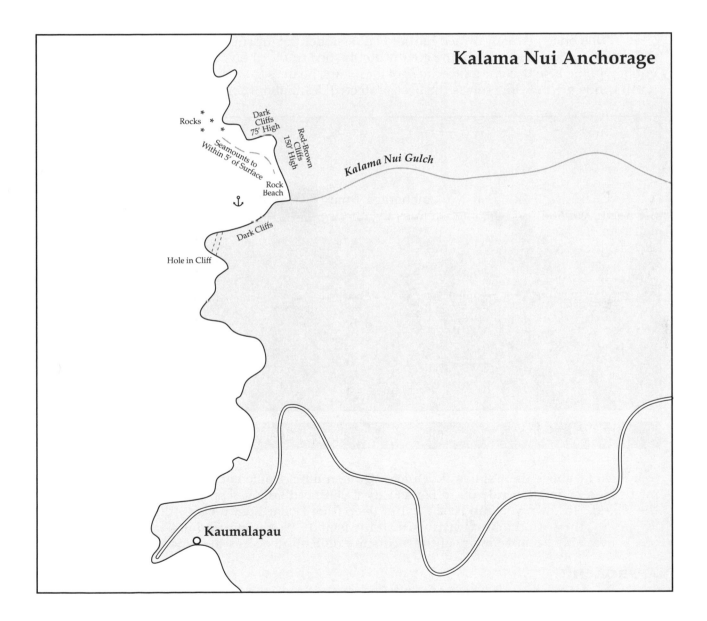

KAUMALAPAU HARBOR
CHART #19340, #19347, OR #19351
LAT. N20° 47.120 LONG. W156° 59.625 (ENTRANCE)

Kaumalapau, a small commercial harbor on the west side of Lāna'i, is a man-made harbor constructed by the Dole Company in the 1920s to transport pineapples from Lāna'i to the cannery in Honolulu. When the island of Lāna'i was little more than one gigantic pineapple plantation, barges loaded with pineapples departed from Kaumalapau Harbor so often that cruising boaters felt uncomfortable and in the way. Currently, the island produces only enough pineapples to supply the needs of the island residents and hotels, so pineapple barges no longer come to this harbor. The barge that supplies the island of Lāna'i stops here regularly only on Thursdays, though a barge may stop at other times if the fuel supply on the island is low.

This once privately owned harbor is now under the jurisdiction of the Hawai'i Department of Transportation. Because of the greatly diminished traffic, it has become a good cruising destination. It has also become a favorite spot for fishing boaters to anchor overnight. When trades or north winds are blowing, this is the best-protected destination along this section of coast because of the high cliffs to the north and east of the anchorage. When *kona* or west winds blow, however, get out immediately.

Kaumalapau Harbor has good snorkeling and fishing, both inside and outside the harbor. You can tie your tender to the low ramp on the dock in the northwest corner. If you plan to be gone for several hours, you probably should pull your tender up onto the ramp. Ashore, you can hike up the hill

Abandoned anchors at Kaumalapau Harbor

to a lookout above the Kalama Iki Gulch. Quite a bit of traffic comes down to the dock, so you might be able to get a ride up to Lāna'i City if you need supplies or simply want to see more of the island. In town you can rent a car or Jeep from Dollar Rent a Car. Although these rentals are pricey, they are the best way to see all the island. We recommend a 4-wheel-drive vehicle if one is available because many of the sights are difficult to access in standard vehicles.

APPROACH

From the north or west, go 7.5 miles southeast beyond Keanapapa Point (the northwest corner of Lāna'i) to get to Kaumalapau Harbor. The coastline between Keanapapa Point and Kaumalapau curves to the east, so if you establish a straight line between the two points, you'll be as much as 2 or 3 miles from the coastline in places.

From Mānele Bay or other locations to the east, go 3.5 miles northwest up the coastline after rounding Palaoa Point, the southwest corner of the island. This stretch of coastline, called the *Pali Kaholo*, has cliffs more than 1,000 feet high that rise almost straight up from the water's edge, adding both spectacular beauty and drama to this part of your passage.

Once you're close to the harbor, identification is easy. The south side of the entrance is marked by a light 66 feet above the water. Numerous fuel tanks and buildings are on the hill immediately behind the harbor. On the 400-foot dock on the north side of the harbor are two cranes used to load and unload barges. Buoy G"1" 50 yards south of the end of the breakwater marks the north side of the entrance.

ANCHORAGE

Inside the harbor are two red buoys. The first, R"2," is on the south side and marks the reef along the shore. The second, R"4," marks the reef in the center of the harbor.

One large mooring buoy is in the northeast corner of the harbor, and two smaller ones are on the south side. Local residents warn against trusting any of these moorings. The huge one on the north side near the dock has not been checked since 1991, and the smaller moorings were never intended for use by large boats, having been dropped for 17-foot fishing boats. Visiting cruising boaters should use their own ground tackle.

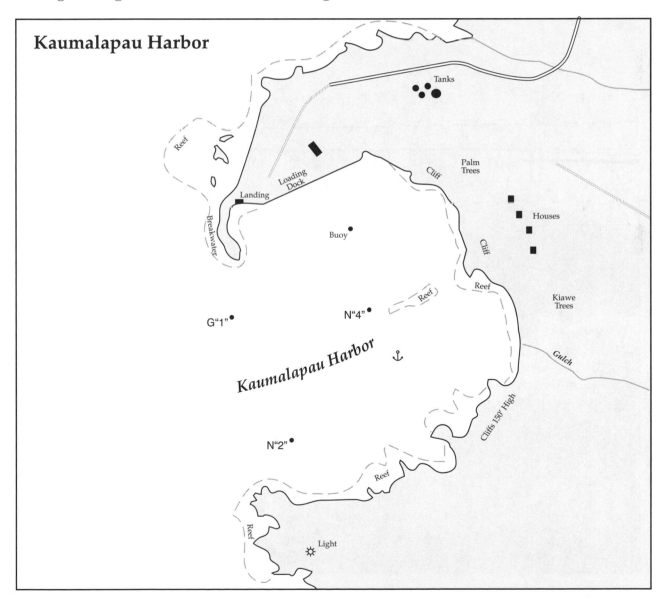

Kaumalapau Harbor

Avoid anchoring in the north half of the harbor because of tug and barge traffic. Though the tug and barge bringing supplies usually arrives on Thursdays, the fuel barge can come in at any time. In any case, the south side of the harbor is more inviting; it has a sand bottom that provides excellent holding, much better than the soft mud on the north side near the barge dock. Anchor in 25-35 feet of water between the red buoy, #4, in the center of the harbor and the shoreline to the southeast.

One local sailor who has extensive experience at Kaumalapau Harbor warns boaters about the frequently shifting winds here when strong trades are blowing. For awhile the winds may come down the canyon from the east; then they may abruptly shift and come over the barge pier. These shifting winds roaring through the harbor at 30 knots can cause boats not well anchored to drag. In fact, this is one of the few anchorages in Hawai'i where a second anchor is advisable—one to meet the force of the east winds and another to hold in north winds.

FACILITIES

None

Loading sugar cane

MĀNELE BAY
CHART #19004, #19340, #19347, OR #19351
LAT. N20° 44.250 LONG. W156° 52.850 (ENTRANCE)

Mānele ("sedan chair") Bay was probably named for the daughter of Kuakini, governor of Hawai'i, the chiefess Ka'ua'umokukamānele, who died in 1834 at age 20. Ashore, a large fishing village once extended from Mānele to Hulopo'e Beach Park. The lava rock foundations of some of the structures lie hidden among a grove of *kiawe* trees about 200 yards up the road from the harbor. The village had already been deserted when a group of Mormons established a church at Mānele in 1853; in 1854 this group moved inland to the Pālāwai Basin, leaving Mānele uninhabited once again.

This small boat harbor, the only all-weather harbor on the island of Lana'i, is sunny virtually year around, with only 10-15 inches of rainfall; the island residents are friendly; and the pace of life is relaxed. All these attributes work together to make it a busy harbor, where visiting boaters can rarely find an open slip. The Expeditions Passenger Ferry between Lahaina and Mānele arrives and departs 5 or 6 times daily, Trilogy charter boats arrive at all hours of the day, and a variety of other boats, both private and commercial, arrive and depart regularly. Despite all the traffic, life at Mānele is still relaxed because everyone works to keep it that way.

The water inside the harbor will not tempt you to jump in: it's a muddy reddish brown color, the same color as the red dirt covering much of the island. Outside the breakwater, though, the water along the cliffs on both sides of the bay is clear, with abundant coral stands and tropical fish. Cave diving is particularly good along these cliffs, and the sea mount, *First Cathedrals,* near Pu'u Pehe Point is a popular snorkeling and diving site.

In the eroded volcanic cone that separates Mānele Bay and Hulopo'e Beach Park is another fine swimming, snorkeling, and diving area. Offshore of the east point of this cone, the sea stack Pu'u Pehe ("Puupehe" on NOAA charts), gives its name to the cove, where a lovely white sand beach goes largely unused.

This sea stack, also called *Sweetheart Island,* was the legendary home of a beautiful young wife named Pu'u Pehe, whose husband hid her there because he feared losing her. In a violent storm that swept over the islet, she drowned.

Hulopo'e was named "Vancouver Bay" on charts until 1921, when an archaeologist working on the island recorded the Hawaiian name of the bay. Oddly enough, Vancouver never anchored in the bay but merely sailed by in 1792. In more recent years this bay became a popular anchorage among cruising boaters and was known as *White Sand Mānele,* or shortened to *White Mānele.* The sugary white sand beach at Hulopo'e is a striking contrast to the black sand at Mānele, then called *Black Mānele.*

Mānele, Pu'u Pehe, and Hulopo'e are now part of the Mānele-Hulopo'e Marine Life Conservation District. At Hulopo'e, only swimming, snorkeling, and diving are permitted, with boating strictly prohibited.

From Mānele, the walk along the road to Hulopo'e takes only 10-15 minutes and will reward you many times over with the beauty of this beach park. The white sand sweeps from the black lava shores in a gentle crescent. Inland from the beach the park has numerous trees and flowering shrubs to add color—and to host a number of birds in their branches and under their boughs. Among the birds you might see and hear are the descendants of the chukkars, francolins, pheasants, quails, and turkeys that Dole had brought to the island when it was a pineapple plantation.

The snorkeling at Hulopo'e is outstanding on the reef off the eastern shore. In the lava beds that constitute the east boundary of the bay are numerous tidepools with water so clear and still you can almost imagine it doesn't exist.

The walk from Hulopo'e up to the Mānele Bay Hotel Resort is along a pathway highlighting some relics of the ancient culture of Lāna'i. At the hotel, you may simply walk around the grounds where Hawaiian artifacts are displayed or wander through the reception area, appreciating the tasteful mixture of Hawaiian, Asian, and Mediterranean appointments.

You can order a drink to enjoy in the library or have a meal at either the Hulopo'e Court restaurant or the much more elegant (and expensive) Ihilani Dining Room. The Pool Grill serves up salads, soup, sandwiches, and light meals for the most casual dining. You can have an even more exotic eating experience by catching the free shuttle up to the Resort golf course, where you can dine on a terrace overlooking the entire bay. The view is breathtaking.

If you can get a slip for a day or two at Mānele Bay, or if you feel comfortable leaving your boat anchored outside the breakwater at Mānele, we strongly recommend you splurge and rent a 4-wheel drive vehicle. This island has much to see that you can't get to by any other means. As you drive along the island's dirt roads, you'll undoubtedly see several species of the birds that were brought to the island. The animals with which the island was stocked are a bit more difficult to spot, but you may catch glimpses of axis deer, pronghorns, or Mouflon sheep grazing on the upper slopes.

APPROACH

Mānele Bay is on the southeast corner of the island of Lāna'i. From the islands of Kaua'i, O'ahu, or Moloka'i, most boaters come counterclockwise around the island as they approach Mānele. Those coming from Maui, Molokini, or the Big Island usually approach from the opposite direction.

Regardless of the direction of your approach, you'll see from some distance the large Pu'u Pehe Rock 110 feet above the water. It lies 0.5 mile southwest of Mānele Bay. Be cautious if you're approaching from the west because rocks extend east and south from Pu'u Pehe Rock for 300 yards.

The entrance to Mānele Bay is on the east side of Pu'u Pehe Rock. A red buoy, "R2," is in the middle of Mānele Bay, warning of the rock half way between the buoy and the cliffs to the northeast. Pass to the port side of the red buoy, and you'll see the breakwater in the northwest corner of the bay. Immediately off the end of the breakwater are a series of buoys to guide you into the harbor. The end of the breakwater is marked by a white concrete tower with a white light flashing 4 seconds.

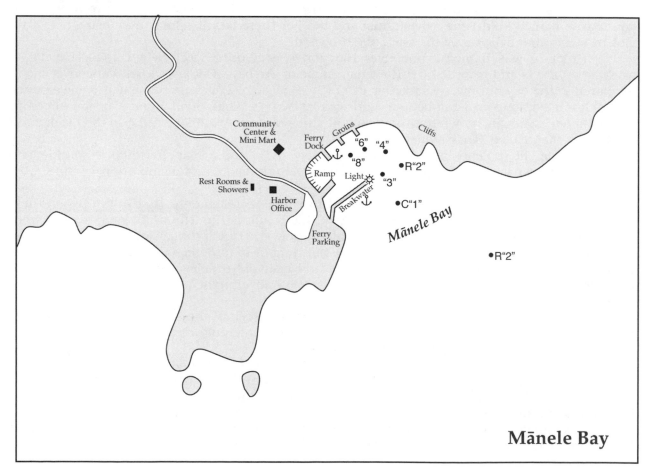

Mānele Bay

ANCHORAGE

With only 24 berths in the harbor, all of them leased out to local boaters, the chance of visitors finding slips is understandably slim.

The harbormaster at Mānele Bay assigns visiting boaters to empty slips when boats are out of the harbor for a few days, but the harbor is small, and these vacancies are rare. Another problem for visiting boaters is the size of the slips at Mānele: most of accommodate only small boats. A beamy 45-foot boat, for example, will fit into few of the slips in the harbor.

You must take into account the surge in Mānele Bay. In case you do get a slip, you'll need sturdy mooring and spring lines. And use all of the fenders you have, too. The docks at Mānele have tires on them to cushion the blows, so you can expect to have some black marks on your hull when you leave Mānele.

When the winds pipe up at Mānele, your boat will be safe, but covered with an unsightly dirt that will take you months to remove the last traces from your boat. We rode out a 40-knot blow in Mānele and never once worried about our boat. After the winds had subsided, however, our boat, which had been white before, was a dull shade of reddish brown. Some stains remained on many of our lines until we replaced them.

If you wish to try for a slip at Mānele Harbor, proceed to the slips area at the extreme west end of the harbor. If you can find an empty slip that will accommodate your boat, you might tie up in it while one of your crew goes to check with the harbormaster. However, remember you are in someone else's slip, so be sure the skipper remains aboard to move the boat should the owner of the slip return.

If the prospects of getting a slip at Mānele seem bleak, consider using your anchor. Inside the breakwater, the Murdoch Company has leased the area

Anchorage at Mānele Harbor

to the north of the channel for the development of a marina. Until that marina is constructed, boaters may anchor here—but for a hefty fee of $1.25 a foot of boat length each day. Most of us will not want to pay that fee. You may also anchor to the north of the entrance channel, outside the breakwater, and take your dinghy ashore to check in with the harbormaster. In addition to avoiding the possibility of upsetting another boater, you will also find less surge at anchor than in a slip. The surge causes boats tied to the docks to jerk back and forth all day and night, while the boats at anchor are relatively unaffected.

When anchoring inside the breakwater, drop your bow hook in the entrance channel and back toward the rock wall to the north. Have a dinghy ready so someone can take a stern line ashore to tie to one of the iron mooring rings on the sea wall. The water depth in this anchorage is generally about 8 feet, but be alert to any shoaling, a continuous problem in Mānele Bay. The anchorage has room for at least eight boats. By rafting up, as many as fifteen boats have used this anchorage at one time.

Even if you can't get a slip or find a place inside the breakwater at Mānele, you can still enjoy Lāna'i by anchoring outside the breakwater. Boaters have been doing so for years. Anchoring outside has some distinct advantages, among them the beautiful clear water you will anchor in and the absence of dirt on your anchored boat.

If you visit Mānele in calm weather, the anchorage outside the breakwater will most likely be calm. When a south swell is running, however, the anchorage is usually too rolly to be comfortable. The best outside anchorage area is in front of the breakwater. Anchor in 20-30 feet of water, being careful to select a sand patch large enough to drop your anchor in without damaging the coral.

Mānele Bay Harbormaster   808-559-0723

FACILITIES

At the harbor:
Restrooms
Showers (cold water)
Snack stand
Water
At Hulopo'e:
Restaurants (at the hotel)
Restrooms
Showers (cold water)
Telephone

ISLAND OF MOLOKA'I

THE FRIENDLY ISLE

Anchorage at Wailau Valley

Moloka'i nui a Hina
("Great Moloka'i, land of Hina")

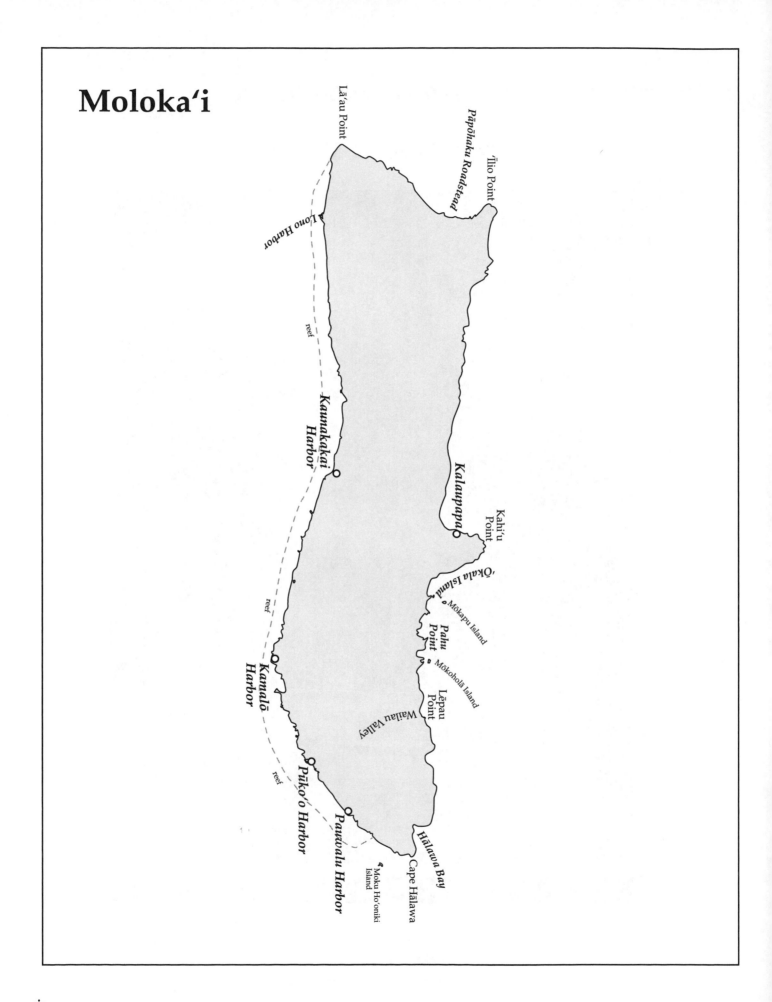

Moloka'i

Lā'au Point

Pāpōhaku Roadstead

'Īlio Point

Lono Harbor

reef

Kaunakakai Harbor

Kalaupapa

Kahi'u Point

'Okala Island

Mōkapu Island

Pahu Point

Mōkohola Island

Lēpau Point

Wailau Valley

reef

Kamalō Harbor

Pūko'o Harbor

reef

Pauwalu Harbor

Moku Ho'oniki Island

Cape Hālawa

Hālawa Bay

THE ISLAND OF MOLOKA'I

Each island in the Hawaiian Chain has an individual character, based in part on the way the island culture has evolved into a 20th century culture and in part on the particular role of the island in Hawaiian history and legend.

In the 19th century Moloka'i became for many "the Lonely Island," the place chosen by the Hawaiian government to isolate the victims of Hansen's Disease, then called leprosy. Beginning in 1866, the government, acting on the advice of the missionary doctors, quarantined hundreds of men, women, and children on the Kalaupapa Peninsula. During the early years of the colony, the diseased were left on the peninsula to fend for themselves, lending to Moloka'i the further epithet "the Forgotten Island." The policy of isolation continued until 1969.

The peninsula, an anomaly of geography, was formed much later than the remainder of the island. A small shield volcano, Kauhakō, erupted from the side of a sheer cliff, leaving behind this flat peninsula. Before the Hawaiian government acquired the peninsula, it had been the site of fishing and farming villages in three *ahupua'a* (land divisions): Makanalua ("double gift"), Kalawao ("announce mountain area"), and Kalaupapa ("the flat plain"). This peninsula had two advantages as a quarantine site: It is relatively close to O'ahu, the most heavily populated of the islands, and at that time access to the peninsula was only by water, making escape nearly impossible.

The people of Moloka'i today call it "the Friendly Isle," and most of the residents warmly receive visitors to this still largely undeveloped island, geographically the closest to O'ahu but culturally perhaps the farthest. On the entire island of Moloka'i is only one resort hotel and condominium, Kaluako'i Villas, on the northwest coast. The island has only two major highways, the Kamehameha V and the Maunaloa highways, with a few other paved roads around the three largest towns, Kaunakakai, Kualapu'u, and Maunaloa. In all the island is not one stoplight! Some people still call it "the Forgotten Isle" because the developers have largely ignored it.

Kalaupapa Peninsula

For the early Hawaiians, Moloka'i had yet other epithets. They called it *Moloka'i nui a Hina* ("great Moloka'i, land of Hina") and *Moloka'i pule o'o* ("Moloka'i of the potent prayer"). Both names refer to the spiritualism and sorcery the Hawaiians ascribed to this island. The island was a place of refuge for those who broke the *kapu* on any of the islands, for the *mana* ("divine power") of its *kāhuna* ("priests, sorcerers") was the oldest, strongest, and most respected throughout the Islands. Kamehameha I was but one of the powerful leaders throughout Hawaiian history who relied on the power of the *kāhuna* of Moloka'i.

Ancient Moloka'i had another, more physical face. Its early residents were legendary athletes, their quickness alluded to in a proverb, "Up rose the smoke of the experts of the island of Hina." The first *hula* dancers were reputedly from Moloka'i. (While the dance itself is physical, it was, and, for some Islanders, still is, an entirely spiritual activity, and its legendary origin on this most spiritual of islands seems natural.)

According to other legends, Moloka'i is also the site of the first settlement of the Polynesian explorers to the Hawaiian Islands. These earliest sailors, believed to have come from the Marquesas, were almost certainly settled in the Hālawa Valley, on the northeast end of the island, as early as the 7th century. This rich valley had a large population for many centuries, its fertile taro fields destroyed by the tsunami of 1946, which deposited salt all the way up to the cliffs sheltering the valley.

Here in the Hālawa Valley, the most famous of ancient *kāhuna, Lanikāula*, practiced the art of Pahulu, a goddess predating even Pele and believed to be the forebear of all the *'aumakua* ("personal gods") of Moloka'i. Pahulu also created the "ocean highway" along which the ancient sailors traveled between Kahiki (Tahiti), the lost homeland of the Hawaiians, and the Kalohi Channel, separating Moloka'i and Lāna'i.

Of all the inhabited islands except Ni'ihau, which is privately owned and thus off limits to visitors, Moloka'i has the largest percentage of native Hawaiians. Among its approximately 7,400 permanent residents, almost half have at least 50% Hawaiian blood, making this island, at least in some respects, the most Hawaiian of the islands.

The physical geography of Moloka'i has determined much of its history; it has also given this island several ideal cruising destinations. The island of Moloka'i resulted from the joining of two shield volcanoes. The earlier of the two eruptions created Mauna Loa, a tableland at the west end of the island; the second eruption formed what is now East Moloka'i. Much later, in an epilogue, Kauhakō erupted, leaving behind the Kalaupapa Peninsula.

The west end, the older of the two eroded volcanoes, has the best beach on Moloka'i and one that can compare to any on the other islands. The silky white sands of Pāpōhaku Beach stretch for 2 miles between Pu'u o Kaiaka and Pu'u Koa'e. North of the beach are the Pāpōhaku Roadstead and Kawākiu Nui Bay Anchorage, both sheltered by 'Īlio Point.

On the south side of West Moloka'i, the only safe anchorage for cruising boaters is in the man-made harbor at Hale o Lono. Generally, the reef along this shoreline has no large openings through which boats can be taken to anchor in its protection, and the bottom behind the reef is generally rocky and shallow.

The one exception to the generally rocky and shallow shoreline is Kolo Wharf, 3 miles east of Lono Harbor. A pocket of water with depths of approximately 8 feet is behind the reef, where the remains of the old wharf are still visible. However, with the long disuse of this wharf, the pilings formerly marking this pocket have largely disappeared, and the water depths are suspect, since heavy shoaling is common along this coast. As disconcerting to the cruising boater considering Kolo as an anchorage is the disappearance of the pilings marking the boundaries of the 100-yard-wide opening through the reef.

East Moloka'i, on the other hand, has the geographical characteristics that provide for many safe anchorages. First, the reef along this coastline is much farther offshore, leaving ample space for anchoring between the reef and the shore. Second, the water behind the reef is often as deep as 25 feet. Finally, at several points along this reef are large passageways through the reef. Though these are not always marked, they are readily visible in daylight. In fact, this coastline between Kaunakakai and Waialua was the site of the longest string of ancient fishponds in the Hawaiian Islands for the same reasons it is now the site of many fine anchorages.

The first of the anchorages on East Moloka'i, Kaunakakai Harbor, is also the most favored anchorage on the island in all weather conditions except a south wind. The channel here is well marked with lighted buoys, the anchorage area is large enough for three or four boats to anchor comfortably, it is well protected by a reef, and its water depth is ample. The harbor also has a few slips.

Pāpōhaku Roadstead

Kaunakakai has another distinction: it is the only harbor on the island that is near a town where boaters can obtain most of the services and provisions they need.

From Kamalō to Waialua are several small anchorages behind the extensive reef of East Moloka'i. These share some other attributes to appeal to the cruising boater. On the shore are white sand beaches with a backdrop of the deeply eroded slopes of the East Moloka'i volcano, the vegetation behind the beach and on the slopes increasingly lush as one travels east.

Ashore at each anchorage is a cluster of houses. Children play on the beaches behind the houses, and a few small fishing boats pass through the anchorages each day.

The north shore of East Moloka'i also has several enticing anchorages, all sharing one quality with those on the south shore: the stunningly rich greens of the backdrop. Otherwise, though, these anchorages differ in striking—and pleasing—ways. Instead of being sheltered behind reefs, these anchorages are in the shelter of the jagged coastline or enormous boulders that have landed at or near the beaches. Any sand on the beaches of the north shore is black or dark gray, though rocks rather than sand predominate. Immediately behind the beaches are sea cliffs, some of which are the tallest in the world. The highest waterfall in Hawai'i is also along the *pali*, falling 1,750 feet. The gulches slicing through the volcanic shield are far deeper than those on the more gentle south shore; they disappear into the mysterious mists of the mountain.

You'll not see any clusters of houses until you reach Kalaupapa, but you'll see the larger fishing boats along this coast, where fishing is as good as it is anyplace around the inhabited islands.

The Moloka'i *pali*

The last safe anchorage as one proceeds west along this coastline is that in 'Awahua Bay, or Kalaupapa. Here, the dramatic sea cliffs are still in evidence, but a large peninsula rather than a jagged coastline, a boulder, or an island shelters the large bay west of the village of Kalaupapa. Here is the only anchorage along this coast with a white sand beach nearby, one that is off limits to visitors, however, as is the entire peninsula, where approximately 60 former victims of Hansen's Disease (or leprosy) still live voluntarily, even though the disease is now controlled by drugs.

If you take the time (and wait for the right weather) to visit all these anchorages on Moloka'i, you may conclude that this island still deserves some of its nicknames. The warmth of the people you meet along the west and south shores will convince you that the island is indeed a friendly place. As you find yourself alone in anchorage after anchorage, you may conclude (but probably not unhappily) that most boaters seem to have forgotten about this island. Finally, you may agree with us that the *mana* of Moloka'i remains powerful.

PĀPŌHAKU ROADSTEAD ('ĪLIO POINT)
CHART #19340 OR #19351
LAT. N21° 11.668 LONG. W157° 15.027 (ANCHORAGE)

Most cruising boaters refer to the roadstead in the lee of 'Īlio Point, at the northwest tip of Moloka'i, as 'Īlio Point, but the charts indicate it is properly called *Pāpōhaku* ("stone wall or enclosure") Roadstead. Whatever you choose to call it, it is both a convenient and comfortable layover anchorage and an excellent cruising destination.

Boaters traveling from the island of O'ahu to Maui, Lāna'i, or the Big Island often stop here to avoid an overnight passage. Other boaters make Pāpōhaku their cruising destination, where they can enjoy a quiet day or two in an anchorage that seems remote, in spite of the fact that a large hotel, the Kaluako'i Villas, sits just 200 yards away from the boats in the anchorage. The guests at the hotel are primarily golfers; rarely will you see more than a handful of people on the beach or in the water, and you'll be anchored far enough out to be away from any noise ashore. As viewed from the anchorage, the tasteful Polynesian architecture of the hotel intrudes little on the natural landscape. In fact, the imported palm trees and other greenery surrounding the hotel add much to the beauty along the coast of this otherwise somewhat barren corner of Moloka'i.

At night, you'll see spectacular sunsets on the western horizon. After dark, the soft lights around the hotel, from the anchorage looking more like torches than incandescent lights, will not detract from the brilliant star show you can observe in the clear air at Pāpōhaku. Out to the northwest the faint glow above the horizon emanates from the lights of O'ahu.

A number of sport-fishing boats typically anchor at Pāpōhaku. They usually leave early in the morning to fish around 'Īlio Point, reportedly one of the best places around Moloka'i to hook a fish.

Pāpōhaku Roadstead can be excellent when trade winds are light or when calm conditions prevail. However, a south swell, generated by storms in the Southern Hemisphere, can enter the roadstead in any weather. While this swell is not in itself dangerous, it can make the motion uncomfortable on boats. When heavy trade winds are blowing, the water in the anchorage also becomes a little rolly, but even so Pāpōhaku is still a safe anchorage. On the other hand, when *kona* or west winds blow, this roadstead is not safe.

For going ashore, take your tender into Kawākiu Nui ("big spy place") Bay, where you can land in the middle of the gently sloping sand beach; or you can land at the north end of the sand beach directly in front of the Kaluako'i Villas. The rock outcropping at this end of the beach gives good protection for making a dry landing in calm weather.

Ashore, you have several options for enjoying the water. Kawākiu Iki ("little spy place") and Kawākiu Nui have gradually sloping sand bottoms and water generally protected from the elements. Snorkeling and diving are also good here. Directly below the resort hotel is Kepuhi Beach, another good choice for swimming and snorkeling. Experienced snorkelers and divers will find even more excitement in the deep water south of Kawākiu Nui Bay, beneath the steep cliffs of Pōhakumāuliuli, called by locals *Make* ("dead") *Horse* because of a horse that fell to its death from the cliffs here.

One of the longest and widest beaches in all Hawai'i is Pāpōhaku Beach, a short distance south of the resort. This expanse of powdery white sand stretches for 2 miles and averages 100 yards wide. The sands at Pāpōhaku Beach are so abundant they were routinely dredged for transporting to O'ahu for construction and for the beach at Waikīkī until 1975. Though Pāpōhaku is beautiful to look at and to walk on, it is often not safe for swimming because of the large waves that roll in here unimpeded.

This west coast of Moloka'i has the island's finest archaeological sites, some of those accessible from the anchorage. Kawākiu is one of the richest archaeological sites in all Hawai'i. The remains of a *heiau* sit above the southern point forming the Kawākiu Nui Bay. Pu'u o Kaiaka, the point separating Kepuhi Bay from Pāpōhaku Beach, was the site of another *heiau*, bulldozed in the 1960s. The site remains a spiritual place for the Hawaiians.

In 1952, Pāpōhaku Beach was the starting point for the first Aloha Week canoe races from Moloka'i to O'ahu. Because of the remoteness of the beach and the difficulty of launching the canoes in the heavy surf, the organizers of the races changed the starting point to Hale o Lono Harbor in 1963.

Make Horse, the cliff behind the anchorage

One cultural event of interest is the festival held each year in May at the nearby Pāpōhaku Beach County Park. This festival honors Moloka'i for its legendary role as the site where hula dancing originated in the Hawaiian Islands.

APPROACH

Approaching the anchorage at Pāpōhaku Roadstead from O'ahu, first identify 'Īlio Point, the northwestern corner of the island of Moloka'i. The anchorage area begins 1.0 mile south of the point and extends for a distance of 1.0 mile.

From the south, proceed north 6.0 miles from Lā'au Point on the southwestern corner of Moloka'i.

During daylight hours, the most noteworthy landmarks to help you locate the anchorage area are two geological formations that are obvious from the ocean. The southernmost of the two is Pu'u o Kaiaka, a 100-foot-high rocky point extending into the ocean some 300 yards from the coastline. The second of these formations is a dark red-brown cliff .90 mile north of the first; this cliff begins its almost vertical rise near the water's edge, reaching a height of over 200 feet. The larger of the two anchorage areas at Pāpōhaku Roadstead is between these two easily identifiable landmarks.

If you arrive after dark, the lights of the Kaluako'i Villas will help you locate the anchorage at Pāpōhaku Roadstead. The flashing red lights on the radio towers 1.5 miles inland of the Villas will also help you locate the anchorage from miles offshore. Since 'Īlio Point has no light, these other lights will be your only navigation aids as you make a night approach.

ANCHORAGE

The larger of the two anchorages is Kepuhi Bay, lying between Pu'u o Kaiaka and the 200-foot-high rocky formation to the north. Many boaters put their hooks down in the water directly in front of the Kaluako'i Villas, in the bight just above Pu'u o Kaiaka. Another desirable place to anchor in Kepuhi Bay is in the lee of the high red-brown cliff to the north. This area has the advantage of being protected from the full force of the tradewinds that often blow here. For some boaters, it also has the added attraction of being farther from the resort.

The depths here range from 15-30 feet, depending on how far you anchor off the beach. The bottom at Pāpōhaku is sand and rock. When you drop your anchor and back down on it, your anchor often digs in instantly. Don't be surprised, however, if you hear your anchor rumbling over a few rocks before it digs in; in many areas only a thin layer of sand covers the rocks.

Another 900 yards north of the large red-brown cliff is a second area where boaters regularly anchor. Called by the locals Kawākiu Nui, this bay is recognizable by the small beach set back in a little bight some 150 feet wide and deep. Drop a hook here in 20-30 of water, in the same sand and rock bottom as in the larger area of the Pāpōhaku Roadstead. This anchorage has the added advantage of being completely removed from the resort activity.

Make your beach landings in this area with caution. Many boaters have found themselves quite wet when the heavy surf has caught their tenders.

FACILITIES

Convenience store at Kaluako'i Villas
Restaurants
Showers (cold water; at Pāpōhaku Beach County Park)
Telephone

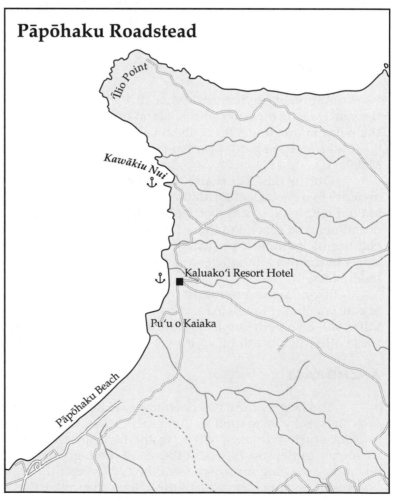

Pāpōhaku Roadstead

'Īlio Point

Kawākiu Nui

Kaluako'i Resort Hotel

Pu'u o Kaiaka

Pāpōhaku Beach

LONO HARBOR
CHART #19340, 19347, 19351, OR 19353
LAT. N21° 05.070 LONG. W157° 15.060 (ENTRANCE)

Lono, on the southwest coast of Moloka'i, is the shortened version of *Hale o Lono*, the name of the ancient *heiau* that once stood here to honor the god Lono. Each of the Hawaiian islands had a *heiau* of this name. Lono, a benevolent god of agriculture, medicine, clouds, and weather, was one of the four major gods of the Hawaiians. A large fishing village was near the *heiau.*

Hale o Lono was also the home of the demigod La'amaomao, Hawaiian god of the winds, who called forth the winds from his calabash and sent them out in any direction and force he desired.

In 1959 the Honolulu Construction and Draying Company began construction on a harbor here for the company barges that would carry sand and gravel from Moloka'i to O'ahu. Since the State of Hawai'i banned the removal of aggregates from Moloka'i in 1975, barges no longer use the harbor. Although the cessation of the barge traffic in Lono has created a more peaceful and trouble-free anchorage for pleasure boaters, the harbor has suffered serious neglect since the commercial operation moved out. Almost all the wood facings on the concrete wharf have fallen off, making the prospect of tying to the wharf most unappealing.

Until quite recently, the only land access to Hale o Lono was through a locked gate on the Moloka'i Ranch. Now, however, the isolation of Lono Harbor has changed: the locked gate that prevented people from driving to the harbor has been permanently unlocked to give Hawaiians free access to both the small beach and the spiritual site where Hale o Lono once stood. Lono Harbor has subsequently become the newest tourist attraction for an island that has few.

Another change going on at Lono Harbor is a small charter operation. So far, only one 30-foot catamaran and one RIB dive/snorkel boat are tied up in the harbor. indeed.

Lono Harbor

At this time, though, Lono Harbor remains fairly quiet. Another cruising or fishing boat or two may be in the small anchorage area. A few local people may be picnicking on the beach, and the occasional rental car with tourists will pass through. Still, with no hotel and no long stretch of sandy beach, Lono has not yet become a tourist mecca. You can be sure of a fairly quiet day and an entirely quiet night—unless you have happened into the harbor during the last weekend of September or the second weekend in October. The Aloha Week Outrigger Race, first for the women and then, two weeks later, for the men, begins at Lono Harbor. Teams from all around the Pacific rim enter this rigorous 42-mile race across the Kaiwi Channel to the Hilton Hawaiian dock in Honolulu.

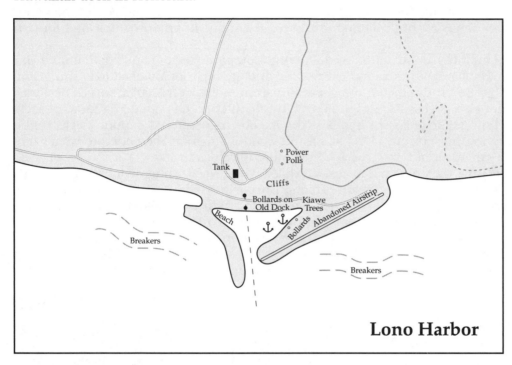

Lono Harbor

On a quieter weekend, you can easily land your tender on the small beach at the northwest corner of the harbor, where you can swim. For more vigorous exercise, hike up the road for a full view of the harbor below or along the rocky shore to the west of the breakwater. If the water is calm outside the breakwater, abundant reefs on both sides of the harbor promise excellent snorkeling, diving, and surfing.

APPROACH

Approaching Lono Harbor from the west, first identify Lāʻau Point, the southwestern corner of Molokaʻi. Lono is 3.5 miles east of the point. Immediately behind Lono Harbor is a bluff with three tall poles (one communications, one unused, and one with three unused transformers). The bluff, reddish brown and gray, is about 150 feet high. These poles and the bluff are easily visible from the sea.

Approaching from the east, Lono is 12.3 miles west of Kaunakakai Harbor. If you are approaching from the east, give a wide berth to the reef along the south shore of Molokaʻi.

Two breakwaters extend out from Lono Harbor, the westernmost one being 300 feet longer than the eastern one. The entrance channel is about 20 feet deep in most areas. The channel is a little more than 300 feet wide.

When entering Lono Harbor, use the range marks as guides. The range marks are 4-foot by 8-foot plywood sheets painted white, with large red stripes indicating the center of the channel. Once you have your boat lined up in the center of the channel, you can steer a course of 332° magnetic if you have trouble seeing the ranges. The ranges at Lono Harbor have no lights, so if you're thinking of making a night landfall, don't count on any help from the ranges.

ANCHORAGE

Inside the harbor, the area to the port side of the channel is too shallow for anything other than a tender. Anchor inside anywhere to the right of the channel. The bottom is mud, offering reasonably good holding in some areas but not in all. We recommend using an anchor designed to hold well in soft bottoms: a Danforth, a Fortress, or an anchor of a similar design. You can expect to anchor in about 18 feet of water.

Many boaters who visit Lono Harbor regularly drop a bow hook and then back up and tie to one of the trees at the extreme east end of the harbor. Another option is to tie to one of the bollards on either side of the harbor and then drop a hook out in the middle of the harbor. However, when you tie to a bollard, you may have a problem if the wind shifts (as it may well do during the course of a day). When we arrived one day at midmorning, the wind was out of the east. We tied a stern line to a bollard on the breakwater and set a bow anchor. Within minutes, the wind began to blow out of the north, pushing us uncomfortably close to the rocks of the breakwater. Luckily, we were aboard when the wind shifted, so we set a second anchor to pull our boat away from the rocks.

Another cruising boater told us he prefers to set a single anchor and not tie to either a tree or a bollard when he visits Lono Harbor because of the problems caused by the shifting winds. He also said he always puts down his largest anchor when he anchors here.

FACILITIES

None

Boats anchored and stern-tied to bollards

KAUNAKAKAI HARBOR
CHART #19340, #19351, OR #19353
LAT. N21° 04.640 LONG. W157° 02.120 (ENTRANCE)

For the boater who visits Moloka'i, Kaunakakai Harbor is almost certain to be the favorite stop. The anchorage is calm in most weather conditions, the coral reef on the west side is one of the most extensive and beautiful in the islands, and life aboard or ashore in Kaunakakai is slow and easy. It is also the only harbor on the island where you can go ashore to shop, get fuel, find someone to make repairs to the boat, or rent a car and go sightseeing.

Kaunakakai Harbor has a few slips, and, although they are all rented out, the harbormaster will try to get the visiting boater into a slip if one is vacant. In addition, the turning basin on the west side of the pier contains adequate anchoring space for three or four boats.

Some of the state's boaters have a negative opinion of Kaunakakai because of the wind that regularly howls in the harbor. However, the reef protects the harbor from any heavy waves generated by the strong winds, and the sand and mud bottom provides excellent holding.

If you anchor on the west side of the pier at Kaunakakai, you'll see tugs bringing barges in on a regular basis. One tug may bring in a barge mid-morning and leave by late afternoon; then another tug may arrive with a barge that same evening. After dark, the tug crews shine bright lights into the turning basin when they are maneuvering to get the barge against the dock to ascertain the position of any anchored boat. Be sure you anchor at the back of the turning basin so your boat won't be in the way.

The barges bring to the island all the goods and supplies needed for the residents and the tourists on Moloka'i. For Kamehameha the Great, Kaunakakai (formerly Kaunakahakai, meaning "beach landing") was a convenient layover for his warriors on their way to invade O'ahu. After the construction of the dock, pineapples were the primary cargo shipped out on the barges tying up here. Now that the pineapple plantations are all gone, the outgoing cargo is cattle and some local produce, such as cucumbers, melons, sweet potatoes, and coffee. Sometimes, the noise of unloading and reloading the barges continues long into the night, but it is not bothersome.

Kaunakakai Harbor is the scene of much activity. People of the island come to the harbor to swim from the swim platform near the turning basin. Day and night, young and old alike drive their vehicles out the mole to the pier, where they may stop for awhile, or, more frequently, they turn around and drive back toward town. Large trucks carrying produce or cattle begin to arrive at the dock shortly before the next barge comes in.

The main street of Kaunakakai

The water, too, has steady though not intrusive traffic. Fishing boats, sailboats, outrigger canoes, kayaks, and surfboards make daily appearances in the harbor. Luckily, few PWCs (personal water craft, or jet skis) disturb the peacefulness of the anchorage.

Daily, fishermen pole their small boats over the shallow reef that protects this harbor to the west as men have done for centuries all along this south shore of the island. One of the old sayings around the Islands is, *Moloka'i ko'o lā'au* ("Moloka'i [the place of] poling with a stick"). The reef has numerous varieties of healthy coral, where colorful tropical fish feed. Although the water is sometimes murky, the snorkeling is nevertheless good because the coral is so close to the surface of the water.

You must do whatever shopping you plan to do on the island at Kaunakakai. This town is one of a kind. Its one-block main street lined with old buildings with dilapidated wooden false fronts is the urban center of Moloka'i. You can see all the town, stopping to chat with the friendly locals as you walk, in well under a half a day.

If you want a longer walk, follow Kamehameha V Highway west to what remains of the formerly 10-acre coconut grove where 1,000 coconut palms were planted for Kamehameha V. Kapuāiwa ("mysterious taboo") Grove, as it is called, comes properly labeled with signs posted warning of the dangers of falling coconuts.

Before he became King Kamehameha V, Prince Lot lived on Moloka'i at a site near the harbor. As king, he continued to spend his summers here at his vacation home called *Malama* ("moon"). The state has established a cultural park on this site, where you may learn more about the ancient culture of Moloka'i.

Commercial dock and warehouse at Kaunakakai

One of the best features of Kaunakakai is the friendliness of the people. Everyone seems eager to help, from the harbormaster and the other boaters in the harbor to the local residents who happen to be driving by while you're walking to town. People who live on the island tend to wave if you look even a little friendly, and we were offered a ride to town numerous times when we were walking, in spite of the fact that town is only a 15-minute walk from the harbor.

If you can schedule your stop at Kaunakakai Harbor during the first week in October, you'll have great fun watching the activities during Aloha Week. As do all the other islands, Moloka'i has a parade featuring *pā'ū* riders (women on horseback, dressed in flowing satin skirts and adorned with exquisite *lei*). Instead of marching bands, a small group of local women play *'ukuleles* and guitars and sing Hawaiian songs as the parade passes along the main street of Kaunakakai. Perhaps the most entertaining of the events is the mule drag, the name describing exactly the activity. Teams of two or three young people drag a mule from one end of the main street to the other and back, with the fastest team winning. After two or three heats, many of the mules have had enough and will barely budge.

APPROACH

Approaching from the west, identify Lā'au Point, the southwest corner of the island, and go east along the south shoreline of Moloka'i for 16.5 miles. To avoid the hazard presented by the reef along the south shore of Moloka'i, stay at least a mile offshore. When you're within 2 or 3 miles of the harbor at Kaunakakai, you'll be able to see the green warehouse on the pier and the houses of the town on the hillside behind the harbor. Kaunakakai is the first town visible from the water as you go east along the south shore of the island.

From the east, identify the buoy at Kamalō and go 9.5 miles to the west. The reefs to both the east and the west sides of the harbor deserve respect.

Again, the warehouse on the pier is the primary identifying feature of the harbor; however, from some vantage points at sea, the two fuel tanks north of the warehouse are also easily visible.

Lighted buoys and rangemarks will help you get into the harbor safely if you're making a night landfall. The light on the outermost buoy is red, and a green light marks the other side of the channel through the reef. Two range marks with red lights guide you into the anchorage area after you pass through the reef. Whenever a barge is in the harbor being loaded or unloaded, the bright lights on the barge and dock make the harbor even more easily recognized.

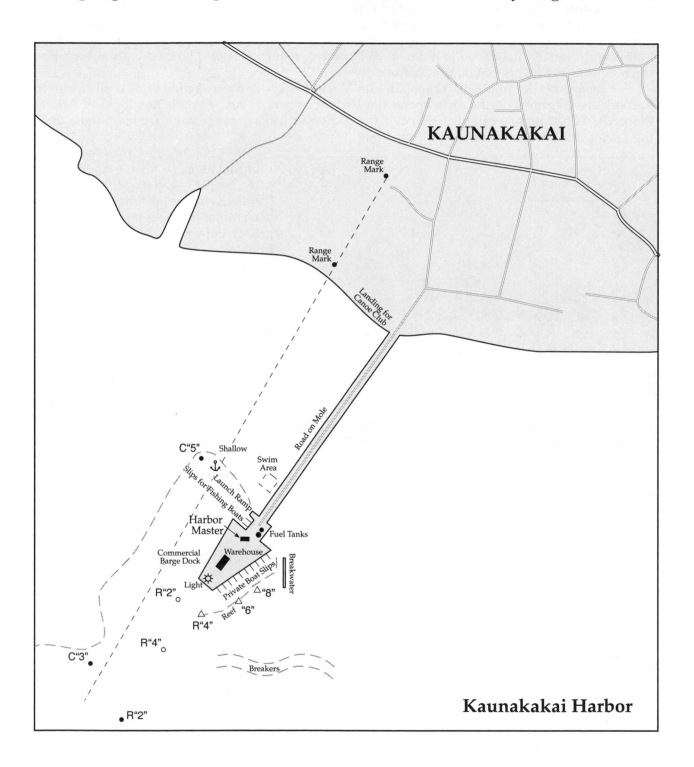

Kaunakakai Harbor

ANCHORAGE

All visiting boaters should anchor in the turning basin and go ashore to check in with the harbormaster. The preferred location for visiting boaters to anchor is at the back of the turning basin, between the green buoy, C"5," and the launch ramp to the east of the basin. You will anchor in about 20 feet of water. The bottom of the harbor has a thick layer of mud, which offers excellent holding but leaves a terrible mess on the anchor when you hoist it.

Do not anchor west of the green buoy marking the western side of the turning basin on the west side of the pier. The reef is no more than 30 feet west of that buoy, and water barely covers the reef at high tide. At low tide you will have no doubt why you should not anchor beyond the green buoy. Also, be cautious not to anchor too far north of the line between the green buoy and the launch ramp. Water gets shallow approximately 100 yards north of that line.

Three or four boats can anchor in this area without creating problems for the tug crews bringing in barges. After you have your anchor down, take the tender to the launch ramp and tie alongside it. The harbor office is out on the pier, to your right after you leave your tender at the launch ramp. If the harbormaster is not in the harbor office when you arrive, plan to stay put in the back of the turning basin. You may agree with us that life doesn't get much better than anchored in this area, but, if you would rather be tied Tahiti-style in one of the slips, ask the harbormaster if a slip is available.

The best news about the anchorage at Kaunakakai is the calm water. Even when the winds are blowing at 25 knots just outside the harbor, your boat will sit calmly in the anchorage.

Kaunakakai Harbormaster 808-553-1742

FACILITIES

Bank
Car Rental (from airport)
Fuel (diesel by truck; gasoline by jerry jug)
Grocery Stores
Hospital
Launch Ramp
Laundromat
Library

Pharmacy
Post Office
Propane
Restaurants
Restrooms
Showers (cold)
Telephone

St. Joseph Church, built by Father Damien

Fishing boat anchored in Kamalō

Reef along the south coast of Moloka'i, near Lono Harbor

KAMALŌ HARBOR
CHART #19351, 19353
LAT. N21° 02.040 LONG. W156° 52.538 (BUOY AT ENTRANCE)

Not many boaters visit Kamalō Harbor, perhaps because they must navigate a narrow, unmarked channel through a reef to get into the anchorage or perhaps because the harbor is completely isolated. Whatever the case, we have yet to see another cruising boat anchored here. All those other boaters are missing a beautiful cruising destination and a legendary place for the Hawaiians of many centuries past.

To the north of the anchorage are reddish brown slopes, with little vegetation, no doubt inspiring the ancient Hawaiians to name this place *Kamalo'o*, or "the dry place." Although these slopes appear to rise immediately behind the beach, the sandy flat land around Kamalō extends inland for almost a mile.

Kamakou, the peak of the shield volcano that formed eastern Moloka'i, at 4,970 feet has the highest elevation on the island. Because of this height, the island east of Kamalō receives

Kamalō Anchorage

considerably more rainfall than the western half. Thus, the landscape east of Kamalō becomes increasingly green and the gulches much more deeply eroded. The once rounded shield is now strips of lush green alternating with green valleys below cliff sides of vivid burnt red volcanic soil.

Near the anchorage is a thick stand of *kiawe* and palm trees. Little remains of the old pier in the north corner of the anchorage. Kamalō was once a major port for the island, before Kaunakakai assumed that role.

You can go ashore inside the cove northwest of the old pier by taking your tender over the reef, carefully checking depths. After you tie your tender to a tree or pull it up on the beach near the Kamalō Canoe Club, you can hike 150 yards to the road that goes from Kaunakakai to Hālawa Valley. The small village of Kamalō is .25 mile west of the harbor. The village has no stores or services, only a few residences. From Kamalō to Kaunakakai is 10 miles.

One mile to the east of Kamalō Harbor is Saint Joseph Church (1876), the second of the two small churches Father Damien built on the south side of Moloka'i. This wood-frame structure has a fresh coat of white paint on it and well-tended grounds around it. A statue of Father Damien, often draped with fresh *lei,* stands by the door. Between the harbor and the church are a few homes but no businesses.

'Ili'ili'ōpae Heiau is farther along on this road, too far for most people to want to hike. The largest temple on the island and, according to some legends, the oldest, it was the site of human sacrifice. The Menehune, the legendary race of small people who worked at night building various kinds of structures for the Hawaiians, reportedly built this platform-type *heiau,* passing the stones from hand to hand from the Wailau Valley, on the other side of the island. The trail from the *heiau* over the mountain to Wailau Valley still exists. These master builders worked only one night on a project and then moved on to the next job.

A powerful *kahuna* ("priest") was named after Kamalō. The *kahuna* had two sons who were put to death for playing the temple drums in the 'Ili'ili'ōpae Heiau. In retribution, the *kahuna* sought the help of the shark god Kauhuhu, who sent a great storm that destroyed the *heiau* and washed all the people out to sea except for the *kahuna*, in legends called Kamalō, and his family.

White A-frame house at Kamalō

Some boaters consider Kamalō the only all-weather anchorage on the island. The Hawaiians used this natural harbor as a canoe landing for centuries. The extensive reef protects the anchorage from the open water of the Kalohi Channel outside so that the water inside is calm in all but the most violent weather. Even when the winds are blowing at 25 knots and whitecaps curl all around your boat, the motion is delightfully calm.

The water behind the reef shows turquoise above the sand bottom. The reef, so near the surface, glitters golden in the sun. Snorkeling is good along the reef on the inside. Outside by the buoy is a good diving site.

Although the anchorage at Kamalō has much to commend it to the cruising boater, it does get windy. If the sound of the wind playing with your rigging bothers you, you might want to choose another anchorage.

APPROACH

When approaching Kamalō from the west, travel the 9.5 miles from Kaunakakai Harbor, following the reef line but staying at least one mile out from the reef. Coming along this coast from the west is the hard way to get to Kamalō Harbor, however. The wind and waves virtually always present along the southeastern shoreline of Moloka'i will slow your forward progress to almost nothing. Some boaters say the more practical way to get to Kamalō from the west is to sail from Kaunakakai to the north shore of Lāna'i, across the 'Au'au Channel to Lahaina, up the west shoreline of Maui, and then across the Pailolo Channel to Kamalō. Following this route from Kaunakakai to Kamalō makes for an all-day trip, but the trip would give you the opportunity to do some sailing, and it would certainly be much more comfortable than plowing into the waves going east along the reef line.

Approaching from the east, you will travel 12.5 miles along the shoreline from Cape Hālawa or make the easy 15.0 mile trip from Lahaina.

The landscape changes dramatically at Kamalō. To the west, the terrain is arid, with sparse vegetation. To the east of Kamalō, the terrain is green, especially on the higher slopes. Directly north of the anchorage the mountain is reddish-brown and barren. Slightly east of this barren mountain is the highest mountain on the island, Kamakou, at 4970 feet a beautiful shade of green.

Kamalō is marked by a red buoy, R"2." The entrance through the reef into Kamalō Harbor is about 100 yards north of the buoy and is at least 200 feet wide. Breaking water normally marks the position of the reef on either side of the entrance, but proceed slowly, checking continuously to be certain you're not too close to the reef. When the sun is high, you can easily

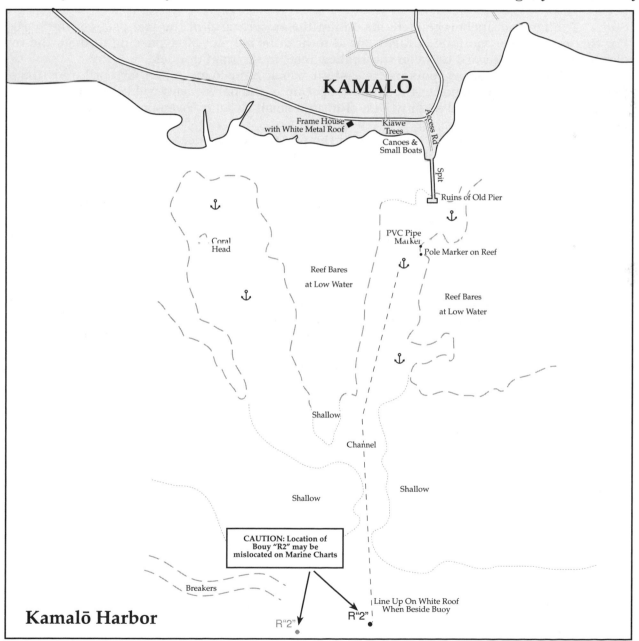

Kamalō Harbor

spot the reef, provided you are entering at low water. At high tide, finding the reef may be more challenging; however, generally, the water in the channel is a turquoise color while the water over the reef appears golden brown. The minimum depth is 10 feet as you pass through the reef.

The easiest way to find the channel is to line up on the white A-frame house with a white metal roof at the back of Kamalō Harbor when you are just east of the buoy. From the buoy, you'll also be able to spot the remains of the old pier.

As you proceed toward the house, you'll pass a part of the reef that appears to extend out into the channel from the starboard side. When you're abeam of it, you can change course slightly to starboard and head directly for the old pier or turn abruptly to port and head into the west basin of this harbor.

The depths in the channel, surprisingly deep after you pass through the opening in the reef, are as much as 48 feet and as little as 26 feet as you enter either of the anchoring areas.

ANCHORAGE

The favored anchorage at Kamalō is in the eastern arm of the two parts of the harbor. For this anchorage, continue straight ahead toward the old pier after passing through the reef; slowly proceed northward between the shallow reefs to the right and left.

The best anchorage spots in the eastern arm at Kamalō are in the far north near the old pier. When you drop anchor in the farthest spot up in the harbor, you will be within 100 feet of the end of the old pier and slightly east of it, in a small circular cove some 100 yards in diameter.

A second anchorage is just south of the pier in the channel leading to the pier. Anchor west of the marker shown on the chart as "4." This marker now is only a piling at the edge of the reef; it has no color, no number, and no light. This anchorage offers particularly good protection because of the reef 150 feet or so off your bow. The motion here is excellent. You may be a little nervous at first when you look behind your boat and see another reef only 100-150 feet behind you, but you will soon relax and thoroughly enjoy this marvelous anchorage.

In the unlikely event that you arrive at Kamalō and discover these two areas filled with other boats, you can anchor in the channel a little farther from the old pier. The protection and holding are just as good.

You can also try the western arm of the anchorage, where your boat will have more room to swing. Between the reef to the east of the anchorage and the reef to the west is easily 150 yards. Another advantage of the western arm is that you can anchor closer to the beach and therefore farther from the reef protecting you from the heavy seas rolling through the Pailolo and Kalohi channels, which converge just outside the harbor. The depths in the western arm are 25-40 feet, depending on how close you are to the beach. You can easily land your tender on the beach at the north end of the anchorage, but, when we were there, we couldn't find a way from the beach to the highway that connects Kamalō with Kaunakakai.

Set your anchor securely because the winds do blow with authority at Kamalō. If you don't trust your primary anchor, set a second bow hook. The holding here is excellent, but given the wind and the proximity of your boat to the reef, you must have complete confidence in whatever ground tackle you put down.

FACILITIES

None

PŪKOʻO HARBOR
CHARTS #19347, 19353
LAT. N21° 03.550 LONG. W156° 47.482 (ENTRANCE)

Pūkoʻo Harbor offers challenges and beauty for the cruising boater. The first challenge is finding this lovely but unmarked harbor. The second challenge is figuring out how to get inside the reef and get an anchor down in a comfortable spot. Although these challenges might make this anchorage sound intimidating and therefore cause some boaters to pass it by, Pūkoʻo ("support hill") gives enough pleasure to make up for the challenges. The dramatic backdrop of green mountains above sparkling white beaches set off by palm trees swaying in the wind creates a memorable destination.

Pūkoʻo Harbor

Behind the outer anchorage is an inner anchorage, located in the old Pūkoʻo Fishpond, one of the dozens of fishponds along the southern coast of Molokaʻi where the ancient Hawaiians practiced a sophisticated form of aquaculture. This clover-shaped inner anchorage is a posted private lagoon, so it is off limits to cruising boats. Inside the eastern-most "leaf" of this inner anchorage is a thriving modern aquaculture operation, where seaweed is grown, harvested, and bagged for shipment to a hungry market in Honolulu, so hungry, in fact, that the market needs far more seaweed than the operators on Molokaʻi can produce. The west side of the harbor belongs to a private investor who saved the area from developers some years ago. He has put in a dock that appears to be well over 60 feet long for his private yacht.

As tempting as the inner harbor sounds as an anchorage, the three parts of the outer anchorage at Pūkoʻo are all more than serviceable anchorages in most weather conditions. In these outside areas your boat will sit in sparkling turquoise water near the shallow golden reefs, far enough offshore to hear nothing more than an occasional loud vehicle on the Kamehameha V Highway, a short distance from the beach. You'll most likely have your own private swimming pond, though an occasional fishing boat will slowly pass by. The only disappointment here is the snorkeling: most of the coral on the inside of the reef appears to be dead. Both snorkeling and scuba diving are reported to be much better along the outer edges of the reef.

In addition to the anchorage, the surrounding area is also inviting for the cruising boater. You can land your dinghy at the public access beach in the southwestern corner of the anchorage and explore along the beach and up along the Kamehameha V Highway. Within a short distance is a small market with a busy lunch counter that serves excellent food, including fresh fish sandwiches and plate lunches. The market is well stocked, considering its size; it has many items cruising boaters want, such as vegetables, dairy products, bread, and brew. To the west of the market not more than 100 yards is a home market that sells fresh fruit and vegetables. Pūkoʻo has no other markets.

In the early 1900s Pūkoʻo was one of the major villages on Molokaʻi. Lighters from steamers anchored offshore docked regularly at the wharf, bringing goods for the island. The village had a courthouse and jail, a bakery, a dairy, an ice plant, a hotel, and several residences.

Several historical remains are in this homesite of many ancient Hawaiians. The remnants of fishponds line the shore in a continuous string for miles in both directions from Pūkoʻo.

Lava rock walls of ancient fishpond

Across the highway from the beach is the ʻIliʻiliʻōpae Heiau, the largest and perhaps the oldest temple on Molokaʻi. In Hawaiian mythology, the Menehune, the little people who built roads, fishponds, and temples, built this *heiau*. They brought the stones for the *heiau* from Wailau, on the north shore of Molokaʻi, passing them from hand to hand over the mountain along a trail that remains today.

This ancient trail from the North Shore to the *heiau* is still the only land access to the Wailau Valley from the leeward side of the island. Though a portion of it is on private property and therefore closed to the public, you may be able to get permission to cross the property to visit the *heiau* and to hike farther on the 8-mile trail that follows the Punaʻula Gulch to the ridge and then the Wailau Stream down to Wailau.

APPROACH

Pūkoʻo Anchorage is about 5.0 miles east of the entrance buoy at Kamalō Harbor. From the west, the trip is either a long period of pounding into head seas or an even longer trip of tacking out toward the west end of Maui and then back to Pūkoʻo. The long trip out and back is far more comfortable, if you have the time to spare.

From the north, Pūkoʻo is about 7.5 miles southwest along the shore from Cape Hālawa. From the east Pūkoʻo is about 13 miles from Lahaina.

On shore at Pūkoʻo are few major landmarks to let you know when you're close to the anchorage. When you're directly off the anchorage, however, you can see a large grove of palm trees just to the west of the area and a pair of good-sized houses on the hillside directly behind the anchorage, one with a slate gray roof and the other with a bright green roof. Close to the beach are a number of other houses.

If your GPS and the houses on the hill suggest you are at Pūkoʻo, begin to look for the break in the reef. The breaking water on each side of the entrance is obvious; the lack of breaking water at the entrance is also usually evident. The opening through the reef is at least 150 yards wide, leaving plenty of room for even the most cautious cruising boater to be comfortable. Other boaters have reported, though, that occasionally, when the winds and swells are heavy, water does break across the opening. The deepest water in the entrance is toward the eastern side, so favor that side as you enter. As you proceed into the anchorage, stay in the center between the two reefs. Depths in the entrance are between 10-20 feet.

ANCHORAGE

Pūkoʻo has three anchorage areas for visiting boaters. The smoothest water and best protection are in the small area in the northeastern corner. This part of the anchorage is so small, however—about 250 feet in diameter—that it can accommodate no more than one boat, unless two small boats raft up. A channel about 100 feet wide at its narrowest point and 15 feet deep at its most shallow connects this circle of water to the central area. Both the channel and the anchorage area are easy to see when the sun is high. The water in the channel is a deep blue while the water over the reefs is a distinct golden brown.

If you choose this area, anchor about 50 feet from the reef at the eastern end and allow the wind to blow you back as you let out anchor rode. The bottom here is dead coral with patches of sand; the trick is to find one of those patches of sand in which to bury your hook. You might hear your anchor skipping across rocks on the bottom before it finally buries itself. A local boater told us that the owner of a sailboat kept his boat moored in this little cove until recently and that his mooring is apparently still down there but with no chain or line attached to it. We didn't look for this mooring since the search would have required us to get out our scuba equipment and spend a long time looking in water that was somewhat murky that day.

The second anchorage at Pūkoʻo is larger, with room for 2 boats. This larger area is between the entrance through the reef and the private lagoon at the back center of the harbor. A boat can comfortably anchor about 150 feet from the lagoon entrance. The water depth in this larger area is about 12 feet, and the bottom is similar to that of the smaller anchorage, a mixture of rocks and sand. Look carefully for the sand patches before you drop anchor.

Farther out toward the entrance through the reef, perhaps halfway between the blue water at the entrance and the rock wall of the private lagoon, is a third anchorage area. Another boat or two can anchor safely here. This area offers the most swinging room of any of the three areas at Pūkoʻo Harbor. In addition, the bottom in this part of the anchorage is almost exclusively sand, giving excellent holding. Anchor in about 20 feet of water in a sand bottom. The only disadvantage to this part of the harbor is that the boat motion is a bit rolly when the winds and waves in the Pailolo Channel are up. Although few cruising boaters would complain much, the gentle roll here is noticeable compared to the almost imperceptible movement of boats anchored in the two other anchorage areas.

FACILITIES

Groceries
Lunch Counter
Telephone

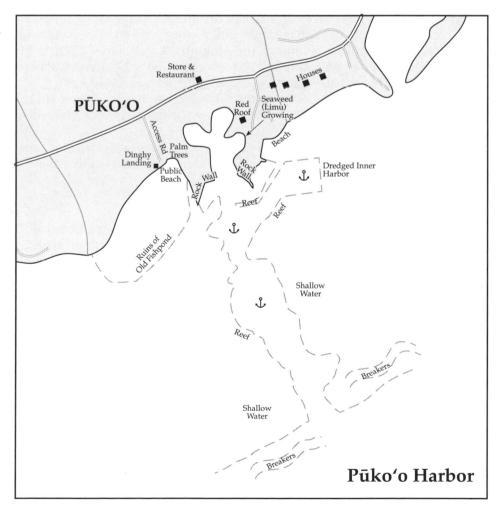

Pūkoʻo Harbor

PAUWALU HARBOR
CHART #19347
LAT. N21° 05.065 LONG. W156° 46.010 (ENTRANCE)

As do Pūko'o and Kamalō, its closest neighbors, Pauwalu Harbor benefits from the reef protecting most of the shoreline on the south shore of the eastern half of Moloka'i. An opening in the reef at Pauwalu allows boaters to slip through and enjoy the protected waters inside, though the reef at Pauwalu does not provide enough protection to make the water inside as calm as it is in either Pūko'o or Kamalō. When we anchored at Pauwalu in moderate trades and a strong north swell, our boat rolled quite noticeably, although not objectionably. If we had planned to be anchored here overnight, we would have deployed a roll stabilizer.

Pauwalu has the same exquisite interplay of colors as has Pūko'o. The green foliage and red soil of the volcanic slope that ascends from the inland side of the highway contrasts with the white beach and small aquamarine cove. From this anchorage, you can look across to the green checkered cane and pineapple fields on the slopes of West Maui and identify majestic Haleakalā touching the clouds.

Much of the population of ancient Moloka'i lived along this southeast coast of the island, where the fishponds flourished in the protected water behind the reefs and the taro grew abundantly in the fertile valleys beyond the beaches. Some taro fields remain in cultivation today, but the village of Pauwalu is little more than a name on the map. The legendary origin of that name, however, survives among the Hawaiian people. The story of the naming of Pauwalu ("eight finished") is a sad one. A shark-man killed seven children here. To rid the village of this terror, the residents sent out the eighth child as bait so they could capture and kill the shark-man.

For a taste of this ancient culture, walk about a mile northeast along the Kamehameha V Highway to the village of Waialua, where you may explore the remains of two *heiau*, Maileola and Welokā. There, too, are the remains of the later, post-contact culture, the Waialua Congregational Church (1855) and the ruins of the Moanui ("big chicken") Sugar Mill (1870s). The processed sugar from this mill was shipped out in barrels on schooners at Pauwalu. When a fire destroyed the mill in the late 19th Century, the plantation was closed.

At Waialua, too, is one of the island's best beaches for swimming, snorkeling, and beginners' surfing. You can also enjoy all three water activities right beside your anchored boat at Pauwalu.

For mountain hiking, two trails are near Pauwalu Harbor, one across the highway to the north and the other, to the south. They are both short—only about a mile long.

APPROACH

If you must come to Pauwalu from the southwest, you will have a 1.84 mile run from Pūko'o Harbor, short enough to be bearable when going to weather. Even so, you may want to keep your mainsail up as you go to make the boat motion more comfortable.

The best approach is from the north or east, of course. From Cape Hālawa to Pauwalu is a 5.8-mile downwind ride. When coming from this direction, stay out a mile or so from shore because of the reef.

Coming from the east, if you depart from Lahaina, you'll have a 13.75-mile beam reach. If strong trades are blowing, consider staying along the coast of West Maui as long as possible to minimize the distance you must cover in crossing the Pailolo Channel.

Recognizing Pauwalu will give you a challenge. No buoy marks the entrance, and shore-side features are not so distinctive as to make this harbor easy to spot. Still, the following might help. To the west, 1.0 mile from the Pauwalu Harbor, is a house with a bright blue roof. Also, a large stand of palm trees is on the beach about .25 mile west of the anchorage. In the back of the anchorage beside the highway is a small green house with a gray roof. Once you're close, you can see the 500-foot-wide opening through the reef and the breaking water on either side of this opening.

ANCHORAGE

From the center of the break in the reef, head directly for the green house with the dark gray roof. From the reef line to the anchorage area is no more than 750 yards. A reef about 150 yards from the beach marks the inside boundary of the anchorage area. When you're approximately 100 yards from the reef in the back, turn up wind (normally to the northeast) and drop your anchor in 30-35 feet of water close to the reef on the east side of the anchorage. Check carefully to be sure you aren't dropping your hook on coral. The bottom here is primarily sand, providing excellent holding.

You can take your tender ashore by going around the reef in the northeast corner of the anchorage and landing on one of the beaches. The calm water behind that inside reef promises you a dry landing.

FACILITIES

None

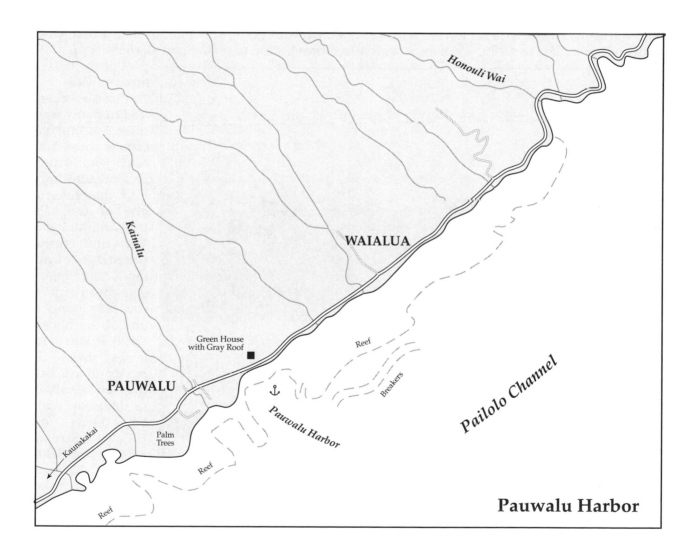

Pauwalu Harbor

Both times we were in Hālawa Bay by boat, moderate trades were blowing and a 10-foot north swell was rolling in. We went in, sat in the cockpit for a while, and finally motored out and around the east end of Moloka'i to friendlier waters. We were sorry to have to leave without spending some time in this bay that has everything to delight the eyes. It is also a much-touted swimming, snorkeling, and surfing site.

The most imposing of the natural wonders are the precipitous cliffs on either side of the entrance into the bay. Then the slender V-shaped valley opens up, its floor a mass of tropical plants flourishing in this moist corner of Moloka'i. The emerald spires atop the cliffs beyond the valley form a tableau that finally disappears into the clouds. Among those cliffs one discerns two vertical ribbons of shimmering silver: Moa'ula ("red chicken") Falls, 250 feet high, and the 500-foot Hīpuapua ("tail flowing") Falls.

Two stories concern these two waterfalls. The first, and oldest, is that a *mo'o*, or lizard woman, who lives in the pool at the base of the falls on occasion pulls a bather into the depths of the pool. To test whether you'll be safe swimming here, throw a *tī* leaf into the water. If it floats, she will let you swim without harm. If it sinks, swim at your peril. The second story is that, when Queen Emma died in 1885, a violent storm caused beach sand to be washed all the way up to the pool at the base of Moa'ula Falls.

Cape Hālawa and Hālawa Valley

For a closer and in many ways more spectacular view of these falls, take your tender ashore at the inner cove and hike on one of the best trails on Moloka'i. This trail crosses privately owned land, so, before you head up to the falls, stop at one of the houses down a side road across from the park and ask permission to walk up to Moa'ula Falls. You must ford Hālawa Stream, but once you have done so, the trail along the north side of the valley is well-defined, paralleling the stream about 50 feet below and following crumbling stone walls and a water pipe. The trail itself is worth the journey, as it winds through mango groves and old taro patches overgrown with guava. The pool at the base of the falls, some 2 miles from the trailhead, is much favored by swimmers (though you'll want to be sure to test the waters with a *tī* leaf!). You might want to be content with viewing Hīpuapua Falls from the trail rather than make the treacherous climb over rocks to get to its base.

Hālawa ("curve") is credited by legend with being the first permanent settlement of the Polynesians who sailed to the Hawaiian Islands. The date of the arrival of these ancient sailors may have been as early as the beginning of the Christian era, but almost certainly they came at least as early as the 7th century. In either case, Hālawa has a long history. The remains of two early *heiau*, Pāpā ("forbidden") and Mana ("supernatural power"), overlook the bay from the cliffs to the north.

For centuries taro terraces filled this fertile valley home of hundreds of Hawaiians. In 1946 a tremendous tidal wave inundated the valley, killing several people and leaving a deposit of salt that rendered the once-fertile valley sterile for years. The jungle has reclaimed this valley land once bountiful with taro.

We have known people who have anchored in Hālawa Bay in both calm and *kona* conditions, but we can't tell you from personal experience how to do so. We have been in Hālawa from the land side and seen 30-foot fishing boats at anchor in the inner harbor. This anchorage looks ideal, but the bar between the inner and outer bays is reported to be only 4 feet deep, too shallow for most cruising boats to cross.

What we know for sure is that the anchorage outside the bar at Hālawa Bay is not a safe or comfortable place to anchor when moderate to heavy trades are blowing and/or when a north swell is running. The best time to try Hālawa is in early fall or late spring when the trades are light and the swell from the north is not running.

APPROACH

Hālawa Bay, in a large indentation of the northeast corner of Moloka'i, is easily located from any direction. From the southwest, Cape Hālawa is 5.8 miles from Pauwalu Harbor; from the cape, the bay is 1.5 miles west. Coming along the south coast is bad enough, but rounding Cape Hālawa can be particularly nasty. If you're approaching from this direction, leave early in the day before the Pailolo Channel becomes too roiled up. Swing wide as you round Cape Hālawa to avoid rough seas that bunch up at the point.

The easier approach to Hālawa is usually from Lahaina or one of the other anchorages on the northwest coast of Maui. By traveling up Maui's western coastline early in the day and crossing the Pailolo Channel where it joins the Pacific Ocean at Honolua Bay, you can make the 20-mile trip quite comfortably.

ANCHORAGE

When large fishing boats are anchored here, they are typically just outside the inner cove in the small cove along the south coast of the bay. The bay has 45 feet of water that shallows abruptly to 10-12 feet in this cove.

FACILITIES

None

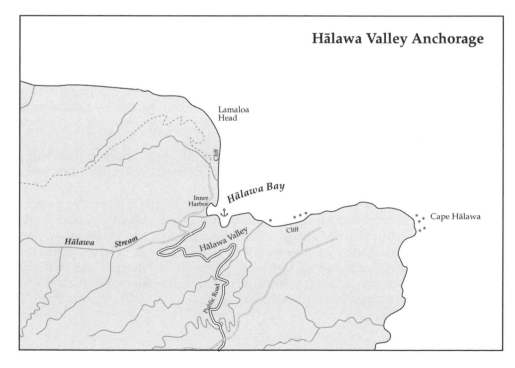

Hālawa Valley Anchorage

All the anchorages along the north shore of Moloka'i afford the cruising sailor spectacular views. This north coast easily rivals the more widely acclaimed Nā Pali Coast of Kaua'i. On Moloka'i the Hawaiians express their admiration for a stately and regal person by saying, *"Hanohano na pali ki'eki'e o Wailau,"* or, "Majestic are the tall cliffs of Wailau." Despite the beauty of this coast, it attracts few sightseers, probably because it is virtually inaccessible by land and too far from a commercial harbor to be a practicable tourist site for the charter boats. Hence, for the cruising sailor, this coast is ideal: it has all the beauty of the Nā Pali Coast but no charter boats competing for the good anchorages.

Fishing boats are usually in evidence up and down this north coast of Moloka'i. In fact, the Jackpot International Fishing Tournament, held in October each year, begins at Lahaina, Maui, but all of the hundreds of boats entered in the tournament head around Cape Hālawa to this north shore.

Poi pounding

Wailau Bay is a good-sized bay at the mouth of the Wailau Valley, the largest valley amphitheater on Moloka'i. The Wailau Stream and its tributaries that flow from the mountain ridge have carved out this valley. Numerous waterfalls cascade down its walls, the highest falling from 4,970 feet above. The Wailau Trail follows this stream up and over the mountain, ending at Pūko'o, on the opposite side of the island.

In the Wailau Valley from the earliest times a large community of Hawaiians grew taro, continuing to produce it commercially until the 1920s. The villagers supplemented their diets by traveling to Kalawao and Kalaupapa to catch fish and dry it there, since their valley had so few hours of sunshine even on a clear day. (On an average this valley has rain between 10 and 15 days each month.) They must have also used the Wailau Trail to cross the mountains to the south shore of Moloka'i. The early Hawaiian residents of this now deserted valley were reputed to be excellent climbers.

Wailau Valley figures in several ancient stories concerning fish. In one, the fishing god 'Ai'ai punished the people for not protecting the fish spawn by hiding all the shrimp under a ledge at Wailau called *Kōkī.* From that story came the proverb, "At *Kōkī* at Wailau is the stairway of the shrimp."

The people began to move away in the late 1800s. The village was already entirely abandoned when the 1946 tsunami swept through the valley and destroyed the few structures remaining.

Boaters who have anchored at Wailau regularly over the years say that they especially like being anchored here when the tradewinds are blowing. Their boats sit comfortably behind Lēpau Point, while the whitecaps go rolling by just a few yards away. According to their reports, the motion aboard their anchored boats is comfortable even in these conditions.

Clearly, though, you'll not want be anchored here if the north winds begin to blow or a north swell sets in. In such conditions, you will want to be anchored on the south side of the island.

APPROACH

The anchorage at Wailau Valley is easy to spot from a mile or two offshore. Lēpau Point, on the east side of the bay, extends .10 mile northward; two rocks off the point extend even farther out.

From Cape Hālawa, the anchorage at Wailau is a 7.0-mile downwind trip. About 2.0 miles east of the anchorage, the magnificent Papalaua Falls drops 1,200 feet into a lush green valley. Surprisingly, the rushing stream one would expect to see carrying all this volume of water into the ocean is not in evidence.

From the west, the anchorage is about 8.5 miles upwind from Moloka'i Light on the Kalaupapa Peninsula. If light tradewinds are blowing, of course, this will be an easy up-wind trip, but the trip is sure to be miserable in moderate or heavy tradewinds.

We recommend that you not transit this coastline at night or with limited visibility because of the numerous small offshore islands.

When you're adjacent to the anchorage, you'll see the trees at the east end of the beach. Also, the Wailau Valley behind the anchorage is the largest of the amphitheater valleys on Moloka'i. Immediately to the west of the anchorage, a large, precipitous cliff constitutes the west wall of the valley.

ANCHORAGE

The best anchorage at Wailau Valley is behind the 150-foot high Lēpau Point. Anchor in 12-20 feet of water as close as you can to the shoreline and to the high, green Lēpau Point. Just behind the shoreline at this point is a stand of about a half dozen palm trees.

Much of the bottom here is covered with rocks that will not provide good holding; therefore, look carefully for a sand patch before you drop anchor. When the anchor is set in the sand here, the holding is excellent.

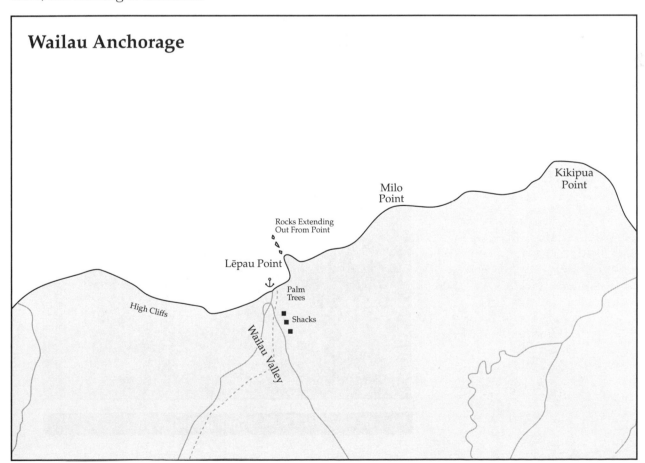

Wailau Anchorage

Kikipua Point

Milo Point

Rocks Extending Out From Point

Lēpau Point

Palm Trees

High Cliffs

Shacks

Wailau Valley

When we anchored at Wailau, we couldn't get into the ideal anchorage up tight against the cliffs because of the boat that had arrived minutes before we did, so we anchored about 100 yards off the beach, 300 yards west of the huge hill that extends out to become Lēpau Point. The day we were there the winds were blowing light and variable, and the motion we experienced was gentle if slightly rolly.

Considerable swell breaks on the shore at Wailau Anchorage, so be careful if you decide to go ashore. Rather than a sand beach, the beach is large rocks, and it is steep enough to make landing a real challenge.

FACILITIES

None

"Waterfall"

PAHU POINT ANCHORAGE (LAEOKAPAHU POINT)
CHART #19347
LAT. N21° 10.028 LONG. 156° 53.578 (ANCHORAGE)

The anchorage at Hā'upu Bay, in the lee of Laeokapahu ("point of the drum"), called on NOAA charts simply *Pahu Point*, is another of the dramatic Moloka'i north shore anchorages. High mountains on three sides of the bay painted gloriously, as one writer put it, "a thousand shades of green" and the sapphire water breaking white on the rocks blend in perfect harmony. About 200 yards inside the bay are 100-foot-high boulders, said to have been kicked into the bay by a giant demigod, Kana, after he had defeated an enemy up on the ridge.

Hā'upu Peak rises 1,022 feet above Laeokapahu. A legendary Moloka'i chief, Kapepe'ekauila, built a fortress on this peak, where he imprisoned Hina, called the "Helen of Hawai'i," after he had abducted her from her husband's home on the Big Island. After spending 20 years discovering where Hina was being held captive, her two sons came to rescue her.

The hill with the fortress stretched higher and higher, but Hina's giant son, Kana, the stretching *kupua* ("demigod"), learned that the hill was a turtle whose stretching power lay in its flippers. Kana broke these off, crushed the turtle, and rescued his mother. The crushed pieces of Hā'upu Peak became the turtles of the Hawaiian waters. Kūka'iwa'a ("canoe extension") Point, about a mile west of Laeokapahu, was so named because, when Kana anchored his canoe at Laeokapahu, the stern reached all the way to this point.

A cable stretches across Hā'upu Bay.

Now for the practical story about this anchorage. When the trades are blowing, the cliff that extends out 400 yards on the east side of the bay protects the anchorage. The water in the anchorage is generally a bit rolly, but most cruising boaters are willing to put up with a little roll for beauty. If you plan to spend the night, you might want to put out roll stabilizers.

The beach at the back of this bay is rocky and steep and not suitable for taking a tender ashore. The water, though, offers opportunities for exploration. You can snorkel along the cliff faces or take the tender along the shore to three fairly large caves. The photo opportunities, too, are compelling.

This anchorage provides great protection when light or moderate trades blow; it could be rough inside in strong trades. The anchorage at Pahu Point is absolutely unsafe when north winds and swell are up.

APPROACH

Pahu Point is 11.0 miles west of Cape Hālawa, along some of the most scenic coastline in the state, if not in the world.

The distance from the north end of the Kalaupapa Peninsula, just off the Moloka'i Light, to Pahu Point is 6.0 miles. Boaters can also hold a course of 109° magnetic from Mōkapu Island, 2.75 miles west of Pahu, to locate the anchorage.

A house sits on a cliff on the southeast side of the bay, at least 200 feet above the level of the boats in the anchorage. A hoist system on a cable from the back of the bay is apparently used to get people and supplies up to the house.

ANCHORAGE

Enter the bay about 200 feet west of Pahu Point, turning southeast and proceeding approximately parallel to the cliff face to the east. You'll be heading directly toward the house on the cliff. As you pass Pahu Point, the water behind the cliff becomes quite calm.

Anchor in the small cove below the house, about 150 feet from the rocks at the back of the cove. Plan to drop in about 50 feet of water in this deep anchorage. Make sure you leave enough room for the boat to swing without hitting the rocks. If you have enough visibility, pick a sand patch to drop anchor in and set your anchor carefully.

Caution: Some boats have been washed ashore and destroyed on the rocks when a north wind and swell set in unexpectedly. One local boater recommends diving down and setting the anchor by hand in this cove.

When we anchored behind Pahu Point, the day was heavily overcast, so we couldn't see the bottom. As a result, we can't give you a good report about it. Our anchor held well, but then the weight of the chain alone would probably have held us in place with the slight breeze that wafted through the anchorage area. However, as we backed down to set the anchor, the chain rumbled across rocks as it straightened out. Before going to bed or leaving the boat to go exploring, you may want to get into the water and check the bottom.

In the southwest corner of the bay, some 500 yards from Pahu Point, is another potential anchorage. It doesn't have the great protection of the other anchorage, but it could be a better anchorage if it has a good sand bottom. This potential anchorage can be identified by the beach in the back of the area.

FACILITIES

None

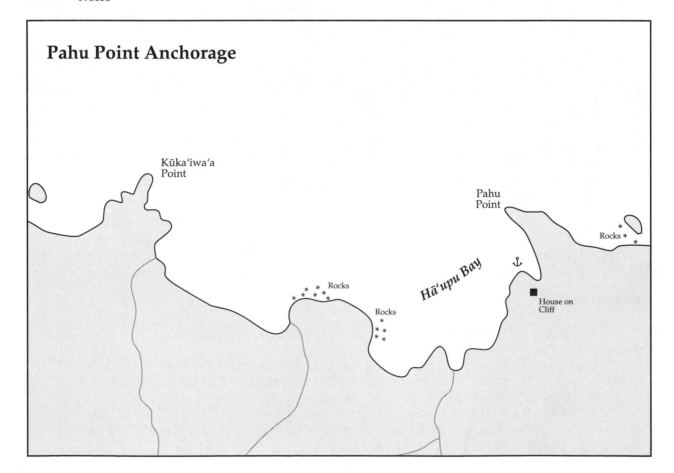

ʻŌKALA ISLAND ANCHORAGE (KALAWAO ANCHORAGE)
CHART #19347
LAT. N21° 10.475 LONG. 156° 55.940 (ANCHORAGE)

The anchorage on the eastern side of Kalaupapa Peninsula is variously called the ʻŌkala or *Kalawao* anchorage. ʻŌkala Island shelters the anchorage from the tradewinds, and the anchorage is a short distance across the bay from Kalawao, the original site where the victims of Hansen's Disease, or leprosy, were exiled.

By any name, this anchorage is one of the best along the north coastline of Molokaʻi. In addition to ʻŌkala Island, Mōkapu Island and Leina o Papio Point also shelter boats anchored here. We were recently anchored in the Kalaupapa Anchorage, a much better known anchorage, when a northwest swell set in, causing the boats to roll throughout the night. One fishing boat had come into the anchorage before dark, sized up the situation, and left. The next morning when we went around the point, we saw that fishing boat sitting motionless at ʻŌkala.

The high cliffs to the east and west give this anchorage much of the same beauty as the other anchorages on the north shore of Molokaʻi. The cliffs are not as close to the water here, leaving a long expanse of flat (or at least relatively flat) ground, where feral goats sometimes browse and gambol.

Ashore, somewhat hidden by the trees, are historic sites from the days when the leper colony was at Kalawao. The two churches are well-known landmarks. The Protestant church, Siloama, the Church of the Healing Spring, built in 1871, is named for Siloam, a spring near Jerusalem where, at Jesus's bidding, a blind man bathed and recovered his sight. St. Philomena Church was completed after Father Damien's arrival in 1873. A monument behind a fence in the cemetery marks where Damien was buried, but his remains were removed to his native Belgium in 1936. The Baldwin Boys' Homesite, for the young boys sent to Kalawao, is also here.

Signs on the shore at the head of the bay at ʻŌkala warn that it is illegal to go ashore there, just as the signs do at Kalaupapa. But you can enjoy swimming and snorkeling or exploring with your tender without going ashore.

Like all of the other north shore anchorages, Kalawao is not recommended during the winter because of the frequency of north winds and swells. The anchorage is open to the north.

Egrets ashore at ʻŌkala

APPROACH

From Cape Hālawa to ʻŌkala Island is 12.5 miles, and, when trade winds are blowing, a fast trip for those who don't stop along the way. When only 6 miles from Cape Hālawa, you'll be able to distinguish Mōkapu Island, approximately 0.5 mile seaward of ʻŌkala Island, and head directly for it.

From the west, round Kahiʻu Point, the northern tip of Kalaupapa Peninsula, and follow the east side of the peninsula south to ʻŌkala Anchorage. The distance from Molokaʻi Light to the anchorage is 3.3 miles.

The two islands immediately north of the anchorage, Mōkapu and ʻŌkala, make identification of this anchorage easy. Approaching from the east, you can safely pass between these two islands before turning into the anchorage. When coming from the west around Kahiʻu Point, keep both islands on your port side.

Another landmark is St. Philomena Church at Kalawao, to the starboard when you're abeam of Mōkapu Island.

ANCHORAGE

The best place to drop anchor is in the southeastern corner of the anchorage. Anchor in 30 feet of water about 200 feet from the rocky beach at the south and about 150 feet from the peninsula to the east. Be careful to find a sand patch among the rocks to drop in. Your anchor chain will undoubtedly rumble over the bottom if your boat moves about while you're anchored here, but the anchor should nonetheless hold well if you have indeed dropped in a sand patch.

Although we've not anchored at ʻŌkala when strong tradewinds are blowing, our boat moved little when light to moderate trades were blowing. This anchorage is almost as well protected from the trades as Kalaupapa Anchorage.

ʻŌkala Anchorage is not safe when north winds or swell set in.

FACILITIES

None

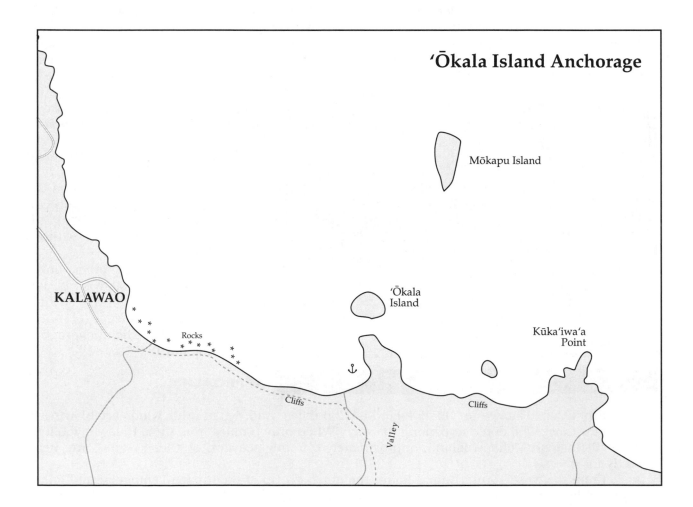

KALAUPAPA ANCHORAGE ('AWAHUA BAY)
CHARTS #19340, 19347
LAT. N21° 11.306 LONG. W156° 59.178 (ANCHORAGE)

Kalaupapa, the best known anchorage on the north shore of Moloka'i, should perhaps be called 'Awahua Bay Anchorage, but we have heard it referred to only as Kalaupapa. Fishing boats regularly anchor here at night when they are working the waters north of Moloka'i. An occasional cruising boater also spends a night or two here.

The primary reason for the popularity of Kalaupapa Anchorage can be summed up in one word: protection. The peninsula, on a flat map looking like a shark's fin, extends out from the remainder of the island almost 3 miles. Formed by the eruption of the Kauhakō volcano long after the two other volcanoes created the eastern and western ends of Moloka'i, this geologic afterthought provides excellent protection when even strong tradewinds are blowing. The vertical *pali* along the north coast of Moloka'i shelters the anchorage from south winds. Open to the north and west, this anchorage becomes untenable when winds from either of those directions are blowing.

Before the State of Hawai'i acquired the peninsula, it was the home of Hawaiians living in fishing villages in three separate *ahupua'a* (land divisions), called Makanalua, Kalawao, and Kalaupapa. The state acquired Makanalua and Kalawao in 1848 and began exiling victims of Hansen's Disease here in 1866. The exiles settled around the village of Kalawao. The state purchased the third *ahupua'a*, Kalaupapa, in 1873.

Unlike all other north shore Moloka'i anchorages, you can sit on your boat and watch the activity on shore. From the anchorage, and from ashore, too, for that matter, Kalaupapa looks like a model village. Its well-tended grounds festooned with blossoming bougainvillea, plumeria, and ginger and the neatly painted wood-sided houses belie the tragic history of this former leper colony. Looking at Kalaupapa from the water, you may have little sense of how isolated

The village and anchorage at Kalaupapa

this peninsula has always been until you begin to search for a way out by land. A solid mass of green conceals even the mule trail that is the only access by land. Only sixty or so residents continue to live at Kalaupapa; if you anchor here, you'll see some of them doing what Hawaiians all around the Islands do—standing on the rocks casting their fishing lines into the water.

A sign on the warehouse by the pier warns boaters, "Restricted area. No landing without permission." Apparently, this restriction is enforced. Only those boaters who have secured permission ahead will be allowed to visit. We haven't tried to go ashore from the anchorage, but obtaining permission should be possible since visitors routinely go in by mule and by plane.

APPROACH

The most notable landmark on the Kalaupapa Peninsula is Moloka'i Light, standing atop a tall white lighthouse some 213 feet above the water. With a range of 25 miles, this is one of the most powerful lights in the state. At the base of the lighthouse standing out sharply against the black lava of the peninsula are two sparkling white buildings with bright red roofs. The lighthouse and the buildings make finding Kalaupapa easy, day or night.

Moloka'i Light is 15 miles from Cape Hālawa, the direction from which most cruising boats will be approaching because the winds also come from that direction. If you are approaching from the east, be sure to stay well offshore as you round Kahi'u Point on Kalaupapa Peninsula to avoid the rocks along that shoreline. Also, continue to stay well offshore as you travel from Kahi'u Point down the west side of the peninsula. Rocks, coral heads, and parts of a ship that went on the rocks are a hazard along this shoreline.

For those boaters who find a good weather window and can approach from the west, the

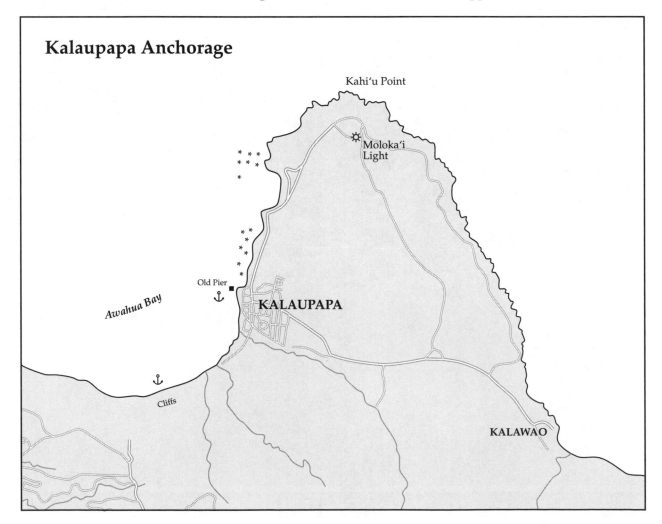

anchorage at Kalaupapa is 16 miles from ʻĪlio Point on the northwestern corner of Molokaʻi.

For boaters approaching from either direction, the town of Kalaupapa is visible from 2 or 3 miles out and makes final identification easy. Especially easy to see is the old white warehouse near the pier on the west side of town. A church is also easy to spot from some approaches. The palm trees scattered around the town stand out, too.

ANCHORAGE

The best anchorage at Kalaupapa is 150 feet west of the old pier. The old pier, once used by the tugs and barges bringing supplies to the colony of exiles on Kalaupapa, has only 2-4 feet of water alongside it. Even when the tugs and barges were still tying up here, the water was shallow. A tug captain who once towed barges to Kalaupapa says towing in here was a nightmare. Because of the shallow water, he couldn't take the barge all the way up to the pier; instead, the people of the town had to use a truck onshore to pull the barge the final 100 feet to the dock.

However that may be, the anchorage off the pier is excellent. Water depths range from 25-40 feet. If that area has already been taken when you get there, you can also anchor just south of the old pier 200 feet from shore in 40-50 feet of water. Others have told us that the area off the beach at the south end of ʻAwahua Bay, some .50 mile southwest of the old pier, also provides good anchorage in about 25 feet of water.

The bottom at Kalaupapa is sand with some rocks, but, if you set the hook well, you're not likely to have any surprises in the night. The winds typically come from the east, over the town, but they can also come from the south, over the island. When they do come from the south, they tend to be inconsistent in strength and direction.

In almost all conditions except in north or west winds, the boat motion is comfortable in this anchorage.

FACILITIES

None (Boaters can't go ashore without securing prior permission.)

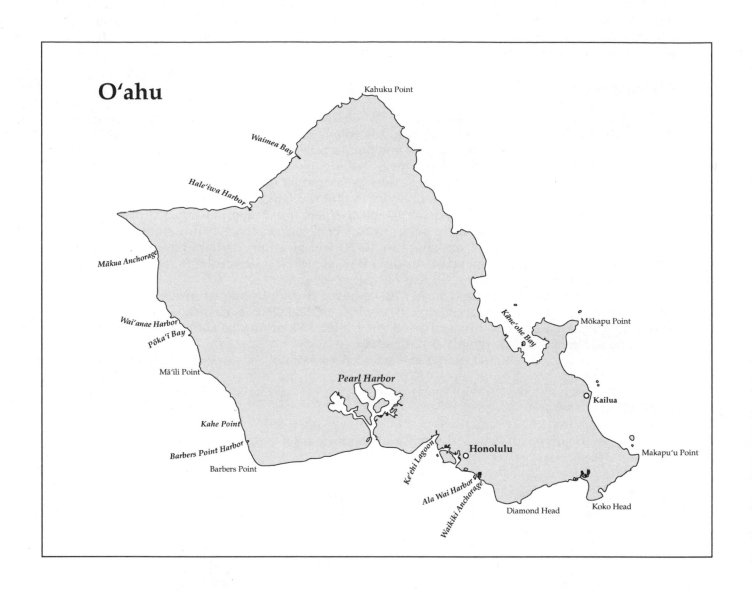

O'ahu

Kahuku Point

Waimea Bay

Hale'iwa Harbor

Mākua Anchorage

Kāne'ohe Bay

Mōkapu Point

Wai'anae Harbor

Pōka'ī Bay

Mā'ili Point

Pearl Harbor

Kailua

Kahe Point

Honolulu

Barbers Point Harbor

Makapu'u Point

Barbers Point

Ke'ehi Lagoon

Ala Wai Harbor

Waikīkī Anchorage

Diamond Head

Koko Head

THE ISLAND OF O'AHU

THE GATHERING PLACE

Entering Ala Wai Channel, with Diamond Head as the backdrop

Oahu ka 'ōnohi o na kai
("O'ahu, the gem of the seas")

THE ISLAND OF OʻAHU

Oʻahu, ka ʻōnohi o na kai. This Hawaiian proverb, "Oʻahu, the gem of the seas," accurately reflects what Oʻahu is to many visitors, whether they come by land or by sea.

In one Hawaiian legend, the man-child Oʻahu, the sixth of the great island children, was the child of the Hawaiian earth mother, Papa. Angered by the infidelity of her husband, Wākea, Papa found a handsome young lover, Lua, and from their brief union came Oʻahu.

Scientists tell a different story. They say two separate shield volcanoes formed the island of Oʻahu. The older of the two resulted in the Waiʻanae Range that extends from the southern Ewa plain to the North Shore. In this range is the highest spot on the island, Kaʻala, at 4,020 feet elevation. The remnants of the younger of the two volcanoes is the much wetter Koʻolau Range that form windward Oʻahu and is the magnificent backdrop for the city of Honolulu. Lava flows from the two volcanoes joined to create the fertile central plain, the Leilehua Plateau.

Other prominent physical features on Oʻahu appeared much later in its geological history. When volcanic activity resumed after long periods of quiescence, ash built up around the vents and then solidified, resulting in the "tuff cones" now called Diamond Head, Koko Head, Punchbowl, Hanauma Bay, and Ulupaʻu Head. The sheer cliffs of the southeastern and north-western ends of Oʻahu are the result of erosion, while the magnificent *pali* that soars above Kāneʻohe Bay developed from both erosion and the coalescence of migrating valley heads.

With 607.7 square miles, Oʻahu is third in size among the Hawaiian Islands. Yet it has more miles of swimming beaches than any of the other islands in the state, and its surfing beaches along the North Shore are unparalleled anywhere in the world.

It also has far more people than all the other islands put together. With more than 900,000 residents, 80 percent of the population of the State of Hawaiʻi, and, on an average day, close to 80,000 visitors, Oʻahu earns its popular designation as "the Gathering Place."

Sailors who come to the Hawaiian Islands today from all around the Pacific Ocean almost invariably gather eventually at this place. Honolulu, the county seat of Oʻahu and the capital of Hawaiʻi, has the widest range of boating facilities in the state. The two small boat harbors in Honolulu—Ala Wai and Keʻehi—have between them over 1,600 slips. Though a number of slips in each harbor were out of service in mid-2005, one of the remaining spaces will almost surely be available for a visiting boater. In Honolulu, boaters can choose from two boatyards for haul-outs and other marine repairs. Two chandleries as well as several small marine supply stores can provide needed boat parts and service. At or within walking distance of the Ala Wai are all the other facilities required or desired by boaters.

Oʻahu is more than just Honolulu, even though, in the governmental organization of the state of Hawaiʻi, the island and Honolulu City and

Early scene of Honolulu Harbor

County are synonymous. For sailors Oʻahu has much more in store, and, for those who soon tire of city lights, much of it is more appealing than the city. Once you've made all the necessary repairs, stocked up on provisions, and generally enjoyed the city, you can head for other harbors on this island, all of them in a more serene environment than either Ala Wai and Keʻehi.

On the east side of the island is the largest bay in the State of Hawai'i, and one of the most picturesque, Kāne'ohe Bay, with a small boat harbor, a yacht club with its own docks, and four designated anchorages. On the north shore Hale'iwa Small Boat Harbor is in the heart of surfing country, and Wai'anae, the site of another small boat harbor, is on the west coast, said to be the most "Hawaiian" of any area on O'ahu. In Barbers Point Harbor, on the southwest corner of O'ahu, is the new first-class Ko Olina Marina, where visiting sailors can often secure a temporary slip. This marina has all the facilities one could want without the surrounding bustle of a city. Across the harbor channel is the even newer Phoenician, a large, full-service boatyard. And, if you prefer the even greater solitude that comes with anchoring out, you have several coves and bays from which to choose on this diverse island.

At the time Captain William Brown, of the English merchant ship the *Jackall*, discovered the harbor at Honolulu in 1792, O'ahu was far less important politically than either Kaua'i, Maui or the Big Island. Its place in the *mele*, ("chants") that have preserved pre-contact Hawaiian history, though, is easily as significant as that of any of the other islands.

O'ahu was home to many powerful chiefs whose fame spread throughout the Islands. One of the earliest was Nanakaoko, who, along with his wife Kahihiokalani, is credited with having built the sacred birthplace called *Kukaniloko* in the Ewa District of O'ahu. So powerful was the *mana* of this sacred place that centuries after the erecting of the structures Kamehameha I had arranged to have his son and successor born here, but the illness of Queen Keōpūolani prevented her being taken there for the delivery.

On January 1, 1795, the last great chief of O'ahu, Kalanikupule, led an attack on two British ships that resulted in the deaths of Captain Brown, the discoverer of Honolulu Harbor, and his second in command, Captain Gordon of the ship *Prince Lee Boo*. Kalanikupule had hoped to use the two ships, their guns, and the crew to attack the powerful advancing forces of Kamehameha I, king of the Big Island. Once out to sea, the British crew aboard the captured vessel *Jackall* overcame the 40 Hawaiian warriors, forcing them overboard, and sent Kalanikupule ashore in a canoe.

A few months later Kamehameha and his warriors landed on O'ahu. Kalanikupule and his men had taken a stand on high ground, but they were unable to deter the march of Kamehameha and suffered their final and bloody defeat in the Battle of Nu'uanu Valley.

The ascendancy of O'ahu as the economic and political hub of the islands began with Brown's discovery of Honolulu Harbor, where, he noted in his logbook, *"a few vessels may ride with the greatest safety."* That "few vessels" grew to hundreds of ships yearly in this safest of harbors within a 2,000-mile radius. Inevitably, this harbor drew to its shores many Hawaiians, including Kamehameha I, lured by the gain to be had from the thousands of foreign sailors coming ashore. In 1850 Kamehameha III officially declared Honolulu the capital of the Kingdom of Hawai'i.

Sugar mill at Waialua

Because O'ahu has been the political and economic center of the State of Hawai'i since the early 1800s, it has attracted immigrants from all over the world, beginning with the Americans and Europeans who arrived on merchant and whaling ships. American missionaries, primarily from the East Coast, followed in the 1820s.

To meet the growing need of the pineapple and sugar cane industries, contract workers began to arrive: the Chinese in 1852, other South Pacific Islanders in 1859, Japanese in 1868, Portuguese in 1878, Koreans in 1903, and Filipinos in 1906. These workers were scattered throughout the Islands, wherever their work was needed, but inevitably many of them and their descendants ended up in Honolulu, giving this city and county a rich ethnic diversity. Immigrants of many other nationalities have arrived in this century, most of them settling in the city. Yet even cosmopolitan Honolulu retains some of its Hawaiian flavor. At this place called *Kou* by the early Hawaiians, a sailor can still find *honolulu* ("a protected bay") and much *aloha.*

ALA WAI HARBOR
CHART #19351, 19357, 19364, 19380,
LAT. N21° 16.600 LONG. W157° 50.720 (ENTRANCE BUOYS)

For most cruising boaters, Ala Wai Harbor in Honolulu is the most important harbor in the Hawaiian Islands. The reasons for its importance are many: it has slips for over 1,000 boats, shopping nearby, two major yacht clubs offering reciprocal privileges, all-weather protection, a fuel dock, one of the four boat yards on Oʻahu with a chandlery, and a wide range of options for activities, both physical and cultural.

After cruising the more remote locations in the Islands for a few weeks or months, most visiting cruisers, even those who dislike large harbors, come to the Ala Wai. Some come to spend some time with family or friends who fly in to visit; others come here to get some boat work done before heading on to the next destination. And for all, the Ala Wai is the place to reprovision, go shopping, see movies, listen to live music, and socialize with other boaters.

Honolulu has been the hub of activity around the Islands since the early part of the 19th century, as European and American sea captains discovered the truth of its name: *Hono* is "bay" and *lulu* is "sheltered." Either late in 1792 or early in 1793, an English merchant captain, William Brown, found a narrow channel in the reef on the south coast of Oʻahu and led his three ships into what he called "Fair Haven," the harbor of Honolulu.

The Honolulu Harbor that Brown found was not one that had been favored by the Hawaiians. It was hot and humid, with sparse vegetation between the coast and the lower slopes of the *pali*. The beaches were primarily mud flats and exposed coral reefs. But for ships it was ideal. Besides the channel through the reef and its sheltered waters, this harbor had deep water in close to shore. Other sea captains were soon to follow Brown into Honolulu Harbor.

After Kamehameha I conquered Oʻahu in 1795, he began to spend more and more time in his royal beach house in Honolulu, no doubt in response to the growing commerce between the Hawaiians and the Europeans and Americans. Finally, in the 1840s Kamehameha III moved the royal court to Honolulu from Lahaina.

Overview of the Ala Wai Harbor

Waikīkī, its name "spouting waters" said to have come about because of the springs there, had not yet become the world's most famous beach, and the Ala Wai Canal and harbor did not yet exist. About the several months he spent in Honolulu in the 1890s, Robert Louis Stevenson, who had a house at Sans Souci Beach, on the east end of Waikīkī, wrote, ". . . I am always out of sorts, amidst heat and cold and cesspools and beastly haoles" *(Travels in Hawaiʻi 128)*.

In the wetlands between the beach and the *pali* were several fish-ponds spread over 50 acres, surrounded by fields of taro and rice paddies, excellent breeding grounds for mosquitoes. With the construction of the Ala Wai ("fresh water way") Canal between 1919 and 1928 "to reclaim a most unsanitary and unsightly portion of the city," the wetlands drained into the ocean, and Waikīkī began its ascendancy as a world-class resort.

Another significant result of the canal was the creation of the Ala Wai Harbor, with its large public marina and two yacht clubs, each with a few slips for visiting boaters. With Waikīkī Beach to the southeast, the Ala Moana Beach Park on the northwest, and the city of Honolulu spreading inland from the shore, cruising boaters can satisfy all their needs and desires.

Within walking distance from the harbor are, in addition to Waikīkī, the beaches of the Ala

Moana Beach County Park, these swimming beaches favored by the locals over the more crowded Waikīkī. In the park are wide, winding trails for jogging, biking, roller blading, or walking, and well-maintained tennis courts. For snorkeling or scuba diving, the reef near the entrance to the Hilton Hawaiian Village has long been a favorite spot.

A biking and walking trail also follows the south bank of the canal. From the harbor you can reach this trail by taking the steps that go down on the south side of the Ala Moana bridge over the canal. The trail goes through an urban area but also, after crossing over the canal at McCully Street, passes a park and a golf course. And many of the buildings on the other side of the canal are in garden-like settings.

On Oʻahu, the bus system, simply called TheBus, allows visiting boaters to go all around Honolulu, and the entire island for that matter, without the expense of renting a car. And the price is right: only $2 per person, one way, with one transfer. You'll need a guide book to enumerate all the many sites of interest to which TheBus gives you access in this culturally diverse city of about 400,000 residents.

Among the outdoor adventures accessible by TheBus are some of the several hikes in the hills above Honolulu, the best known one to the rim of the Diamond Head crater. The reef around the base of Diamond Head is also a much touted snorkel and scuba site. Beautiful Kapiʻolani Park, too, is a pleasant place to walk near Diamond Head. TheBus will also take you to Hanauma Bay Nature Park, a marine sanctuary where you can snorkel or scuba with approximately 450 species of tropical reef fish.

The rainbow painted on the Hilton Hawaiian

A short bus ride from the harbor is the Hawaiʻi Maritime Center, where the nautical history of the Islands is attractively displayed and clearly described. The *Falls of Clyde*, an old square rigger partially restored, is moored at the dock alongside the Maritime Center. The one site you'll not want to miss if you're curious about the natural and cultural history of the Hawaiian Islands, as well as of the Pacific Basin, is the Bishop Museum. Other sites of cultural interest are the ʻIolani Palace, the only royal palace in the United States, and the Mission Houses Museum.

For a look at one of the rich sub-cultures of Hawaiʻi, take TheBus to Chinatown, formerly peopled by Chinese but today a mix of Chinese, Vietnamese, Filipinos, Koreans, and others. Here you can simply stroll around, taking in the sights and sounds, or you can do some shopping and have an authentic Asian meal.

The role of the Hawaiian Islands in more recent U. S. history is poignantly displayed in two military memorials. Pearl Harbor, the site of the Japanese attack on the United States on December 7, 1941, includes the *Arizona* Memorial, the Pacific Submarine Museum, and the restored submarine the USS *Bowfin*. The second memorial, the National Memorial Cemetery of the Pacific inside Punchbowl Crater, is one of the most popular tourist attractions in all Hawaiʻi. The early Hawaiians called this extinct volcano, with its 112-acre crater floor, *Puowaina* ("hill of

THE ISLAND OF OʻAHU 225

placing") because it was the site of human sacrifices.

Boaters moored in the Ala Wai Harbor have a myriad of choices of outdoor activities and cultural and historical sites to keep themselves pleasantly occupied for months, if they choose to stay that long. We've given you no more than a start for your list of "Things to do in Honolulu."

APPROACH

Approaching from the west, go 16.0 miles after you pass the Barbers Point Light. If you're arriving from the neighbor islands to the east or from the Mainland, you'll most likely come around the south end of the island, pass Diamond Head, and continue 2.5 miles to the entrance to Ala Wai Harbor.

The seaward end of the Ala Wai Channel is marked by a pair of buoys: G"1" and R"2." Three pairs of channel markers show the edges of the channel as it goes through the reef. In the park beyond the harbor are range marks.

According to government charts, the channel is 150 feet wide and 22 feet deep. In fact, the channel is that deep where it goes through the reef, but it is significantly more shallow inside the harbor. Those areas with little current or tidal flow tend to silt in, as do most harbors in Hawai'i, but the primary passageway from the entrance through the reef to the Ala Moana Bridge, over the Ala Wai Canal, is dredged whenever the silting becomes a problem. For cruising boats with 6- or 7-foot drafts, depths are rarely a question in the Ala Wai, but for large race boats with 13-foot drafts, water depths could be an issue.

Since the channel into the Ala Wai is wide and deep, you can make a night entrance without too much danger, provided you've been into the harbor before. The two buoys at the outer end of the channel are lighted and relatively easy to spot, but the range marks are difficult to identify. The lower (closer) range mark has a continuous red light, and the upper (back) range mark has a flashing red light. When you see them for the first time, you may not be sure whether they are range mark lights or the lights of the shopping center directly behind them. (Note! Unless your charts are current as of 1998, they will show the range lights as yellow, not red.)

Regardless of the direction of your approach during daylight hours, you can locate the entrance channel easily by identifying the high-rise Hilton Hawaiian Hotel; it has a vividly colored rainbow painted on the full height of its seaward end. The entrance to the Ala Wai is about 200 yards west of this hotel. When you're close enough to identify the Hilton, you'll also be close enough to see the sailboat masts in the harbor and the entrance buoys to the Ala Wai.

You can safely enter Ala Wai Harbor in all weather except when *kona* storms are blowing. Furthermore, once your boat is inside the harbor, it will be safe during all but the most severe weather.

ANCHORAGE AND BERTHING

The Ala Wai Harbor has no anchorage area within its confines. Outside the harbor, the state has sunk five moorings about 850 yards east of the entrance buoys to the Ala Wai Marina. The white buoys for these moorings are approximately 10 feet below the surface, so you'll have to dive down to tie your line to one. The water depths here range from 17 to 36 feet. (See the section on Waikīkī Anchorage.)

When coming into this harbor for the first time without having made prior arrangements for a slip, stop at the fuel dock as you enter. (Most of us fuel up every time we enter the Ala Wai because it is one of the few opportunities in the Islands to tie up to a dock and stick a hose in the fuel tank: no jerry jugs and no tank truck.) While one person fuels up, someone else can call to find a place to park the boat. If you don't choose to fuel up or if you have to vacate the fuel dock before you've secured a slip, you can take the boat to the loading dock behind the huge 'Ilikai Hotel at the extreme southeast end of the harbor. You may tie up for only 30 minutes at this location, but that is often enough time to find a slip.

If you're a member of a yacht club, call the Hawai'i Yacht Club or the Waikiki Yacht Club

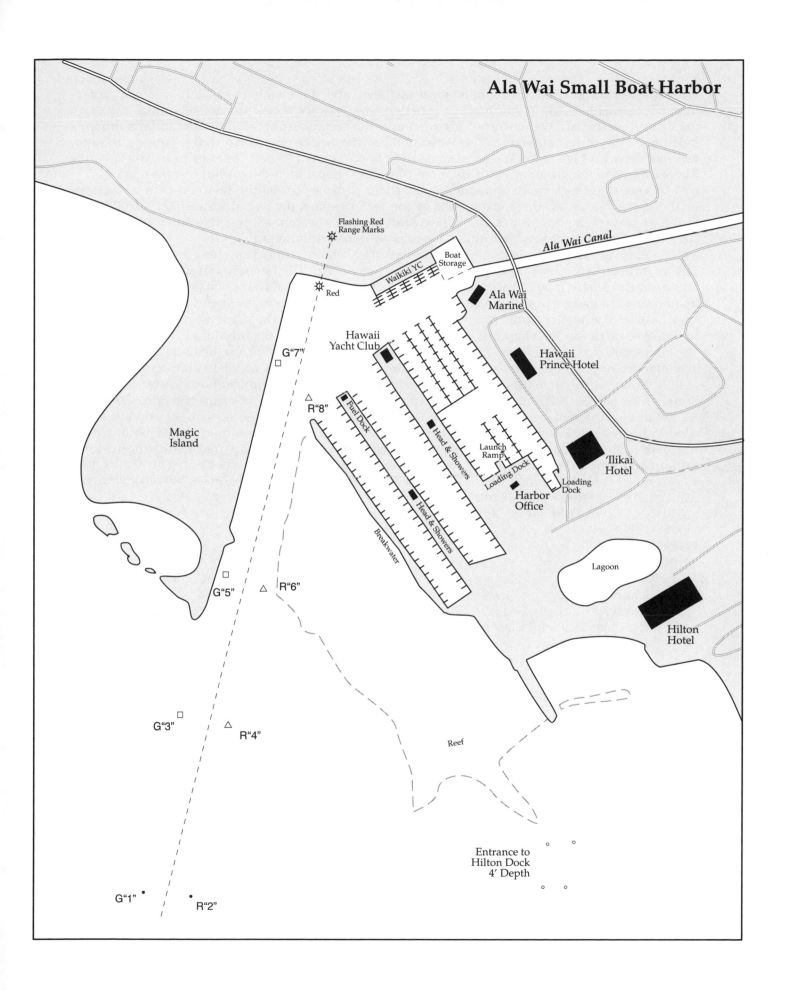

Ala Wai Small Boat Harbor

Flashing Red
Range Marks

Ala Wai Canal

Boat
Storage

Waikiki YC

Red

Ala Wai
Marine

G"7"

Hawaii
Yacht Club

Hawaii
Prince Hotel

R"8"

Fuel Dock

Magic
Island

Head & Showers

Launch
Ramp

Ilikai
Hotel

Loading
Dock

Loading Dock

Harbor
Office

Loading Dock

Breakwater

Head & Showers

Lagoon

G"5"

R"6"

Hilton
Hotel

G"3"

R"4"

Reef

Entrance to
Hilton Dock
4' Depth

G"1"

R"2"

for guest berthing. Both clubs have good facilities, and the members of both welcome visitors from other yacht clubs. If you prefer the better view, Hawai'i YC is the choice because the guest docks are on the Ala Wai entrance channel and the second-storey dining area affords diners a splended view of the sunsets. The Waikiki YC is the better choice for those wanting to enjoy the more modern guest docks, accommodating boats up to 155 feet long, or to be closer to the Ala Moana Shopping Center, with its more than 200 shops, including a large supermarket.

One of the two yacht clubs is usually the first choice of visiting boaters. The advantages of the yacht clubs are the convenience of the facilities and the social atmosphere around the club. However, the Ala Wai Harbor office staff is most accommodating to visiting boaters, and the boating community on the public docks is congenial and helpful.

Ala Wai Harbor is also unique in that visiting boaters can stay as long as 120 days a year on the public docks, *provided the harbormaster has space.* The harbor staff will put the visiting boater in the slip of a boater who is hauled out or on a cruise. Although visiting boaters should be prepared to move from slip to slip every week or two, they can often spend two or three weeks here during the winter while the weather is less pleasant for exploring the neighbor islands, heading back to the Mainland, or continuing on to more distant destinations.

Unless you arrive during the time that the TransPac, Pacific Cup, or Kenwood race boats are also arriving, you can be fairly confident one of the three calls will get you a temporary slip.

Note: At the time this edition of the *Cruising Guide to the Hawaiian Islands* went to press, many of the slips at Ala Wai Harbor were out of service. Though the governor has released almost $2 million for the replacement of some of the condemned docks, those new docks are not scheduled to be in service until spring 2008. If you can't get a temporary slip in the Ala Wai, try the marinas in Ke'ehi Lagoon or Ko Olina Marina, at Barbers Point.

Ala Wai Small Boat Harbormaster	808-973-9727
Hawai'i Yacht Club	808-949-4622
Waikīkī Yacht Club	808-949-7141

FACILITIES

In the harbor:
- Chandlery
- Electricity
- Fuel (gasoline and diesel)
- Haul-out
- Launch Ramp
- Laundromat
- Marine Supplies and Service
- Propane
- Pumpout Station
- Restrooms
- Showers
- Telephone
- Water

Hawai'i & Waikīkī Yacht Clubs
- Bar
- Showers
- Restaurant
- Restrooms

Within walking distance:
- Banks
- Grocery Stores
- Movie Theaters
- Public Transportation
- Restaurants
- Shopping Center
- Shops and Department Stores

All other facilities are available by bus.

WAIKĪKĪ ANCHORAGE
CHARTS #19357, 19364
LAT. N21° 16.200 LONG. W157° 49.900 (ANCHORAGE)

Waikīkī! Is there a cruising sailor anywhere who hasn't heard of this most famous of all Hawaiian beaches? Waikīkī translates as "spouting waters," the name the Hawaiians gave to this stretch of the O'ahu coastline as well as to the marshy lowlands between the beach and the base of the Ko'olau Range. The Mānoa and Pālolo streams flowing into these marshes frequently caused extensive flooding, or "spouting waters," during the rainy season. In these lowlands were taro fields and duck ponds.

Over the centuries various members of the Hawaiian royalty had residences along the 2-mile expanse of Waikīkī Beach, as did a few wealthy residents in the late 19th Century, and the ideal surfing waves and wide sand beach made Waikīkī a favorite recreation area for the locals. However, not until 1901, with the opening of the first hotel on Waikīkī, the Moana, did the beach become a tourist attraction.

After the digging of the Ala Wai Canal between 1919 and 1928 "to reclaim a most unsanitary and unsightly portion of the city," according to a publication of the Waikīkī Reclamation Project, and the subsequent draining of the wetlands, Waikīkī began its ascendancy to a world-class resort. Instead of mosquito-ridden wetlands, duck ponds, and taro fields, scores of hotels and condominiums stand between Waikīkī and the mountains.

Waikīkī Anchorage below Diamond Head

For boaters who love to people watch, Waikīkī Anchorage is the destination of choice in Hawai'i. Surfers ride the waves near the anchorage, swimmers swim out around the boats, and sunbathers spread themselves along the beach.

If you don't want to watch the hordes of people on Waikīkī, you can enjoy the snorkeling around the reef south of the breakwater at the west end of the beach.

The anchorage is good because it offers calm water and modest winds. Even when strong trades blow, Waikīkī has relatively flat water. If *kona* winds blow, of course, this anchorage is uncomfortable at best and unsafe at worst.

Boaters who use this anchorage are limited to a maximum stay of 72 hours, as in all other anchorages in the State of Hawai'i.

APPROACH

Waikīkī Anchorage is easy to locate: from the buoys marking the entrance to Ala Wai Harbor to the mooring buoys at Waikīkī is only about .30 mile and, to the east end of the anchorage area, less than 1.0 mile.

If you're approaching from the east, continue along the shoreline for about 1.0 mile after you round Diamond Head. The hotels and the busy beach make identifying Waikīkī simple.

ANCHORAGE

Even though the Waikīkī Anchorage appears to stretch from the Ala Wai entrance buoy all the way to Diamond Head, only some of this expanse of water offers good anchoring ground. Most of the bottom off Waikīkī is sand with rocks and patches of coral.

The best area is where the five state-owned moorings are, in water depths ranging from 17 to 36 feet. The submerged buoys for these five moorings are approximately 850 yards east of the entrance buoys to the Ala Wai Channel. These buoys are approximately 10 feet below the surface, so you will have to dive down to tie your line to one. These buoys are most commonly used by dive boats, though they are available to all boaters, on a first-come, first-served basis.

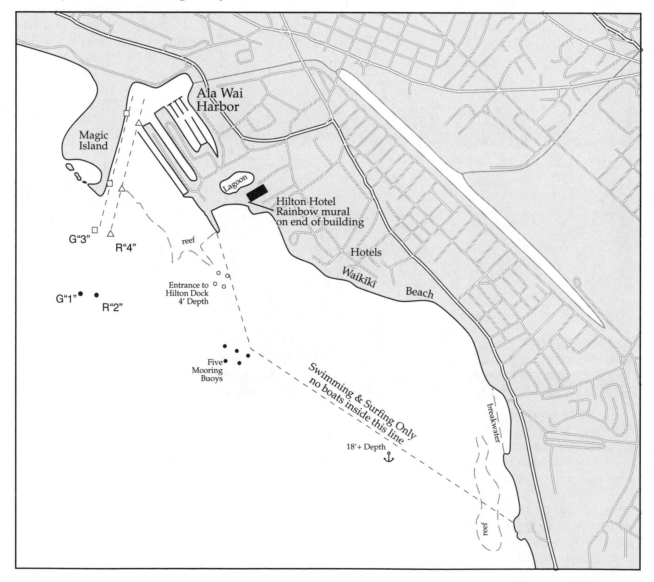

The State of Hawai'i installed these moorings so boaters could enjoy Waikīkī without dropping their anchors and possibly damaging the delicate coral. Because these buoys were correctly installed, they are safe to tie to, unlike many other moorings in Hawai'i that were privately installed. If you don't mind diving down to pick up these moorings, the moorings to the south of the Hilton Hotel are almost surely the more attractive option.

The most appealing area for anchoring, however, is at the most easterly end of Waikīkī Beach, where you'll find a good sand bottom and the best protection from the swells that occasionally wrap around Diamond Head. Be careful to stay clear of the reef paralleling the shoreline here.

The bottom is shallow far out from shore along Waikīkī, so you can expect to be a considerable distance from the beach when you drop anchor. Because the water shallows abruptly from 20 feet to 6 feet or less, do not anchor in less than 20 feet. Closer in, you'll be endangering swimmers and surfers. If you see surfers in the place where you're considering anchoring, you'll know you're in too close to the beach.

Going ashore from Waikīkī Anchorage presents problems. The only place to leave your tender while you go ashore is in the Ala Wai Harbor. If you drop your hook at the east end of Waikīkī, you'll be about a mile from the Ala Wai entrance buoys. While the harbor has no dedicated dinghy docks, you may be able to get permission from one of the yacht clubs to leave your dinghy there if you are a yacht club member. Or you can tie up at the temporary dock in front of the Ala Wai Small Boat Harbor office while you check with the harbormaster about accommodations for your tender.

FACILITIES

(See the list of facilities of the Ala Wai Small Boat Harbor.)

Diamond Head and Waikīkī Beach

KĀNEʻOHE BAY
CHARTS #19357, #19359
LAT. N21° 31.065 LONG. 157° 48.135 (SHIP CHANNEL)
LAT. N21° 28.100 LONG. 157° 46.375 (SAMPAN CHANNEL)

Kāneʻohe Bay, the only good anchorage area on the east side of Oʻahu, is one of the premier boating areas in the Islands. Though this body of water is called a bay, it is, in fact, an estuary. This largest of estuaries in the Islands, covering 11,000 acres and extending over 4.6 miles wide at its mouth, has many attractions for the cruising boater.

The water itself is the first attraction. It is so clean that coral grows remarkably fast in the bay. Divers must periodically remove coral from the marinas, where it becomes a navigational hazard, and transplant it elsewhere in the bay. This clear, clean water makes for jewel-like colors around the bay: sapphire where the water is deep, emerald near some shores where the bottom is mud, and turquoise where it shallows over the sand bars.

The water in this bay is calm, even when heavy trades blow. Outside the bay is the only true barrier reef in Hawaiʻi. Especially in the southern half of the bay, this reef breaks the swells, producing a wonderfully comfortable anchorage, here on the windward side of the island. This protection also provides a smooth, clear pond, outstanding for swimming, snorkeling, and diving.

The ease of navigating these waters appeals to boaters, too. Within Kāneʻohe Bay, buoys, channel markers, and range marks denote the boundaries of the channel. Pipes driven into the water by private boaters rise a few feet above the water surface wherever coral heads are dangerously close to the channels.

Another great attraction is the number and variety of options where cruising boaters can anchor or tie up. Kāneʻohe Bay has four anchorage areas, with room for approximately 25 boats on a hook or a mooring. In addition, it has four marinas—Heʻeia Kea, Kāneʻohe Yacht Club, Makani Kai, and Kāneʻohe Marine Corps Air Station, though only Heʻeia Kea and KYC are options for most visiting boaters.

Mokoliʻi, or Chinaman's Hat

The surpassing beauty of Kāneʻohe Bay is one of its most persuasive appeals. The emerald cliffs of the Koʻolau Range ring the town of Kāneʻohe, their sharp peaks usually shrouded in clouds. The thematic green color repeats itself along the shores of the bay, where vegetation conceals much of the activity of the town.

Islands and reefs add even more variety. One site particularly attractive to visitors is Ahu o Laka ("altar of Laka [the god of forest growth and patron of the *hula*]"). The northwest corner of Ahu o Laka is popularly called "Turtle Haven" because of the number of sea turtles seen here. This "island" is, in fact, a sand bar of 3.1 acres awash at high tide. You can drop anchor at the edge of the bar and then walk or swim above the shallow sand, or, if the tide is out, set up your chairs and have a picnic.

In the southern third of the bay is Moku o Loʻe, more popularly known as Coconut Island. This island could be the prototype for our mythical vision of tropical islands. If you've seen the opening scene of the television series *Gilligan's Island,* you've seen Moku o Loʻe and its covering of swaying coco palm trees. This island is now off-limits for boaters, just as it was *kapu* for the ancient Hawaiians.

The shape of the other island has given it its English name. At the northernmost extension of the bay, this small island called "Chinaman's Hat" sits about 500 yards offshore from Kualoa Point. You can't fail to recognize it. The Hawaiians called it *Mokoli'i*, for, according to their legends, the island is the tail of the evil *mo'o Mokoli'i*, which was crushed by the goddess Hi'iaka, Pele's favorite sister. The body of the lizard is the flat area near the old sugar mill north of the point.

Sailing on Kāne'ohe Bay

This story is but one indication of how culturally rich Kāne'ohe Bay and its surroundings are. The shores of this bay known to the Hawaiians as *Ko'olau* ("windward") were the most heavily populated region on O'ahu in the pre-contact era. At least twelve *heiau*, two from as early as the 12th Century, were located here. Fishpond aquaculture thrived along the coast in the shallow, calm waters of the bay. (The Sampan Channel front range light stands atop the walls of an old fishpond.) In the northwest corner of the bay is Mōli'i Fishpond, the only fishpond on the island in continuous operation since the ancient Hawaiians constructed it.

The peninsula at Kualoa Point, a place of refuge for *kapu* breakers and defeated warriors, was one of the most sacred sites on the island. The chiefs throughout O'ahu brought their children here for training. Anytime a chief was here, he, too, became sacred, so the masts on all passing canoes had to be lowered out of reverence.

When Kamehameha I conquered O'ahu in 1795, he retained for himself this beautiful bay and its environs, so abundant in both its cultural importance and in its food production from the taro fields and fishponds.

Kāne'ohe ("bamboo husband") at that time was the name of but one of several land divi-

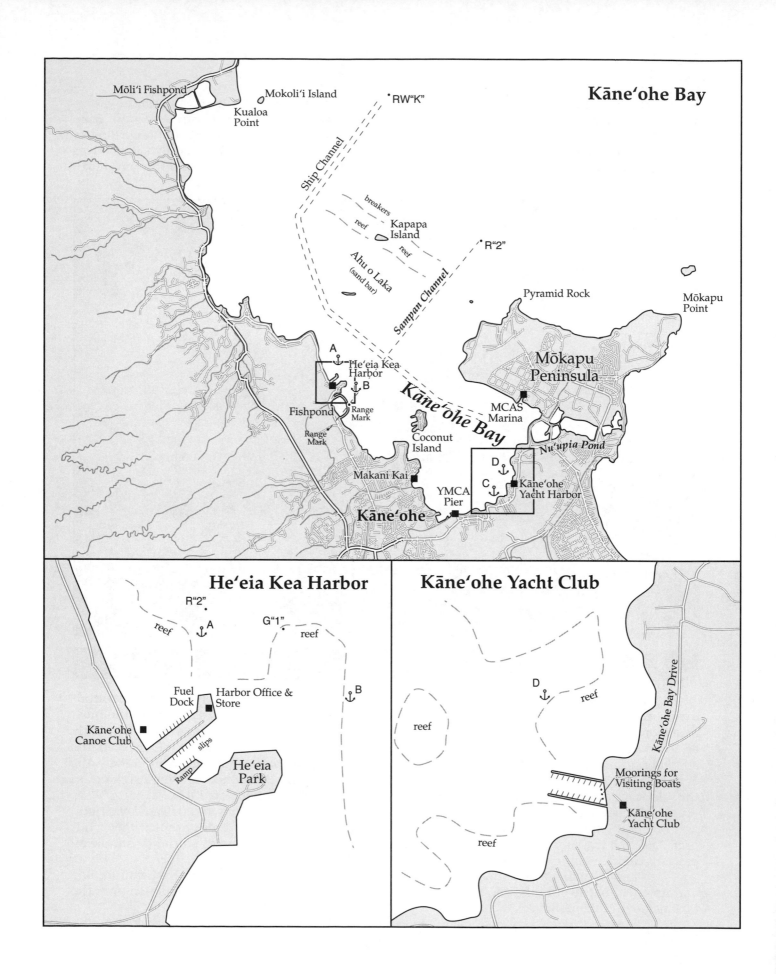

Kāneʻohe Bay

Mōliʻi Fishpond
Mokoliʻi Island
• RW"K"
Kualoa Point
Ship Channel
breakers
reef
Kapapa Island
reef
R"2"
Ahu o Laka
(sand bar)
Sampan Channel
Pyramid Rock
Mōkapu Point
Mōkapu Peninsula
A
Heʻeia Kea Harbor
B
Fishpond
Range Mark
Range Mark
Kāneʻohe Bay
MCAS Marina
Nuʻupia Pond
Coconut Island
D
Makani Kai
C
Kāneʻohe Yacht Harbor
YMCA Pier
Kāneʻohe

Heʻeia Kea Harbor

R"2"
reef
A
G"1"
reef
Fuel Dock
Harbor Office & Store
B
Kāneʻohe Canoe Club
slips
Ramp
Heʻeia Park

Kāneʻohe Yacht Club

Kāneʻohe Bay Drive
D
reef
reef
reef
Moorings for Visiting Boats
Kāneʻohe Yacht Club

sions of Ko'olaupoko. In legend, a woman who lived here gave this name to her husband, whose cruelty she compared to the sharp edge of a bamboo knife. When the Protestants established a mission here in 1835, they named it Kāne'ohe Mission; by the 1840s the bay became better known by that name than by *Ko'olau.*

Closer to the southern portion of the bay is the He'eia Kea State Park, an interpretative park on this site rich in cultural history. The 14-acre park exhibits several varieties of indigenous and exotic plants. Perhaps as compelling a reason as any to visit this park is for the view it affords of Kāne'ohe Bay, including the He'eia Fishpond directly below. At He'eia Kea in ancient times the souls of the dead came to be judged and, as a result, separated into two groups. From the cliff overlooking the bay, they then leapt into eternity, the white souls going to He'eia-kea ("white"), and the black, to He'eia-uli ("black"). (*He'eia* means "to have washed.")

You can easily visit these many sites around the bay by sportboat. To go ashore at He'eia Kea Harbor, you can land your tender near the canoe club on the west shore. Note, however, in Kane'ohe there is no secure landing ashore for tenders.

APPROACH

If you're approaching Kāne'ohe Bay from the south, going counterclockwise around the island, you can enter the bay through the south entrance channel, better known as the Sampan Channel. The Sampan Channel is located .90 mile north of Pyramid Rock Light on Mōkapu Peninsula. The seaward end of this channel is marked by an entrance buoy, R"2."

The Sampan Channel is well marked but has less depth than the ship channel. The Sampan has a minimum depth of 8 feet at the inner end but at least 12 feet toward the outer end, where the swells are most likely to be encountered. In spite of this depth, boaters should be cautious when a heavy swell is running and the tide is out. (Remember to compensate for the tidal difference between Kāne'ohe and Honolulu—minus 2 hours.)

For boaters making a clockwise passage around the island and approaching from the north, Kāne'ohe Bay is relatively easy to spot. The entrance buoy—RW"K" Mo (A)—is 15.6 miles from Kahuku Point, the northernmost point of the island. When making this passage, be sure to stay far enough offshore to avoid the rocks that are as much as .50 mile from land.

On the passage down the coastline, you'll see Mōkapu Peninsula almost as soon as you've cleared the north end of the island and assumed the course that will take you to the entrance to Kāne'ohe Bay. Mōkapu Peninsula will at first look like an island, and you'll be convinced it's closer than the entrance to Kāne'ohe. By the time you reach the north entrance to Kāne'ohe, though, you can see that it is indeed a peninsula extending eastward from the island of O'ahu.

Within 3 or 4 miles of Kāne'ohe Bay, you will see Mokoli'i Island (Chinaman's Hat), a 206-foot-high conical-shaped islet in the northern part of the bay. Mokoli'i is .45 mile north of the north entrance channel. A lighted buoy marks the seaward end of this channel. Buoys, channel marker poles, and range marks indicate the channel itself, but, since these marks are sometimes a considerable distance apart, you may need to use your binoculars to keep your boat in the center of the channel at some times of the day. Although the channel marks may be a little hard to pick out at times, this channel is the ship channel and has a minimum depth of 26 feet.

If for some reason you do have difficulty seeing the channel markers, follow a compass course of 216° mag., and you'll soon see the range marks at the west end of the first reach. The channel turns to port just before those range marks and wanders off down the bay in a southerly direction, but changing directions occasionally.

As you proceed southward through the bay, you will pass anchorage areas and the He'eia Kea Small Boat Harbor.

ANCHORAGE AND BERTHING

If you're a member of a yacht club, you can find superb hospitality and facilities at the Kāneʻohe Yacht Club. Boaters arriving at this yacht club for the first time must look carefully for the reefs immediately before the entrance to the club, located in the southeastern corner of the bay. Pipe markers and buoys warn of the shallow water. Use the range marks as you pass through the reef into the yacht club.

The club manager assigns visitors to any of the 140 slips that are temporarily vacant. You can also tie your boat Tahiti-style between the seawall in front of the yacht club and the five mooring buoys when no slips are available. For a refundable deposit of $25, you can get a gate key that will allow you to take a car in or out of the premises. Club rules limit visiting boaters to 14 days per year at the club.

From the club to the nearest market is 1.7 miles, so walking to provision is possible if you have a cart and a desire for some serious exercise. TheBus stops in front of the club, allowing you to get easily to nearby towns such as Kāneʻohe, Kailua, or even Honolulu.

The second marina where you can stop is Heʻeia Kea Small Boat Harbor. Located almost due west from the Kāneʻohe Bay end of the Sampan Channel, this public harbor offers boaters an opportunity to get fuel and water. All the slips in this busy marina are leased out, of course, but, if any tenants are temporarily out of the harbor, the harbormaster will assign visiting boats to a slip. While Heʻeia Kea Harbor has few accommodations for large boats, it does have a few slips for boats up

He'eia Kea Harbor

to 55 feet, with a maximum of 7-foot drafts. The main dock at the outer end of the marina is for loading and unloading or for disabled vessels. Water depths throughout the marina are 6-7 feet, so deep draft vessels should go no farther than the fuel dock, where depths are about 12 feet.

The third marina in Kāneʻohe Bay is Makani Kai, a private marina for the owners of the Makani Kai condominiums. Because not all the owners have boats to put in the slips, visiting boaters can occasionally lease a space for their boats. However, the Makani Kai Marina has a strict no-live-aboard policy. If you want to leave your boat while you go elsewhere—for example, back to the Mainland—call the manager of the Makani Kai facility to determine the availability of a slip.

The last of the four marinas in Kāneʻohe Bay is the one attached to the Kāneʻohe Marine Corps Air Station in the eastern corner of the bay. If you're active duty or retired military, you can possibly find a guest slip at this marina. Although the marina has only about 30 slips and a few moorings, it is in a well-protected area and is certainly worth checking into.

If no slips are available at the four facilities mentioned above, you can anchor out in Kāneʻohe Bay. Few anchorages anywhere have calmer water; boats anchored in the southern part of Kāneʻohe Bay particularly have an almost imperceptible movement.

One problem with anchoring here, though, is that much of the bottom is covered with about 4 feet of soft mud. Most anchors do not set well in such a bottom. After you've dropped anchor anywhere in Kāne'ohe Bay, use reverse gear for at least a full minute to check the set. If your anchor drags, hoist and try again—and again and again, if you must. Don't leave your boat unattended until you're confident the hook is securely set.

One important precaution to take when anchoring in the mud bottom of Kāne'ohe Bay is to put out plenty of scope. Boats with insufficient scope drag anchor here regularly. In the average depths in the bay, 35-40 feet, you'll need to let out at least 150 feet of an all-chain rode or 250 feet of a nylon and chain rode.

Because of frequent tide and wind shifts in the bay, boats face one way and then the other, often fouling their anchors and then dragging them. All-chain rodes and Bruce anchors can minimize this problem, but the best solution is to set two anchors. The harbormaster suggests one anchor to the north and one to the south of the boat.

Though you may legally anchor for 72 hours anywhere in the bay that is not a traffic zone, the state has designated four specific areas that are deemed the safest in the bay. (The other areas, some of which were popular in the past, have exceedingly poor holding, where unwary boaters can get into trouble.) Of the four approved anchoring areas, the two most commonly used by visiting boaters are areas A and B, both adjacent to the He'eia Kea Small Boat Harbor. Areas C and D are small and fairly well taken up by boats on permanent moorings.

After being anchored for 72 hours anywhere in the bay, you must obtain a temporary permit. The harbormaster at He'eia Kea Small Boat Harbor issues permits for a period of 30 days at a time, up to a maximum total of 90 days. When you apply for a temporary permit, the harbormaster will come aboard the boat and check it out, specifically checking anchor tackle to be sure it will withstand the conditions at Kāne'ohe. While regulations prohibit permanent liveaboards in Kāne'ohe Bay, visiting boaters may stay aboard their boats.

Local boaters warn visitors who anchor by the sandbar in the middle of the bay to set a stern anchor if they plan to spend the night. Those who don't will likely end up aground when the winds shift during the night.

If you're considering anchoring in a particular spot, check with the harbormaster right away to ascertain the safety of your choice. The current harbormaster stresses that he wants to share his knowledge of the bay with visitors. He recommends that, no matter where you anchor, you keep mast lights on at night for safety; both day and night, numerous fishing boats transit the bay, many at high speeds.

If you plan to keep your boat in Kāne'ohe for any prolonged period, you should probably see the harbormaster and arrange to set a mooring in one of the designated mooring areas.

Unfortunately for cruising boaters who want to go ashore, the shoreline near the anchorages has few suitable places for landing a tender. Generally, the land around the southern part of the bay is either private property or part of the military reservation. The Kāne'ohe Yacht Club does not allow anchored boaters to use the club facilities or to leave their tenders at club docks.

The harbormaster suggests that the best place to leave your tender, no matter where your boat is anchored, is on the beach by the canoe club at He'eia Kea. When you go in, be cautious of the shallow water at low tide; if you have an outboard on your tender, consider tipping up your motor and rowing in. However, there is no protection for tenders left at the canoe club; no one monitors boats left on this beach. Check in at the harbor office before you leave your tender here. You can catch TheBus on the highway right alongside the canoe club if you want to go farther than you care to walk.

Kāne'ohe Yacht Club	808-247-4121
He'eia Kea Small Boat Harbor	808-233-4606 (or CB 23)
Makani Kai Marina	808-235-4416
Kāne'ohe Marine Corps Air Station	808-254-7667

FACILITIES

At Kāne'ohe Yacht Club:
- Launch Ramp
- Public Transportation
- Restaurant (limited hours)
- Restrooms
- Showers
- Snack Bar (limited hours)
- Swimming Pool
- Telephone
- Water

At He'eia Kea:
- Fuel (diesel and gasoline)
- Launch Ramp
- Mini-market
- Public Transportation
- Pump-out
- Restrooms
- Showers
- Telephone
- Water

In Kāne'ohe or Kailua, accessible by bus, all other services are available.

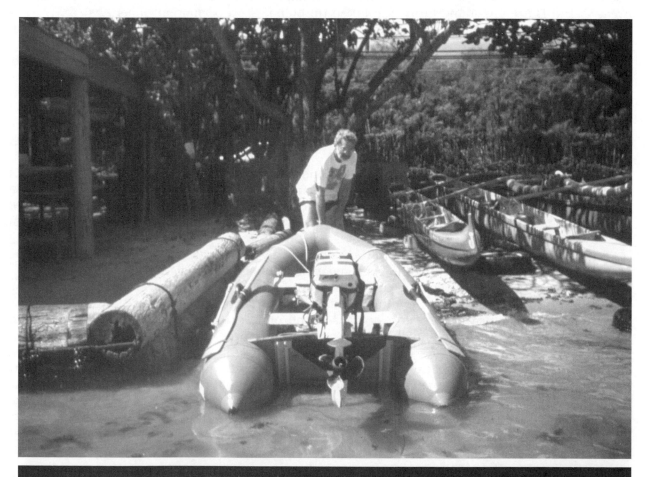

Beaching the tender at He'eia Kea

Offerings on a shrine at Pu'u o Mahuka

Waimea Bay is one of the most frequently photographed bays on O'ahu. The lush green cliffs of the Ko'olau Range snugly ring the smooth, white sand beach. At the north end of the bay the Waimea River disappears into the thickly forested Waimea Valley. Perhaps after a heavy storm, the river runs red, as its name, meaning "reddish water," suggests. Near the beach on the south side of the bay, an enormous black boulder, or islet, sits at the water's edge, where locals dive from what they call "the Rock." Underneath the Rock is a large underwater tunnel.

In the spring, summer, and fall, when the surf breaks gently on the reef and then washes up on the beach in creamy scallops, swimming, snorkeling, and diving at Waimea Bay are generally ideal, At the north end of the beach, the Waimea River provides beach goers a freshwater lagoon at low tides.

Few people swim or dive here in the winter, when the surf and rip tides are dangerous for even the most skilled of swimmers. This northwest coast then becomes the surfers' heaven. Waimea Bay has the largest rideable surfing waves in the world, reaching heights of 20-30 feet during the winter months.

Waimea Bay is another of those sites on O'ahu rich in history and legend. Atop the cliff above the river are the well-preserved remains of the Pu'u o Mahuka Heiau, one of the largest on the island. This *heiau*, in Hawaiian legend built by the Menehune, was a place where chiefesses came to give birth. Today, people still leave their offerings, usually wrapped in sacred *tī* leaves, on the rock walls of the temple.

Historians believe this site of human sacrifice for the early Hawaiians is where three of the crew of the British ship *Dedalus* were offered in sacrifice in 1794. George Vancouver, the ship's captain, had sent the men ashore to fill water barrels up the Waimea River. In an altercation over the sailors' firearms, some of the local residents killed the three men; the sailors were subsequently sacrificed, probably at Pu'u o Mahuka.

In pre-contact Hawai'i, each island was separated into *ahupua'a*, approximately wedge-shaped divisions of land extending from the mountains to the ocean. The people of Ahupua'a o Waimea had a fertile valley for growing taro and medicinal herbs and a bay replete with fish. As much as a thousand years ago, according to legend, this *ahupua'a* became the province of the *kāhuna* ("priests") and thus a sacred place.

The first foreigners to land on O'ahu did so on the beach at Waimea. After Captain Cook's death at Kealakekua, on the Big Island, in 1779, his ships, the *Resolution* and the *Discovery*, anchored here while the crew went up the Waimea River for water before going on to Kaua'i.

After Kamehameha I and his warriors from the Big Island conquered O'ahu, Ahupua'a o Waimea was bestowed on his high priest. In 1894, a flood destroyed the fields and homes and washed a large quantity of silt down the river so that it no longer flows unimpeded into the ocean.

The most popular tourist attraction nearby is without question Waimea Valley Park, a privately operated botanical garden and cultural center. The park has one of the largest botanical collections in the Pacific, with 36 separate collections. Historical sites in the park include Ahu Pohaku, a stone platform marking an undetermined but undoubtedly important spot; Hale Iwi, a burial spot and probable site of a temple; Hale o Lono Heiau, dedicated to the god of agriculture, weather, medicine, and peace; and the reputed site of the fight between the sailors off *Dedalus* and the native Hawaiians.

Demonstrations of ancient Hawaiian arts and crafts go on throughout the park. Visitors can learn about medicinal herbs and the sacred art of healing, ancient and contemporary *hula,* and early fishing techniques. They can play the games of the early warriors, and watch the divers who perform acrobatic dives from atop the 55-60-foot rock walls of Waihe'e (Waimea) Falls.

Of a much later vintage is Saints Peter & Paul Mission, its steeple prominent on the cliffs north of the bay. This building was originally a rock-crushing plant used during the construction of the highway.

To see any of these points of interest around Waimea Bay, you'll have to be a fairly good hiker. Everything is uphill, a mile or more from the beach. You may decide to be content savoring the *mana* of the Waimea Valley and Bay from the decks of your anchored boat or from the sand and water of the beach and river.

Church tower above Waimea

During the summer and early fall when the trades blow consistently, you can be almost sure to find a safe anchorage here. You will also have a splendid feeling of isolation. Some noise from the highway and the beach goers will reach your boat, but the noise is not so loud as to be objectionable, and it all disappears when the sun goes down.

A mere handful of boaters visit Waimea Bay during the summer, perhaps because it is open to any north swell that develops. Even when the strong trades are blowing in the summer months, some swell wraps into the bay. Boaters without some device to control the roll might find this a less desirable anchorage than we have found it.

For boaters wishing to explore the north side of O'ahu, the anchorage at Waimea is one of only two viable destinations, the other being Hale'iwa.

If you anchor at Waimea Bay during the winter or early spring months, be cautious of north winds and swell. Be ready to leave the anchorage at the first sign of a weather change.

APPROACH

If you're proceeding counterclockwise around the island, Waimea Bay is 6.3 miles southwest of Kahuku Point. In making a passage around the north end of O'ahu, be particularly careful of off-lying reefs and rocks along this stretch of coastline.

A red-roofed church tower is on the cliff at the north end Waimea Bay, the only landmark

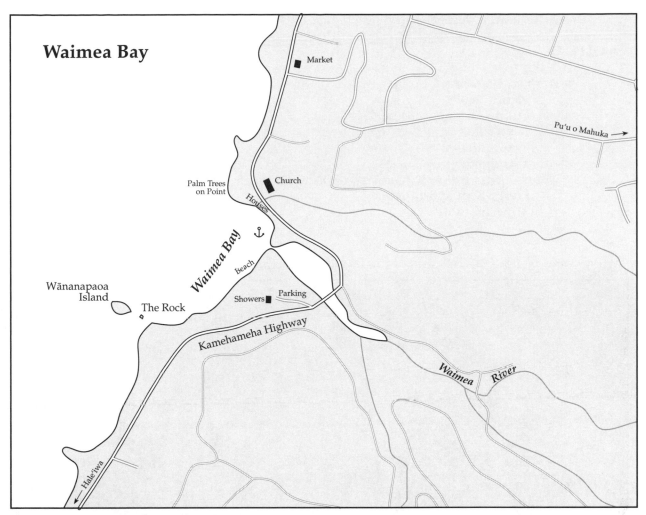

Waimea Bay

you'll have other than the configuration of the bay itself. You may not be able to see this tower until you've made your turn into the bay.

Clockwise around the island, Waimea Bay is 3.6 miles northeast of the entrance buoy at Hale'iwa. From the Hale'iwa buoy, you can easily see the church tower on the cliffs above Waimea. Stay far enough offshore to avoid the rock and surf along this shoreline; otherwise, you need only to aim for the white church tower with the red tile roof.

If you're still uncertain of the location of Waimea Bay, use the power line towers on the mountain tops to the east and west of the bay. The towers consist of three poles with timbers between the tops.

ANCHORAGE

DLNR regulations prohibit the use of engines on boats entering or leaving Waimea Bay. These regulations also prohibit anchoring closer than 200 feet from shore or anchoring where your anchor or chain may damage the coral.

Enter Waimea Bay as near the middle as possible. Since the opening of the bay is .35 mile wide, identifying the exact center is not imperative. What is imperative is to avoid the rocks at the western and eastern sides of the bay.

A reef extends a short distance from the eastern point, but it is covered by perhaps 15 feet of water. Still, water does break in the area, so most boaters will give the reef a wide berth.

The best anchorage in the bay lies about 200 yards from the north shore of the bay, roughly south of the church tower, and 100 yards from the beach to the east. Anchor in 15-20 feet of water. Most of the bay has excellent holding in sand, but if you get too close to the north side of the anchorage, you will be anchoring in coral.

You can land a tender on the beach east of the anchorage.

FACILITIES

At Waimea Bay Beach County Park:
    Picnic Tables
    Public Transportation
    Restrooms
    Shower (cold)
    Telephone
In Waimea (also called Maunawai), approx. 1.0 mile:
    Public Transportation
    Supermarket

The Queen at Waimea

Kāneʻohe Yacht Club

The *Tole Mour*, a training ship for young people

HALE'IWA SMALL BOAT HARBOR
CHART #19357
LAT. N21° 36.360 LONG. W158° 06.980 (ENTRANCE BUOY)

The only harbor on the North Shore of O'ahu, Hale'iwa is a refuge for boaters in all but extreme weather. This harbor is especially good when heavy trades pipe up because the coastline here has a northeast to southwest orientation and Waialua Bay, where Hale'iwa Harbor is located, has a .50-mile indent into the coastline. From this anchorage, you can sit comfortably on your boat in heavy trades and watch gigantic white caps marching down the coastline just outside the harbor by the entrance buoy.

Hale'iwa Harbor has no dedicated guest dock, but visiting boaters can sometimes get a berth for a night or two. If no slips are available, visitors can almost without fail find a place to anchor.

The town of Hale'iwa attracts locals and tourists from around the island. One draw in the winter is the surfing beaches spread along this northwest coast. Another, though, is the somewhat funky town itself. It's a good town for walking around and exploring. Plantation-era buildings with falsefronts line the main street, which is also the Kamehameha Highway. Many of these buildings house arts and crafts shops and restaurants. In plazas off the main street are more modern buildings with additional arts and crafts shops and restaurants.

At the northern edge of town is the wonderful old art deco bridge over the Anahulu Stream. From the walking path on this narrow bridge, you can look up this waterway shaded by the arching branches of monkeypod trees in the backyards of the houses on either side of the river. You can also take your tender up Anahulu Stream (carefully negotiating around the bar that covers all but a few feet of the mouth of the river), where, in only a few minutes, you'll have escaped the busy town.

Up the Anahulu Stream

Beaches and beach parks provide another ideal walking ground, and little Hale'iwa has three of them, one along the north side of Waialua Bay and two others south of the harbor. Especially during the week, they are largely unoccupied.

A more distant walk will take you to the old sugar town of Waialua, the site of the last of the sugar mills on O'ahu.   The stacks of Waialua Sugar, which closed in 1996, dominate the skyline. Whereas Waialua was a prosperous plantation town and the commercial center of Waialua Bay, Hale'iwa became a seaside resort. In 1899, the Hale'iwa Hotel opened here at the terminus of the railroad line from Honolulu, and the town remained a popular resort until after World War II.

The name *Hale'iwa* ("house of the frigate bird") is a fairly recent one for this settlement. A Protestant missionary established the Waialua Female Seminary on the banks of Anahulu Stream in 1865. He called the dormitory for the seminary *Hale'iwa,* perhaps for the frigate bird, much revered in ancient legends for its role as a messenger of the gods and for its beauty when it spreads its wings as much as 7 feet to glide over the ocean. Soon, the district of Waialua became better known as *Hale'iwa.* Hale'iwa, though small by Mainland standards, is the principal town on the North Shore. It has the majority of the shops, restaurants, and services available in this region.

If you're anchored out and want to go ashore, you can tie your tender on the inner Temporary Dock south of the harbor office.

Hale'iwa Harbor

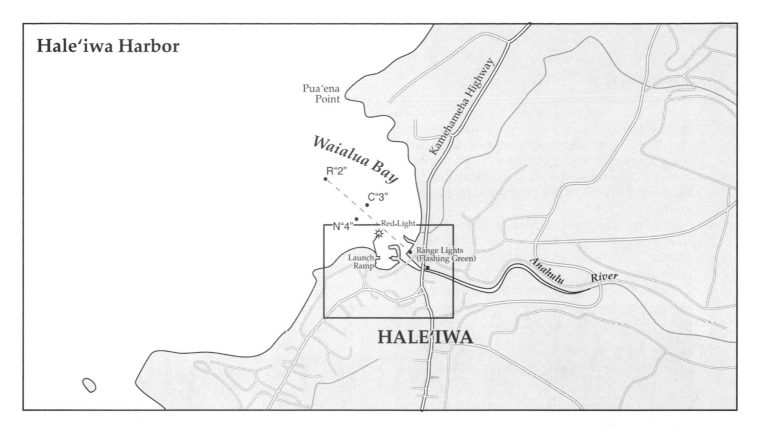

Pua'ena Point

Waialua Bay

R"2"

C"3"

N"4"

Red Light

Launch Ramp

Range Lights (Flashing Green)

Anahulu River

Kamehameha Highway

HALE'IWA

Detail of Hale'iwa Harbor

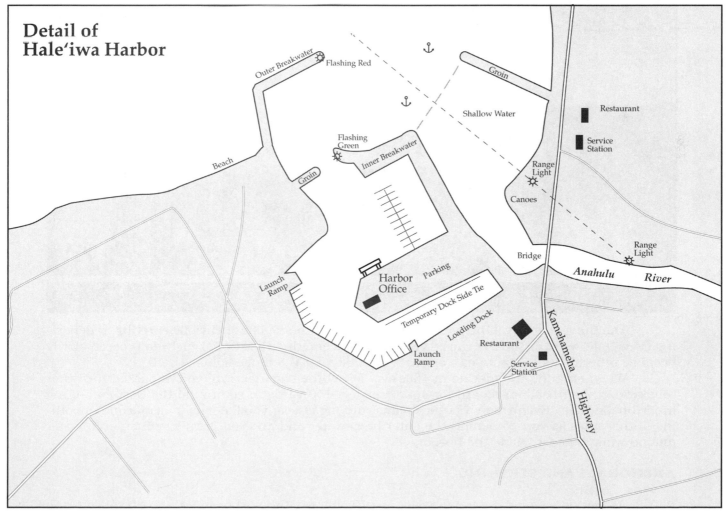

Outer Breakwater

Flashing Red

Groin

Beach

Flashing Green

Inner Breakwater

Shallow Water

Restaurant

Service Station

Range Light

Canoes

Launch Ramp

Harbor Office

Parking

Temporary Dock Side Tie

Bridge

Range Light

Anahulu River

Loading Dock

Restaurant

Launch Ramp

Service Station

Kamehameha Highway

APPROACH

Hale'iwa Small Boat Harbor is easy to find. Going counterclockwise around the island, you will travel southwest past Kahuku Point, at the northern tip of O'ahu, for 10.0 miles to Hale'iwa. Proceeding clockwise around the island, you'll travel 9.2 miles east along the coastline from Ka'ena Point Light to the entrance buoy at Hale'iwa.

This buoy marking the entrance is red and has an identifying numeral of 2, but the numeral is hard to read because of the large number of booby birds that have visited it over the years.

Be cautious because charts do not accurately represent the buoys and lights. A pair of buoys—G"3" and R"4"— are half-way between the entrance buoy and the breakwater, as shown on charts. The green buoy that is reported to be off the end of the outer breakwater, however, is not there. Rather, a red light is now mounted on the end of the outer breakwater, and a green light is on the end of the inner breakwater.

Winter swell over the Hale'iwa breakwater

The range marks will help you stay in the middle of the channel while entering or departing from Hale'iwa. One boater warns visiting sailors entering Hale'iwa at night to proceed slowly because other lights on shore can be easily mistaken for the range lights.

When entering the marina at Hale'iwa, follow the channel until you've passed the outer breakwater; then head starboard for approximately 150 yards to go around the west end of the inner breakwater. Even when a large swell is running at sea, you'll detect a significant smoothing of the water as you go behind the outer breakwater and an even greater reduction in water motion when you get inside the harbor.

ANCHORAGE AND BERTHING

As you go around the inner breakwater, you'll see the harbor office straight ahead. All slips in the marina are leased out, but occasionally the harbormaster will be able to accommodate cruising boats on the temporary dock. Before departing on a trip to Hale'iwa, you can make arrangements for a guest slip by calling.

Hale'iwa Small Boat Harbor has a minor silting problem, as do all the harbors in Hawai'i. If your boat draws more than 6 feet, be cautious at low water. Also, the harbor has no facilities for boats over 50 feet long.

If no space is available on the temporary dock and the harbormaster is not in his office, you can anchor outside the inner breakwater for up to 72 hours. The anchorage outside the harbor has good holding in mud and sand, in about 15 feet of water. Much of the time the motion will be calm. The water depths between the end of the groin and the corner of the inner breakwater, on the other hand, are only 4-6 feet. Likewise, the shallowness of the bar at the mouth of the river eliminates the option of anchoring up the river for most cruising boats.

If you anchor out and want to go ashore, you can tie your tender on the Temporary Dock on the south side of the Harbor Office, being careful not to block the commercial boats that have slips on this dock.

Since this anchorage is open to the north and west, we cannot recommend it in the winter. If you cannot get temporary berthing inside, do not plan to stay at Hale'iwa during winter months or any time a north swell is running. (Sometimes in the winter, when waves can break as high as 25 feet at the entrance, boats cannot get into or out of this harbor at all.)

Hale'iwa Harbormaster   808-637-8246

FACILITIES

Bank
Fuel (diesel and gasoline, by jerry jug)
Grocery Stores
Launch Ramp
Medical Clinic
Pharmacy
Post Office

Propane
Public Transportation
Restaurants
Shops
Shower (cold)
Telephone
Water

Hawaiian woman and her grass house

MĀKUA ANCHORAGE
CHART #19357
LAT. N21° 32.000 LONG. W158° 14.090 (ANCHORAGE SPOT)

The anchorage at Mākua has all the attributes to make it the ideal destination for boaters wishing to enjoy a quiet, isolated spot. Exactly 3.8 miles southeast of Ka'ena Point Light, the anchorage is tucked in where the coastline bends from its southeast bearing and goes south toward Kepuhi Point. Few boaters come to this remote anchorage. Ashore are no homes and no businesses; in fact, the Farrington Highway ends within sight of boaters anchored at Mākua—about 1.5 miles northwest.

Once densely populated, the Mākua Valley, with abundant fresh water from springs and streams, was rich with fruit trees and feral pigs. The Hawaiians from all around the west coast treasured its fine-leafed *maile*, a twining shrub with shiny, aromatic leaves used in *lei* and other decorations. Because the *maile* became as popular with the feral goats as it was with the Hawaiians, it is now almost non-existent here. First Captain Cook and then Captain Vancouver brought goats to the Islands. Because the goats were *kapu* for many years and thus couldn't be killed, they multiplied wildly, becoming pests on seven of the eight islands.

'Ōhikilolo Mountain and Mākua Valley

Mākua, which translates as "parents," was the name of a legendary priest, Makuakaumana, who was on the first canoe to come to Hawai'i from the homeland, Kahiki (probably Tahiti). The last person to board the canoe, he had to sit in the only available space, the *moamoa*, the sharp point at the stern of the canoe. One of the early ancestors of the Kamehameha line was also named *Makua* (the singular of Mākua).

Whether this valley and bay were named after either of these figures is uncertain; perhaps it was called "parents" for some other reason. What is known about Mākua is that it was the gathering place for the *lua* fighters, the bodyguards for the chiefs. These elite fighters perfected secret techniques for hand-to-hand fighting. Specifically, they tried to overcome their opponents by breaking bones, dislocating bones at the joints, and pressing on painful and disabling nerve centers.

During World War II, the military took over Mākua Valley for a bombing range. Across the highway from the anchorage are a military observation tower with two small buildings nearby. Nothing remains of the village of Mākua except the graveyard. The valley is still restricted to the military.

Except for the tower and the two buildings, the view from the anchorage is of a magnificent white sand beach and a wide green valley gently sloping up into the more narrow valleys between the ridges of the Wai'anae Range, where misty clouds drift down the slopes to keep the valley green. So photogenic is Mākua Bay and Valley that it was the location for filming the scenes set in Old Lahaina for the motion picture *Hawaii*, based on James Michener's novel of the same name.

To anchor here is to be close to the Old Hawai'i of our imaginations. Serenity prevails in Mākua today. Any activity you perceive will be in the winds and clouds coming down the canyon, the surf breaking ashore in rolls of aquamarine and white, and the spinner dolphins feeding in the waters around your boat.

When you do want a bit more activity, you can take a tender ashore and walk or swim off the beach. Just south of the anchorage, .25 mile, is a cave to explore, the Kāneana, in Puʻu o Hulu hill. This large cave, 100 feet high in places and 450 deep, was carved out by the action of the sea about 150,000 years ago. The demigod Māui and his grandmother lived in this cave, perhaps the reason the cave was subsequently *kapu* (taboo). Or perhaps it was *kapu* because it was the mythical home of a shark-man, Kamahoaliʻi, who would adopt his human form to capture people and drag them into his cave for a tasty meal. A second cave is 2.0 miles northwest of the anchorage.

The nearest town, Mākaha, is about 4 miles south on the Farrington Highway. Since 1952, it has been the home of the Mākaha International Surfing Competition.

Mākua Anchorage, with dolphins, and the military tower

APPROACH

From the light at Kaʻena Point, Mākua Anchorage lies southeast 3.8 miles. Follow the southeast line of the coastline after Kaʻena Point, staying about 1.0 mile offshore. When the coastline turns directly south, you'll see the military tower surrounded by a few trees.

From the south Mākua Anchorage is 5.8 miles north of Waiʻanae Small Boat Harbor. The coastline to the northwest of the anchorage is easily distinguished because a large canyon goes off to the east, while a mountain rises immediately north of the anchorage.

ANCHORAGE

The best anchorage at Mākua is just off the sand beach to the west of the tower. Anchor in 30-40 feet of water. The sand bottom provides excellent holding.

A south or west swell would make Mākua an uncomfortable anchorage. You would do well to think of this anchorage when trades are blowing or when only a light north swell is running in the winter.

We anchored here when the trades were blowing strongly and enjoyed a comfortable motion. The wind came down the canyon strongly at times, but the boat motion remained slight.

At the south end of the beach by the volcanic outcropping is the best place to land your tender.

FACILITIES

None

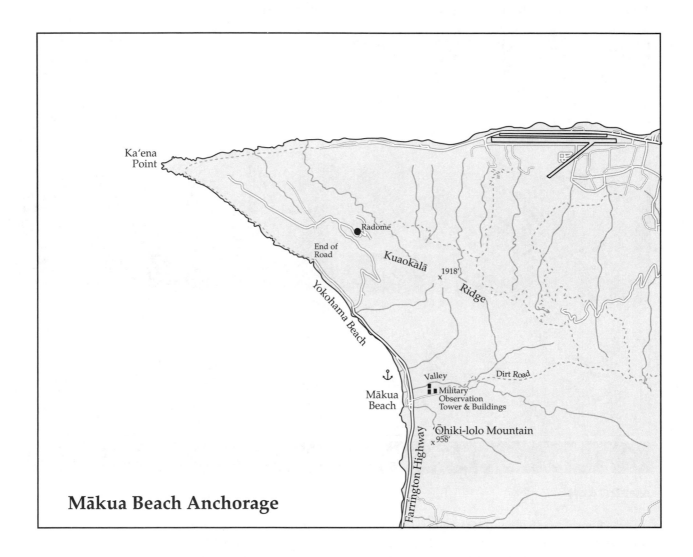

Mākua Beach Anchorage

WAI'ANAE SMALL BOAT HARBOR
CHART #19357 OR 19361
LAT. N21° 26.900 LONG. W158° 11.800 (ENTRANCE)

Wai'anae Harbor, at the north end of Pōka'ī Bay, is a busy place. With 146 slips in the marina, it is larger than many harbors in the Islands; however, the boats in the slips are not the primary source of all the activity in the harbor. Rather, it is the launch ramp, the busiest we have seen. Local boaters begin launching and retrieving boats long before dawn, and the action scarcely ceases until well after dark.

Busy launch ramp at Wai'anae Harbor

If you tire of the wet weather in other harbors, you'll find Wai'anae a good destination. From the harbor on this dry side of the island, you can look up the canyon to the east and see rain falling on the Wai'anae Range, but the clouds rarely reach far enough down the slopes of the high mountains to wet the boats. Those same high mountains to the east also protect the harbor from the heavy trades when they blow. In fact, the entire coast along the west side of the island frequently suffers from a lack of wind. Still, the typically light breezes here keep boaters in the area comfortable.

As a cruising destination, Wai'anae Harbor has many qualities to recommend it, but the one feature that will fail to please is the surge in the harbor. In a state where the surge creates hazards in many harbors, the surge in this harbor is still noteworthy. It is especially hazardous when the south or northwest swell is up. When you visit this harbor, take along extra heavy dock lines, and secure your boat by using spring lines.

While the prevalence and ferocity of the surge may keep some pleasure boaters away from Wai'anae Harbor, it has never hampered the fishing enthuiasts along the Wai'anae Coast. This region was one of the most important centers of population on O'ahu for many centuries past. The broad, sheltered plain extending to the foot of the Wai'anae Range, along with the rich fishing grounds, must have made this an ideal place for the earliest settlers to this island.

Wai'anae figures in a number of Hawaiian legends, beginning with stories of that most popular of demigods, the trickster Māui. He and his mother, the great goddess Hina, lived in a cave on the south side of Wai'anae, where she kept busy making *tapa*.

Other myths concern *kupua*, cultural heroes, usually with supernatural powers, who lived at or came to Wai'anae on a mission of some sort. One such *kupua* was Kawelo, who exhibited his extraordinary powers early on in his mastery of kite flying and toy boat sailing. Later, he defeated all opponents at boxing and out-fished all the men. He built a temple at Wai'anae to honor his god, Kāne'ikapualena. The greatest of fishermen, though, was the *kupua* Niho'olaki, born on the Big Island but later a ruling chief at Wai'anae. His famous pearl fishhook named *Pahuhu* and his double canoe ten fathoms long, manned by twenty paddlers, enabled him to catch enough fish to feed the people of the entire island.

Besides being the site of extraordinary feats of fishing, Wai'anae is a place where girls and women came to become expert in the *hula*. Hi'ilaniwai taught the *hula* at Wai'anae by instructing the students to watch the swaying of leaves and blossoms in the wind and the movements of the clouds and the shadows they cast.

Contemporary Wai'anae retains much of its traditional Hawaiian flavor, perhaps more so than any other region on O'ahu. It has not become a tourist mecca; rather, it is a place of small family farms, modest houses, and authentic family *lū'au*.

Ashore at the harbor is a small park, where you can watch the young locals play soccer. You'll not want to miss a walk around the town, its proximity to the beach no better illustrated than by the sign on the door of the Tamura Super Market: "If you are dripping wet, you are not allowed to enter the store."

One boater's response to the surge at Wai'anae

The water is, of course, the grand attraction here, and the Pōka'ī Bay beach is as pretty as any on this coast, if not as large as some. Snorkeling and diving are especially good outside the breakwater or in the small cove south of Kāne'īlio Point, called Lualualei Beach.

For a more demanding hike or bike ride, follow Mākaha Road, to the north of the harbor; then climb the hill for about 3.0 miles to visit one of the best of the reconstructed *heiau*, Kāne'ākī. Constructed between 1450 and 1650, the *heiau* was first dedicated to agriculture and then later to the war gods. In addition to the lava rock walls and platform are thatched huts, fish shrines, and *ki'i* ("totems").

The *heiau* is on private property in a gated community. You must show picture identification to the guard at the gate for admittance.

APPROACH

If you're approaching Wai'anae Harbor from the north, the best landmark is Lahilahi Point, 1.5 miles northwest of the harbor entrance. When you pass Lahilahi, follow the coastline southeastward until you see the breakwater with the sailboat masts inside and the two-storey beige harbor office.

Wai'anae Harbor is 10.4 miles northward from Barbers Point Light and .40 mile from Kāne'īlio Point. Locating the harbor from this direction can be difficult because the topography along this part of the coastline does not vary much. Use your knotmeter to determine when you have traveled 10 miles from Barbers Point. You'll then be abreast of Kāne'īlio Point. Directly behind Kāne'īlio Point .25 mile is an 8-storey apartment building. Just north of the apartment building is a 646-foot-high hill, Pu'u Pāhe'ehe'e, easily distinguished by the large water tank on its south slope. The triangular-shaped face of the slope above the tank is the result of engineers' having cut into the hill to reduce erosion. From Kāne'īlio Point, Wai'anae Harbor is easily visible in good weather.

ANCHORAGE AND BERTHING

Guest slips are often available at Wai'anae Harbor, but the harbor has only a few slips that can accommodate large boats. If the harbormaster can't provide you with a guest slip, you can go across the bay to Pōka'ī and anchor. Many boaters who have tried both anchoring at Pōka'ī and using a guest slip at Wai'anae have found they get a better night's rest at Pōka'ī, where the motion is far more gentle. Sometimes in the winter months, in fact, boats can neither enter nor exit Wai'anae Harbor because of the size of the waves breaking at the entrance.

Wai'anae Harbormaster   808-697-7095, VHF 16, and CB

FACILITIES

At the harbor:
- Launch Ramp
- Restrooms

In Wai'anae:
- Bank
- Fuel (diesel and gasoline, by jerry jug)
- Grocery Stores
- Laundromat
- Library
- Medical Clinic

- Telephone
- Water

- Pharmacy
- Post Office
- Propane
- Public Transportation
- Restaurants
- Shops

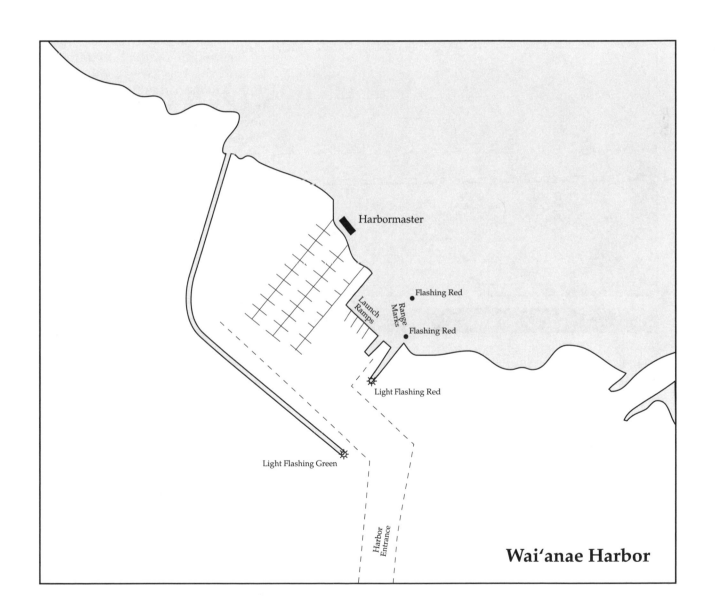

Wai'anae Harbor

PŌKAʻĪ BAY ANCHORAGE
CHART #19357, #19361
LAT. N21° 26.554 LONG. W158° 11.460 (ANCHORAGE)

Located on the West Shore of Oʻahu at Waiʻanae, Pōkaʻī Bay may be the best destination for boaters from Honolulu. In all except strong northwest winds, Pōkaʻī has excellent protection and calm water, especially behind the breakwater. Hurricane ʻIwa in 1982 and Hurricane ʻIniki in 1992 almost destroyed this breakwater built in the 1950s and extended in the 1960s; however, even though it has fallen down in a number of places, the breakwater still functions well.

Anchoring behind the breakwater presents two problems. First, the *Coast Pilot* states flatly that only swimmers and outrigger canoes may use that portion of the bay behind the breakwater. On the other hand, the harbormaster says that boaters may anchor behind the breakwater whenever no organized outrigger canoe activity is scheduled. To check on such activity, call the harbormaster at Waiʻanae Small Boat Harbor or read the "Notices to Mariners."

The second problem has to do with the size of the anchorage area. This bay is small to begin with, and, with half of it marked off for swimmers, the remaining area behind the breakwater will comfortably accommodate only about two boats. However, when boaters from one of the local yacht clubs have had cruise-ins to Pōkaʻī, they have gotten as many as ten boats behind the breakwater by rafting up.

The anchorage at Pōkaʻī Bay

Neither problem should dissuade you from taking your boat to Pōkaʻī Bay. If you arrive when a canoe activity is scheduled or when the inner bay is crowded, you can anchor outside the protection of the breakwater, in water almost as calm as that inside.

Pōkaʻī Bay is much more than just an anchorage. In the shelter of the old breakwater is a beautiful beach that is heavily used by local residents. On weekends, the beach swarms with children playing, and numerous families picnic in the park. Outrigger canoes, launched from the beach, glide in and out of the bay, the crews practicing for an upcoming race. When the *halalū* (juvenile *akule*, a type of scad fish), come into the bay, as many as a hundred locals set up their fishing stations on the breakwater. These small fish suddenly appear in the bay, swimming together in large, swarming balls; the fishermen and women can then catch them as quickly as they can cast their baited lines into the water. Hawaiian residents like to eat *halalū* raw in a tomato and onion mix or deep-fried whole.

Pōkaʻī Bay, the bay of Waiʻanae, has for many centuries been a busy place. A seaside *heiau*, unusual because water surrounds it on three sides, is at the tip of Kāneʻīlio ("the god Kāne in dog form") Point, the southern boundary of the bay. Constructed of coral and lava rock in the 15th or 16th Century, this *heiau* called Kūʻīlioloa was named after a legendary *kupua*, whose supernatural powers included changing himself into a dog. Ku the Long Dog, as his name translates, protected travelers from ferocious cannibals who preyed on passersby in Waiʻanae. The *kāhuna* at this temple trained others in astronomy, navigation, and religious traditions. Kamehameha I paid homage to the gods at this *heiau* before making his first attempt to cross the channel and invade Kauaʻi.

In a sea cave in the bay lived another *kupua*, Puhinalo, an eel-man, whose body the jealous men of Waiʻanae hacked into pieces because he seduced one of the women of Waiʻanae. The pieces of his writhing body left huge marks on a cliff at Kō'Olina as they tried to reconnect.

The shores of this bay were also the site of an extensive and well-known coconut grove, Ka Ulu Niu o Pōka'ī, said to have been planted by a chief named *Pōka'ī*, who came from Kahiki, the lost homeland, around 1300; a few trees from the grove (though perhaps not the original 700-year-old trees!) still grace the southern side of the bay. At this grove a priest prophesied that Kamehameha would conquer O'ahu by saying, "The land shall belong to those over the sea."

In Pōka'ī the sparkling, calm water will lure you in to swim, and the long white sand beach is ideal for either walking or lying on. Outside the breakwater, the waves attract surfers, especially during the winter months. Diving, as well, is reported to be good outside the breakwater.

For a change of scenery, you can go around to the other side of Kāne'īlio Point and swim or walk at Lualualei Beach County Park. From this beach park, you'll have a better view of the dramatic Kāne'īlio Point and the crashing white water on its black lava rocks.

If you anchor in Pōka'ī Bay rather than get a slip in Wai'anae Harbor, you'll be considerably closer to the town of Wai'anae. (For attractions in Wai'anae, see the entry for Wai'anae Small Boat Harbor.)

Beach at Pōka'ī Bay

APPROACH

Pōka'ī Bay can be difficult to locate. The bay is almost halfway between Barbers Point and Ka'ena Point, the south and north points on the west shoreline of O'ahu. Pōka'ī Bay is 8.0 miles from Ka'ena Point and 10.0 from Barbers Point Light, but, because of the unvaried terrain, you may not readily identify Pōka'ī until you're within a mile or two of the breakwater. The boats in the Wai'anae Small Boat Harbor, .33 mile north of the anchorage, may be the first confirmation you have that you've arrived.

You can also use the 8-story apartment building just behind the anchorage. It stands out clearly when you're 2 or 3 miles out to sea. Another good landmark is the 652-foot-high pyramid-shaped hill, Pu'u Pāhe'ehe'e, 1.0 mile directly east of the anchorage. On this hill is a water tank one-third of the way up its southern side. The final landmark that identifies Pōka'ī Bay is the old breakwater itself, completed in 1953. You can easily spot the places where powerful waves have washed away some of the coral and lava rocks of the breakwater, leaving it no more than a few inches above the surface of the water. On the end of the breakwater is a red light 30 feet above the water.

ANCHORAGE

The best anchorage area is immediately inside of the breakwater if no organized canoe activity is planned. If the canoeists are practicing in the bay when you're there, anchor north or northeast of the end of the breakwater. The water depths here are between 10 and 25 feet, and the bottom is sand with good holding. If a west wind is blowing, consider trying to get a slip in the Wai'anae Small Boat Harbor because the anchorage at Pōka'ī Bay will not be comfortable.

Wai'anae Harbormaster   808-697-7095 and VHF 16

FACILITIES

At Pōkaʻī:
- Restrooms
- Shower (cold)
- Telephone

For additional facilities, see the Waiʻanae section.

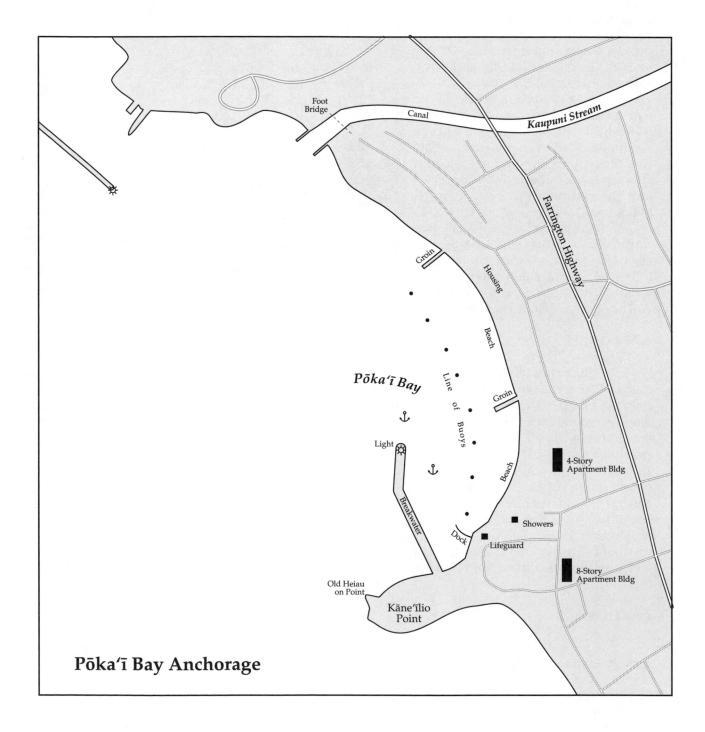

Pōkaʻī Bay Anchorage

KAHE POINT ANCHORAGE
CHART #19357
LAT. N21° 21.280 W158° 08.140 (ANCHORAGE)

Charter boat captains who wish to take clients to a quiet place to dive and snorkel regularly use Kahe Point Anchorage. When trades blow strongly, the mountains to the east of Kahe Point reduce the winds to a near whisper in the anchorage close to shore.

This anchorage offers little in the way of scenery; the mountains to the east are dry and somewhat barren, and the trees around the Kahe Point Beach County Park are sparse. The three stacks of the Hawaiian Electric power plant across Farrington Highway dominate the landscape.

The attraction of this anchorage, though, is its water, both for its tranquillity as an anchorage and its swimming, snorkeling, and diving possibilities. As well as the water of the anchorage, another small beach, Hawaiian Electric Beach, lies to the north. Popularly called "Tracks" by island surfers because of the old railroad tracks that run along here, the gentle waves off Hawaiian Electric Beach have long attracted novice surfers. When the train still ran along this coast, youngsters from Honolulu rode here to surf during the summer.

APPROACH

From the north, Kahe Point Anchorage is 6.5 miles after Kāne'īlio Point. From the south, it is 2.0 miles north of the entrance buoy to Barbers Point Harbor.

You can recognize the anchorage by the three prominent stacks at the Hawaiian Electric power plant at Kahe Point. As you approach the anchorage, identify the outfall from the power plant about 150 yards seaward from the shoreline. The water around the outfall is turbulent, seeming to boil up vigorously.

ANCHORAGE

When you've identified the power plant outfall, begin looking for the sand patch about 100 yards south of the main area of turbulence and 150 yards from shore. Drop anchor in 30 feet of water. The sand bottom provides excellent holding.

This anchorage is only a roadstead, and, because it is open to the waves on three sides, you must watch the weather constantly and plan to leave if *kona* winds come up or a south or west swell sets in.

If the swell is minimal, you can land a tender at Hawaiian Electric Beach.

FACILITIES

Public Transportation
Restrooms
Showers (cold water)
Telephone

Hawaiian Electric power plant at Kahe

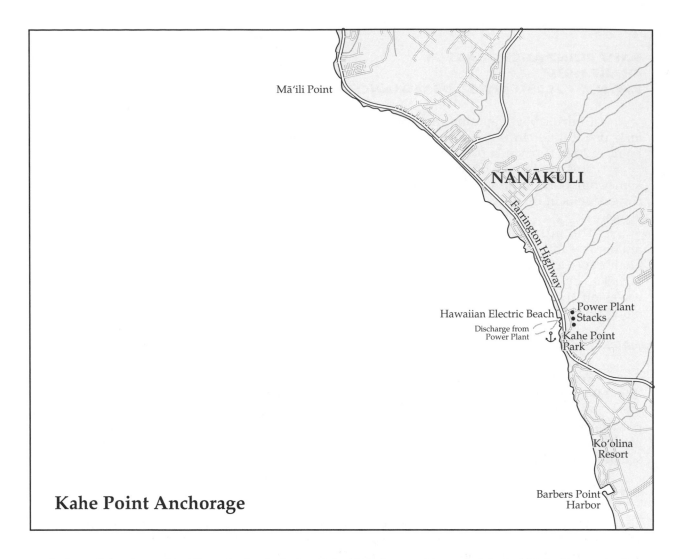

Mā'ili Point

NĀNĀKULI

Farrington Highway

Power Plant
Stacks

Hawaiian Electric Beach

Discharge from
Power Plant

Kahe Point
Park

Ko'olina
Resort

Barbers Point
Harbor

Kahe Point Anchorage

View of O'ahu from Ewa

KO OLINA MARINA (BARBERS POINT HARBOR)
CHART #19357
LAT. N21° 19.300 LONG. W158° 07.810 (ENTRANCE BUOY)

Barbers Point Harbor, a man-made harbor, is about 2 miles north of Barbers Point, the southwest tip of O'ahu. This point, called by the Hawaiians *Kalaeloa* ("the long point"), was another one of those accidental discoveries unfortunate sailors sometimes make. Captain Henry Barber's ship *Arthur* went aground on a coral reef here on October 31, 1796, and the point has since been his, Barbers Point. Hawaiian divers salvaged the cannons from the sunken vessel, and Kamehameha I installed them in the new fort at Lahaina, Maui.

Barbers Point Harbor was open to only commercial traffic for many years, but the new Ko Olina Marina opened for business in 2001 with 267 slips and added another 63 in 2005.

Fishing boat entering Ko Olina Marina

Though slip rental prices at Ko Olina are significantly higher than those at state-owned marinas in Hawai'i, the marina has no difficulty in keeping all the slips full. The facilities at the marina include concrete docks and electricity, water, cable, and telephone hook-up at each slip, as well as centrally located showers, a laundry room, a fuel dock, and a deli. And directly across the harbor is the Phoenician, a full-service haul-out and repair facility.

Visiting as well as local boaters can enjoy this new marina. It not only offers excellent protection in heavy weather but is located on the dry side of the island, which is especially pleasant in winter months. The town of Kapolei, with an extensive shopping center, is only 4 miles away. Marina occupants can catch TheBus along the highway about a mile from the marina, or they can call for a taxi. TheBus also goes on to Honolulu, a one-hour trip from Ko Olina Marina.

This marina is a welcome addition to the list of cruising destinations in the Islands. As well as its first-rate facilities, the marina gives boaters here access to a golf course and luxuriant grounds that include 1.5 miles of paved walkways winding through the resort complex. Along the pathway toward the Ihilani Hotel, a small visitors center introduces guests to the history of the region. The seven exquisite lagoons behind the reef north of West Harbor are suitable for swimming, snorkeling, and fishing. Four of the lagoons alongside the marina were excavated at the site of three historically sacred pools, where Ka'ahumanu, the favorite wife of Kamehameha I, reportedly bathed and performed sacred rituals. And offshore, divers can find some of the best diving on O'ahu.

APPROACH

From the north, Barbers Point Harbor and Ko Olina Marina is 8.1 miles south of Kāne'īlio Point. After you pass the power plant with its three stacks, the harbor entrance is 2.2 miles farther. From the south, the harbor is 1.8 miles north of the Barbers Point light. You'll see a number of large fuel tanks at the refinery that is .9 mile from the entrance. When close to the entrance channel, you can see the 300-ton travel lift at the Phoenician boat yard situated on the south side of the channel.

An R"2" buoy approximately 100 yards offshore marks the channel. Two buoys, R"4" and G"5," mark the halfway point between the entrance and the shore. Range lights make staying in the channel easy. Expect to see breakers on both sides of the channel when large seas are running. The channel has a depth of almost 40 feet, so you'll have no concern with depth.

Depths inside the barge harbor are 40 feet throughout. This is a busy harbor, with ships, tugs, and barges entering and exiting regularly. A ship or two and tugs will usually lie alongside the long dock on the southeast side of the harbor. A large floating drydock is near the Mariscos warehouse on the starboard side of the channel in the barge harbor.

ANCHORAGE

The entrance into the Ko Olina Marina is to the north side of the Barbers Point Channel, about 100 yards east of the "7" marker on the end of the breakwater. Water depths in the entrance channel and around the dock areas are usually 13 feet. However, with shoaling a persistent problem in most marinas in the Hawaiian Islands, we recommend asking the Harbormaster for advice before entering the harbor if you're sailing a large boat with a draft over 10 feet.

The marina can accommodate boats up to a length of 140 feet. Although all slips at Ko Olina Marina are currently leased, the Harbormaster can usually find a vacant slip for a visiting boat. Nevertheless, he requests visitors call, if at all possible, before coming to the marina to confirm the marina has vacant slips. Boaters who call and get a slip assignment will be told to tie up at the fuel dock if they will be arriving after dark.

No anchorage area exists inside Barbers Point Harbor or Ko Olina Marina. If no space is available in the marina, boaters can anchor at Kahe Point, 2 miles north of the Barbers Point Harbor entrance, or at Poka'i Bay, some 8 miles north of the Barbers Point Harbor entrance.

The Phoenician, located immediately south of the Ko Olina Marina entrance off the Barbers Point Harbor channel, has the capability of hauling and repairing boats up to 300 tons and 150 feet in length.

Ko Olina Marina Harbormaster	808-679-1050 and VHF 71
The Phoenician	808-564-0705

FACILITIES

In the harbor
- Convenience Store
- Electricity
- Fuel (gasoline and diesel)
- Haul-out
- Launch Ramp
- Laundromat
- Pumpout Station
- Restrooms
- Showers
- Telephone
- Water

Nearby
- Banks
- Beach
- Public Transportation
- Rental Cars
- Restaurants
- Shopping Center

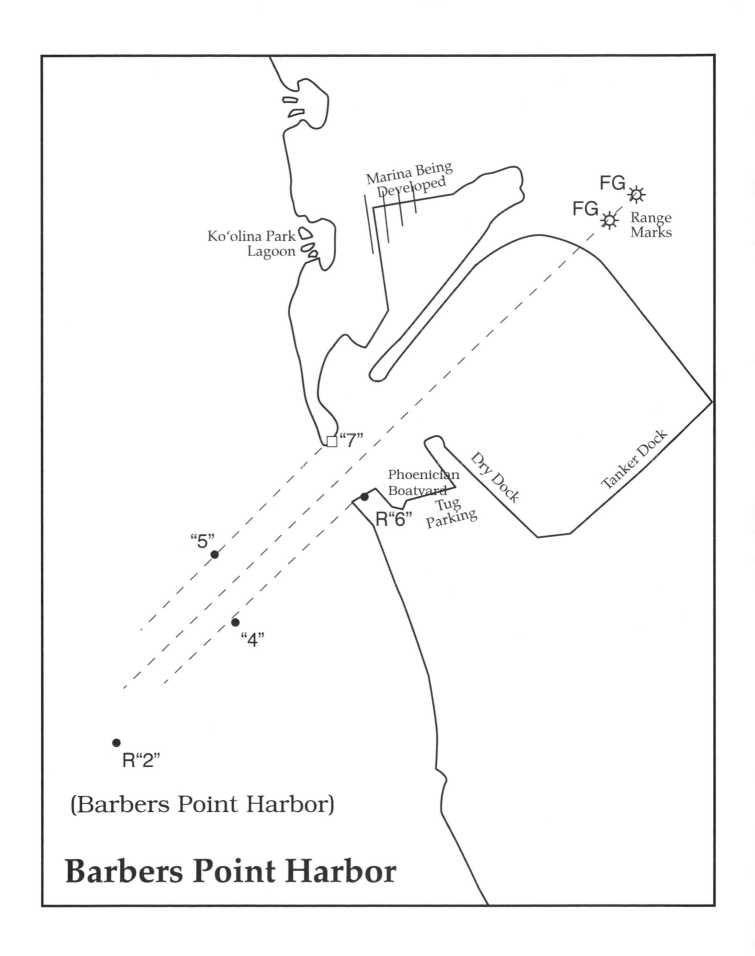

Marina Being
Developed

FG ☼

FG ☼ Range
Marks

Ko'olina Park
Lagoon

□ "7"

Phoenician
Boatyard
Tug
Parking

Dry Dock

Tanker Dock

R"6"

"5"

"4"

R"2"

(Barbers Point Harbor)

Barbers Point Harbor

KE'EHI LAGOON
CHARTS #19357, 19367, 19380
LAT. N21° 17.400 LONG. W157° 53.900 (ENTRANCE BUOY G"1")

Ke'ehi Lagoon offers cruising boaters four possible places to leave their boats while they're exploring the island, making repairs, and provisioning. This lagoon has long been a favorite of boaters because of the casual atmosphere at the marinas and the strong breezes that cool the boats.

Two of the problems that boaters have always complained about at Ke'ehi still exist: noise and dirt. The noise emanates from the jets that take off over the marina day and night. When the jetliners depart from Honolulu International Airport, they go almost directly over the boats at Ke'ehi. To make matters worse, they are only a few hundred feet above the boats when they pass overhead, leaving boaters aboard their boats almost deaf. But since nothing can be done about this problem, boaters at Ke'ehi soon learn to stop talking mid-sentence when a plane goes over and resume where they left off a minute later. The other problem, the dirt, can't be helped either. This problem goes along with the wonderful winds that rip through the area nearly 12 months a year, cooling the boats and providing abundant electricity to boats with wind generators.

An airplane taking off over Ke'ehi Lagoon

All the disadvantages aside, Ke'ehi Lagoon is still popular among Hawaiian boaters. Unlike many harbors in the state, this one is well protected in virtually all weather. When Hurricane 'Iwa struck the Islands in 1982, some boats in the anchorage did suffer serious damage, but most of the boats there at the time remained intact, despite the 80-knot winds that tore through the harbor. Besides its wonderful protection for boats, the lagoon has other appeals as a cruising destination. For many boaters, one of the most appealing qualities of Ke'ehi is its large and friendly boating community. With slips or moorings for more than 800 boats, this facility is the second largest in the state, exceeded only by the Ala Wai Harbor.

The cooling winds make it a more comfortable place than Honolulu in the summer, yet all the amenities of the city are readily accessible via public transportation. The lagoon has an open feeling; from a boat on a mooring here, you can watch the sun set into the ocean on one side and look up into the *pali* of the Ko'olau Range on the other. Though you're still in the city, you can easily imagine yourself elsewhere.

From the docks at the boat harbor, you have an easy walk across the bridge to Sand Island, largely man-made from the material dredged in the harbors. Originally *Sand Island* was the name given to the larger of two separate islands that were artificially joined in 1940. The smaller of the two, Mauliola Island, was a quarantine station set up in 1869 for ships and passengers arriving from suspected plague areas; hence the name *Mauliola,* a god of health. The Sand Island State Recreation Area borders the west and south shores of this roughly triangular-shaped 500-acre island. Hiking, biking, fishing, and picnicking are popular activities in this park. (It lacks a good swimming beach.)

Like much of the Honolulu area, Ke'ehi was once marshland with a large fishpond behind the reef. The U. S. government dredged portions of the lagoon for a seaplane landing area during World War II.

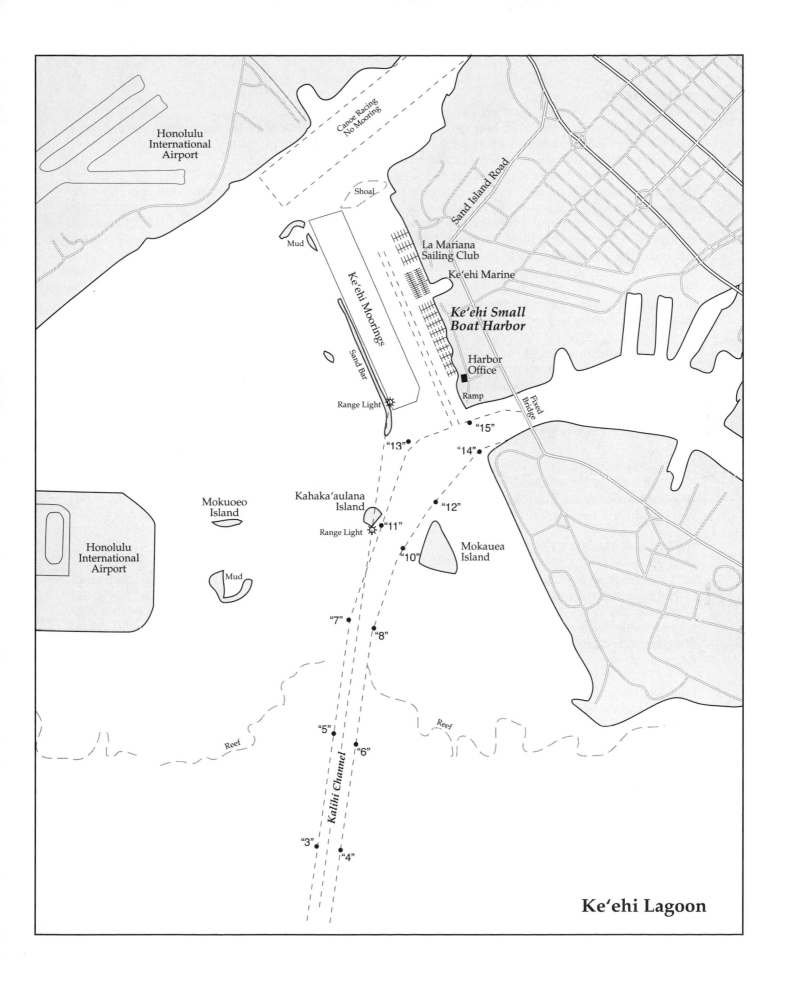

Honolulu
International
Airport

Canoe Racing
No Mooring

Shoal

Sand Island Road

Mud

La Mariana
Sailing Club

Ke'ehi Marine

Ke'ehi Moorings

*Ke'ehi Small
Boat Harbor*

Sand Bar

Harbor
Office

Ramp

Fixed
Bridge

Range Light

"15"

"13"

"14"

Mokuoeo
Island

Kahaka'aulana
Island

"12"

Honolulu
International
Airport

Mud

Range Light

"11"

"10"

Mokauea
Island

"7"

"8"

Reef

"5"

Reef

"6"

Kalihi Channel

"3"

"4"

Ke'ehi Lagoon

APPROACH

The entrance to Ke'ehi Lagoon is through the Kalihi Channel. Approaching from the west, go 11.8 miles after passing Barbers Point Light. Between Barbers Point and the Kalihi Channel, watch for ship traffic around the entrance to Pearl Harbor.

If you're approaching from the east, look for the channel 5.2 miles from the Diamond Head Buoy and 3.0 miles from the entrance to the Ala Wai Harbor. From this direction, be careful not to mistake the Honolulu Ship Channel for the Kalihi Channel. The channel entrance buoy at Honolulu is a red and white buoy identified as "H." The entrance buoy at the Kalihi Channel is a green buoy identified as "1." If you look up the channel and see the Aloha Tower, you'll know you're in the wrong channel.

The passage through the reef and into the Kalihi Channel is clearly marked by a number of buoys, channel markers, and range marks. From the entrance buoy to the beginning of the gradual turn to the right is .90 mile. After that, the distance to the Ke'ehi Small Boat Harbor is slightly more than .50 mile.

During daylight hours the trip northward up the Kalihi Channel is straightforward. The buoys are easy to see, and the boat harbor is clearly recognizable long before you get there. Local boaters also enter and leave the harbor during the hours of darkness, but unless you know the entrance well, we do not recommend attempting to enter at night. The lights on shore make identifying the buoys and range marks difficult.

ANCHORAGE AND BERTHING

Anchoring is not permitted in Ke'ehi Lagoon. However, a visiting boater can usually obtain a slip or a mooring at one of the three marinas in the lagoon: Ke'ehi Small Boat Harbor, Ke'ehi Marine, or La Mariana Sailing Club. Call before you set sail for Ke'ehi to ascertain where you can find a berth or mooring.

KE'EHI SMALL BOAT HARBOR

The first marina you'll see off the starboard bow as you pass between the small islands of Kahaka'aulana and Mokauea is the state-owned Ke'ehi Small Boat Harbor, which has 389 slips and 202 moorings. Make a turn to port as you approach the boat ramp at the harbor, and proceed slightly west of north, leaving the docks to starboard and the moorings to port. Call the Harbormaster on VHF 16 for instructions. (The harbor office is at the foot of the first dock you come to as you enter.)

The Harbormaster attempts to find temporary berths or moorings for visiting boats. However, because several docks at the Small Boat Harbor are currently in desperate need of repair, many slips have been taken out of service. At the time this edition went to press, the legislature had allocated money for the repairs, but no date for the reconstruction to begin had been set. If no slips are available, one of the moorings likely will be. (If you take a mooring, you may leave your tender at the dinghy dock in the Small Boat Harbor.)

Ke'ehi Small Boat Harbor   808-832-3464 (pager 844-5405) or VHF 16

KE'EHI MARINE CENTER

Immediately north of the Small Boat Harbor are the 160 slips privately owned and operated by Ke'ehi Marine Center. All these slips have permanent tenants, but visiting boaters are welcomed when slips are temporarily open. (This marina has the only laundry facility in Ke'ehi; however, this facility is reserved for boaters renting slips at the Marine Center.)

Ke'ehi Marine Center   808-845-6465

LA MARIANA SAILING CLUB

The last set of docks, adjacent to those of Keʻehi Marine Center, belongs to the La Mariana Sailing Club. Although La Mariana has only 100 slips, it often has openings for visiting boaters. The atmosphere at this club is down-to-earth and unpretentious. A popular restaurant at the club features live piano music nightly. In the past some boaters have joined the club to have a place to leave their boats for an extended time.

La Mariana Sailing Club   808-845-7738

FACILITIES

At the marina:

Dinghy Docks	Public Transportation
Fuel (diesel and gasoline)	Pump-out
Haul-out	Restaurant
Marine Service and Supplies	Restrooms
Launch Ramp	Showers
Propane	Telephone

Docks and moorings at Keʻehi

Mother and child on the black sand beach at Ho'okena

Māhukona Harbor on a quiet day

THE ISLAND OF KAUAʻI

THE GARDEN ISLE

Boats at anchor in Hanalei Bay

Maika ʻi nā kuahiwi,
Nani nā pae puʻu e olo nei ka makani.
("Majestic are the mountains,
Beautiful is the row of hills breasting the wind.")

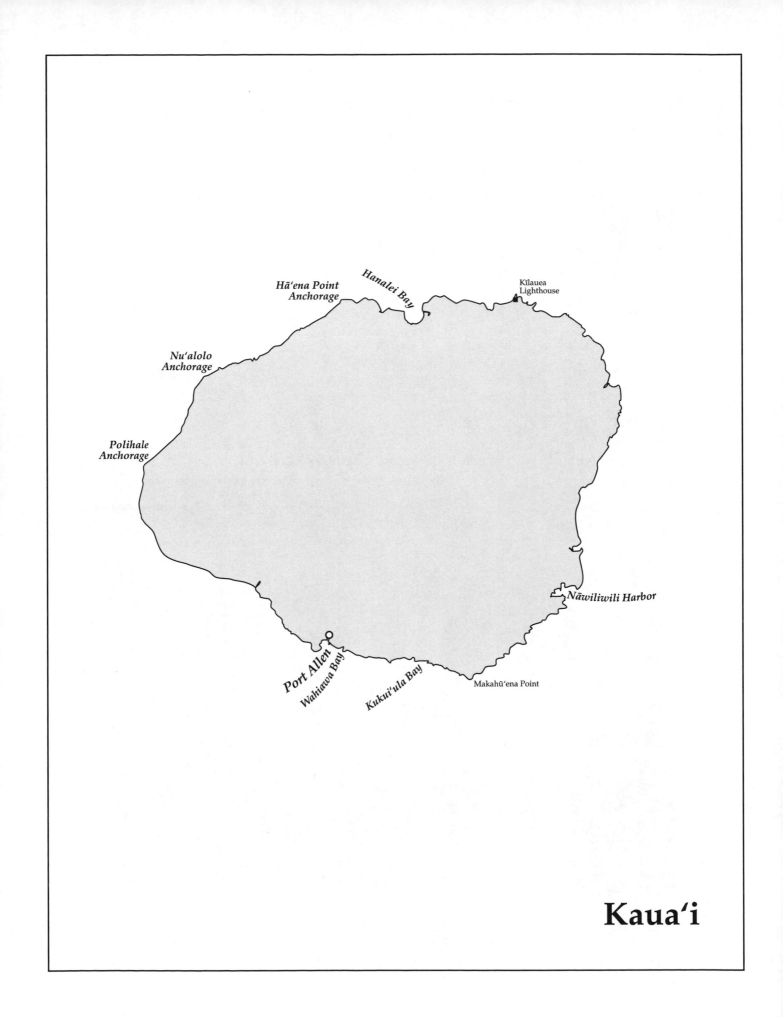

Hā'ena Point
Anchorage

Hanalei Bay

Kīlauea
Lighthouse

Nu'alolo
Anchorage

Polihale
Anchorage

Nāwiliwili Harbor

Port Allen

Wahiawa Bay

Kukui'ula Bay

Makahū'ena Point

Kaua'i

THE ISLAND OF KAUA'I

At the northwest end of the inhabited Hawaiian Islands, Kaua'i richly deserves its nickname "the Garden Isle." To cruise along any of its shores—past spectacular waterfalls cascading from vertical cliffs, valleys rising gently toward deep green mountains, white sand beaches lined with palm trees—will convince you this island is a fertile Eden.

The Garden Isle, though surely an appropriate name, is a recent invention. Ancient Hawaiians called Kaua'i and its tiny neighbor Ni'ihau "the leeward islands," placing all the islands to the southeast in another group which they called "the windward islands." While "leeward" may not be as evocative a name as "garden," it suggests something important about the distinctiveness of Kaua'i.

Kaua'i, the oldest of the inhabited Hawaiian Islands, is also the most remote, 100 miles across a tumultuous channel from O'ahu, the nearest of the other major islands. The result of that distinction is that Kaua'i was, until the 20th Century, relatively isolated and thereby protected from the ambitions of the rulers of the other islands.

Even the great warrior Kamehameha I, who conquered all the other islands, was unable to conquer Kaua'i; during the planned invasion of 1796, the boisterous winds and waves in the Kaua'i Channel forced Kamehameha and his warriors to turn back to Wai'anae on O'ahu after several of their canoes overturned. In 1804 Kamehameha prepared for another invasion. He had composed a rallying cry to inspire his men: *"Let us go and drink the water of Wailua, bathe in the water of Namolokama, eat the mullet that swim in Kawaimakua at Ha'ena, wreath ourselves with the seaweed of Polihale, then return to O'ahu to dwell there."* But this time a deadly foreign disease, perhaps typhoid fever, struck his warriors assembled on O'ahu.

Hanakāpi'ai Beach and Nā Pali Coast

Perhaps Kamehameha was left to ponder the warning of the *kahuna* who had advised against his going to Kaua'i or to acknowledge the superior lineage of the king of Kaua'i, Kaumuali'i. Too, he might have gained respect for the legendary *pule o'o* ("potent prayers") of the people of Kaua'i and for the powerful prayer that Kamakahelei, the mother of Kaumuali'i, possessed. For whatever reason, he made no further attempts to invade the leeward island.

In 1810, faced with the preeminent power Kamehameha had garnered, Kaumuali‘i agreed to become a part of the new kingdom, though he retained the governance of Kaua‘i.

In 1816 Kaumuali‘i entered into an alliance with a Russian, Georg Scheffer, to conquer the other islands, to which Kaumuali‘i had ancestral claims. Kaumuali‘i would supply men and food for the campaign, and the Russians would supply guns and ships. The only tangible result of this failed scheme was the star-shaped Fort Elizabeth, built by Scheffer on the banks of the Waimea River and above which flew the Russian flag for a few months.

The people of Kaua‘i still proudly exclaim that theirs is the only Hawaiian island never to have been conquered.

The geologic age of this island has given it other attributes besides its remoteness. The most nearly round-shaped of the Islands, approximately 33 miles long and 25 miles wide, it is also the most deeply, and, some would say, the most beautifully, eroded.

The dramatic Waimea Canyon has been called "the Grand Canyon of the Pacific." Though it is only a fraction of the size and only about a third as old as the Grand Canyon, the Waimea Canyon is second to none in its splendor. Kaua‘i also has the only navigable river in Hawai‘i, the Wailua. The

Waimea Canyon

highest peak on the island, Wai‘ale‘ale (5,148 feet), is reputed to be the wettest spot on earth, in some years having as much as 480 inches of rainfall.

Another distinction of the physical geography is that Kaua‘i has more sand beaches per mile of shoreline than any other island in Hawai‘i: 50 miles of its 113-mile circumference, or 44 percent, almost twice the percentage of O‘ahu, a distant second.

Some legends support the claim that Kaua‘i was the first inhabited island in the chain, as well, having been populated by Polynesian explorers as early as A. D. 200. The Menehune, the legendary "little people" of Hawai‘i, popularly depicted as close relatives to the Irish *leprechaun*, are believed by some historians to have been a distinct group of settlers who came to Kaua‘i from Central Polynesia. Later subjugated by the Tahitian explorers, the original settlers, according to this theory, were called *Manehune*, a derisive Tahitian term for commoners.

In Hawaiian lore, Kaua‘i (or Ni‘ihau, in other legends) was also the first Hawaiian home of the goddess Pele, who moved down the chain, from the leeward islands to the Big Island, digging pits on each island, until she found a fiery volcano, Kīlauea, where she and her family could live.

This island's cruising potential is as rich as its natural and cultural history. Though Kaua‘i has fewer cruising destinations than any of the other major Hawaiian Islands except for Lāna‘i, these destinations give Kaua‘i as much variety as any of the others have.

The two small boat harbors—Nāwiliwili and Port Allen—have the advantages of security and easy accessibility for sightseeing and provisioning. Hanalei Bay, on the North Shore, is easily the most popular cruising destination on the island. Boaters from around the Islands flock to this lovely, commodious bay throughout the summer months. Along the North Shore are two other picturesque anchorages, as stunningly beautiful as Hanalei but much smaller—Nu‘alolo and Hā‘ena. These three anchorages on the North Shore are outstanding for water sports and for the views of the steep cliffs and lush green valleys along the coast.

On the west end of the island is the roadstead at Polihale, sometimes a little less comfortable than the other destinations, but its attributes compensate for the little roll you might experience. Anchored here, you'll have the best of both coastal worlds of Kaua'i: the cliffs to the north and the island's longest sand beach and the beginning of the Mānā Plain to the south. Polihale is notable for its sounds as well as its sights. From the roadstead, you may hear the feral goats bleating on the slopes. Go onto the beach and listen to the "barking sands," a rare natural phenomenon.

For the quietest of the destinations, turn to Wahiawa, less than a mile east of Port Allen but seemingly in another world. Tucked in between low lava cliffs and secluded from the cane fields by a low plateau above the beach, this anchorage feels as cozy as a cocoon.

Everything you could want from a cruising destination is on Kaua'i except big city lights. This island has nothing that approximates a city, and the brightest lights you'll see from most anchorages will be the moon and the stars.

The prospect of crossing the Kaua'i Channel has undoubtedly deterred many sailors from visiting Kaua'i. With careful planning and the flexibility to change those plans as necessary, however, you can cross the channel in either direction without trauma and savor the fruits of this lush garden isle.

View of Waimea, Kaua'i

NĀWILIWILI HARBOR
CHARTS #19381, 19383
LAT. N21° 57.130 LONG. W159° 20.000 (ENTRANCE)

Famous is Nāwiliwili
Your beauty is greatly admired
A genuine beauty.

These lines from a traditional Hawaiian song describe but one of the appeals of this most important harbor on the island of Kaua'i. Beautiful Hawaiian *wiliwili* trees, with their flowers of red or orange, yellow or white once covered the mountain slopes to the south of Nāwiliwili Harbor. The Hawaiians used the red, oblong seeds of *nā wiliwili* to make *lei* and the light *wiliwili* wood for surfboards, canoe outriggers, and net floats. Today few of these treasured native trees remain above the harbor, but the beauty of Nāwiliwili the place remains.

Up the Hulē'ia Stream

Another appeal of Nāwiliwili Harbor for cruising sailors is its security. It is the one genuinely all-weather harbor on the island. Only storms of the magnitude of the hurricanes 'Iwa (1982) or 'Iniki (1992) can threaten boats moored in this harbor. In normal tradewind conditions, the water in Nāwiliwili is calm, even when the wind whistles in the rigging of boats moored or anchored here.

One reason for the security of Nāwiliwili Harbor is its location in the lee of the magnificent 779-foot Kalanipu'u ("the royal hill"), where the goddess Pele's elder sister, Nāmakaokaha'i, planted *kava* and bananas. In a presumably much later era, the Hawaiians used Kalanipu'u as a "calling hill," from atop which they could watch the movements of the fish and call out directions to the fishermen with nets below.

Built between 1921-1930, the commercial docks at Nāwiliwili are used by the barges and ships that supply the island. (On December 31, 1941, the Japanese shelled Nāwiliwili Harbor, but the facilities sustained little damage.) Across the harbor channel from the commercial docks is an anchorage area for small boats. Behind the inside breakwater, the small boat harbor, built in 1980, has 88 slips for sail and power boats and a Coast Guard facility.

An interesting excursion from Nāwiliwili is to take your tender up the Hulē'ia Stream that flows into Nāwiliwili Bay. You'll glide under the branches of trees forming a canopy over the stream and pass groves of banana and papaya trees. So picturesque is this stream that it was the site for some of the filming of the movies *Jurassic Park, Uncommon Valor,* and *Raiders of the Lost Ark.*

Along these banks Kamapua'a, the hog-man, ravished the fire goddess Pele, giving the stream its name, formerly *Hulā'ia,* meaning "pushed through." Hidden by the trees and bushes are the remains of the Alakoko (Menehune) Fishpond; its ancient stone wall extending for 2,700 feet off a bend in the river has been attributed to the Menehune, those mythical builders of ancient Hawai'i. Mullet, the fish of the *ali'i,* were plentiful in this river and bay until recent times.

As you slip quietly up and down the stream, perhaps you'll see some of the birds from the Hulē'ia National Wildlife Refuge beyond the trees. The endangered Hawaiian coot, stilt, and duck make their homes in the flats and estuary inside the refuge.

Kalapakī Beach, an excellent and exquisite swimming and surfing beach behind the Kaua'i Marriott, is a short walk from the harbor. Ancient Hawaiians surfed here, and for many years the beach was the site of the Rice family beach home, built in 1870 by the son of William and Mary Rice, who had come to Hawai'i in 1841 as missionaries. Beyond the white sand beach is a grassy area under swaying palms where you can spread out your beach towel. The open-air bar behind the palms may be too inviting to pass up.

Sailing canoe *Hawai'iloa* at loading dock

While in Nāwiliwili, find a way to see the town of Līhu'e, some 2 miles from the harbor. The written history of Līhu'e begins in 1839, when the Reverend Doctor Thomas Lafon, a missionary, moved from Kōloa and built a church here. The governor of the island, Kai'kioewa, and his wife had a "straw palace" here at the time. In 1850 the planting of sugar cane began around Līhu'e, and the plantation town grew. Today it has close to 12,000 residents. Many of the businesses have moved to outlying shopping centers, but the heart of this town is still along Rice Street.

A visit to the Kaua'i Museum, on Rice Street, may well be the highlight of your sojourn in Līhu'e. Here are exhibits illustrating the variety of cultures of historic as well as contemporary Kaua'i and Ni'ihau, from the Menehune to the missionaries. It's a small museum but large in its effect.

If you can arrange to be in Līhue in late September, you can participate in the Kaua'i Mokihana Festival. Hawaiian music, *hula*, and *lei*-making competitions are highlights of this two-week festival.

A weekly event that might be easier to plan for is the Sunshine Market, sponsored by the County of Kaua'i. The Līhu'e Sunshine Market is at the Vidinha Stadium at 1530 on Fridays. The fresh fruits, vegetables, and flowers go quickly, so plan to be there early.

APPROACH

Nāwiliwili Bay is on the southeast corner of Kaua'i. The entrance to the harbor is almost directly under the flight path of the interisland jetliners. You can spot the approximate location of the harbor when you are still 10 miles from Nāwiliwili. Air traffic to Kaua'i is heavy, day and night.

Ninini Point, marked by a 24-mile light on a 112-foot-high white tower, extends from the island immediately north of the entrance to Nāwiliwili Bay. At night, you can see the light for many miles before you reach the harbor. A red hilltop clearance light is also evident near the top of Carter Point, on the south edge of Nāwiliwili Bay.

From Ninini Point to the entrance channel that is between Kūki'i Point on the north and the end of the breakwater to the south is .70 mile.

Turn to port after passing the green buoy off the end of the breakwater. The small boat harbor is in the southwestern corner of the harbor, 1,100 yards from this green buoy.

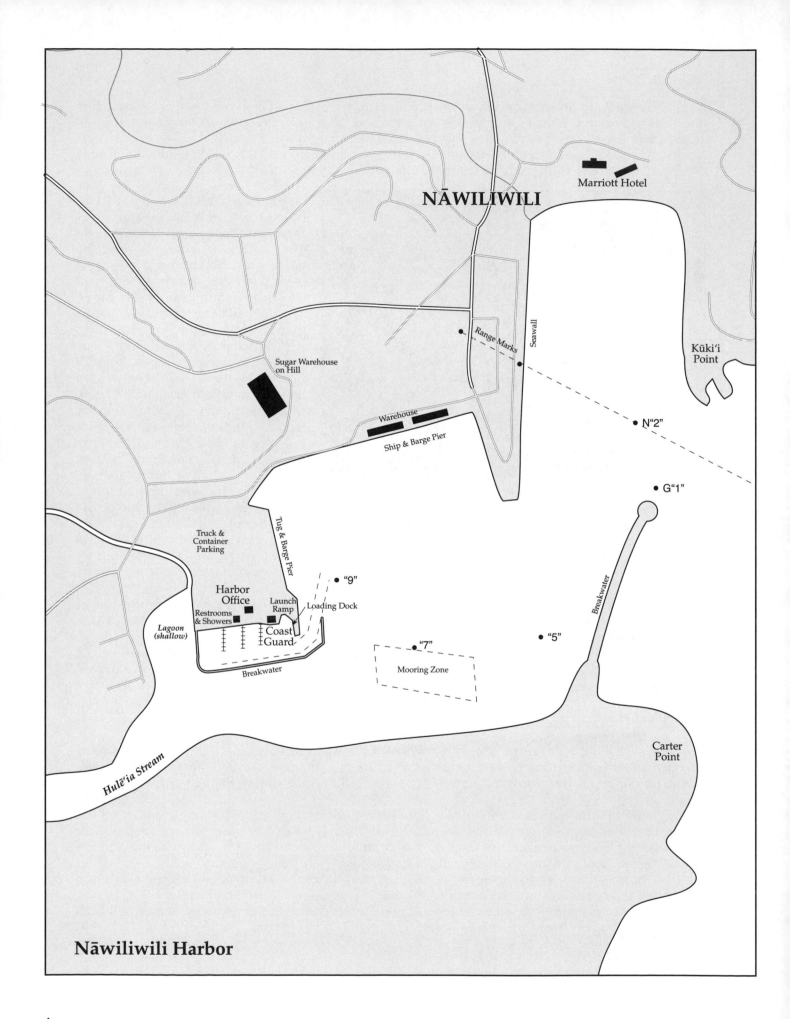

NĀWILIWILI

Marriott Hotel

Kūki'i Point

Range Marks

Seawall

Sugar Warehouse on Hill

Warehouse

Ship & Barge Pier

N"2"

G"1"

Truck & Container Parking

Tug & Barge Pier

"9"

Harbor Office

Launch Ramp

Loading Dock

Restrooms & Showers

Coast Guard

"7"

"5"

Breakwater

Lagoon (shallow)

Mooring Zone

Breakwater

Carter Point

Hulē'ia Stream

Nāwiliwili Harbor

ANCHORAGE AND BERTHING

Once inside the small boat harbor, you can tie up at the loading dock east of the launch ramp while you check with the harbormaster for a possible guest slip. The harbormaster's office is in the temporary structure north of the docks in the small boat harbor. Do not plan to stay on the loading dock as it is normally busy.

If the harbormaster has no guest slips available, you can anchor outside the small boat harbor breakwater but inside the main breakwater. Anchorage space for 15 boats is southward from Buoy G"7," located 250 yards east of the breakwater protecting the inner harbor. The mud bottom in this anchorage provides good holding in 10-25 feet of water. Anchoring up Hulē'ia Stream is illegal, and boats anchored there are subject to eviction.

Do not anchor in any other area of the commercial harbor, or you will certainly be in the way of the ships and tugs that move about in the harbor.

Nāwiliwili Harbormaster   808-245-4586

FACILITIES

At Nāwiliwili:
- Fuel (diesel by truck; gasoline & diesel by jerry jug)
- Hardware Store
- Launch Ramp
- Mini-market
- Produce Market
- Restaurants
- Restrooms
- Showers (cold)
- Telephone
- Public Transportation

In Līhu'e:
- Airport
- Banks
- Car Rental
- Grocery Stores
- Laundromat
- Library
- Shopping Centers
- Movie Theaters
- Post Office
- Propane

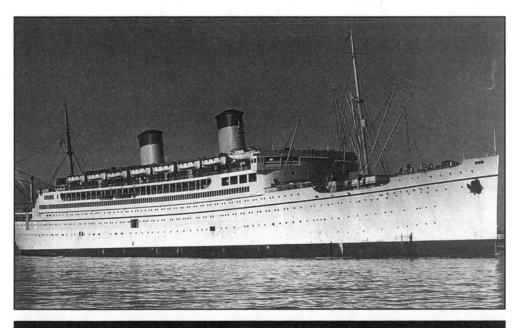

SS *MONTEREY*, 1935

HANALEI BAY
CHART #19385, 19381
LAT. N22° 13.950 LONG. 159° 30.650 (ENTRANCE)

By any standard, Hanalei Bay is one of the premier summer anchorages in the state of Hawai'i. The large size of this deeply indented bay encourages many boaters to visit because they know they can always find room to anchor.

And this lovely bay typifies the beauty of Kaua'i. As its name suggests, Hanalei is like a Hawaiian *lei*, a crescent of silk and jewels, foliage and flowers. A 2-mile-long beach of silky white sand curves *lei*-like along the gracefully breaking sapphire and turquoise water between Pu'u Pōā and Makahoa points. Along the edge of the beach grows a second strand of trailing beach morning glories and low *naupaka* bushes, behind which are taller bushes and trees flowering red and orange and yellow. Beyond the neat homes tucked in among the trees and bushes rise precipitous mountains, some covered with emerald trees, others showing the brilliant red of the volcanic soil. Puffs of white clouds that darken with moisture almost every day hang over the peaks and spill down the ridges, bringing cooling rain with them as far as the busy little village of Hanalei. A rainbow, often double, arches over the mountains ringing the crescent bay.

Another reason for the popularity of Hanalei is that boaters can choose from such a wide variety of activities here. Once the anchor is down, you can sit in the cockpit and watch the spectacular natural drama over the *pali* and the human drama of boats moving in and out and around the bay.

The anchorage at Hanalei

The Hanalei River, emptying into the east side of the bay, makes an inviting excursion in your sportboat, dinghy, or kayak. Yellow and melon-colored blossoms from the *hau* trees hanging over the river float downstream, adding to the tropical allure.

Opportunities for swimming, snorkeling, and surfing abound in this large bay. With two miles of sand to choose from, you can always find an uncrowded beach for swimming; snorkeling is good on the reef off Makahoa Point, on the west end; and the major winter and spring surfing site on the north shore of Kaua'i is Pine Trees, a shorebreak off Wai'oli Beach Park, where the Wai'oli Stream flows into the bay near the center of the 2-mile beach. (Incidentally, at Wai'oli is also the site where the first royal Hawaiian yacht, Kamehameha II's *Ha'aheo o Hawai'i,* or "Pride of Hawai'i," went aground on a reef in 1824.)

Ashore, you have but a short 3-block walk to the village of Hanalei, assiduously kept small by the local residents. They have resisted any attempt to build a large condominium on the east end of the bay at Black Pot Beach, named for the large black cooking pot formerly kept on the beach for fishermen, yachties, and picnickers to cook and share their food. Many of the townspeople are also determined to keep down the number of charter boat companies operating out of Hanalei Bay.

Taro fields in Hanalei Valley

Another successful ploy for minimizing the number of tourists is the one-lane Hanalei Bridge at the east entrance to Hanalei Valley. The old bridge, built in 1912, with a supporting truss added in the late 1960s, limits the weight and height of vehicles that can cross the river. Thus large trucks and tour buses cannot enter the valley.

In town are numerous restaurants and shops and a funky little museum. At the west end of town is the Wai'oli Mission House, built in 1837, its Southern-style exterior the design of a missionary architect from Kentucky. The house became the home of Abner and Lucy Wilcox, missionaries who arrived in 1846, and was owned and occupied by members of the Wilcox family until a few years ago.

At Hanalei, too, you can catch a bus that runs hourly between Hā'ena and Līhu'e. Taking this bus is perhaps the best way to see some of the spots that are not near another anchorage. West of Hā'ena is the National Tropical Garden in Limahuli Valley. In this garden you can walk through ancient taro terraces, built possibly as long as 1,000 years ago, and view plantings of endangered Hawaiian species.

At beautiful Kē'ē Beach you can swim with the turtles and tropical fish or, across the road from the beach, begin the Kalalau Foot Trail that traverses the magnificent sea cliffs, Nā Pali. A 2-mile hike on the trail will take you to Hanakāpī'ai Valley, where a white sand beach lies at the mouth of the Hanakāpī'ai Stream. At the head of the valley, 2 miles inland on an unimproved trail, are a waterfall and pool. Along the trail are coffee trees planted in the late 1800s and the ruins of a coffee mill. Earlier, this valley was the site of a Hawaiian fishing and farming village, the taro terraces of which are still visible. Continuing on the main trail, you'll have another 9 miles to reach Kalalau Valley, a trek not be undertaken without careful planning and a permit for staying overnight at the beach. Kalalau Valley was home to a fishing and farming village; the last inhabitants left the valley in 1919.

Hanalei, too, was originally a fishing and farming village. In the 1860s the moist valley where taro had flourished for centuries was judged to be ideal for growing rice. Rice soon became the major export from Hanalei, leading to the construction of a commercial pier in the 1890s.

The commercial use of the pier ended in 1933 when the rice growers here could no longer compete with the California growers.

In 1861-1862 Robert Wyllie constructed a state-of-the-art sugar mill next to the Hanalei River, much of the machinery brought over from Glasgow, Scotland. He named the large-scale sugar plantation *Princeville* to honor the young son of Kamehameha V and Queen Emma. The mill and plantation were not fiscally successful, and in 1867 the entire estate was sold at auction.

Today Hanalei Valley has, at least in one way, returned to the way it was when Hawaiian villagers fished and farmed here: the taro fields are once again prospering. In fact, the Hanelei Valley supplies about half the *poi* consumed in Hawai'i.

However, no longer do the fishermen and farmers paddle their canoes across the bay, carrying goods for trade with the other villages on the North Shore of Kaua'i or on the island of Ni'ihau. Nor, for that matter, do commercial ships carrying rice or sugar still tie up at the pier.

Instead, pleasure crafts of all sorts fill this bay in the summer months. Local canoe clubs and charter boat companies make Hanalei their home. Hawaiian boaters from other islands visit year after year, some leaving their boats in the bay for the summer and commuting back and forth. Many of the boats that compete in the Transpac and Pacific Cup races from the Mainland to Honolulu stop at Hanalei on their way home. All this activity makes the bay a wonderful place to people and boat watch.

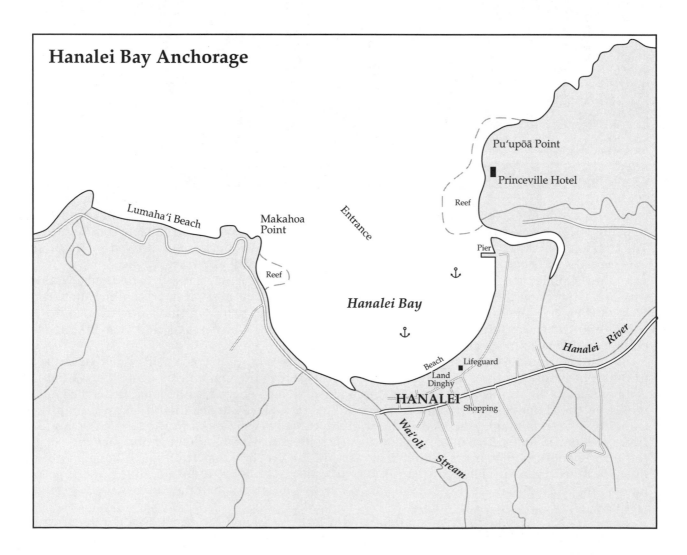

APPROACH

Hanalei Bay is approximately in the center of the north coast of Kaua'i. For boaters coming from the east, as most visitors to this bay will be, the entrance is 6.0 miles west of Kīlauea lighthouse.

Coming from the east or west, you'll see the imposing Princeville Hotel, its several storeys stepping down the cliffs of Pu'u Pōā Point on the eastern side of the entrance.

Entering Hanalei requires attention to the reefs on either side of the entrance, but if you line up with the center between the reefs before you enter, you'll have no trouble. The distance between Pu'upōā Point to the east and Makahoa Point to the west is 1.0 mile; the distance between the two reefs is .70 mile, making Hanalei one of the easiest anchorages to get into and out of. In fact, boaters here regularly enter and leave the bay under sail.

ANCHORAGE

The most popular anchorage in the bay is on the east side near the old pier. (Boats may not be tied to the pier; it is for fishing and swimming only.) Unless you want to be part of a large crowd, however, consider anchoring in another part of the bay. Our preferred anchorage is in the southeast part of the bay; it is usually less crowded than the east side. Drop anchor in 20-30 feet of water. The sand bottom provides excellent holding.

Land your tender by the lifeguard station in the southeast corner of the bay and drag it high up on the beach near the beach cats. The lifeguards typically put flags out to mark where boaters should take their tenders ashore. The second location for landing a tender is between the old pier and the mouth of the Hanalei River. In both these locations, swimmers are usually in the water, so be careful.

From May through October, this anchorage is generally comfortable and safe. During the remaining months, the north swell and the storms make Hanalei Bay a potentially dangerous anchorage. If you do take your boat to Hanalei on a calm day in the winter, you and your crew will not want to be far from your boat because conditions along this coast can change rapidly.

Hanalei Harbormaster   808-645-6178 (cell)

FACILITIES

Bank	Restaurants
Car Rental (by calling Princeville)	Restrooms
Grocery Stores	Shops
Laundromat	Showers (cold)
Post Office	Telephone
Public Transportation	

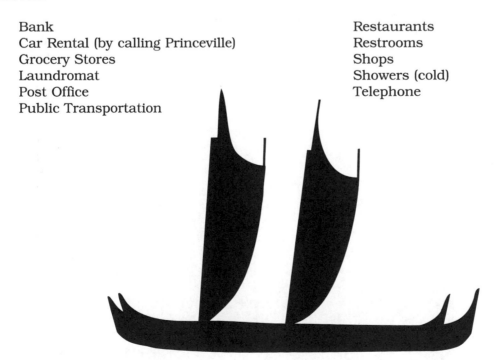

Nāwiliwili Harbor

Kē'ē Beach, where Nā Pali of Kauai'i begins

Kalalau Valley, Nā Pali

HĀʻENA POINT ANCHORAGE (ALSO CALLED TUNNELS BEACH)
CHART #19381
LAT. N22° 14.020 LONG. W159° 34.085 (ENTRANCE)

Hāʻena Point Anchorage has one of the most breathtaking settings in all of Hawaiʻi. The backdrop for this anchorage looks as if it were designed as a movie set, and, in fact, the scenes of the Bali Hai cliffs and ocean in the movie South Pacific were shot immediately west of the anchorage.

Not to be outdone by the cliffs behind the anchorage, Mākua Reef, east of the anchorage, is also a sight to behold. The large waves spawned by the winds that race across the Pacific Ocean and sweep around the north end of Kauaʻi send up a crescendo of white foam and mist when they meet Mākua Reef. When you approach the anchorage, you may well wonder if the reef can protect your boat from these forceful waves. But once your boat comes to rest behind the reef, you'll recognize what a calming effect a reef can have. Your anchored boat will head east into the winds, as the huge waves break on the reef not more than 100 yards off your port bow. What may amaze you most is the gentle boat motion behind that reef.

Hawaiians knew the bay behind the reef as *Maniniholo* ("traveling *manini*, or reef surgeon-fish"); it was a popular place for *hukilau*, or fishing with a seine. Today the name *Maniniholo* is primarily associated with the dry cave across the road from Hāʻena Beach Park.

Hāʻena ("red hot") is apparently the older name for the area where Hawaiians fished and farmed as much as 1,000 years ago. Hāʻena figures in myths and legends of ancient Kauaʻi; perhaps the name derived from the legend of Pele and Lohiʻau, king of Kauaʻi. In searching for a place with fire in the earth where she could live, Pele traveled along the Nā Pali Coast until she came to Hāʻena. She followed the sounds of *hula* drums to a gathering of people, among whom was the handsome young king. Pele asked him to become her husband, but she had to find a suitable place to live before he could join her. Pele finally found her home at Kīlauea on the Big Island, but, through a series of mishaps, Lohiʻau ended up back at Hāʻena with Pele's

"Bali Hai" cliffs and Mākua Reef

sister Hiʻiaka. Lines from a *hula* song suggest the naming of this place: *A Lohiʻau-ipo i Hāʻena lā, ʻenaʻena ke aloha ke hiki mai,* or "Lohiʻau the sweetheart at Red-hot, hot the love that comes."

The remains of a stone wall near the cliffs are still known as the house of Lohiʻau. Beyond the house on the boulders are the remains of a *heiau,* Kaulu Paoa, the most famous of its kind in all Hawaiʻi, for at this shrine Hawaiians from all the Islands came to learn the art of communicating through dances and chants. Paoa, the legendary *hula* master, was a friend of Lohiʻau. An upper terrace was dedicated to Laka, the patron deity of the *hula.*

The *hula* temple is no longer the major attraction to this spot at the east end of the magnificent Nā Pali Coast. In the early 1970s quite a different kind of industry arose here. Hāʻena is the place where *puka* shell jewelry was born. The heavy winter surf along the north shore breaks the tops off small cone shells, and then repeated poundings by the surf erode holes, or *puka,* in the flattened shells. The hippies who lived at Taylor Camp in the late 60s and early 70s discovered the shells and gave them their name. The story is that Howard Taylor, who owned the property

At anchor behind Makua Reef

around the bay, sent a necklace of these shells to his famous sister, Elizabeth Taylor. When she wore it in public, the popularity of the jewelry was assured.

Now, the crystal turquoise and azure waters and the fertile reefs bring most tourists and locals to the beaches of Hāʻena Bay to swim and snorkel. Surfing and windsurfing are excellent here, too. Net and spear fishermen dive near the reef, particularly inside the lagoon. The divers call the site *Tunnels* because of the underwater tunnels along the side of the reef.

Sightseeing, too, is a big draw. In addition to the archeological sites are two wet caves, Waikapalaʻe and Waikanaloa, between Hāʻena and Kēʻē Beach, as well as the dry cave, Maniniholo. For a strenuous hike and the most stupendous view of this exquisite coast, the Kalalau Trail begins nearby and traverses 11 miles of the Nā Pali Coast.

Because the anchorage at Hāʻena Point is so close to the ever popular Hanalei Bay and because it is so small, few boats anchor here, making it an even better destination.

Like Hanalei Bay, the anchorage at Hāʻena is reliable only in the summer and early fall when the trades are blowing. In the winter and early spring, use all north shore anchorages with extreme caution.

APPROACH

From the Hanalei Bay entrance to Hāʻena Point is 3.0 miles. Finding the anchorage at Hāʻena can be challenging because of the lack of easily recognized landmarks. Just prior to arriving at the point, the breaking water on the reef extending .50 mile out from shore is the best indication you'll have. After swinging out from shore to avoid the reef, turn south into the anchorage.

No distinctive features mark this anchorage if you're traveling clockwise around the island either. However, when traveling northeast along the Nā Pali coastline, you'll have cliffs down to the ocean almost continuously for the 12 miles from Polihale to Ka'ilio Point, but at Ka'ilio Point the topography changes. (Note! Ka'ilio is labeled as *Kailiu* on some charts.) At Ka'ilio, the cliffs are .30 mile inland from the beach, and palm trees grow behind the beach and back toward the cliffs. From Ka'ilio to Hā'ena Point Anchorage is 1.2 miles. As you approach the anchorage, you can see the waves breaking on the reef.

ANCHORAGE

The first anchorage area at Hā'ena is in the lee of the east side of the bay, about 300 yards from the beach, approximately one-half of the way from the beach to the outer edge of the reef. Although you could anchor anywhere in the lee of the reef, the closer the boat is to the reef, the better the boat motion will be. Be careful to avoid the patches of coral. If you get too close to the reef, you'll find more coral than sand. We have anchored in 15 feet of water about 150 feet from the reef, allowing the wind to keep us away from the reef. The holding at Hā'ena is excellent, and the boat motion is minimal in the shelter of the reef, even when the winds are blowing 15-20 knots.

A small anchorage that will hold two or three boats is in the lagoon between the reef and the beach, but the passage into this anchorage is difficult to spot. When we were last in Hā'ena, a charter boat company had sunk mooring buoys inside the reef, where the company's large rubber boats tied up while their passengers snorkeled, and one sailboat was anchored in the lagoon. Department of Land and Natural Resources administrative rules specifically state that anchoring in the lagoon inside the reef is allowed only during daylight hours. If you decide to anchor in the lagoon, watch for swimmers and snorkelers in the area.

FACILITIES

Restrooms
Showers (cold water)

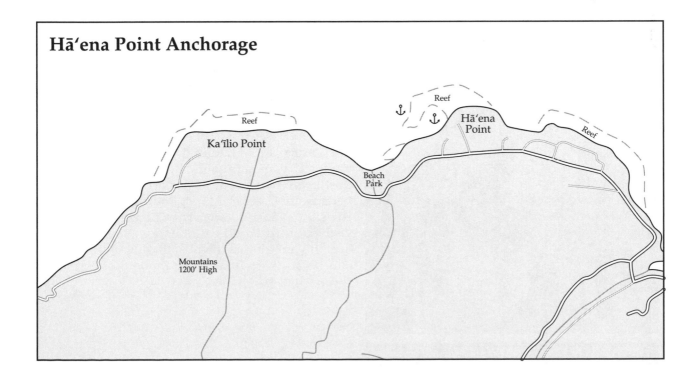

Hā'ena Point Anchorage

NU'ALOLO STREAM ANCHORAGE (CALLED NU'ALOLO KAI)
CHART 19381
LAT. N22° 10.000 LONG. W159° 42.400 (ENTRANCE)

An earlier cruising guide to the Islands referred to this anchorage as the "crown of a small boat trip to Kaua'i." Having read this description, we eagerly set sail for Nu'alolo. What we found was an anchorage too crowded with commercial traffic to allow us to get our boat in behind the reef. The operators of the charter boats have set buoys behind the reef so they can easily tie up while their customers snorkel. When we arrived at Nu'alolo, four of these boats were there, leaving only marginal room for another boat the size of ours.

While interviewing a charter boat captain, we were told to use the moorings of the charter boats at night since they do not make night trips. He also suggested that boaters who want to anchor there should do so before the charter boats begin arriving at 0830. He said he regularly sees as many as 10 charter boats moored at Nu'alolo.

The reasons for the crowded conditions at Nu'alolo are the unparalleled scenery along the Na Pali Coast, the unmatched snorkeling around the reef, and the protection the reef at Alapi'i Point affords from the swells that run along the coastline.

This reef that once provided nourishment for a village is a remarkable example of a fringing reef still in pristine condition. Because of its remote location, it has suffered little of the abuses of civilization so damaging to other reefs in the Islands. Numerous varieties of coral make up the reef, home to over fifty species of fish. Octopus and eels hide in the crevices, and shellfish grow along the slopes.

On the narrow coastal flat between the precipitously steep sea cliffs was the site of the small fishing village that was connected to the farming village on the plateau above by a swinging ladder and trail up the face of the eastern cliff at Alapi'i ("ascent") Point. The fishing village was Nu'alolo Kai ("[of the] sea"); the village on the plateau was Nu'alolo 'Āina ("[of the] land").

APPROACH

The anchorage at Nu'alolo has no easily identifiable features. Going counterclockwise around the island, it is 7.8 miles from Ka'ilio Point (shown as *Kailiu* on some charts). From the south it is 5.0 miles from the northern end of Polihale Beach, the point at which the cliffs begin to rise precipitously out of the water.

Alapi'i Point is immediately to the east of the anchorage and Makuaiki Point .25 mile to the west. If you approach the anchorage from the northeast, be alert after passing the Nā Pali coast because the reef at Alapi'i Point extends out from the shore some 250 yards. The reef will be easily visible, but proceed cautiously.

If you approach Nu'alolo during the day, you can be fairly certain to see moored charter boats there when you arrive.

Nā Pali to Alapi'i Point

284   THE ISLAND OF KAUA'I

ANCHORAGE

The best place to anchor at Nu'alolo is close to the reef. As you might guess from what we have said earlier, however, that may present problems because at least seven moorings take up much of the space in that area. If you anchor here, be careful that your boat will not endanger boats on one or more of the moorings.

Another precaution you must take is to be sure you do not drop your anchor on live coral. To do so is both illegal and imprudent.

A safer alternative is to anchor in the large sand patch about 200 feet west of the reef and 300 feet off the shore. It has no moorings in it and is well clear of the coral. When that area is too crowded, you might try the area close to Makuaiki Point, reported to have a good sand bottom. However, it will be less comfortable because it is not in the lee of the reef at Alapi'i Point.

If you anchor for the night at Nu'alolo, make sure you have enough room to swing without hitting the reef; the east wind typical during the day generally changes to a west wind after dark.

You can ignore the range marks on the shoreline that are evident when you are entering the anchorage at Nu'alolo. They are only to help the skippers of the inflatable charter boats get through the inner reef to land their customers on the beach.

FACILITIES

None

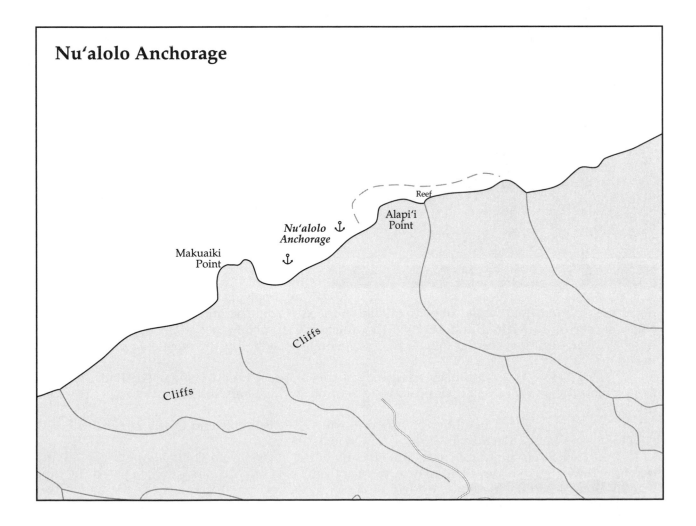

POLIHALE ANCHORAGE
CHART #19381
LAT. N22° 06.140 LONG. 159° 45.081 (ANCHORAGE)

When going counterclockwise around the island from Hāʻena Anchorage, you are treated to the entire length of the indescribably beautiful Nā Pali Coast. The Nā Pali begins just past Kaʻīlio Point and lovely Kēʻē Bay. Interspersed among the gloriously green ridges and peaks and valleys, set off by exposed strips of bright red volcanic soil, are dozens of waterfalls, many cascading into the ocean from a great height while others high above fall into unseen caverns and disappear. Local lore says that after a good rainy season you should be able to count more than 170 waterfalls on the Nā Pali Coast.

At the northeast end of Polihale Beach, the cliffs make a turn inland, giving way to one of the longest expanses of white sand beach in all Hawaiʻi. Beginning with the 2.25-mile Polihale, the beach skirts the Mānā Plain for 15 miles, all the way to Kekaha. Mammoth sand dunes, some as high as 50-100 feet, separate the beach from the plain. Perhaps better known than the name *Polihale* is *Barking Sands,* the beach at the southwest end of Polihale State Park, which the Hawaiians called the "Sounding Sand of Nohili," or *Ke one kani o Nohili.* When this unusual sand is moved by the wind or an object, it makes a unique sound, sounding to some like the dull woofing of a dog, to others like singing.

A young woman of Hawaiʻi

The Hawaiians had another explanation for some of the sounds the sand makes. They believed ghosts haunted Keonekani o Nohili. In one legend those ghosts are the warriors from Kauaʻi and from Oʻahu who were killed in a battle for the beautiful queen Leilani. The lagoon behind the reef where Leilani bathed is still called *Queen's Pond;* it is the best swimming spot at Polihale. Polihale ("house bosom") is memorialized in chants and songs for its *pahapaha* ("sea lettuce"), highly favored for *lei* because its green color can be revived by immersion in salt water. Pele's older sister, Namakaokahaʻi, is credited with introducing the practice.

Polihale Anchorage has much to recommend it. Some boaters go there to get away, knowing that they will almost certainly never see another boat while they are anchored there. From the anchorage on a clear day, you can look across to Niʻihau and Lehua. The quiet in the anchorage will generally be broken at dusk by the bleating of the feral goats climbing along the slopes at the northeast terminus of the beach.

Long before the goats took occupancy of this slope, it was the site of the Polihale Heiau, from which the souls of fallen warriors were sent off into eternity to the drumbeat of the *kāhuna.*

A wholly modern sending off may occur at the southwest end of the beach, where the Pacific Missile Range Facility at Barking Sands tests missiles.

No missile, though, can match the beauty of the sunset from Polihale Anchorage. With a perfectly unobstructed view, you may have one of your best opportunities ever to catch the much sought after "green flash" that is evident on a cloudless horizon at the moment the barest tip of the sun disappears into the ocean.

APPROACH

Recognizing the anchorage is a matter of finding the place where the cliffs no longer rise straight up out of the water and where the white sand beach stretching as far as the eye can see commences. Polihale Beach begins 5 miles from Nu'alolo. Proceeding clockwise around the island, you will travel about 20 miles beyond Port Allen to reach Polihale.

ANCHORAGE

The best anchorage is in the lee of the cliffs at the northeast end of Polihale Beach in 20-30 feet of water, 150-200 feet offshore. Even though most of the bottom is sand, watch for the few patches of coral and rock.

The anchorage most often used, though, is not off Polihale at all but is .50 mile north of the beach at the little cove known as *Treasure Beach*. In tradewind conditions, in fact, all the area just north of Polihale Beach is in the lee of the island and could thus be used as an anchorage.

Polihale is a good place to drop a hook, but since it is only a roadstead, the motion can be rolly if any swell develops. You should be ready to depart if a west or north swell begins.

FACILITIES

Restrooms
Showers (cold water)

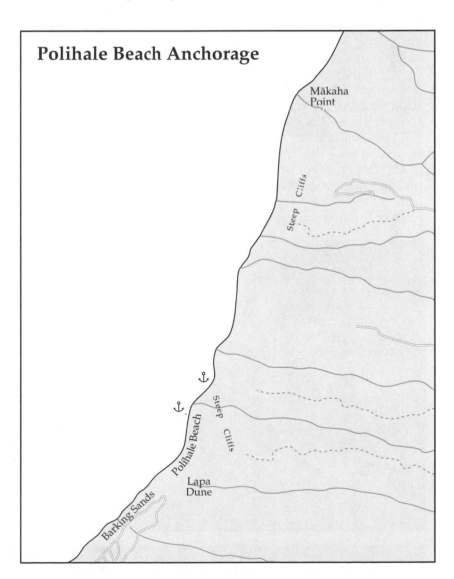

Polihale Beach Anchorage

Mākaha Point

Steep Cliffs

Steep Cliffs

Polihale Beach

Lapa Dune

Barking Sands

PORT ALLEN HARBOR
CHART #19381, 19382
LAT. N21° 53.980 LONG. W159° 35.650 (END OF BREAKWATER)

Another 20 miles counterclockwise around the island from Polihale is Port Allen, a noteworthy stop because it has one of the two small boat harbors on the island. Before 1909 this site in Hanapēpē (meaning "crushed bay," for the landslides common here) was called 'Ele'ele Landing.

Samuel C. Allen, a Honolulu businessman who financed much of the improvement to the harbor and for whom the harbor is named, had hoped this port would become the principal harbor on the island, but the U. S. Army Corps of Engineers recommended Nāwiliwili as the site of major construction. The Kaua'i Railway Company owned Port Allen Harbor until the early 1930s. Congress authorized improvements to the harbor in 1935 and again in 1948. In 1982 Hurricane 'Iwa completely destroyed the facilities at the Port Allen Small Boat Harbor. The state rebuilt the harbor in 1985.

This harbor has good protection from all except south winds, but an uncomfortable surge develops when a south swell is running. Still, despite the surge, once you've secured your boat in a slip here, you will surely enjoy Port Allen and the nearby towns of 'Ele'ele and Hanapēpē.

Because of the constant runoff in the bay, swimming and snorkeling are not popular inside Hanapēpē Bay. However, the best swimming, snorkeling, and windsurfing sites on this end of the island are at Salt Pond Beach County Park, on the other side of the airport west of the bay. Scuba diving and surfing are also good at Salt Pond under the right weather conditions.

This park merits a visit also because nearby are the only salt ponds still in use in the Hawaiian Islands. Local Hawaiians work the salt ponds, using the same methods their forebears used for hundreds of years, resulting in salt with a reddish cast that comes from particles of the red soil along this coast. The salt, called *alae*, is not pure enough to have commercial value, but the Hawaiians prize it precisely for its unique qualities.

Across the Hanapēpē River Bridge from the harbor is historic Old Hanapēpē, once one of the largest communities on Kaua'i. In the second half of the 19th Century Chinese farmers planted rice in the valley where the Hawaiians had cultivated taro for generations. Stores and other commercial ventures sprang up in Hanapēpē; at one time it had as many as 60 stores, as well as the largest airstrip on the island.

Harbor entrance at Port Allen

A road sign at the edge of town welcomes visitors to Hanapēpē, "Kauai's Biggest Little Town"; fortunately, the "Biggest" describes only the charm of this rustic little town and the monkey pod tree spreading its blossoming branches in a towering canopy from one side of the street into town to the other. On the main street through Old Hanapēpē the false front buildings retain their look of another era so convincingly that this street was the set for the films *The Thornbirds* and *Flight of the Intruder*. Behind these false fronts today are arts and crafts shops and restaurants. You should not be put off by this apparent appeal to tourists, however. Old Hanapēpē streets remain surprisingly quiet.

In the moist valley the rice fields are gone, the rice farmers unable to compete with California rice growers, and taro is once again king. A *poi* mill nearby processes the taro harvest.

APPROACH

Port Allen is in the middle of the south coast of Kaua'i. A light on Pū'olo Point to the west of the entrance, a buoy in the center of the bay, and a light on the end of the breakwater to the east make identifying the harbor straightforward. A number of fuel tanks are prominent on the point of land just east of the harbor entrance, and a large pinkish-colored warehouse with a rust-colored roof sits in the harbor on the starboard side just inside the breakwater.

Proceeding counterclockwise around the island, Port Allen is almost exactly 20 miles from the anchorage at Polihale. Clockwise from Nāwiliwili, Port Allen is about 17.5 miles.

NOTE: Boaters passing by the Pacific Missile Range at Barking Sands, on the extreme western end of the island, should check with the facility before transiting this restricted area. If personnel at the Range have an activity scheduled, they may ask you to time your passage at a later hour for your safety.

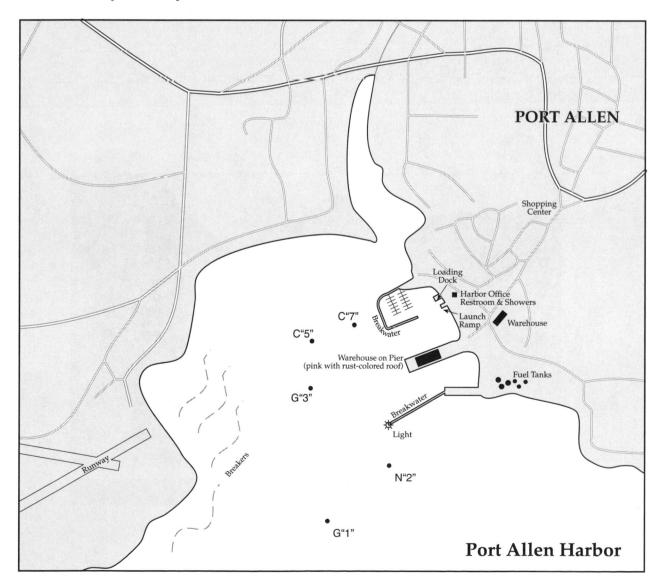

Port Allen Harbor

ANCHORAGE AND BERTHING

The small boat harbor is on the eastern side of the harbor immediately behind the warehouse. You may tie up temporarily at the loading dock to starboard after entering the small boat harbor while getting a slip assignment from the harbormaster. Although the Port Allen Small Boat Harbor is relatively small, the harbormaster can usually find visiting boaters a slip for a few days.

The harbormaster responsible for Port Allen is also responsible for other harbors, so he may not be on-site when you arrive. He asks boaters who plan to stop at Port Allen to call ahead a few days so he can give them slip assignments before they come in. Although he is in the office at other times, the only time you can be relatively certain of catching him is between 0745 and 0845.

Some boaters have anchored northwest of Buoy "5" to the west of the small boat harbor, but the Port Allen harbormaster strongly recommends against doing so. Anchors commonly drag there, and some boats have washed ashore as a result.

Pacific Missile Range	808-335-4667 or VHF 16
Port Allen Harbormaster	808-335-5361 (hours 0745-0845)

FACILITIES

Bank	Post Office
Electricity	Restaurants
Fuel (diesel by truck; gasoline by jerry jug)	Restrooms
Grocery Store	Shopping Center
Medical Clinic	Showers (cold)
Pharmacy	Water

Waimea Gulch, Kaua'i

WAHIAWA BAY
CHART #19381
LAT. N21° 53.845 LONG. W159° 34.780 (ENTRANCE)

Cruising boaters rarely stop at Wahiawa, perhaps because it is so close to Port Allen. But for a getaway to an isolated bay, Wahiawa is unsurpassed. The little beach at the head of the bay begs for exploration, and the bougainvillea growing along the cliffs to the east and west is a feast for the eyes.

The anchorage at Wahiawa

Wahiawa, only 150 yards wide and 400 yards deep, gives one a wonderful sense of seclusion. In addition, the small size and location provide excellent protection except from south winds and swells, producing an ideal anchorage on most summer and winter days and nights for the boater who wants simply to bask in the beauties of this sweet little bay.

Land access to the beach is along a sugar cane road on the property of the McBryde Sugar Company, so you'll see no more than a few people on the beach, taking advantage of its excellent conditions for swimming, snorkeling, and fishing.

Both sugar and coffee grow on the wide plain between Port Allen and Nahunakuea Point. The McByrde Sugar Mill is at Numila, a mile up the road from the bay. Before sugar and coffee proved more profitable than taro, the taro terraces of the Wahiawa *ahupua'a* ("land division") once extended all the way down to the mouth of the Wahiawa River.

In earlier times, this land division, river, and bay were called *Ahulua*, perhaps referring to two shrines that might have been here. Later, the name became *Wahiawa* ("milkfish place") because of a stone basin in the valley where milkfish the fishermen had caught were kept alive until they were eaten. This legendary stone, as well as others, has been preserved in Kukui o Lono Park in Kalāheo, a few miles north of the bay.

APPROACH

Wahiawa is .90 mile to the east of the entrance buoy at Port Allen Harbor. On either side of the entrance to Wahiawa are 60-foot reddish-brown bluffs. Waves break on rocks at the base of these bluffs, warning boaters to keep to the middle. Water depth in the entrance is about 25 feet, but that shallows gradually to 8-10 feet in the middle of the bay. Local boaters say five or six boats can anchor in this bay at the same time, but we think a more comfortable maximum is three boats unless the boats are rafted up.

Wahiawa is a superb destination for seclusion and relaxation but not so good for any extensive sight-seeing. Behind the beach and the trees is a gravel pit through which you would have to walk to get to the road leading to Numila, the nearest small town.

ANCHORAGE

The middle of the bay is the best spot to drop your anchor. If someone already has that spot when you arrive (a remote possibility), you can easily find a comfortable anchorage farther into the bay or out closer to the entrance.

Wahaiwa has a mud and sand bottom that provides good holding. You will be anchoring in only 10-20 feet of calm water, so you'll not have to let out a tremendous amount of anchor rode to be secure.

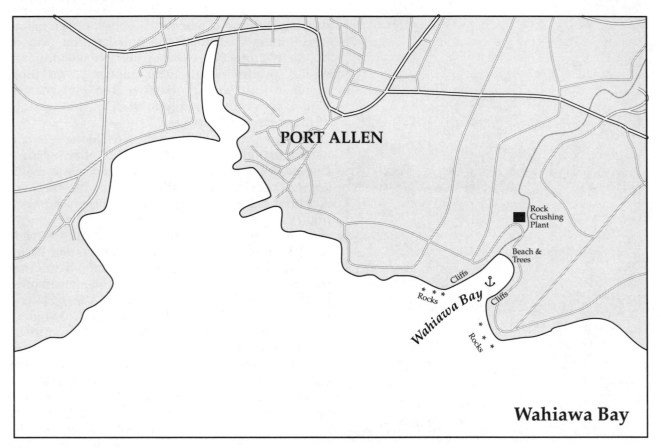

PORT ALLEN

Rock
Crushing
Plant

Beach &
Trees

Cliffs

Rocks

Wahiawa Bay

Cliffs

Rocks

Wahiawa Bay

KUKUI'ULA BAY
CHART # 19381
LAT. N21° 53.160 LONG. 159° 29.585 (ANCHORAGE)

Kukui'ula Bay is located on the south coast of Kaua'i near Po'ipū, the most popular tourist area on the island. Blue skies and warm weather prevail on this coast. Kukui'ula ("red light") may have been so named because the early Hawaiians built beach fires here to signal boats into the bay. An ancient *heiau* of the same name is near Makahū'ena Point.

With an entrance width of 150 yards and an inland extent of 300 yards, Kukui'ula can accommodate no more than 8 or 9 boats. On a typical day in Kukui'ula, 9 boats, 2 of them large multi-hull charter sailboats, are on permanent moorings, so little anchoring space remains for visiting boats. Some boaters do anchor for a day or two at Kukui'ula, but they must anchor outside the protection of the breakwater. If you do go to this charming bay, plan to arrive early enough so that, if you cannot find a secure spot, you'll have time to go on to Port Allen, Wahiawa, or Nāwiliwili.

Besides the beauty of Kukui'ula Bay, you'll find many other attractions to this anchorage. The coastline between Lāwa'i, west of Kukui'ula, and Po'ipū to the east has some of the best snorkeling and sport diving on the island. Surfing on the reef outside the breakwater is also good. For swimming, the beach in the bay is but one possibility. Around Ka'iwa Point, at the west end of the bay, is Lāwa'i Bay, with a wide crescent beach where both swimming and snorkeling are good. You can follow an ancient Hawaiian shoreline trail along the low cliffs from Spouting Horn Beach Park to get to this beach.

Kukui'ula Bay

Spouting Horn is a blowhole whose mournful sounds, according to legend, emanate from a *mo'o,* or lizard-man. As he was returning from Ni'ihau, the *mo'o* learned of the deaths of his two sisters. His eyes blinded by tears, he missed his landing and was trapped forever in the blowhole. Whenever high surf forces water through the narrow chimney in the roof of the lava tube, you can still hear his voice.

The nearest town is Kōloa, about 2 miles north of Kukui'ula. Old Town Kōloa has been carefully restored, including the wooden sidewalks and western-style store fronts of the plantation era. Across the street from these buildings still stands the chimney of the first commercial sugar plantation in Hawai'i, Ladd & Company, which began operation here in 1835. Kōloa is notable, too, for its number of old churches: St. Raphael's Roman Catholic Church, founded in 1841; the Koloa Church, built in 1859; and the Hongwanji Mission, built in 1910 by master carpenters from Japan.

APPROACH

From the entrance buoy at Port Allen to Kukui'ula Bay is 5.8 miles to the east, and from Makahū'ena Point to Kukui'ula Bay is 2.8 miles to the west. When within 1-2 miles of the entrance, you can see the Spouting Horn along the shore .25 mile west of the bay. A red light on a white pole at the end of the breakwater will also help you recognize the anchorage area at Kukui'ula Bay.

ANCHORAGE

If your boat is small enough, you might be able to find a spot to anchor among the boats moored there. Don't expect an exceptionally calm anchorage at Kukui'ula. Even behind the breakwater the surge keeps boats moving. In fact, the Port Allen Harbormaster recommends using extreme caution when anchoring at Kukui'ula because of the surge and the obstructions underwater. If you do attempt to go inside the breakwater, proceed dead slow.

You can anchor at the entrance to Kukui'ula if you fail to find enough room behind the breakwater. In calm winds or light trades, anchoring at the entrance will be fine, but if a south swell is running or even if an east swell is wrapping around Makahū'ena Point, you'll not want to be anchored in this bay.

Kukui'ula Bay has water depths ranging from 10-20 feet. The bottom is primarily sand, but watch closely for the patches of rock and coral when you drop your anchor.

FACILITIES

Launch Ramp	Showers (cold water)
Telephone	Restrooms

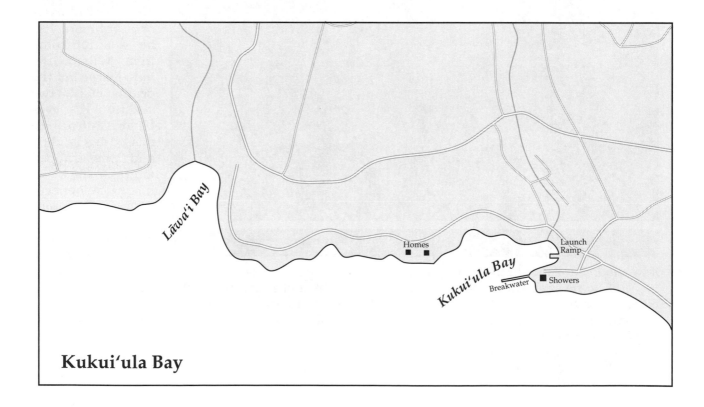

Kukui'ula Bay

THE ISLAND OF NI'IHAU

THE LAST HAWAIIAN ISLAND

Landing at Ni'ihau

"The ground through which I passed was in a state of nature, very strong, and the soil seemed poor. It was, however, covered with shrubs and plants, some of which perfumed the air with a more delicious fragrance than I had met with at any of the other islands visited by us in this ocean." (Captain James Cook, 1779)

Ni‘ihau

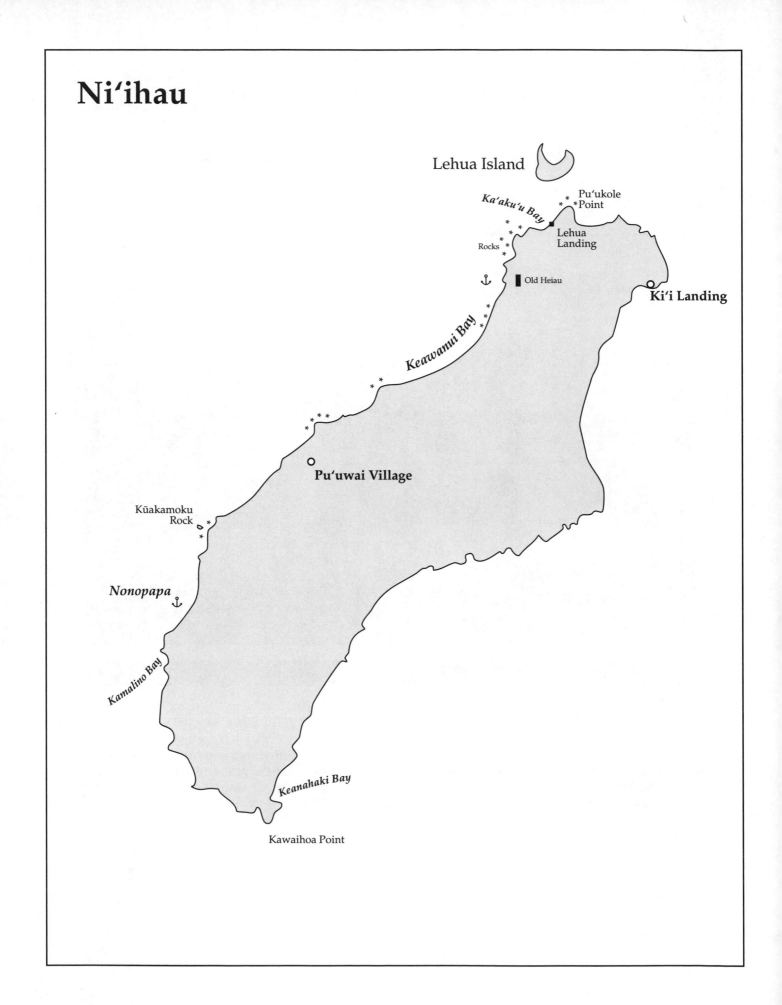

Lehua Island

Ka‘aku‘u Bay

Pu‘ukole
* *Point

Rocks

Lehua
Landing

⚓

Old Heiau

Ki‘i Landing

Keawanui Bay

Pu‘uwai Village

Kūakamoku
Rock

Nonopapa

⚓

Kamalino Bay

Keanahaki Bay

Kawaihoa Point

Ni'ihau, the only privately owned island in the Hawaiian Chain, has some limitations as a cruising destination. Nevertheless, some local Hawaiian boaters tout its many appeals. Needless to say, it is secluded. If you go there, you almost certainly won't see another boater anywhere around the island. You'll see instead an island of distinct beauty and, off its shores, Hawaiian monk seals and Hawaiian green sea turtles, both endangered species. Ni'ihau and Lehua, the small uninhabited island .75 mile off the north shore, have many excellent sites for fishing, swimming, snorkeling, and surfing.

Though arid and somewhat barren, Ni'ihau has several lovely bays with deep white sand beaches. Oddly enough, it also has the two largest natural lakes in the state, Hālāli'i and Halulu. It also has two distinguishing geologic features that compare to Diamond Head and Koko Head on O'ahu. These two, called Kawaihoa and Lē'ahi (also the Hawaiian names for the two heads on O'ahu), are celebrated in song as "the beautiful places of Ni'ihau." Some boaters know Kawaihoa, the massive 500-foot high tuff cone, as "South Point."

The unfortunate part about Ni'ihau as a destination is that outsiders, including boaters, are not allowed to go ashore for any reason. In 1863 King Kamehameha IV sold Ni'ihau to Mrs. Elizabeth McHutchison Sinclair, the matriarch of a family of thirteen who came to Hawai'i from New Zealand. When Aubrey Robinson, a nephew of Mrs. Sinclair's son, took over the management of the island in 1883, he decided to restrict access to the island in order to preserve the Hawaiian language and culture. Anyone going ashore on the island will be arrested.

Whether access to Ni'ihau will remain restricted is often debated. Since 1973, Hawaiian beaches inland to the vegetation line have by law belonged to the public. The owners of the island claim their deed is unique, giving them ownership of all the land on the island. If the island is sold, as is rumored, a new deed would surely settle the debate.

Tropicbird over Ni'ihau, "the island of the birds"

Subsequent to her acquisition of Ni'ihau, Mrs. Sinclair purchased thousands of acres of land on Kaua'i, including the 21,844-acre Makaweli *ahupua'a* (a land division, generally extending from the sea to the mountains). Today, the family holdings include the Makaweli Ranch, the Ni'ihau Ranch, the Olokele Sugar Mill, and the Gay and Robinson Sugar Company, all managed from the family headquarters at Makaweli.

The slightly more than 250 residents of Ni'ihau, most of them of Hawaiian ethnicity, live in the village of Pu'uwai, near the southwest end of the island. They live simple rural lives similar to those of their ancestors. Though the language of instruction in the elementary school on Ni'ihau is English, the residents regularly speak Hawaiian. The island has no community electricity and no telephones, though residents have generators and two-way radios; the drinking water comes from cisterns or, in a dry season, from shallow wells.

The people on the island work on the ranch as their ancestors in the 19th and 20th centuries did, herding cattle and sheep, harvesting honey, and making charcoal from *kiawe* wood. They fish and pick *opihi* (limpits), a Hawaiian delicacy usually eaten raw. The exquisite shell *lei* they make from the tiny shells washed up on the shores of the beaches, particularly at Keawenui, are noted throughout the Islands.

Ni'ihau, as well as the two uninhabited islands off its shores, Lehua and Ka'ula, is part of the county of Kaua'i, reflecting a history of political and cultural links between these two islands. In Hawaiian lore, these connections are as ancient as the islands themselves. When Papa, the Hawaiian earth mother, gave birth to Kaua'i, Ni'ihau came out as the afterbirth. Geologists, too, believe in an ancient connection between Kaua'i and Ni'ihau, theorizing that the two islands, Ni'ihau then much larger than it is now, were once joined.

The inhabitants of these two islands have also shared some pronunciations of the Hawaiian language that are unique in the Hawaiian Islands. These differences suggest to some linguists an earlier settlement on the windward islands from Central Polynesia, probably from the Marquesas, before the later arrival of the Tahitians to the other islands.

With only 17 miles separating the two closest points of the two islands, their residents

photo by Matt Klocek

Ni'ihau and Lehua from Keawanui Bay

have apparently always traveled freely back and forth, the people of Ni'ihau moving to Kaua'i when their island became too arid to sustain their villages.

Politically, too, Ni'ihau has apparently always had close ties to Kaua'i. In chants, the chiefs of Ni'ihau proudly trace their lineage back to the high, pure-blooded chiefs of Kaua'i. Thus connected to the chiefs of Kaua'i, those of Ni'ihau apparently acknowledged the sovereignty of the *mō'ī* (highest chief, or king) of Kaua'i and supported him against external foes.

Though few boats anchor off the coast of Ni'ihau now, such has not always been the case. When Captain James Cook discovered these islands he named the Sandwich Islands in 1778, he landed first at Waimea Bay, Kaua'i, where he found fresh water and provisions. After a few days a southerly storm with rain forced him to seek another anchorage, which he found off the west point of Ni'ihau, immediately south of Kamalino. Here, he gave the natives a ram and two ewes, a boar and a sow, and melon, pumpkin, and onion seeds.

After Cook's death, James King, who assumed command of the expedition, returned to Ni'ihau and found the anchorage at Nonopapa, north of Kamalino, to offer more protection. Later in the 18th Century other sailing ships came into Nonopapa, seeking provisions, and the bay became known as "Yam Bay," for, when the island had had sufficient rain, yams, sweet potatoes, sugar cane, and plantain grew abundantly.

In dry years, though, the island could not support even its own residents. When Captain George Vancouver landed here in 1783, he found that the island was barren and that most of the people had moved to Kaua'i.

Nonopapa Bay was the first choice of visiting captains seeking anchorage at Ni'ihau, but the Navy LCM that transports supplies from Makaweli, Kaua'i, lands at Ka'aku'u, or Lehua Landing, on the northwest coast. To the south of Ka'aku'u lies Keawanui Bay, at 3.5 miles long the longest bay on the island and the choice anchorage of some local cruising sailors.

When *kona* winds blow, sailors also anchor at Keanahaki, on the southeast corner of Ni'ihau. Here, on the low sea cliffs are the remains of several cottages of the Robinson family's former summer retreat.

Another possible anchorage is Ki'i Landing, at the north end of Pōlelo Beach, on the northeast coast. When the surf is too high for a safe landing at Lehua Landing, the landing craft can usually anchor safely at Ki'i because of the excellent protection in the lee of Kaunuopou Point.

APPROACH

To the north end of Ni'ihau from Port Allen, on the southern coast of Kaua'i, is 27 miles and from Hanalei, on the north coast, 35 miles. Generally, the trip to Ni'ihau is a fairly easy run, provided strong trades are not blowing. The return trip, however, can be rough. If you decide to visit the waters around Ni'ihau, plan to go when the weather forecast calls for light and variable trades.

Since the preferred anchorage on the island is at Keawanui Bay, on the northwest coastline, most boaters go between Lehua Island and Ni'ihau Island to get to the anchorage. The pass between the two islands has coral and coral heads close to Ni'ihau. Stay close to Lehua Island if you decide to use this pass to avoid the underwater obstructions. Some boaters recommend going around the south end of Ni'ihau and up the west side to the anchorage at Keawanui Bay.

ANCHORAGE

Although we did not anchor at Ni'ihau before this book went to press, the boaters with whom we spoke agreed that their favorite anchorage is Keawanui Bay, on the northwest coastline. One boater who has anchored here a number of times cautions boaters to be alert when entering this bay because the charted position of the island does not agree with the GPS coordinates. The coordinates in the heading for this section are this boater's GPS position when he was last anchored off Ni'ihau.

When anchoring, do not come into the anchorage from the north, for rocks are under the surface along this route. Instead, stay offshore about a mile until you are south of the anchorage; then proceed slowly until you are in less than 20 feet of water. The anchorage is west of the lava rock foundation of an old *heiau* behind the beach.

If this anchorage is uncomfortable, you can move to an anchorage in the lee of Kūakamoku Rock, some 8.0 miles along the coastline to the southwest, or off Nonopapa Beach, 1.5 miles farther. Ni'ihau has no protected bays, so take along your flopper stoppers.

MIDWAY ATOLL

NATIONAL WILDLIFE REFUGE

Feeding time on Sand Island

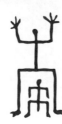

MIDWAY ATOLL
CHARTS #19480, 19481
LAT. N28° 11.640 LONG. W177° 21.380 (CHANNEL ENTRANCE)

Midway Atoll has only recently become a cruising destination. From 1940 to 1997 it was a military installation, and the atoll and its waters were off-limits to pleasure boaters. While it was under military jurisdiction, the atoll was known as the Midway Islands.

On June 30, 1997, the C5A aircraft carrying the last group of Navy personnel lifted off, leaving the islands in the hands of the U.S. Fish and Wildlife Service. The Fish and Wildlife Service has the responsibility to protect the wildlife on the atoll.

The Fish and Wildlife Service also has the responsibility of keeping the airport open, maintaining the infrastructure on the island, and providing accommodations and services for visitors to the atoll. To handle these responsibilities, the USFWS has a staff of approximately thirty to forty people on Sand Island at all times, including biologists, foreign nationals, and volunteers. In the near future the FAA will take over the maintenance and operation of the Midway Airport, an emergency stop for aircraft making the long flights between the U.S. and the Orient.

As a cruising destination, Midway Atoll is not for everyone. To begin with, the trip to Midway Atoll is 1,100 miles from Kaua'i, and that's the easy part. After leaving Midway, boaters will then face a long, hard trip back to Kaua'i, to the Mainland, or to some South Pacific destination. The shortest is the trip back to Kaua'i, a difficult upwind passage.

Another consideration is the fact that you will have to get permission from the Fish and Wildlife Service to make the trip and then follow the guidelines of the service. You must agree to stay outside the 20-fathom line as you pass by the islands and reefs in the chain northwest of Kaua'i, all of which are national wildlife refuges. Thus, the passage to Midway must be nonstop.

Gardiner Pinnacles

The restriction to stay outside the 20-fathom line, however, need not be an impediment to your seeing the other islands. The islands and atolls rise so precipitously from the sea that at 20 fathoms you will often be only a few hundred yards offshore. An impediment to seeing all eight of the islands will likely be one of timing. You may find, as we did, that you can't easily arrange your sailing schedule to pass by them all in the daylight. But you'll likely be able to see five or six.

Of the eight refuges, the first two you'll pass after leaving Kaua'i—Nihoa and Necker—are "high islands." You'll see hundreds of petrels, shearwaters, boobies, frigatebirds, terns, noddies, and tropicbirds swarming like bees above these mostly barren rocks.

The next refuge, French Frigate Shoals, is a low reef barely rising above sea level except for its one prominent pinnacle, named La Perouse after the French captain who discovered these shoals in 1786. Gardiner Pinnacles, 120 miles northwest of French Frigate Shoals, is the last of the high islands in the chain.

The remaining four refuges are all low. Maro Reef is a large, oval-shaped reef about 31 miles long and 18 miles wide, discovered in 1820 by the captain of the whaling ship *Maro*. Laysan and Lisianski are both small sand islands, where palm trees, vines, and bushes grow near the white sand beaches. Thousands of seabirds nest on these latter two islands, and millions of flies keep the birds company. Lisianski was named for the Russian captain whose ship the *Neva* went on the reef here in 1805. The last of the refuges before you reach Midway Atoll is Pearl and Hermes Reef, a large oval-shaped atoll 40 miles in circumference. This reef was discovered when two British whaling ships, the *Pearl* and the *Hermes,* went aground on the coral reefs here on the same night in 1822.

Throughout the Hawaiian archipelago northwest of Kaua'i, only Nihoa and Necker show definite signs of having once been inhabited by early Hawaiians.

World War II anti-aircraft gun and gooneys on Eastern Island

The discovery of Midway Atoll in 1857 was a direct result of the Guano Act passed by the U.S. Congress in 1856. This act claimed for the United States any previously unclaimed islands with guano deposits. The search for significant deposits of guano, a valuable source of fertilizer, drew Captain N. C. Brooks (originally *Middlebrooks*) to Midway, though the atoll's guano deposits turned out to be disappointingly meager. Nevertheless, the United States annexed the atoll in 1867.

The seabird eggs and feathers on the three small islands comprising Midway Atoll—Sand, Eastern, and Spit—proved attractive to Japanese sailors, so, to protect the wildlife, President Theodore Roosevelt placed Midway under the jurisdiction of the U.S. Navy in 1903.

Between 1903 and 1941 Midway figured in two other commercial ventures. The Commercial Pacific Cable Company completed a cable station on Midway in 1903, providing the last link in the Pacific cable between the United States and the Philippines. Four bungalows built by the company in 1905 remain on Sand Island.

In the second venture, Pan American World Airways established a fuel stop for its Clipper seaplanes on Midway in 1935. Though the era of the Clipper seaplanes, flying between San Francisco and Hong Kong, was short-lived, ending with the onset of World War II, Midway has continued to be a fuel stop for both government and private planes flying between the Americas and Asia.

The military history of the atoll will fascinate many boaters. Pillboxes, anti-aircraft artillery, underground concrete bunkers, and a few shrapnel holes in the old seaplane hangar are about all that remain to remind visitors of the role this atoll played in the defense of the Pacific. But these are sufficient to imbue the islands with a World War II atmosphere. The Fish and Wildlife personnel show films made during the war that help remind visitors of the importance of Midway to the outcome of the war in the Pacific.

For many boaters the birds and animals on the islands will make the trip worthwhile. The islands belong to the wildlife. The number of species of sea birds staggers the imagination:

Laysan albatross (gooney birds), black-footed albatross, frigate birds, booby birds, white terns, sooty terns, gray terns, brown noddies, black noddies, tropic birds, and more. Many of these birds have so little fear they will let people walk up to them.

The Laysan albatrosses, or gooney birds, reign on Sand Island from November, when over 400,000 nesting pairs begin to return to the island, to July, when the last of the year's crop of chicks take to the air. While on the island, the gooneys have so little fear of people that they wander everywhere—on all the streets and sidewalks, into yards and gardens, and through any open doors. The only place they're not tolerated is on the runway when a plane is landing or taking off, where the danger to both birds and plane is great.

Endangered monk seals and threatened Hawaiian green sea turtles and a large pod of spinner dolphins reside here. The seals loll on the beaches when they're not swimming in the lagoons, and the green sea turtles cruise near the docks and beaches. The large pod of spinner dolphins spend their days resting in the protection of the atoll after hunting for food all night in the open ocean outside the reef.

Cruising sailors who anchor at Midway will have generally free access to Sand Island, though some beaches may be restricted for the protection of the monk seals. Old Navy roads crisscross the island, wonderful trails for hiking or biking. (You can rent vintage bicycles on Midway if you don't have your own.) The swimming beach on the north side of the island, North Beach, is a tropical fantasy: almost a mile of powdery white sand, unsullied by even the smallest rocks or gravel, gently curving around aquamarine and sapphire water so clear you can see the sand or coral bottom at 40 or 50 feet, and generally unoccupied.

Eastern Island, once covered with non-native trees, radio towers, and other World War II structures, has now been returned to its natural state. Exclusively a wildlife refuge now, Eastern Island hosts hundreds of red-footed boobies and frigatebirds nesting in the beach heliotrope and sooty terns, gray-backed terns, brown noddies, and wedge-tailed shearwaters nesting on or under the ground.

The wide white sands of North Beach

The Fish and Wildlife Service, with only a few people to watch out for millions of birds, seals, turtles, fish, and other critters, has little time to spend with visitors. If USFWS personnel have planned a trip into the lagoon or to the reef while you are visiting Midway, however, you might be invited to accompany them in your own sportboat, assuming you have expressed an interest. The reef is remarkably healthy and beautiful, despite all that has been dumped, dropped, or sunk in these waters over the past century. You'll see a number of the more than 200 species of tropical fish that live inside the lagoon, among them the colorful parrotfish, angels, butterflies, wrasses, and damsels.

The unique wildlife species at Midway are matched by the unique geography. This spectacular atoll is made up of three small, remote tropical islands roughly midway between Japan and the West Coast of the USA. It is one of the most isolated places on earth, one that will probably never be popular among the cruising community because it's not en route to anywhere. Those dedicated cruisers who do visit Midway Atoll will go there because they want to see these islands, not because the Atoll is a convenient place to refuel and reprovision.

In many ways the appearance of the "town" on Sand Island is as American as one can imagine, with its infrastructure devised by the U.S. Navy during its 56 years of tenure at

Midway. The white two-storey houses where some of the USFWS employees live, formerly the officers' quarters, could have come right out of a Norman Rockwell painting; the cinder-block barracks and administrative buildings remaining for the use of the USFWS are the same nondescript structures of WW II vintage found on any U.S. military base. The asphalt streets have street signs identifying them with the names of American heroes: Roosevelt, Nimitz, Halsey, and Cannon.

At the Midway Mall (generously called a *mall*) you'll not find any of those icons of American culture such as McDonald's or Walmart, but you'll find the just-as-American bowling alley; the All Hands Bar (no alcoholic drinks are served on Midway), having a game room with free access to pool and Ping-Pong tables, shuffleboard, foose ball, and a dart board; a barbershop open one night a week; and a small market where you can purchase snacks, drinks, and a few necessities such as laundry detergent. Across the street from the mall are a gymnasium with showers and sauna and a tennis court, all available free of charge to both residents and visitors.

Cyclists must yield right of way to gooneys

Most of the island's residents eat their meals at the Clipper House, a facility with a postcard-perfect view of North Beach. Visitors are invited to take their meals with the staff at Clipper House if they wish. The charge for three meals a day is currently $32 per person, but this charge will be pro-rated on days when the visitors are arriving or departing. The USFWS employees welcome visiting boaters and accommodate their wishes whenever they can, but their busy schedules prevent them from offering any special services, such as tours, to visitors. The foreign nationals who work at the restaurant, the various shops, and the airport are remarkably cheerful and enthusiastic, despite their isolation from family and friends and culture for at least eleven months of the year. The people add to the uniqueness of this tropical island.

In planning a trip to Midway, you must carefully consider the weather because it will impact the time of year of the scheduled trip. Unfortunately, what many people would find among the most exciting events on Midway—the mating and nesting of over 400,000 pairs of Laysan albatrosses, or gooneys—occurs during the winter and spring, when weather conditions suggest boaters not schedule a trip to the atoll.

The rainy season in the Hawaiian chain generally runs from November through April. Winds during those months will often be stronger and more northerly than during the remainder of the year, making the trip a beat instead of a downhill run and increasing the possibility of storms with gale-force winds.

The weather on the atoll will be the same, of course. Much of the 42 inches of average annual rainfall on Midway falls between November and April. These months are also cooler (though certainly not cold) and windier.

With these weather considerations in mind, most boaters will schedule their visits during the months of May through September. Of these months, perhaps May and June are preferable because many of the adult and juvenile gooney birds are still on the islands. Many other species of birds

The anchorage in the Inner Harbor

will still be on the islands after all the gooneys have departed, but that may be little consolation to most visitors, who want to see the fabled and fascinating gooneys.

APPROACH

To visit Midway Atoll, you'll most likely depart from Kaua'i. You can't stop at any of the islands and reefs enroute to Midway, but you can use them for waypoints and take pictures of them as you pass by.

Even though some traditionalists will use a sextant as they make the trip to Midway, most will use a GPS. Before we departed from Kaua'i, we programmed our GPS with a route that included a waypoint for each island and reef enroute. Virtually every 24 hours we passed a waypoint, although we passed some during the night. Having each island and reef in the GPS as a waypoint enabled us to know with some certainty that we wouldn't accidentally encounter one too closely some dark night.

All that is absolutely required, of course, is the waypoint for Midway Atoll. The channel entrance is on the south side of the atoll. You can easily spot the channel between Sand and Eastern islands by sailing west on the south side of the atoll until the gap between the two islands comes into view. Stay south of the atoll at least a mile until the channel markers and range markers become evident; then proceed up the channel following a course of 341° mag.

Warships transited the channel at Midway for over 50 years, so you should have no trouble getting safely through the reef and into the anchorage. Buoys G"1" and G"2" are located in shallow water where the channel goes through the reef. The size of the channel—150 yards wide and 37 feet deep—makes the entry into Midway Atoll easy. The rusted skeleton of a shipwrecked barge on the starboard side of the channel is visible from a mile or two at sea, even before you can see the buoys or range marks.

Boaters entering the atoll should turn to port after passing Buoy 7. This turn is approximately .75 mile from the first buoys, "1" and "2," on the main channel. The breakwater protecting the Inner Harbor is approximately .25 mile from the center of the entrance channel.

ANCHORAGE

No berthing facilities exist at Midway Atoll, though the USFWS has 6 moorings in the inner harbor for visiting boats. The charge for tying up here is $1 per foot per day. An additional charge of $5 per day per person must be paid for Park fees (a maximum of $25 per person while at the Refuge). At first glance, the fees might seem exorbitant, but the pleasure of being moored at Sand Island in the huge Inner Harbor, tucked in behind the ironwood trees and the encircling reef, will surely justify the expense.

The USFWS manager requests that, before you head for Midway, you contact the Honolulu office or the Midway office to give the personnel there your approximate date of arrival and to obtain special instructions. At that time you will be asked to agree not to stop at any of the islands in the Hawaiian chain between Kaua'i and Midway. Another request is that you enter the channel at Sand Island only during daylight hours, standing off the entrance until daylight if necessary. At the entrance, call on VHF 16 for final instructions for entering the channel and the moorage in the Inner Basin.

As soon as your boat is tied to a mooring, a USFWS official will set up a time for you and your crew to receive an orientation about the Atoll. You can land your dinghy at the small dock in the west end of the Inner Harbor. The manager of the Preserve will also come aboard your boat to inspect for pests. The USFWS is determined to avoid the accidental introduction of any pests that might precipitate an ecological disaster on any of the islands it protects. NO PETS ARE ALLOWED ON THE ISLANDS.

MAKING THE RETURN PASSAGE FROM MIDWAY

Some who visit Midway will want to return to Kaua'i or O'ahu. The 1,100-mile trip to

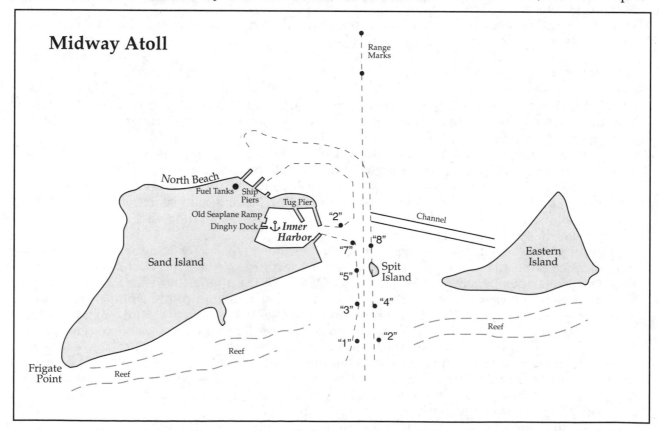

weather will certainly be less enjoyable than the outward leg. Despite the long upwind leg, though, the rigors of the passage are somewhat lessened by the generally light winds, typically 10-18 knots, in the summer months.

When we departed from Midway, we made the most of a rare three-day south wind, heading straight east on the 28th parallel. After those first three days, our goal was to make as much easting as we could, tacking northeast whenever the winds came directly out of the southeast and east but maintaining our track between the 28th and the 30th parallels of latitude for as long as possible. Eventually, when we were faced with the inescapable steady east wind, we had made enough easting to fetch Kaua'i without tacking.

MAKING THE DECISION TO VISIT MIDWAY ATOLL

Because of the distance alone, you should not undertake a trip to Midway without considerable planning. During the 1,100-mile trip from Kaua'i to the atoll, for example, boaters will consume most of their fresh provisions—fruits, vegetables, and dairy products. Almost no replacement provisions will be available at Midway for the trip back to Kaua'i or another destination.

The USFWS understands that sailboats visiting the island might be low on diesel fuel when they arrive, and, although the Service isn't in the business of selling fuel, visiting boaters are able to purchase enough to get them safely to their next destination. Transporting fuel to Midway Atoll is expensive and difficult, however, so the current charge is $5 a gallon. By the way, the fuel you fill your tanks with will be JP-5 jet fuel. Although some boaters have told us they don't like to put jet fuel into their tanks, our old Ford Lehman loved the stuff, and we'll be glad to fill our tanks with it once again when we return.

The second problem with the location of the islands is the destination of the boat after it departs from Midway if the boat doesn't return to Kaua'i. For example, from Midway to Seattle, San Francisco, or Los Angeles is over 3,000 miles, making the total trip from Kaua'i to the final destination about 4,000 miles. That's a long trip, especially so considering that you'll make no stops enroute except for Midway.

Because of the distance between Kaua'i and the final destination and the absence of repairs and supplies enroute, only boats that are in excellent condition should be taken on the trip.

Finally, boaters who would like to embark on the trip to Midway should think seriously about the USFWS restrictions and requirements before committing to the trip.

U.S. Fish and Wildlife Service, Honolulu office   808-782-5940
U.S. Fish and Wildlife Service, Midway Atoll 808-674-8237x100 and
                                     808-693-8041 x102

FACILITIES

Fuel (under 100 gallons)	Restrooms
Internet	Showers
Laundromat	Souvenirs
Medical Clinic (PA only)	Telephone
Mini-mini-market (limited hours)	Water
Restaurants	

A NOTE ON THE HAWAIIAN LANGUAGE

Though few children in the Hawaiian Islands today learn Hawaiian as their first, or native, language, it remains alive in chants, proverbs, poetical sayings, and even popular contemporary songs. It is the primary spoken language only on Niʻihau, the small privately owned island where the people have preserved much of the old Hawaiian way of life.

Linguists classify Hawaiian as a Polynesian language, closely related to the languages of Tahiti, the Marquesas, and other nearby island groups in the South Pacific. It apparently changed only slightly over the hundreds of years after the earliest settlers brought it from the islands to the south.

The most significant change came after Western contact. The Hawaiians had never had a written language, having preserved their histories, genealogies, poems and songs, and myths in a rich oral form. To communicate their religious beliefs more widely to the Hawaiians, the American missionaries soon began to develop an alphabet for the language. Because the missionaries didn't agree on the the equivalent English letters to represent some sounds of the language, they met in 1823 and voted on the letters that would represent the Hawaiian language. This language-by-committee had the seven consonants—H, K, L, M, N, P, and W—and five vowels—A, E, I, O, and U—that we know today as the Hawaiian alphabet. Some scholars of Hawaiian culture and language contend that the ancient Hawaiians used other sounds that the missionaries could not detect.

The consonants have the same sound as in English, with the exception that the W sounds like a V when it follows a stressed vowel in the middle of a word. The vowels are pronounced as they are in the Romance languages—Italian or Spanish, for example. Spoken Hawaiian also includes the frequent use of a glottal stop, similar to the break in the exclamation "Uh-oh!" An *ʻokina* (ʻ) indicates this stop. Careful writers of the language also use a *kahakō*, or macron, a bar over a vowel (as over the "o" in *kahakō*) to indicate that it is a long vowel in this word.

Following are a few Hawaiian words that you will hear or see frequently in Hawaiʻi:

ʻaʻā. jagged fragments of clinker lava
ʻahi. Hawaiian tuna fishes, especially the yellow-fin
ahu. shrine made of pile of stones
ahupuaʻa. land division usually extending from the uplands to the sea
aliʻi. Hawaiian nobility
aloha. love, affection, mercy, sympathy, pity; kindness; greetings; farewell
ʻaumakua. family or personal gods; deified ancestors who might assume other shapes
ʻekahi. the number one
halalū. young of the akule, or big-eyed scad fish
hālau. long house, as for canoes or hula instruction
hale. house, building
haole. white person, American, English, Caucasian, formerly any foreigner
hapa. portion, fraction
hau. a lowland tree, with petals that change from yellow to dull red during the day
heiau. pre-Christian place of worship; shrine
holokū. long fitted dress with a yoke, usually with a train
holomū. long fitted dress, a combination of holokū and muʻumuʻu
honu. turtle
huki. to pull or tug
hukilau. a seine; to fish with the seine
hulihuli. to turn repeatedly; to barbecue
iʻa. fish
iki. small; slightly
ʻīlio. dog
imu. underground oven

ipo. sweetheart

kāhili. feather standard

kahuna. priest; sorcerer; magician; wizard

kalo. taro, a plant grown for food since ancient times

kālua. to bake in the imu

kama'āina. native born; resident of Hawai'i

kāne. male; husband

kapa. tapa, as made from wauke or māmaki bark

kapu. taboo; prohibition

keiki. child; offspring

koa. the largest of native forest trees, a valuable lumber tree

koholā. whale

kōkua. help; aid; assistance

kona. leeward sides of Hawaiian Islands; leeward wind

kūkū. (also tūtū; often said affectionately) grandmother; grandfather; any relative or close friend of the grandparents' generation

kumu. teacher

kupua. demigod or cultural hero

kupuna. grandparent; ancestor

lehua. the flower of the 'ōhi'a tree

limu. edible seaweed; all kinds of underwater plants

loa. distant; long; tall; far; permanent

lomi lomi. massage; salmon or fish, usually raw, worked with the fingers, mixed with onions and seasoned

lua. the number two

mahalo. thanks; gratitude

mahimahi. dolphin fish; dorado

maile. a native twining shrub

makai. ocean (used when giving directions)

makani. wind

malihini. stranger; foreigner; newcomer

mana. supernatural or divine power

manō. shark

mauka. inland (used when giving directions)

mauna. mountain

Menehune. legendary race of small people who worked at night building fishponds, roads, temples

mele. song; anthem; chant

milo. a tree found on coasts; used for shade; the wood for calabashes

moana. ocean; open sea

mō'ī. sovereign; monarch; ruler

mo'o. lizard; reptile of any kind

mu'umu'u. a woman's loose gown,

nui. large; great; grand; important

ohana. family; social organization

one. sand; silt; poetical name for the land

ono. large mackerel-type fish

'ono. delicious

'opihi. limpits

'ōpakapaka. blue snapper

pāhoehoe. smooth, unbroken type of lava

pali. cliff

paniolo. cowboy

pau. finished

pāʻū. skirt worn by women horseback riders

poi. starchy food made from kalo, pounded and thinned with water

pono. goodness; uprightness

puaʻa. pig

puhi. eel

puka. hole; door; entrance; gate

pule oʻo. potent prayers

pūneʻe. movable couch

pūpū. relish; appetizer

ulua. certain species of crevalle, jack, or pompano

waʻa. canoe

wahine. woman

wai. fresh water

wiki. quick; fast

SELECTED BIBLIOGRAPHY

Atlas of Hawaii. 2nd ed. Department of Geography, U. of Hawaii. Honolulu: U of Hawaii, 1983,

Balder, A. P. *Marine Atlas of the Hawaiian Islands.* Honolulu: U of Hawaii, n.d.

Beckwith, Martha. Hawaiian Mythology. Honolulu: U of Hawaii, 1970. Orig. pub. Yale UP, 1940.

Bisignani, J. D. *Hawaii Handbook: The All-Island Guide* . 4th ed. Honolulu: Island Heritage Pub., 1995.

Chisholm, Craig. *Hawaiian Hiking Trails.* 8th ed. Lake Oswego, OR: Fernglen, 1994.

Clark, John R. K. *The Beaches of the Big Island.* Honolulu: U of Hawaii, 1985.

—-. *The Beaches of Kaua'i and Ni'ihau.* Honolulu: U of Hawaii, 1990.

—-. *The Beaches of Maui County.* Rev. ed. Honolulu: U of Hawaii, 1989.

—-. *The Beaches of O'ahu.* Honolulu: U of Hawaii, 1977.

Cox, J. Halley with Edward Stasack. *Hawaiian Petroglyphs.* Honolulu: Bishop Museum, 1988.

Cruising Guide for the Hawaiian Islands. ed. Arlo W. Fast & George Seberg. Honolulu: Pacific Writers Corp., 1980.

Daws, Gaven. *Shoal of Time: A History of the Hawaiian Islands.* Honolulu: U of Hawaii, 1968.

Dean, Love. *The Lighthouses of Hawai'i.* Honolulu: U of Hawaii, 1991.

Fornander, Abraham. *Ancient History of the Hawaiian People to the Times of Kamehameha I.* Honolulu: Mutual, 1996.

Hawaii. Leonard Lueras, ed. 2nd ed. Hong Kong: APA Productions (HK), 1980.

Hawaiian Reader, A. ed. A. Grove Day and Carl Stroven. Honolulu: Mutual, 1984.

Hinz, Earl L. *Landfalls of Paradise: Cruising Guide to the Pacific Islands.* 3rd ed. Honolulu: U of Hawaii, 1993.

Joesting, Edward. *Kauai: The Separate Kingdom.* Honolulu: U of Hawaii, 1987.

Kalakaua, David. The Legends and Myths of Hawai'i. Honolulu: Mutual, 1990.

Kumulipo, The. trans. Lilu'okalani. Kentfield, Ca: Pueo Press, 1997. Rpt. of first ed., 1897.

London, Jack. *Stories of Hawaii.* ed. A. Grove Day. Honolulu: Mutual, 1986. Rpt. of stories pub. in 1906, 1908, 1909, 1916.

Markell, Jeff. *The Sailor's Weather Guide.* Dobbs Ferry, NY: Sheridan House, 1995.

Oliver, Anthony Michael. *Hawaii Fact and Reference Book.* Honolulu: Mutual, 1995.

Pager, Sean. *Hawaii: Off the Beaten Path.* 2nd ed. Old Saybrook, CT.: Globe Pequot, 1995.

Pukui, Mary Kawena. *Nā Mele Welo: Songs of Our Heritage.* Honolulu: Bishop Museum, 1995.

—-. 'Ōlelo No'eau: Hawaiian Proverbs & Poetical Sayings. Honolulu: Bishop Museum, 1983.

Pukui, Mary Kawena & Samuel Elbert. *Hawaiian Dictionary.* Rev. ed. Honolulu: U. of Hawaii, 1986.

Pukui, Mary Kawena, Samuel Elbert, & Esther T. Mookini. *Place Names of Hawaii.* Rev. ed. Honolulu: U of Hawaii, 1974.

Pukui, Mary Kawena, E. W. Hartig, M. D., & Catherine A. Lee. *Nānā I Ke Kumu: (Look to the Source).* 2 vol. Honolulu: Hui Hānai, 1983.

Riegert, Ray. *Hidden Maui.* Berkeley: Ulysses Press, 1996.

Stevenson, Robert Louis. *Travels in Hawaii.* ed. A. Grove Day. Honolulu: U of Hawaii, 1973.

Twain, Mark. *Roughing It in the Sandwich Islands.* Honolulu: Mutual, 1990. Rpt. from *Mad about Islands: Novelists of a Vanished Pacific,* by A. Grove Day. Honolulu: Mutual, 1987.

Westervelt, W. D. *Myths and Legends of Hawaii.* ed. A. Grove Day. Honolulu: Mutual 1987.

Wood, Charles E. Wood. *Charlie's Charts of the Hawaiian Islands.* Rev. ed. Surrey, BC: Charlie's Charts, 1994.

INDEX

313